Financing for Sustainable Development in International Investment Law

This book highlights the intersection between international investment law and sustainable development, particularly in the context of the right to regulate for public interest related to sustainable development.

Addressing key challenges hindering the harmony between investment law and sustainable development, the book unveils a new methodology to assess whether a government measure or foreign investment contributes to sustainable development. The primary question driving this text is: how should investment treaty arbitration tribunals evaluate the sustainable development impact of both government measures and foreign investments affected by those measures? Beginning by establishing a conceptual framework around the right to regulate for public interest, the book also identifies limitations in the typical approach taken in investment treaty arbitration. Additionally, broader systemic constraints within international investment law concerning sustainable development are discussed.

This book will be of interest to students and scholars in the field of international investment law, economic law, and sustainable development.

Soo-hyun Lee is a scholar and a practitioner working at the intersection between international economic law and sustainable development. He explores the nexus relationship between economic governance and Financing for Sustainable Development. While serving the United Nations in different capacities for over a decade, he has been an academic at the University of Suwon and University of Tokyo. This book is the product of his doctoral programme at Lund University, Faculty of Law, and the interdisciplinary 2030 Agenda Programme.

Image a.1 Illustration by Jeannie Lee

Financing for Sustainable Development in International Investment Law

Soo-hyun Lee

Routledge
Taylor & Francis Group
LONDON AND NEW YORK

First published 2025
by Routledge
4 Park Square, Milton Park, Abingdon, Oxon OX14 4RN

and by Routledge
605 Third Avenue, New York, NY 10158

Routledge is an imprint of the Taylor & Francis Group, an informa business

British Library Cataloguing-in-Publication Data
A catalogue record for this book is available from the British Library

ISBN: 978-1-032-75562-5 (hbk)
ISBN: 978-1-032-80185-8 (pbk)
ISBN: 978-1-003-49587-1 (ebk)

DOI: 10.4324/9781003495871

Typeset in Times New Roman
by Apex CoVantage, LLC

Contents

Acknowledgements

From my view atop the Øresund Bridge, I distinctly remember that immeasurable blue horizon, sky and sea taped together by a single column of light. My wife and I, three suitcases each, aboard a train travelling deep into the uncertainty and thrill of the unknowable. This book would not be possible without her grace and patience, silent strength, and resounding spirit. For staying with me undaunted by new lands, unfamiliar faces, pandemic-fuelled paranoia, and doctoral gloom. She reminds me of what is good in this world.

This book is also dedicated to the unfaltering courage and resilience of my mother and sister, standing with resolve from boardroom to courtroom against systemic racial and gender discrimination. I can know no greater fortune than having been raised in a family of strong women.

I extend my deepest gratitude to the 2030 Agenda Graduate School at Lund University, through the graces of which I completed this volume. Kristina Jönsson, a steady voice through the noise. To my role model Daria Davitti and her crystal ball. I am honoured to have written this under her tutelage, and I believe to this day that she is the answer to the world's problems. Ulf Linderfalk, without whose stoic guidance this book would have ever seen the light of day. I endeavour to be such a qualified academic as him.

The friends I've met along the way and will meet again someday. I wonder if you will ever read this, but *gomapda*.

And finally, this book is written for my son and the generations after you. Unborn at the time of writing, yet responsible for protecting this precious world of ours from ourselves.

I may only hope that this volume helps.

1 Introduction

1.1 Background and scope

Between 2015 and 2019, a German photovoltaic power generation investor, SolEs Badajoz GmbH, challenged through investment treaty arbitration a public policy decision by Spain that amended a feed-in tariff meant to support renewable energy generation. The amendment increased a tax and decreased a subsidy to an extent to which the SolEs investment was adversely affected. SolEs claimed that the measure taken by Spain did not have a reasonable or rational connection to the public policy objective that it sought to achieve, which was to support the country's transition to renewable energy.[1] As a result, the losses that SolEs saw through its investment could not be justified as having been necessary to achieve the stated public policy objective. The investment treaty arbitration tribunal, in recalling decisions made in *Charanne and Construction Investments v Spain*[2] and *Saluka v Czech Republic*, identified a core issue in the dispute as the need for balancing the host state's right to regulate on matters concerning the public interest against its obligations to the foreign investor's legitimate expectations concerning rights and protections it received through an applicable international investment agreement (IIA).[3] This, the tribunal claimed, involved "weighing the Claimant's legitimate and reasonable expectations on the one hand and the Respondent's legitimate regulatory interests on the other".[4]

Spain contended that the measures taken were

> part of a set of structural macroeconomic control measures adopted pursuant to recommendations by the European Union and the International Monetary Fund. These measures have affected all Spanish citizens and businesses, which have had to bear certain sacrifices and burdens within a highly negative economic context.[5]

1 *SolEs Badajoz GmbH v Kingdom of Spain*, ICSID Case No ARB/15/38, Award (31 July 2019) para 295.
2 *Charanne and Construction Investments v Spain*, SCC Case No V 062/2012, Award (21 January 2016).
3 In this case the Energy Charter Treaty (1994).
4 *Saluka Investments BV v The Czech Republic*, UNCITRAL, Partial Award (17 March 2006) para 304.
5 *SolEs Badajoz GmbH v Kingdom of Spain* (n 1) para 397.

DOI: 10.4324/9781003495871-1

The central issue in the case arises from the fact that SolEs made its investment in a regulatory setting defined by Spain's objective of promoting renewable energies. Due to changes introduced by Spain, the characteristics of the regulatory setting in which the SolEs investment was evaluated upon the admission of its investment, such as energy saving and efficiency,[6] were in effect replaced by a separate public policy objective, e.g. tariff deficits and economic austerity recommended by the European Union and the International Monetary Fund as countermeasures to a looming balance of payments crisis. The tribunal determined that Spain imposed a measure on the SolEs investment that resulted in losses that could not be justified on the basis of the public policy objective that intended to be served, therefore rendering the government measure a violation of the investor's legitimate expectations concerning their investment. Such expectations were guaranteed at the time SolEs was admitted as a foreign direct investment (FDI) into Spain based on the Energy Charter Treaty. The tribunal thus found that Spain's changes to the regulatory framework disrupted the certainty, stability, and predictability of the investment climate that was guaranteed to SolEs when it decided to invest in Spain.[7]

In effect, the tribunal did not assess the extent to which either government measure, feed-in tariffs or taxation, advanced the public policy objectives that they sought to advance, or even the possibility that they may had served the same objective, such as sustainable development or public welfare, or neither public purpose objective at all. Instead, the tribunal turned its focus to a different set of conflicting interests: Spain's reservation of its sovereign right to conduct policy or regulatory measures to advance its public interest against its obligations to observe a minimum standard of treatment towards SolEs under the Energy Charter Treaty. To do this, the tribunal applied relevant elements of a proportionality test. This involved an assessment of the cost burden of the policy measure passed on to the SolEs investment in proportion to the extent that the public policy objective was advanced. The assessment also sought to determine whether Spain had alternative policy options that would have been less harmful to the investment's performance while achieving similar public policy outcomes.[8]

This aspect of the assessment undertaken in *SolEs Badajoz v Spain* poses a challenging question in investment treaty arbitration to understanding the host state's right to regulate. The government measure implemented by Spain was intended to advance its sustainable development progress by expanding the share of renewable energies in its energy portfolio. Invoking the right to regulate for the public interest in such scenarios involves inter alia determining the material cost to the foreign investment against the extent to which the public policy objective was achieved.[9] If

6 *SolEs Badajoz GmbH v Kingdom of Spain* (n 1) para 103.
7 *SolEs Badajoz GmbH v Kingdom of Spain* (n 1) para 355.
8 *SolEs Badajoz GmbH v Kingdom of Spain* (n 1) para 364.
9 These are cases when implementing a government measure in a manner that is inconsistent to its obligations to provide the foreign investor with minimum standards of treatment results in a direct or indirect adverse effect on the foreign investment, such as the partial or complete loss in profit or control over the investment (see, generally, Rudolf Dolzer and Christoph Schreuer, *Principles of International Investment Law* (2nd edn, OUP 2012) 122–23). As explained in Sections 1.2 and 1.3, if the government measure was implemented for a legitimate public policy objective, however, then the measure may be viewed as falling within the host state's right to regulate for the public interest.

that public policy objective is to advance sustainable development, then the question becomes: how does one assess the extent to which sustainable development, as a public policy objective, was achieved?

Broadening the above question results in a central theme of this book: assessing contributions to sustainable development in international investment law in the absence of standards or a normative definition of sustainable development. More specifically, this book examines the host state's right to regulate for the public interest of sustainable development, especially when both the government measure and foreign investment claim to have contributed to sustainable development.

The right to regulate for the public interest, which finds more comprehensive explanation later in Chapter 2 of this work, is evoked when the host state implements a measure on behalf of the national public interest, such as an amendment in law or policy. However, that government measure may be inconsistent with the host state's obligations to a foreign investor set out by an international investment agreement (IIA) with the investor's home state. Bilateral investment treaties (BITs), the most common form of IIA, will regularly identify these obligations. The Benin-Canada BIT, for instance, identifies as a guiding principle that:

> Each of the Contracting Parties shall ensure the promotion of investments of investors of the other Contracting Party as well as the protection of those investments and investors in its territory, consistent with the provisions of the guiding principles of this Chapter, including national treatment, most-favoured-nation treatment, minimum standard of treatment, compensation for losses, compensation for expropriation, transparency, subrogation and corporate social responsibility.[10]

As explored at greater length throughout this text, if a government measure is implemented legitimately within a state's right to regulate for the public interest, then it may not be inconsistent with the provisions of an IIA on minimum standards of treatment to foreign investors. Flexibilities and exceptions of this kind are derived from multiple sources of law, though located more generally within the international legal principle of state sovereignty.[11] IIAs conventionally do not identify public interest objectives as one may find in the general exceptions (Article XX) of the 1994 General Agreement on Tariffs and Trade (GATT).[12] Yet as explored further in Chapter 3, new generations of IIAs, such as the EU-Canada Comprehensive Economic and Trade Agreement (CETA), more explicitly indicate legitimate public interests in carving out reservations of the right to regulate.

10 Agreement Between the Government of Canada and the Government of the Republic of Benin for the Promotion and Reciprocal Protection of Investments (2013) Art 4.

11 Yulia Levashova, *The Right of States to Regulate in International Investment Law: The Search for Balance Between Public Interest and Fair and Equitable Treatment* (Kluwer Law International BV 2019) 26.

12 GATT Article XX reserves the adoption or enforcement of measures necessary or related to a list of legitimate public policy interests such as inter alia public morals or human, animal, or plant life or health.

Chapter eight of the CETA, for instance, clearly provides for the right to regulate at all levels of government.[13]

Last, the interpretation of the right to regulate has also been taken up in key arbitral decisions in investment treaty arbitration, such as in *ADC Affiliate Limited and ADC & ADMC Management Limited v The Republic of Hungary*, where the presiding tribunal evaluates the right to regulate by the host state and subsequently qualifies that right as "not absolute" and "subject to the duty of compensation . . . [w]here a State fails to act in accordance with the rule of law or breaches of a treaty obligation".[14] When taken up in investment treaty arbitration, tribunals also confront contentious and challenging tasks such as balancing the rights and protections granted to the investor with preserving the regulatory authority of the host state to conduct government measures.[15]

Across these sources of law, the right to regulate for the public interest remains one of the means in international investment law to facilitate the assessment of a government measure or foreign investment in relation to a public interest or public policy objective. This book looks specifically at the transnational public policy objective of sustainable development. However, as further examined in Chapter 3, current assessments of contributions to sustainable development within international investment law following the evoking of the right to regulate remain incomplete. Such incomplete assessments, while specifically examined in Chapter 2, originate from larger systemic attributes of international investment law in general. These are adequately captured in the debate between the "evolutionary" and "revolutionary" approaches to international investment law scholarship, which is explored further in this chapter.

One broader theme that is present in both research and practice, however, is that international investment law remains insufficiently equipped, or as this book identifies as "incomplete", in assessing the extent to which a government measure and/or foreign investment affects sustainable development. This book uncovers the incomplete assessments of investment law, their origins and reasons, and submits proposals for how such incomplete assessments may be addressed. One dimension of incomplete assessment that is core to this work is that sustainable development relies on vague normative content upon which to base any such assessment in international investment law. While further examined in the first pillar of the conceptual

13 'CETA Chapter by Chapter: Chapter Eight—Investment' (*Trade—European Commission*, 24 August 2018) <https://ec.europa.eu/trade/policy/in-focus/ceta/ceta-chapter-by-chapter/index_en.htm> accessed 20 August 2020.

14 *ADC Affiliate Limited and ADC & ADMC Management Limited v The Republic of Hungary*, ICSID Case No ARB/03/16 para 403.

15 See, for instance, *Total SA v Argentine Republic*, ICSID Case No ARB/04/01, Decision on Liability (27 December 2010) paras 123–24, 162, 309, 333, 429; *Plama Consortium Limited v Republic of Bulgaria*, ICSID Case No ARB/03/24, Award (27 August 2008) para 177; *EDF (Services) Limited v Romania*, ICSID Case No ARB/05/13, Award (8 October 2009) para 299; *El Paso Energy International Company v The Argentine Republic*, ICSID Case No ARB/03/15, Award (22 September 2014) para 358; *Joseph Charles Lemire v Ukraine*, ICSID Case No ARB/06/18, Award (8 July 2013) paras 273, 500.

framework offered in Chapter 2, in encountering this dimension of incomplete assessment, this project turns to key multilateral frameworks furnished through the UN system that exposit on the role of foreign investment in sustainable development, such as the *2030 Agenda for Sustainable Development.*[16]

Turning to investment treaty arbitration,[17] a key dimension of international investment law, will help to contextualize the objectives of this project. In *Berkowitz v Costa Rica*, the host state (Costa Rica) reclaimed land in a national park established to "protect the leatherback sea turtle and other species and natural resources".[18] The host state had evoked the right to regulate for the public interest of environmental concerns that was provisioned under Article 10.11 of the prevailing IIA, the Free Trade Agreement between Central America, the Dominican Republic and the United States of America (CAFTA).[19] Despite having been submitted as a claim in the dispute, the investment treaty arbitration tribunal identified in its preliminary decision that evaluating the extent to which the public interest was served by the government measure was beyond its jurisdiction. Yet the tribunal did go on to identify that the government measure was both arbitrary and unfair on the basis of minimum standards of treatment guaranteed by the CAFTA.[20] Furthermore, the tribunal did not consider in its deliberations the fact that both the investor, whose aim was commercial real estate development, and the competent authority, the National Environmental Technical Secretariat (SETENA) and Ministry of the Environment and Energy (MINAE), submitted opposing positions as to their respective contributions to the public policy objective: preservation of the leatherback turtle ecosystem.

The foreign investor claimed that the real estate was meant to cater to an "environmentally conscious clientele"[21] and that it had taken "specific steps to ensure that his estate lots could be developed in an environmentally sensitive and

16 Transforming Our World: The 2030 Agenda for Sustainable Development 2015 (UN Document A/RES/70/1).

17 Other relevant cases are further explored in Chapter 3.

18 Aaron C Berkowitz, Brett E Berkowitz and Trevor B Berkowitz, *(Formerly Spence International Investments and Others) v Republic of Costa Rica*, ICSID Case No UNCT/13/2, Interim Award (Corrected) (30 May 2017) para 2.

19 Article 10.11 reads: "Nothing in this Chapter shall be construed to prevent a Party from adopting, maintaining, or enforcing any measure otherwise consistent with this Chapter that it considers appropriate to ensure that investment activity in its territory is undertaken in a manner sensitive to environmental concerns" (Aaron C Berkowitz, Brett E Berkowitz and Trevor B Berkowitz, *(Formerly Spence International Investments and Others) v Republic of Costa Rica*, ICSID Case No UNCT/13/2, Interim Award (Corrected) (30 May 2017) 28).

20 Aaron C Berkowitz, Brett E Berkowitz and Trevor B Berkowitz, *(Formerly Spence International Investments and Others) v Republic of Costa Rica*, ICSID Case No UNCT/13/2, Interim Award (Corrected) (30 May 2017) 282.

21 Aaron C Berkowitz, Brett E Berkowitz and Trevor B Berkowitz, *(Formerly Spence International Investments and Others) v Republic of Costa Rica*, ICSID Case No UNCT/13/2, Notice of Arbitration and Statement of Claim (10 June 2013) para 9.

profitable manner".[22] Meanwhile, the investor claimed, the Costa Rican government suspended environmental feasibility procedures in the area since 2005 to expand the area for development in the park and permitted construction and development without "environmental sustainability criteria and technical studies" from 2008.[23] Nevertheless, Costa Rican authorities claimed that the roads and utilities that were installed by the investor would "seriously affect the nesting of the leatherback turtles".[24]

The government measure, which was to revoke the license granted to the foreign investor, and the FDI, an environmentally conscious estate, were both contended by their respective party to advance the sustainable development ambitions of Costa Rica. Assessing the right to regulate in light of these opposing positions in relation to applicable multilateral standards related to sustainable development can help to provide the normative basis to evaluate whether the government measures were indeed arbitrary and unfair in their treatment towards the foreign investment or, in fact, important measures in protecting the ecosystem of the leatherback turtles.

Such an effort would find basis in the preamble of the CAFTA, which identifies objectives of preserving the environment, providing flexibility to safeguard the public welfare and "build on their respective rights and obligations under the Marrakesh Agreement Establishing the World Trade Organization and other multilateral and bilateral instruments of cooperation".[25] Other instruments of cooperation may include, for example, the Convention on the Conservation of Migratory Species of Wild Animals (CMS), to which both Costa Rica and the United States (the home state of the investors) are party, which could provide clear conditions for the maintenance of the ecosystem of migratory creatures such as the leatherback turtle, as well as guide the assessment of environmental (biodiversity) impacts of private sector investment.

As this book will show, the *Berkowitz v Costa Rica* arbitration alongside other facets of international investment law demonstrate that the assessment of sustainable development contribution in international investment law remains incomplete. This assessment may benefit from interpreting sustainable development within the context of multilateral agreements and standards of sustainability, especially when such concerns are raised as complaints in a dispute.

22 Aaron C Berkowitz, Brett E Berkowitz and Trevor B Berkowitz, *(Formerly Spence International Investments and Others) v Republic of Costa Rica*, ICSID Case No UNCT/13/2, Notice of Arbitration and Statement of Claim (10 June 2013) 58.

23 Aaron C Berkowitz, Brett E Berkowitz and Trevor B Berkowitz, *(Formerly Spence International Investments and Others) v Republic of Costa Rica*, ICSID Case No UNCT/13/2, Interim Award (Corrected) (30 May 2017) para 41(m).

24 Aaron C Berkowitz, Brett E Berkowitz and Trevor B Berkowitz, *(Formerly Spence International Investments and Others) v Republic of Costa Rica*, ICSID Case No UNCT/13/2, Respondent Response to Notice of Arbitration (26 July 2013) para 6.

25 Free Trade Agreement Between Central America, the Dominican Republic and the United States of America (2004) preamble.

1.1.1 Objectives

The argument advanced by this book is that multilateral approaches related to sustainable development, specifically those resulting from multilateral consensus through the UN system, should serve as a normative contextual framework in international investment law in connection to the right to regulate for the public interest of sustainable development. Such multilateral approaches can act as interpretive tools in international investment law aiding in the assessment of a government measure or foreign investment. Two categories of these multilateral approaches are pivotal to this effort. The first relates to the macroeconomic impact of international investment in the sustainable development process. This approach is formulated in Chapter 3 and referred to as the "International Investment-Sustainable Development Framework" (identified in this work as the "Framework"). The second approach relates to Sustainable Investment,[26] which is a form of portfolio investment that accounts for the means to monitor, report, and verify the impact of investment on the different dimensions of sustainable development. This second approach is formulated in Chapter 4 and referred to as the "Notion of Sustainable Investment" (identified in this work as the "Notion"). The two approaches of the Framework and Notion are synthesized in Chapter 5 into what is referred to as the "Consolidated Method".

A potential objection that might be raised at this juncture is whether international investment law, particularly investment treaty arbitration tribunals, should prefer and adopt any one definition of sustainable development over another. As discussed in Chapter 2, in the absence of a universally accepted and comprehensive definition of sustainable development, there are certain connatural elements that characterize sustainable development and the role that investment can play in it. These connatural elements are found in the corpus of the standards produced by multilateral consensus and facilitated through the UN system, such as the Sustainable Development Goals (SDGs).

The 2030 Agenda with its 17 SDGs is perhaps one of the most representative multilateral standards having been adopted universally by all UN Member States in 2015 to "mainstream sustainable development at all levels, integrating economic, social and environmental aspects and recognizing their interlinkages, so

26 This work refers to "Sustainable Investment" recognizing a lack of uniformity in terminology and scope used mainly in the private sector that classify both the semantic and normative differences between, for instance, "responsible investment" and "environmental, social, and governance (ESG) investments" without specifying a preference for any one moniker. In a comprehensive survey, the Institute of International Finance found that there were 80 variant terms to describe some form of Sustainable Investment circulating in the private sector, making it difficult to quantify with any degree of certainty the true size of these types of investments ('The Case for Simplifying Sustainable Investment Terminology' [Institute of International Finance 2019] IIF Sustainable Finance Working Group Report 2–3). Another study finds that there are 33 definitions of corporate sustainability without notable normative differences in connection to sustainable finance (Johannes Meuer, Julian Koelbel and Volker H Hoffmann, 'On the Nature of Corporate Sustainability' (2020) 33 Organization & Environment 319).

as to achieve sustainable development in all dimensions".[27] As further explained in Chapter 2, standards like the SDGs serve as effective points of departure to substantiating sustainable and inclusive economic growth, social development, and environmental protection—the three dimensions of sustainable development identified in the UN system.

In connection to the role of investment in sustainable development, the 2030 Agenda identifies international investment as a principal means of implementing the SDGs,[28] predominantly in relation to advancing technology, innovation, and infrastructure as stated in SDGs 2.a, 7.a, and 9.5.[29] This connection is further corroborated by SDG 8 (decent work and economic growth), which identifies increased trade and investment as engines of economic growth, but calls for the type of trade and investment that form a "trade-investment nexus"[30] with the social and environmental objectives of sustainable development. These "productive investments" add capacity to the host state through job creation while accounting for social and environmental impact.[31] Through the Consolidated Method, this book reframes the discussion on the role of international investment and international investment law in sustainable development.

As further discussed in Chapter 2 and later in Chapter 5, the need for an interdisciplinary approach is founded on the fact that the economic, social, and environmental impacts of international private sector investment are so diverse and integrative that it is necessary to evaluate them from a comprehensive perspective, which goes beyond laws and regulations and takes into consideration relevant socioeconomic and environmental implications of the investment. Failing to do so would not only limit our understanding of how international investment contributes to sustainable development, but also the capacities of investment treaty arbitration tribunals to uphold a system of dispute settlement that can effectively govern and thereby support those contributions.

The argument advanced by this work moves from the assumption, widely shared in the literature,[32] that in their determinations investment treaty arbitration

27 The Future We Want: Outcome Document of the United Nations Conference on Sustainable Development 2012 (UN Document A/RES/66/288) para 3.

28 Transforming Our World: The 2030 Agenda for Sustainable Development paras 28, 39, 41, 43, 60, 62, 67.

29 Transforming Our World: The 2030 Agenda for Sustainable Development paras 16, 19–20.

30 United Nations Trade and Development (UNCTAD), 'Goal 8: Decent Work and Economic Growth' (*SDG Pulse*) <https://sdgpulse.unctad.org/sdgs/goal-8-decent-work-and-economic-growth/> accessed 27 February 2020.

31 United Nations, 'Promote Inclusive and Sustainable Economic Growth, Employment and Decent Work for All' (*Sustainable Development Goals*) <www.un.org/sustainabledevelopment/economic-growth/> accessed 27 February 2020.

32 This expanded on further in the literature review in Section 1.3 and the conceptual framework in Chapter 2. Also, see generally, Inessa Love and Leora F Klapper, *Corporate Governance, Investor Protection, and Performance in Emerging Markets* (The World Bank 2002); Joshua Robbins, 'The Emergence of Positive Obligations in Bilateral Investment Treaties' (2005) 13 University of Miami International & Comparative Law Review 403; Peter Muchlinski, 'Caveat Investor? The Relevance

tribunals should also take into consideration the conduct of the investor or performance of the investment in assessing their rights and obligations within the host state. Expanding on that research, this book puts forth the position that the assessment of the conduct of the investor and/or performance, as well as the government measure, must consider sustainable development impact when in the context of the host state invoking its right to regulate for the public interest of sustainable development.

In *Bear Creek v Peru*, for instance, a dissenting opinion by one of the arbitrators acknowledged that the conduct of the investor could, in certain circumstances, significantly reduce the compensation awarded to the investor, or quantum, thus to take into account the investor's failure to act with due diligence.[33] The investor's lack of transparency was determined to have been a contributing factor in the "undermining of the conditions" and that the "discontent that followed, expressed by many members of the affected local communities, was foreseeable".[34] While the foreign investor did not have explicit obligations under the applicable IIA for such due diligence review, the view of the tribunal was that this would not excuse private sector actors for engaging in activities that would violate international law beyond the applicable instrument.[35] This meant that the investor, as a private entity, was not exempt from obligations more widely held in multilateral agreements on sustainable development[36] such as, prominently, the Universal Declaration of Human Rights.[37]

---

of the Conduct of the Investor Under the Fair and Equitable Treatment Standard' (2006) 55 International & Comparative Law Quarterly 527; Barnali Choudhury, 'International Investment Law as a Global Public Good Business Law Forum: Balancing Investor Protections, the Environment, and Human Rights' (2013) 17 Lewis & Clark Law Review 481; Lone Wandahl Mouyal, *International Investment Law and the Right to Regulate: A Human Rights Perspective* (Routledge 2016).

33 *Bear Creek Mining Corporation v Republic of Peru*, ICSID Case No ARB/14/21, Partial Dissenting Opinion of Professor Phillipe Sands QC (30 November 2017) para 4.

34 *Bear Creek Mining Corporation v Republic of Peru*, ICSID Case No ARB/14/21, Partial Dissenting Opinion of Professor Phillipe Sands QC (30 November 2017) para 6.

35 *Bear Creek Mining Corporation v Republic of Peru*, ICSID Case No ARB/14/21, Partial Dissenting Opinion of Professor Phillipe Sands QC (30 November 2017) para 10.

36 Such agreements are further explored in the first pillar of the conceptual framework provided in Chapter 2.

37 While beyond the scope of the present study, there has been contention surrounding the binding nature of the obligations of the Universal Declaration of Human Rights in international investment law. In 2016, for instance, the investment treaty arbitration tribunal in *Urbaser v Argentina* stated that a "source of international law that is external to this BIT can provide more favourable rights that are granted . . . and therefore subject to be claimed" (*Urbaser SA and Consorcio de Aguas Bilbao Bizkaia, Bilbao Biskaia Ur Partzuergoa v The Argentine Republic*, ICSID Case No ARB/07/26, Award (8 December 2016) para 1192), referring to customary international law that may be applicable within the circumstances of the dispute. When administrating an instrument with more expansive rights than the international investment agreement, the tribunal observed that while it "must certainly be mindful of the BIT's special purpose as a treaty promoting foreign investments, but it cannot do so without taking the relevant rules of international law into account" (*Urbaser SA and Consorcio de Aguas Bilbao Bizkaia, Bilbao Biskaia Ur Partzuergoa v The Argentine Republic*, ICSID Case No ARB/07/26, Award (8 December 2016) para 1200). The investment

Overall, in the nexus between international investment law and sustainable development, the conduct of the foreign investor and/or performance of the foreign investment ought to be taken into consideration when ascertaining whether a government measure by the host state as well as the foreign investment putatively influenced by the government measure "contributed to sustainable development". The Consolidated Method is constructed throughout this book to ensure that such conduct can be taken into consideration accordingly.

The specific venue within that nexus between international investment law and sustainable development that is at the centre of the present study is the host state's use of the right to regulate for the public interest of sustainable development. As the third pillar of the conceptual framework provided in Chapter 2 further expands upon, the right to regulate for the public interest, whether as provisioned in an IIA or conceded in an investment treaty arbitration, is perhaps the most appropriate venue for the research pursued by this book. This, in brief, is because reserving the right to regulate helps to serve as a safety valve both against foreign investments and government measures that are counterintuitive to the national and transnational public policy interest of sustainable development.[38]

In spite of this, however, investment treaty arbitration tribunals have repeatedly conducted incomplete assessments of contributions to sustainable development by either setting aside the issue or without substantiating relevant considerations in reaching their determinations. This incomplete assessment is illustrated in detail throughout Chapters 2 and 3 by first examining the process through which investment treaty arbitration tribunals determine whether a government measure or investment putatively contribute(d) to sustainable development. As demonstrated therein, a major causal factor is a reluctance towards committing to specific criteria or connatural elements within the scope of advancing sustainable development that tribunals need to take into consideration in making such determinations.

1.1.2 Structure

A primary question aids the reader in navigating this text: in assessing a government measure implemented within the host state's right to regulate for the public purpose of advancing sustainable development, how should investment treaty arbitration tribunals consider the sustainable development impact of both the government measure and the foreign investment affected by that measure?

The above question is answered by deconstructing its main conceptual elements across three phases in this book. The first phase addresses the concept of

---

treaty arbitration tribunal in *Tulip Real Estate v Turkey* went further to identify that not only were such provisions related to human rights "relevant to the interpretation of the concept of a fundamental rule of procedure", but also identified that "authorities stemming from the field of human rights [as] a legitimate method of treaty interpretation" (*Tulip Real Estate Investment and Development Netherlands BV v Republic of Turkey*, ICSID Case No ARB/11/28, Decisions on Annulment (30 December 2015) para 92).

38 This is established in the third pillar of the conceptual framework in Chapter 2.

sustainable development as it is employed in international investment law,[39] which is indispensable to assessing a "contribution to sustainable development" either by a government measure and/or foreign investment within the context of the right to regulate for sustainable development.

This first phase occurs primarily in Chapters 2 and 3, which construct a conceptual framing around the right to regulate for the public interest.[40] On the basis of that framing, Chapter 2 also identifies the limitations in the approach regularly taken up in investment treaty arbitration based on a selection of past arbitration proceedings and decisions. Chapter 3 then draws out broader, systemic constraints facing international investment law and its capacity to respond to the needs of sustainable development. Confronting these constraints, in turn, embodies the broader research and policy implications of this work.

The second phase of the book considers whether an examination of the foreign investment's sustainable development impact could help overcome the limitations facing international investment law and investment treaty arbitration when assessing "contributions to sustainable development". This second phase occurs in Chapter 4, which builds on existing scholarship and investment law practice calling for the conduct of investors to be examined in investment treaty arbitration. This second phase identifies the benefits of integrating the interdisciplinary analysis provided through the approaches employed in Sustainable Investment into international investment law concerning the sustainable development impact of international investment.

The third phase of this book identifies the benefits and challenges of applying the notion of Sustainable Investment to determinations by international investment tribunals on the use of the right to regulate for the public interest in connection to sustainable development. This final phase is found in Chapter 5, wherein the approaches defined in Chapters 3 and 4 are shaped into a single "Consolidated Method" and then applied in right to regulate determinations.

Through the Consolidated Method, contributions to sustainable development are assessed within international investment law and investment treaty arbitration on a platform substantiated with content arising from multilateral consensus and negotiation provided through the UN system. This includes, for example, broad policy commitments such as the 2030 Agenda and its SDGs and technical guidance facilitated through the UN-backed Principles for Responsible Investment (PRI) or the UN Environment Programme's Finance Initiative (UNEP FI).

1.2 Scholarship divided

In the rapidly growing body of research and scholarship examining the interplay between international investment law and sustainable development, there exists

39 Specifically in international investment agreements and in the deliberation of investment treaty arbitration.

40 The third pillar of the conceptual framework in Chapter 2.

a tension arising from a suspected mutual exclusivity between two possible outcomes of an international investment law regime: promoting foreign investment and advancing sustainable development. This suspicion has been further exacerbated by a significant concern regarding transnational corporations (TNCs) and their investments within the purview of sustainable development.[41] Empowering host states with the dynamic policy flexibilities needed to advance national development strategies that centre on sustainable development[42] has been seen as detrimental to the stability and predictability that foster investor confidence to attract foreign investments.[43]

This division in the scholarship arises from a complex dilemma faced by states when embracing the international investment law regime. At one end, states are faced with the challenge of maintaining a regulatory and policy climate that is conducive to international investment as one means of financing national development objectives, whether that is infrastructure upgrading, climate change mitigation, job creation, or pursuit of socioeconomic objectives. In facing that challenge, the host state is tasked with balancing the potential benefits of FDI with the obligations contingent on the admission of FDI expressed in applicable IIAs. At the other end, host states potentially threaten an investment-friendly regulatory and policy climate when they implement government measures in the right to regulate for sustainable development that may not conform to the investment agreement.[44] The challenge for investment treaty arbitration tribunals then becomes examining the extent to which, and in what form, the host state reserves such a policy space in which it can regulate for matters of public interest, such as sustainable development, against established minimum standards often observed in international investment law.

The challenges posed by this balancing exercise can be traced through the ideological history of international investment law. Placing the origins of international investment law and practice in their current form within the ideological landscape of economic neoliberalism is commonplace in the literature.[45]

41 An alternative phrasing of this tension has been whether international investment agreements form exclusively negative obligations, which limit the host state from taking certain actions that may affect the foreign investor, or positive obligations, which do not restrict the host state's regulatory capacities, but rather obliges it to take measures that are consistent with applicable international investment instruments. See, for instance, Robbins (n 32).

42 One of the means to more closely integrate sustainable development into international investment law has been to provide host states exceptions in their observation of minimum standards of treatment to investors, providing flexibility in reserving the right to implement government measures, whether policy or regulatory, intended to advance sustainable development and other legitimate objectives. As a primary pillar in this work, this is explored in significant detail in the conceptual framework in Chapter 2. However, one may see, generally, Srinath Reddy Kethireddy, 'Still the Law of Nations: Legitimate Expectations and the Sovereigntist Turn in International Investment Law' (2019) 44 Yale Journal of International Law 315, 319.

43 Dolzer and Schreuer (n 9) 9.

44 Dolzer and Schreuer (n 9) 8–9.

45 See, generally, Muthucumaraswamy Sornarajah, *The International Law on Foreign Investment* (4th edn, CUP 2017) 5; Sonia Rolland, Alvaro Santos and David Trubek (eds), 'Embedded Neoliberalism

This legacy begins with the need to regulate "[g]rowing competition amongst imperial powers and an increasing use of direct investment [having] fueled a rise in the use of force during the late nineteenth century".[46] One such view links the origins of international investment law and investment treaty arbitration together with arbitration as a tool of imperialistic coercion: "arbitration did not necessarily replace gunboat diplomacy: gunboats were used, as needed, to bring countries to arbitration. Historically, arrangements for arbitration were made after a dispute arose, not in the initial contract or treaty".[47]

Investor-State dispute settlement, its practices and institutions found substantiation through this process of responding to and providing for the needs and demands of the investor over time through "layering", which was to add provisions enabling investor-State dispute settlement into IIAs without adapting those provisions into the substantive context of the treaty.[48] The consequence of layering investment dispute provisions into treaties was an investor-State dispute settlement "architecture that is fragmentary, inconsistent, and hard to reform . . . The haphazardness of contemporary ISDS . . . led scholars and others to assume the system had decentralized origins and was created through investor demand".[49] Adding to this lack of coherence was the application of international economic law standards like most favoured nation, permitting the "importation of more favourable standards from other treaties".[50]

A significant turning point for investment law began with John Williamson and the Washington technocrats of Bretton Woods institutions releasing a list of policy measures in 1989. These measures were seen as the gateway to rapid growth through economic liberalization. One overarching motive behind those measures was to create conditions that would be favourable to investment.[51] They called for the removal of administrative barriers and regulatory restrictions that would

and Its Discontents: The Uncertain Future of Trade and Investment Law' in *World Trade and Investment Law Reimagined: A Progressive Agenda for an Inclusive Globalization* (CUP 2019) 88.

46 Taylor St John, *The Rise of Investor-State Arbitration: Politics, Law, and Unintended Consequences* (OUP 2018) 55.

47 Taylor St John, *The Rise of Investor-State Arbitration: Politics, Law, and Unintended Consequences* (OUP 2018) 57.

48 Taylor St John, *The Rise of Investor-State Arbitration: Politics, Law, and Unintended Consequences* (OUP 2018) 184.

49 Taylor St John, *The Rise of Investor-State Arbitration: Politics, Law, and Unintended Consequences* (OUP 2018) 184–85.

50 J Anthony VanDuzer, 'Can International Investment Agreements Be Instruments of Sustainable Development? Systemic Capacity Challenges for Developing Countries' in Joost Pauwelyn and Mengyi Wang (eds), *Building Legal Capacity for a More Inclusive Globalization: Barriers to and Best Practices for Integrating Developing Countries into The Maze of Global Economic Regulation* (Georgetown Law and The Graduate Institute 2019) 9.

51 Continuing a tradition of neoclassical economics that found a voice through Rostow's *Stages of Growth*, which identified the accumulation of capital, such as through investment, as yielding an "increase in income in the hands of those who not only save at high rates but place their savings at the disposal of those engaged in modern sector activities" (Walt Whitman Rostow, *The Stages of Economic Growth: A Non-Communist Manifesto* (CUP 1990) 8–9).

discourage FDI, foster a competitive market through privatization, and provide formalized property rights to investors.[52]

This "Washington Consensus" was intended to plant the ideological roots of neoliberalism that would subsequently influence all aspects of an economy,[53] successfully affixing many principles of neoliberalism into the core of economic policy and the mechanisms of international economic law[54] under the belief that they were necessary to inbound trade and investment.[55] The law was seen as a vehicle to mobilize the economy towards those policy objectives, permitting FDI through the merger and acquisition of domestic firms, the provision of rights through greenfield investments, and equity options to private investors through portfolio investment.[56] IIAs such as BITs served as means to provide investors with stable and predictable regulatory conditions in relation to their investments, which as a result surged in number.[57]

This approach of viewing states as heralding legal instruments and reform measures to advance overarching policy objectives has gained traction in the legal research and scholarship of Law and Development. Viewing the expansion of international investment law as occurring within the larger movement towards economic liberalization, for instance, is placed within the Law and Development literature as one part of a broader temporal periodization and taxonomical classification following World War II.[58] Other approaches in Law and Development look also to differences in the way that states interpret development, mount policy approaches to pursue those different interpretations of development, and manipulate their legal and regulatory frameworks in service towards those ends.[59] One issue increasingly addressed in the Law and Development literature that is helpful in contextualizing this project is how discursive structures between legal systems and development policy "[mirror] shifts in dominant Western development paradigm and

52 John Williamson, *A Short History of the Washington Consensus* (OUP 2008).

53 Joseph E Stiglitz, 'Whither Reform: Ten Years of the Transition' (Annual World Bank Conference on Development Economics, Washington, DC, 28 April 1999) 22.

54 Julio Faundez, 'International Economic Law and Development: Before and After Neo-Liberalism' in Julio Faundez and Celine Tan (eds), *IEL, Globalization and Developing Countries* (Edward Elgar Publishing 2010) 22–23.

55 Muthucumaraswamy Sornarajah, 'Developing Countries in the Investment Treaty System: A Law for Need or a Law for Greed?' in Stephan W Schill, Christian J Tams and Hofmann Rainer (eds), *International Investment Law and Development: Bridging the Gap* (Edward Elgar Publishing 2015) 50.

56 David Kennedy and Joseph E Stiglitz (eds), *Law and Economics with Chinese Characteristics: Institutions for Promoting Development in the Twenty-First Century* (OUP 2013) 10–15.

57 Sarah Bauerle Danzman, 'The Political Economy of Bilateral Investment Treaties' in Markus Krajewski and Rhea Tamara Hoffmann (eds), *Research Handbook on Foreign Direct Investment* (Edward Elgar Publishing 2019) 14–15.

58 See, generally, Scott Newton, 'The Dialectics of Law and Development' in David M Trubek and Alvaro Santos (eds), *The New Law and Economic Development: A Critical Appraisal* (CUP 2005).

59 An overview of which can be found in John Hatchard and Amanda Perry-Kessaris, *Law and Development: Facing Complexity in the 21st Century* (Routledge-Cavendish 2012) 30.

assumptions about the role of law in relation to these changes in economic theory and practice at key bilateral and multilateral institutions".[60] A conclusion to draw from this literature is that the rigid

> formalism of epistemological approaches to [international economic law in its neoliberal vehicularization] and the messiness of its actual practice [have become] the enduring endeavour to seek analytical coherence in the face of contestation from competing normative values and conflicting legal regimes.[61]

The final step in advancing this liberalized economic regime was the establishment of an international economic legal order that could monopolize an epistemology of legitimate economic governance,[62] embodying a "set of norms regarding correct behaviour" of global economic governance.[63] Developing economies were lured into the regime with the promise of development, which was seen to share a strongly positive correlation with rapid economic growth,[64] and the consolidation of neoliberal measures at the core of efforts to improve socioeconomic conditions.[65]

While this project does not explore in length the institutional and reform challenges facing international investment law, there is a plethora of existing research on the topic.[66] Starting from this background, this chapter provides an overview of the state of the art in the research on the nexus between international investment law and sustainable development, the area of research in which this work is broadly based.

60 Celine Tan, 'Beyond the "Moments" of Law and Development: Critical Reflections on Law and Development Scholarship in a Globalized Economy' (2019) 12 Law and Development Review 285, 285–89.

61 Celine Tan, 'Beyond the "Moments" of Law and Development: Critical Reflections on Law and Development Scholarship in a Globalized Economy' (2019) 12 Law and Development Review 296.

62 Allen Buchanan and Robert O Keohane, 'The Legitimacy of Global Governance Institutions' (2006) 20 Ethics & International Affairs 405.

63 James Brassett and Eleni Tsingou, 'The Politics of Legitimate Global Governance' (2011) 18 Review of International Political Economy 1.

64 William H Branson, Isabel Guerrero and Bernhard G Gunter, 'Patterns of Development 1970–1994' (The World Bank 1998) 19670 31–32. <http://documents.worldbank.org/curated/en/675081468739202610/Patterns-of-development-1970-1994> accessed 18 February 2020.

65 Roberto Zagha and Gobind T Nankani, *Economic Growth in the 1990s: Learning from a Decade of Reform* (World Bank 2005) 207–22.

66 One such an overview can be found in Javier García Olmedo, 'Recalibrating the International Investment Regime through Narrowed Jurisdiction' (2020) 69 International & Comparative Law Quarterly 301; Sergio Puig and Gregory Shaffer, 'Imperfect Alternatives: Institutional Choice and the Reform of Investment Law' (2018) 112 American Journal of International Law 361; Joost Pauwelyn, 'At the Edge of Chaos? Foreign Investment Law as a Complex Adaptive System, How It Emerged and How It Can Be Reformed' (2014) 29 ICSID Review—Foreign Investment Law Journal 372. A more comprehensive overview can also be found in Chester Brown and Kate Miles (eds), *Evolution in Investment Treaty Law and Arbitration* (CUP 2011).

Within international investment law scholarship, increased attention has been devoted to the impact of international investment law on sustainable development.[67] Scholarly research finds that issues of sustainable development permeate throughout the international investment law system.[68] Nevertheless, the wide divergence of opinions concerning the investment law "regime"[69] and its impacts on sustainable development remains a lively debate, particularly when interpretation cuts across disciplines.[70] Current investment treaty practice, for instance, has been flagged as limiting the promotion of sustainable investment,[71] with the Global South shouldering a greater burden within the shifting dynamics of global economic integration.[72] Meanwhile, others believe that sustainable development and international investment law do not share a necessarily "inimical" relationship, instead pointing to possibilities of a "closer nexus" that can guide the future practice of international investment law.[73] While opinions on this issue vastly diverge, the fact that sustainable development has become a central issue in the examination and study of international investment law has been largely recognized in the literature.[74]

The research on the nexus between international investment law and sustainable development can be broadly categorized into two views: (1) there remain opportunities to reform international investment law through embracing sustainability and inclusivity, and (2) international investment law is inherently an impediment to sustainable development needs.[75] The former is connected with the evolutionary view of international investment law research and the latter with the revolutionary view. The usage of these terms within this classification of the research and

67 For different approaches in legal research towards international investment law, see generally, Stephan W Schill and Kerem Gülay, 'Approaches to Foreign Direct Investment in Legal Research' in Markus Krajewski and Rhea Tamara Hoffmann (eds), *Research Handbook on Foreign Direct Investment* (Edward Elgar Publishing 2019).

68 Marie-Claire Cordonier Segger, Markus W Gehring and Andrew Paul Newcombe (eds), *Sustainable Development in World Investment Law* (Kluwer Law International 2011).

69 The use of the term "regime" refers to international investment agreements, domestic and institutional rules governing foreign direct investment, and investment treaty arbitration, following from a similar grouping made in Jonathan Bonnitcha, Lauge N Skovgaard Poulsen and Michael Waibel, *The Political Economy of the Investment Treaty Regime* (OUP 2017) 3.

70 Kate Miles (ed), *Research Handbook on Environment and Investment Law* (Edward Elgar Publishing 2019).

71 Martin Dietrich Brauch and others, 'Treaty on Sustainable Investment for Climate Change Mitigation and Adaptation: Aligning International Investment Law with the Urgent Need for Climate Change Action' (2019) 36 Journal of International Arbitration 7.

72 Fabio Morosini and Michelle Ratton Sanchez (eds), *Reconceptualizing International Investment Law from the Global South* (CUP 2017).

73 Stephan W Schill, Christian J Tams and Rainer Hofmann, 'International Investment Law and Development: Friends or Foes?' in *International Investment Law and Development: Bridging the Gap* (Edward Elgar Publishing 2015) 32.

74 Steffen Hindelang and Markus Krajewski (eds), *Shifting Paradigms in International Investment Law: More Balanced, Less Isolated, Increasingly Diversified* (OUP 2016); Katia Yannaca-Small (ed), *Arbitration Under International Investment Agreements: A Guide to the Key Issues* (OUP 2010); Gus Van Harten and Martin Loughlin, 'Investment Treaty Arbitration as a Species of Global Administrative Law' (2006) 17 European Journal of International Law 121.

75 Schill, Tams and Hofmann (n 73) 8.

scholarship on the relationship between international investment law and sustainable development is further explained in the following sections.

1.2.1 Revolutionary view of the international investment law–sustainable development nexus

Two issues are recurring in the revolutionary view on the nexus of international investment law and sustainable development: (1) the manner in which international investment law is employed as a means to guarantee predictability and stability in the host state, particularly in developing economies, and (2) the general admonishment of the TNC.[76] Together, they add to a terminal diagnosis that reforms are unable to deliver international investment law from "fundamental legitimacy deficits"[77] that "curtail state measures aimed at the protection of the environment, human rights, labour, and social standards, or taken in reaction to financial crises".[78] These legitimacy deficits arise from the practice of approaching international investment law in relative autonomy from the rest of international law. This and the problematization of such were accurately captured by the International Law Commission:

> The fragmentation of the international social world has attained legal significance especially as it has been accompanied by the emergence of specialized and (relatively) autonomous rules or rule-complexes, legal institutions and spheres of legal practice. What once appeared to be governed by "general international law" has become the field of operation for such specialist systems as "trade law", "human rights law", "environmental law", "law of the sea", "European law" and even such exotic and highly specialized knowledge as "investment law" or "international refugee law" etc.—each possessing their own principles and institutions. The problem, as lawyers have seen it, is that such specialized law-making and institution-building tends to take place with relative ignorance of legislative and institutional activities in the adjoining fields and of the general principles and practices of international law. The result is conflicts between rules or rule-systems, deviating institutional practices and, possibly, the loss of an overall perspective on the law.[79]

Many of the challenges set against international investment law arise from different aspects of its emergence as a self-contained regime,[80] elsewhere known as silo thinking,[81] and its treatment of issues that do not fit neatly within those regimes.

76 Bonnitcha, Poulsen and Waibel (n 69) 25.
77 Daniel Behn, 'Legitimacy, Evolution, and Growth in Investment Treaty Arbitration: Empirically Evaluating the State-of-the-Art' (2014) 46 Georgetown Journal of International Law 363, 369.
78 Schill, Tams and Hofmann (n 73) 28.
79 International Law Commission (ILC), 'Fragmentation of International Law: Difficulties Arising from the Diversification and Expansion of International Law' (2006) A/CN.4/L.702 para 8.
80 International Law Commission (ILC), 'Fragmentation of International Law: Difficulties Arising from the Diversification and Expansion of International Law' (2006) 15.
81 The silo effect on international investment law is identified in Michael Waibel, *The Backlash Against Investment Arbitration: Perceptions and Reality* (Kluwer Law International BV 2010) 293;

Generally, the most iconic dismissal of the very institution of international investment law as illegitimate is offered by Sornarajah,[82] who evocatively wrote:

> [I]f the law brings disadvantages to the many and profits the few, democratic legitimacy would be lacking in such a law and it loses its validity to be regarded as law. [T]he view that [international investment law] has often been a purveyor of poverty and other immiserations and the massive distances are emerging within states between the rich and the poor because of its prescriptions is a wholly tenable thesis. If international law is a purveyor of immiserations, the international law on foreign investment demonstrates it very effectively.[83]

These power asymmetries between the private interests of the TNC and the public interests of the host state were born from the imperial origins of investment law, as briefly described earlier in this chapter, but kept "alive" through investment arbitrations by "staying one step ahead of states which do not want to cut the Gordian knot[84] by withdrawing from the system of investment arbitration altogether".[85] Through the interpretation of international investment treaties arising from investment treaty arbitration, doctrinal elements within the practice of investment law were adopted as core features of the regime, such as fair and equitable treatment (FET) and legitimate expectations.[86]

Sornarajah has also been an iconic figure in striking down the possibility of investment law reform, identifying that such measures "accentuate rather than reduce the deep schisms" between developed and developing economies in international investment law.[87] These schisms originated during what he identified as the third phase of the creation of investment treaties and laws between 2001 and 2008. During this period, investment treaties featured expansionary interpretations that "contained wide defences based on subjective assessments" of normative issues concerning the public interest.[88] Such expansionary interpretations, such as those

---

Daria Davitti, *Investment and Human Rights in Armed Conflict: Charting an Elusive Intersection* (Bloomsbury Publishing 2019) 44; Jean Kalicki and Mohamed Abdel Raouf, *Evolution and Adaptation: The Future of International Arbitration* (Kluwer Law International BV 2019) 1031.

82 See, for instance, Muthucumaraswamy Sornarajah, *Resistance and Change in the International Law on Foreign Investment* (CUP 2015); Muthucumaraswamy Sornarajah, 'Power and Justice: Third World Resistance in International Law' (2006) 10 Singapore Year Book of International Law 19.

83 Muthucumaraswamy Sornarajah, John Linarelli and Margot E Salomon, *The Misery of International Law: Confrontations with Injustice in the Global Economy* (OUP 2018) 151.

84 Or "to deal with problems by taking forceful action".

85 Sornarajah, Linarelli and Salomon (n 83) 166.

86 Sornarajah, Linarelli and Salomon (n 83) 167.

87 Sornarajah, *The International Law on Foreign Investment* (n 45) 175.

88 Muthucumaraswamy Sornarajah, 'International Investment Law as Development Law: The Obsolescence of a Fraudulent System' (2016) 7 European Yearbook of International Economic Law 209, 213.

featured in new generation IIAs, fail to strike at the core of the problem, which has become systemic and about the legitimacy of investment law. Fraudulent practices in international investment law move to embody that legitimacy crisis,[89] many of which are outlined in this subsection. Generally, Sornarajah expressed a deep scepticism about the extent to which investment treaties contribute to development as well as the competency and motives of arbitrators.

As per the former, Sornarajah identified fundamental asymmetries in power relations in investment treaties that favour the investor. Foreign investments that receive protections have at times been admitted despite being "clearly deleterious to the interests of the state".[90] Rich economies responded by installing measures to safeguard national public interests against foreign investors. However, developing economies, when employing those same measures, would find themselves facing investment disputes. This was a result of the "considerable subjectivity" of arbitral interpretation combined with the "uncertainty involved in the wide formulation of regulatory space".[91] The investment treaty arbitration tribunal and their application of proportionality were free to apply their judicial discretion independent of circumstantial and contextual factors involving issues in the public interest, such as sustainable development.[92] Sornarajah observed that proportionality "adds indeterminacy and subjectivity" and "impede[s] democratic state functions by arrogating to themselves [the tribunal] a continuing power to review regulation".[93]

In the broader literature in the revolutionary view, questions of legitimacy in international investment law are far-reaching. Some even assert that the very existence of investment law in combination with the ferocious competition for FDI together present insurmountable challenges for lesser developed economies.

Across a panel of capital-importing and commodity-exporting economies, investors are likely to choose countries with the fewest administrative barriers. In competing for highly lucrative FDI contracts, states will then be more willing to relax or waive environmental, social, and/or economic regulation for investors, thereby creating races to the bottom.[94] This reality has called for a rethinking of not only international investment law, but also international trade law, in a "progressive decentering of the world" away from a single worldview about trade and

89 Muthucumaraswamy Sornarajah, 'International Investment Law as Development Law: The Obsolescence of a Fraudulent System' (2016) 7 European Yearbook of International Economic Law 217.

90 Muthucumaraswamy Sornarajah, 'International Investment Law as Development Law: The Obsolescence of a Fraudulent System' (2016) 7 European Yearbook of International Economic Law 226.

91 Muthucumaraswamy Sornarajah, 'International Investment Law as Development Law: The Obsolescence of a Fraudulent System' (2016) 7 European Yearbook of International Economic Law 227–28.

92 Sornarajah, 'Developing Countries in the Investment Treaty System' (n 55) 64.

93 Muthucumaraswamy Sornarajah, 'An International Investment Court: Panacea or Purgatory?' (Columbia Center on Sustainable Investment 2016) Columbia FDI Perspectives 180 2.

94 Lise Johnson, Lisa Sachs and Nathan Lobel, 'Aligning International Investment Agreements with the Sustainable Development Goals' (Columbia Center on Sustainable Investment 2019) 35 <http://ccsi.columbia.edu/work/projects/aligning-investment-treaties-with-sustainable-development/> accessed 25 February 2020.

investment and towards one that is responsive to diverse development models, economic structures, and political regimes.[95]

Alongside questions of legitimacy, the causal or even correlative relationship between IIAs and their projected outcomes, such as FDI inflows and governance upgrading, have also been a regular challenge to the international investment law regime. A study of 20 years of data from 1980 to 2000 demonstrated that when a state enters into an IIA, there are "signalling effects" pertaining to the treatment of a foreign investment, but there lacks "automaticity"[96] or causality. This is because identifying the relational connection between IIAs and FDI inflows must also factor in biases such as, inter alia, the total size of the host state economy or the rigour of tax laws.[97] Moving further on this question would entail probing the relational connection between three factors: IIAs, FDIs, and sustainable development. The dynamics of this nexus are well documented in the troubled odyssey of the Multilateral Agreement on Investment (MAI), which attempted to formulate a harmonized investment law regime in relation to the treatment of international investment, but failed to reach a consensus at home, between Member States. While those states most supportive of the MAI were motivated by the shared objective of protecting outward international investments, they did not sufficiently factor in and/or reflect socioeconomic and systemic realities at home, namely, the potentially detrimental impacts of liberalized trade and investment on the domestic economy.[98]

1.2.1.1 Level playing field and regulatory chill

Concerns of a level playing field have been predominant in challenging the legitimacy of trade and investment law, wherein international economic law has been criticized as a means of institutional convergence towards a neoliberal economic heterodox by means of "disciplining deviation".[99] Such views have also been shared by third-world approaches to international law, which lament the "disadvantaged position when negotiating [bilateral investment treaties] with wealthier countries whose investors can choose between numerous developing countries".[100]

95 Poul F Kjaer and others (eds), 'The End of Trade and Investment Law as We Know It: From Singularity to Pluralism' in *World Trade and Investment Law Reimagined: A Progressive Agenda for an Inclusive Globalization* (CUP 2019) 70.

96 Mary Hallward-Driemeier, *Do Bilateral Investment Treaties Attract FDI? Only a Bit . . . and They Could Bite* (OUP 2009) 360.

97 Mary Hallward-Driemeier, *Do Bilateral Investment Treaties Attract FDI? Only a Bit . . . and They Could Bite* (OUP 2009) 369.

98 Captured in Andrew Kerner, 'Why Should I Believe You? The Costs and Consequences of Bilateral Investment Treaties' (2009) 53 International Studies Quarterly 73, 80–82.

99 Andrew Lang, 'Heterodox Market Orders in the Global Trade System' in Alvaro Santos, Thomas Chantal and David M Trubek (eds), *World Trade and Investment Law Reimagined: A Progressive Agenda for an Inclusive Globalization* (CUP 2019) 74–75.

100 Antonius R Hippolyte, 'Foreign Investment Law and Developing Countries' in Markus Krajewski and Rhea Tamara Hoffmann (eds), *Research Handbook on Foreign Direct Investment* (Edward Elgar Publishing 2019) 108.

Stronger criticism yet comes with the so-called neoliberal straitjacket argument, which describes investment treaty arbitration as an institutionalized means for developed economies to regulate the activities of developing economies through FDI.[101] This is premised on the teleological calculus that states with divergent political-economic systems are structurally unstable and therefore more likely to commit infractions against investors, who therefore must rely on investment treaty arbitration. Contrary to this assumption, however, has been the recent trend in investment arbitration where most cases from the mid to late 1990s were filed against states characterized by established democratic governance and rule of law infrastructures.[102]

Another aspect of levelling the playing field has been that as the "power differentials and constraints in choosing the forum for the resolution of one's dispute" become increasingly skewed, large corporations may find that they always command a comfortable advantage over weaker states in the instance of a dispute (or vice versa with smaller business entities and an abusive state). In addition to the arbitrators, the monopolization of international arbitration cases by large multinational law firms that form the crux of a "new generation of arbitration technocrats" are argued to maintain their hold on the "symbolic capital" of reputation within a rapidly expanding field of legal practice.[103]

Meanwhile, lower- and middle-income states have been shown to suffer from a disproportionate reputational cost following an investment treaty arbitration, threatening future inflows of FDI. Following a dispute at the International Centre for Settlement of Investment Disputes (ICSID), the benefits a respondent state may have seen from entering into an IIA were shown to have been offset entirely and at times forecasting even greater losses following the initiation of the dispute[104] and even greater still following an adverse result for the respondent state.[105] These impacts were shown to be more pronounced when factoring in certain macroeconomic parameters, many of which weigh negatively against developing economies: rates of economic growth, population size, GDP per capita, financial openness, the protection of property rights, external threats, and political and economic shocks.[106]

101 Thomas Schultz and Cédric Dupont, 'Investment Arbitration: Promoting the Rule of Law or Over-Empowering Investors? A Quantitative Empirical Study' (2015) 25 European Journal of International Law 1147, 1151.

102 Thomas Schultz and Cédric Dupont, 'Investment Arbitration: Promoting the Rule of Law or Over-Empowering Investors? A Quantitative Empirical Study' (2015) 25 European Journal of International Law 1161–62.

103 Rebecca Hollander-Blumoff and Tom R Tyler, 'Procedural Justice and the Rule of Law: Fostering Legitimacy in Alternative Dispute Resolution' (2011) 2011 Journal of Dispute Resolution 1, 13.

104 Todd Allee and Clint Peinhardt, 'Contingent Credibility: The Impact of Investment Treaty Violations on Foreign Direct Investment' (2011) 65 International Organization 401, 421.

105 Todd Allee and Clint Peinhardt, 'Contingent Credibility: The Impact of Investment Treaty Violations on Foreign Direct Investment' (2011) 65 International Organization 426.

106 Todd Allee and Clint Peinhardt, 'Contingent Credibility: The Impact of Investment Treaty Violations on Foreign Direct Investment' (2011) 65 International Organization 428.

Furthermore, while investment treaty arbitration may furnish a means to defer juridical capacity out of the national context, motivations propelling the pursuit of such measures have been observed to be more rapacious in nature. Host countries with institutional constraints, such as intensity of the rule of law or corruption, may find themselves facing a greater number of "disputable actions" in investment treaty arbitration deliberations irrespective of the motivation behind the putatively treaty inconsistent government measure taken. Meanwhile, a state with stronger institutions may take the same "capricious policy" measures but be found with fewer disputable actions.[107] This seriously challenges the idea that international investment law provides institutional strengthening because host states experiencing institutional constraints face a greater burden through investment treaty arbitration, regardless if those host states face institutional constraints that are circumstantial and dyadic, rather than intentional and *mala fides*.[108]

Another core criticism has been international investment law and arbitration discouraging good faith efforts by host states to promote legitimate objectives in the public interest.[109] Known as regulatory chill or regulatory freeze, host states find themselves constrained in implementing public policy measures, such as those on behalf of the environment, in fear of arbitration or capital flight, where foreign investors relocate their investment to a different state where such regulatory pressures do not exist.[110] Regulatory chill can take place at different stages and in reference to different factors. A government may alter its approach to a certain regulation should a similar measure implemented by another state in some other instance be identified as expropriatory in an investment treaty arbitration proceeding. In this manner, past rulings in investment treaty arbitration instil reluctance in the regulatory or policy decisions of host states, even if made in the public interest.[111]

In other instances, regulatory chill may arise from the perceived threat of arbitration and the choice to internalize the risk by delaying, amending, or withholding the government measure.[112] This can, for instance, threaten to damage the reputation of having an investor-friendly climate, which may turn away potential

107 Nathan W Freeman, 'Domestic Institutions, Capacity Limitations, and Compliance Costs: Host Country Determinants of Investment Treaty Arbitrations, 1987–2007' (2013) 39 International Interactions 54, 60–62.

108 Nathan W Freeman, 'Domestic Institutions, Capacity Limitations, and Compliance Costs: Host Country Determinants of Investment Treaty Arbitrations, 1987–2007' (2013) 39 International Interactions 75.

109 Johnson, Sachs and Lobel (n 94) 29.

110 Ashley Schram and others, 'Internalisation of International Investment Agreements in Public Policymaking: Developing a Conceptual Framework of Regulatory Chill' (2018) 9 Global Policy 193, 194–95.

111 Ashley Schram and others, 'Internalisation of International Investment Agreements in Public Policymaking: Developing a Conceptual Framework of Regulatory Chill' (2018) 9 Global Policy 195.

112 Gus Van Harten and Dayna Nadine Scott, 'Investment Treaties and the Internal Vetting of Regulatory Proposals: A Case Study from Canada' (2016) 7 Journal of International Dispute Settlement 92, 98–100.

investors. Alternatively, the host state may recognize that it has little to gain from entering into investment treaty arbitration even if it does garner a favourable decision due to high opportunity costs, such as time spent in administrative processes, public resources spent in legal consultation, or the reputational cost from the public for using public resources in this manner.[113] Such regulatory chill effects on states obstruct attempts to implement policies that may advance an aspect of their sustainable development absent of any manner of *mala fides*.[114] Regulatory chill remains an extraordinarily grave consequence of international investment law, restraining policy officials from implementing government measures to advance the public interest for fear of reprisal by putative investors.[115] While serving the perception that signing on to IIAs increases coherence in international investment law,[116] the major concern is that regulatory chill represents "coherence in the wrong direction" that results from unconstrained adjudicative discretion on such matters as FET standards.[117]

A representative dispute involving regulatory chill can be seen in *Philip Morris Asia Ltd v Australia*,[118] where Philip Morris Asia initiated an arbitration with the Permanent Court of Arbitration (PCA) claiming that plain packaging laws for cigarettes violated a ban against breaching trademarks. While Philip Morris Asia was not successful in its claim, it highlighted the troubling way that TNCs use investment treaty arbitration as a means of judicial review against public policy, in this case for legitimate public health objectives.[119] Employing investor-State dispute settlement like in *Philip Morris v Australia* paired with the rise of multinational corporations in goods that easily carry over into multiple markets, such as

113 Kyla Tienhaara, 'Regulatory Chill and the Threat of Arbitration: A View from Political Science' in Chester Brown and Kate Miles (eds), *Evolution in Investment Treaty Law and Arbitration* (CUP 2011) 615.

114 Carolina Moehlecke, 'The Chilling Effect of International Investment Disputes: Limited Challenges to State Sovereignty' (2020) 64 International Studies Quarterly 1.

115 Sornarajah, 'Developing Countries in the Investment Treaty System' (n 55) 45.

116 The common perception has been that a perceived coherence surrounding treaty and arbitral practice paired with an increasing number of international investment agreements has set off a "bandwagon equilibrium", which sets on a converse relationship the time at which a state enters into international investment agreements, such as bilateral investment agreements, and the extent to which it can benefit from that agreement. As more states join an agreement, or embark on the proverbial bandwagon, the merits of being party to that agreement increases. This logic has been employed to explain the economic demise of the Soviet Union and subsequent pariah states (Santiago Montt, *State Liability in Investment Treaty Arbitration: Global Constitutional and Administrative Law in the BIT Generation* (Bloomsbury Publishing 2009) 99–102).

117 Santiago Montt, *State Liability in Investment Treaty Arbitration: Global Constitutional and Administrative Law in the BIT Generation* (Bloomsbury Publishing 2009) 159–60.

118 *Philip Morris Asia Ltd v Australia*, PCA Case No 2012-12, Award on Jurisdiction and Admissibility (17 December 2015).

119 Christopher Knaus, 'Philip Morris Cigarettes Charged Millions After Losing Plain Packaging Case Against Australia' *The Guardian* (10 July 2017) <www.theguardian.com/business/2017/jul/10/philip-morris-cigarettes-charged-millions-after-losing-plain-packaging-case-against-australia> accessed 20 March 2020.

tobacco or fossil fuel energies, pointed to another form of regulatory chill, one that spreads across markets. These companies, established in multiple countries around the world, have at their disposal both the resources and a wide range of treaty instruments to bring into filing an investment treaty arbitration. The attention that investor-State dispute settlement attracts serves also as a warning for states in other markets where these TNCs are active.[120] Partly in response to cases like *Philip Morris Asia Ltd v Australia*, the "no greater rights" principle surfaced, which meant that although foreign investors were granted rights and protections, they were not conferred "greater legal rights" than those available for domestic businesses.[121] In other words, foreign investors were denied absolute protections, meaning that they were required to observe public interest ordinances of the state.[122]

1.2.1.2 Enclave effects and eclipsing

Other literature looks to domestic manifestations of challenged legitimacy as primarily gravitating towards the belief that since international arbitration acts as an alternative to domestic legal mechanisms that can undertake the same function, preference for the former resulted in weakening or obstructing the development of national legal systems.[123] Within this view, domestic legal systems, along with broader regulatory powers of the state, are identified as political risk factors in the good governance concept that centres on stability and predictability.[124]

One common consequence of a reliance on international investment arbitration is that since they traditionally do not require the exhaustion of local remedies, they "eclipse the customary role of domestic legal systems, especially domestic courts in mediating between the international sphere and domestic regulatory relationships".[125] As a result, these systems have the authority to decide "what activities are sovereign and what are not [as well as] whether sovereign actors have acted improperly and unlawfully".[126] This effectively closes in the horizon of the policy space in which states are able to regulate for matters of the public interest. This regularly falls into the argument that one of the key merits of investment treaty arbitration is that it is disconnected from the domestic zeitgeist, which is fraught with national political tensions. What that means in practice, however,

120 Kyla Tienhaara, 'Regulatory Chill in a Warming World: The Threat to Climate Policy Posed by Investor-State Dispute Settlement' (2018) 7 Transnational Environmental Law 229, 238–40.

121 Bonnitcha, Poulsen and Waibel (n 69) 24.

122 Sornarajah, *Resistance and Change in the International Law on Foreign Investment* (n 82) 7.

123 Susan D Franck, 'Empiricism and International Law: Insights for Investment Treaty Dispute Resolution' (2008) 48 Virginia Journal of International Law.

124 Celine Tan, 'Reviving the Emperor's Old Clothes: The Good Governance Agenda, Development and International Investment Law' in Stephan W Schill, Christian J Tams and Rainer Hofmann (eds), *International Investment Law and Development Bridging the Gap* (Edward Elgar Publishing 2015) 153–54.

125 Gus Van Harten, 'Investment Treaty Arbitration, Procedural Fairness, and the Rule of Law' in Stephan W Schill (ed), *International Investment Law and Comparative Public Law* (OUP 2010) 631.

126 Gus Van Harten, 'Investment Treaty Arbitration, Procedural Fairness, and the Rule of Law' in Stephan W Schill (ed), *International Investment Law and Comparative Public Law* (OUP 2010) 632.

is that investment treaty arbitration cases are "typically concluded by executive officials of states who present an agreed treaty text for adoption by their respective legislatures or other domestic authorities, often without extensive legislative deliberation and debate", thereby eclipsing national and local courts by rendering passive their roles in legislative processes.[127] This becomes especially applicable for relevant institutions in not only developing economies, where foreign investors come with demands for law reform that can protect their interests,[128] but also resource-rich authoritarian states that maintain their hold on domestic judicial mechanisms, preventing their capacity to develop into an independent organ of the state.[129]

Another venue through which domestic judicial supervision was and continues to be circumscribed is by seeking enforcement of an arbitral award in another state[130] whose jurisdiction recognizes and enforces arbitral awards on the basis of such instruments as the *New York Convention*.[131] In this manner, the investor need not necessarily go through the respondent state for the enforcement of an arbitral award, which the host state may refuse to do, and instead seek enforcement in another jurisdiction. By forum shopping or engaging in parallel proceedings in this manner, an investor may seek to (re)submit claims in jurisdictions where IIAs with more advantageous terms are in effect.[132] This type of nationality planning expands the legal protections of investors but can be abused to furnish asymmetric benefits over the host state.[133] Investment treaty arbitration tribunals have rejected the *ratione personae* admissibility of such claims based on, for example, the lack of a substantial economic relationship between the investor and the declared home state in cases where investor establish special purpose vehicles or paper companies to benefit from applicable IIAs.[134]

However, unless explicitly barred through denial of benefit clauses[135] on the lack of an economic connection,[136] nationality planning persists due to, in part,

127 Susan D Franck, 'The Legitimacy Crisis in Investment Treaty Arbitration: Privatizing Public International Law Through Inconsistent Decisions' (2005) 73 Fordham Law Review 1521, 365.

128 See Ronald J Daniels, *Defecting on Development: Bilateral Investment Treaties and the Subversion of the Rule of Law in the Developing World* (U of Toronto P, Faculty of Law 2004).

129 See Mark Fathi Massoud, 'International Arbitration and Judicial Politics in Authoritarian States' (2014) 39 Law & Social Inquiry 1.

130 Van Harten, 'Investment Treaty Arbitration' (n 125) 135–37.

131 Convention on the Recognition and Enforcement of Foreign Arbitral Awards (1958).

132 Van Harten and Loughlin (n 74) 139.

133 Olmedo (n 66) 303–4.

134 Jorun Baumgartner, *Treaty Shopping in International Investment Law* (OUP 2016) 93–97.

135 See, for instance, *Tokios Tokelés v Ukraine*, where the Tribunal identified that for the dispute to have arisen from the investment, a nexus between the dispute and the investment in the host state's territory must be established. However, that the investor despite having "incorporated some months previously . . . had not so far performed any functions", which suggested pre-planning. This was identified as a "crucial fact" in establishing the jurisdiction of the investment treaty arbitration tribunal (*Tokios Tokelés v Ukraine*, ICSID Case No ARB/02/18, Award (26 July 2007) paras 109–11).

136 Such as genuine and substantial economic activities that would qualify as an economic bond rather than a more formalistic incorporation or *siège social* establishment (Christoph Schreuer,

wide interpretative spaces around the definition of an "investment" or "investor". This is particularly the case when involving dual nationality and golden visas that largely facilitate forum shopping.[137] These issues become more contentious in application to corporate investors, which can adjust their corporate structure by shifting shareholder control to vehicles in different countries or purchasing equity in holding companies in order to gain access to more favourable IIAs.[138] These practices become especially pronounced in the balance between developing and developed economies: a study of 66 potential treaty shopping cases found that such practices remained negatively skewed against developing economies, with 80% of such cases involving a developing economy host state and 88% involving claimants from developed economy home states.[139]

Yet another area of critical scholarship looks to the institutional drawbacks of investment treaty arbitration within the legitimacy challenge. One recurring concern has been the creation of an exclusive "enclave" of practitioners who exclude diverse participation in international investment law. Such enclaves can form around shared beliefs towards international investment law, such as the primacy of FET, wherein arbitrators may be influenced by the urge to "advance the interest of the [arbitration] industry" in a bid to build themselves a reputation that can potentially lead to more future appointments. Without the security of tenure, case-by-case appointments may influence arbitrators to not only curry favour to the investors that initiate more disputes.[140] In addition to the arbitrators, the monopolization of international arbitration cases by large multinational law firms that form the crux of a "new generation of arbitration technocrats" are argued to maintain their hold on the "symbolic capital" of reputation.[141] Such firms typically enjoy economies of scale, commanding enough legal practitioners so that they can be involved in multiple stages of an investment treaty arbitration at varying levels of publicity. In the 1980s, for example, a single law firm, the Cordero Brothers, was involved at some stage of almost half the investment treaty arbitrations held through the International Centre for the Settlement of Investment Disputes.[142]

This invariably leads to the troubling issue of impartiality in investment treaty arbitration, where arbitrations may demonstrate biases towards "those investors that have enough foreign wealth and access to legal resources to contemplate

'Nationality of Investors: Legitimate Restrictions vs Business Interests' (2009) 24 ICSID Review—Foreign Investment Law Journal 521, 522–23). See more recently, Anil Yilmaz Vastardis, 'Chapter 7: Evaluation of Responses to Nationality Shopping and the Way Forward' in *The Nationality of Corporate Investors under International Investment Law* (Hart Publishing 2020).

137 Olmedo (n 66) 308.

138 Olmedo (n 66) 315.

139 Eunjung Lee, 'Treaty Shopping in International Investment Arbitration: How Often Has It Occurred and How Has It Been Perceived by Tribunals?' (London School of Economics and Political Science 2015) Department of International Development Working Paper Series No 15–167 18.

140 Van Harten, 'Investment Treaty Arbitration' (n 125) 22.

141 Van Harten, 'Investment Treaty Arbitration' (n 125) 30–31.

142 St John (n 46) 242.

claims, because it is they who decide whether and when to activate the system" of international investment law.[143] Arbitrator biases of this kind raise significant systemic concerns as it bends the arc of reasoning towards protecting investors in the "interests of their industry".[144] Such consequences of enclave effects help to illustrate the deep structural challenges facing investment treaty arbitration, especially in consideration of the prominent role of arbitrators based on established legal expertise. Yet an overview of these challenges led one commentator to write, "[e]xpertise should not be confused with bias".[145]

Adding to enclave effects on arbitrators then becomes a matter of transparency. One form through which enclaves are secured has been through a lack of procedural transparency in the resolution of investment disputes as well as in the design of IIAs.[146] At least 39% of investment treaty arbitration awards are kept confidential[147] on grounds of proprietary business information, which continues to be a widely criticized practice as it precludes public discretion concerning matters that involve the public interest.[148] Composite, systemic impacts of the persistence of such enclaves include fostering a "two-tiered regime of investment governance", subjecting foreign and domestic investors to diverging rules and standards[149] on the unified issue of standards of treatment to investors and investments.

Enclave effects and transparency in investment treaty arbitration became issues of much public outcry in the Republic of Korea surrounding *LSF-KEB Holdings SCA and others v Republic of Korea*[150] concerning a claim for USD 4.7 billion as compensation for government measures taken following the 1997 Asian Financial Crisis.[151] *LSF-KEB v Korea* involved an investment in and an eventual acquisition

143 Gus Van Harten, *Investment Treaty Arbitration and Public Law* (OUP 2008) 172.

144 Gus Van Harten, *Investment Treaty Arbitration and Public Law* (OUP 2008) 174.

145 Andrea K Bjorklund, 'The Emerging Civilization of Investment Arbitration' (2009) 113 Penn State Law Review 1269, 1300.

146 See Cristoffer Mollestad, 'See No Evil? Procedural Transparency in International Investment Law and Dispute Settlement' (PluriCourts 2014) PluriCourts Research Paper No 14–20.

147 Behn (n 77) 381.

148 See Joachim Delaney and Daniel Barstow Magraw, 'Procedural Transparency' in *The Oxford Handbook of International Investment Law* (OUP 2008).

149 Tan (n 124) 163.

150 *LSF-KEB Holdings SCA and Others v Republic of Korea*, ICSID Case No ARB/12/37.

151 The following summary is from Soo-hyun Lee, 'In the Habit of Giants: Fair and Equitable Treatment and Structural Risk Factors in Conglomerate-Led Newly Industrialized Countries' in Junji Nakagawa (ed), *Asian Perspectives on International Investment Law* (Routledge 2019). These regulatory delays were argued to have violated FET pursuant to Article 2(2) of the Belgium Luxembourg European Union–Korea bilateral investment treaty (BLEU-Korea BIT). Notable here is that LSF-KEB Holdings SCA is a paper company, or a conduit company, that was established to "treaty-shop", which is an abusive practice used by firms to either enjoy the benefits of a tax haven or have a disputed matter fall into the remit of an international agreement that they believe will be favourable to their side. In this case, that was the BLEU-Korea BIT. The second claim raised by LSF-KEB Holdings SCA fully exploited this standard of protection, which was that it was impermissible under the BLEU-Korea BIT for Korea to apply a transfer tax in the sale of Korean Exchange Bank. LSF-KEB Holdings SCA claimed that there was an unfair acquisition of its asset by the Korean government or an expropriation, which then demanded prompt,

of the Korean Exchange Bank by the US private equity firm Lone Star Funds. While Banking Act Article 15 limited a single entity from holding an excess of 10/100 of the total number of issued voting stocks of a financial institution, LSF-KEB Holdings SCA was exempt from this restriction by the Financial Supervisory Commission of Korea in September 2003. This decision was based on an assessment by the Financial Supervisory Commission that permitting the acquisition of the Korean Exchange Bank would "contribute to the efficiency and soundness of the banking business" in accordance with Banking Act Article 15(5).

Yet the basis on which the Financial Supervisory Commission made this assessment was based on data that was later suspected of falsification, which set the Bank of International Settlements capital adequacy ratio of Korean Exchange Bank at 6.2%, falling short of the internationally accepted minimum of 8% of assets to cover potential losses. LSF-KEB SCA began its attempts to sell its shares in January 2006, though its efforts were frustrated by government intervention in every attempt until 2012 due to ongoing investigations. When it was permitted to unload its shares to the Hana Financial Group (Korea) for KRW 3.9 trillion, it was in steep contrast to the KRW 6.3 trillion (8.18 billion in current USD) offered by Kookmin Bank (Korea) in 2006 or the KRW 5.9 trillion offered by HSBC in 2007.

The group of six Belgian investors including LSF-KEB Holdings SCA submitted its request for arbitration to the International Centre for the Settlement of Investment Disputes (ICSID) in December 2012 under claims that it was subject to "repeated acts of harassment" as well as "arbitrary and contradictory tax assessments" that resulted in "billions of euros in damages" according to the memorandum drafted to the Korean government in the beginning stages of the initiation.[152]

The Korean government advanced that it had exercised its sovereign right to regulate for what it perceived to be in the public interest.[153] Divestment through the sale to a foreign firm or liquidation of a domestic financial institution as large as KEB would result in not only considerable noncyclical impacts to employment, but also the financial sector as a whole. In fully assessing the State's capacity to make good faith arrangements on its due diligence to the investor, one must also consider the circumstances of the State at the time of the accession. In the case of South Korea, the LSF-KEB Holdings SCA investment was permitted during a period of considerable financial restricting following the Asian Financial Crisis of 1997. LSF-KEB Holdings SCA then attempted to sell its KEB holdings during a

adequate and effective compensation (Hee Jun Kim, 'A Study of Core Issues in Investor-State Dispute (Lone Star Funds vs the Republic of Korea) ("Lone Star-Hangook Jeongbugan ISDui Juyo Naeyong-Gwa Jaengjeom")' (2012) 36 Dankook University Law Review 855).

152 MD Thomas, 'Memorandum Required by Article 8.1 of the Agreement Between the Government of the Republic of Korea and the Belgium-Luxembourg Economic Union for the Reciprocal Promotion and Protection of Investments with Respect to the Dispute Between Lone Star and the Republic of Korea' (21 May 2012).

153 The Financial Supervisory Commission delayed approval of the sale under claims of ongoing prudential and tax investigations until HSBC eventually rescinded its offer in 2008 given the increasingly bleak conditions of the world financial system.

period of tenuous economic recovery, which, if permitted, would have very clear and destabilizing economic consequences.

Nevertheless, while the Award went to the claimant,[154] the arbitral tribunal remained divided on whether the measures implemented by the Financial Supervisory Commission, which were viewed as attributable to the Korean state, were implemented in the public interest.[155] The Award did little to quell public discontent concerning the high level of confidentiality concerning the arbitral process, much of it left inaccessible to the public view as well as third-party participation despite calls for transparency and attempts at amici curiae by civil society groups.[156]

1.2.2 Evolutionary view of the international investment law–sustainable development nexus

In contrast to the revolutionary view, the evolutionary view looks to repair and strengthen aspects of the international investment law regime rather than to overturn it entirely. While recognizing its controversies, deficiencies, and failures, the evolutionary view generally subscribes to the belief that FDI continues to play an important role in sustainable development. In following the conceptual approach constructed in Chapter 2, this project finds its basis within the evolutionary view in approaches promulgated in multilateral fora, namely the frameworks of the United Nations system and those pursued in international investment law instruments. Before engaging on this task in Chapter 3, however, this subchapter provides a broader survey of the research and scholarship that fit under the evolutionary view.

The economic argument underlying the evolutionary approach deserves brief mention. When a TNC is granted entry by the host state through the admission of

154 *LSF-KEB Holdings SCA and Others v Republic of Korea*, ICSID Case No ARB/12/37, Award (30 August 2022).

155 Charles N Brower, appointed by the claimant, wrote in his concurring opinion that the Financial Supervisory Commission acted to "avoid purely political criticism rather than act in accordance with its statutory mandate" and thus was due to compensate Lone for violating fair and equitable treatment (*LSF-KEB Holdings SCA and Others v Republic of Korea*, ICSID Case No ARB/12/37, Concurring Opinion of Judge Charles N Brower (30 August 2022) para 9). Meanwhile, Brigitte Stern, appointed by the respondent, found that the Financial Supervisory Commission was "discharg[ing] its task with a measure of discretion" and that the tribunal did not have an "open-ended mandate to second-guess a regulator's decision-making" (*LSF-KEB Holdings SCA and Others v Republic of Korea*, ICSID Case No ARB/12/37, Dissenting Opinion of Professor Brigitte Stern (30 August 2022) para 68). A summary of the decision can be found at Damien Charlotin, 'Analysis: Tribunal Majority in Lone Star v Korea Decides That Financial Regulator Acted in Its Own Self-Interest by Covertly Lowering the Investor's Exit Payment; Dissenter Doubts This Finding on the Facts, and Sees No Wrongful Conduct or Causality' (*Investment Arbitration Reporter*, 10 October 2022) <www.iareporter.com/articles/analysis-tribunal-majority-in-lone-star-v-korea-decides-that-financial-regulator-acted-in-its-own-self-interest-by-covertly-lowering-the-investors-exit-payment-dissenter-doubts-this-findin/> accessed 20 October 2022.

156 Hyejin Jang, 'Government-Lone Star ISD, Final Hearing Concluded . . . If Recognized, Decision This Year ("Jeongbu-Lonseuta ISD, Choejong Byeonlon Mamuli . . . Ileumyeon Olhae Nae Gyeollon")' *Law Times* (7 June 2016).

FDI, some amount of benefit is absorbed into the domestic economy depending on the host state's capacity to take advantage of the investment's effects. In a seminal paper concerning economic geography, Krugman (1991) identifies a connection between manufacturing clusters (in core-periphery dichotomy) and spillover effects of knowledge and technology from research and development based on the number of forward and backward linkages.[157] The spillover and absorption through forward and backward linkages has also been applied to FDI. A host state's absorptive capacities can depend on such domestic economic factors as state of financial services, access to finance such as credit, preference for domestic products and services, market size of competitive goods and services, level of human and physical capital, presence of growth constraints, and so forth.[158] The benefits of FDI through backward linkages rather than forward linkages, which are largely captured by the transnational investor in the end product market, has largely been established in the economic literature.[159]

These arrangements tend to be much less beneficial to the host state than other arrangements that promote backward linkages. Generally, these are agreements that require a domestic partner rather than full foreign ownership, such as in partial ownership or joint ventures, thereby forcing the foreign investor to rely on domestic suppliers and service providers. Empirical studies have identified that such arrangements are associated with an at least 15% increase in output for domestic firms.[160]

However, in addition to absorptive capacities, the type of arrangements between the transnational investor and the domestic enterprises of the host state are also crucial. For instance, developing economies that rely largely on human labour–intensive manufacturing typically attract upstream roles in global supply chains in such sectors as garments.[161] Offshoring labour demand for low-skill labour quickly become captive and asymmetric arrangements between the investor and the host state, where the former retains virtually all of the control and a vast majority of the profits. Arrangements that bolster the absorptive capacities of the host state help to address such asymmetry.[162] Relational and symmetric arrangements have been

157 Paul Krugman, 'Increasing Returns and Economic Geography' (1991) 99 Journal of Political Economy 483, 486–87.

158 Laura Alfaro and others, 'Does Foreign Direct Investment Promote Growth? Exploring the Role of Financial Markets on Linkages' (2010) 91 Journal of Development Economics 242, 243–44.

159 See, for instance, Tomas Havranek and Zuzana Irsova, 'Estimating Vertical Spillovers from FDI: Why Results Vary and What the True Effect Is' (2011) 85 Journal of International Economics 234.

160 Beata Smarzynska Javorcik, 'Does Foreign Direct Investment Increase the Productivity of Domestic Firms? In Search of Spillovers Through Backward Linkages' (2004) 94 American Economic Review 605, 607.

161 Yoshimichi Murakami and Keijiro Otsuka, 'Governance, Information Spillovers, and Productivity of Local Firms: Toward an Integrated Approach to Foreign Direct Investment and Global Value Chains' (2020) 58 The Developing Economies 16.

162 Yoshimichi Murakami and Keijiro Otsuka, 'Governance, Information Spillovers, and Productivity of Local Firms: Toward an Integrated Approach to Foreign Direct Investment and Global Value Chains' (2020) 58 The Developing Economies 7–8.

shown to better facilitate the deepening of capital, such as by providing vertical mobility and growth opportunities through training and knowledge transfer.[163]

The evolutionary view attempts to identify how international investment law can facilitate the types of investments that result in positive correlations between investment and sustainable development. As the UN generally identifies as positive or high-quality investment, when FDI builds on these linkages with domestic capital factors (whether human, environmental, or otherwise), then the host state stands to benefit in ways more than just a one-off injection of foreign capital. While the concept of a positive investment is discussed further in Chapters 3 and 4, these investments come with value-added effects, such as facilitating clean technology transfer and leapfrogging, or have clear accountability standards concerning environmental harm[164] or alternatively are able to preclude negative social consequences of resource-seeking FDI in fragile conflict- and violence-prone states.[165]

One area of increasing interest in the literature has been in the implementation of empirical tools in international investment law, particularly in investment treaty arbitration. For instance, environmental impact assessments of trade and investment treaties have been identified as a way to inform the treaty negotiation process on matters of complementarities and trade-offs with national policy and development agendas. One example of this in practice is Sustainability Impact Assessments employed by the European Union Commission, which examines economic gains arising from trade and investment treaties against a broad range of cross-cutting factors such as energy use, gender equality, and access to education.[166] However, impact assessment also suffers from the same limitations as broader empirical study in providing reliable guidance for investment and/or trade treaty negotiations, namely in being able to forecast the sustainable development impacts of a large increase of investment in a particular sector.[167]

While this chapter does not go further into the topic of empiricism, proponents of such approaches suggest that the "scope for misunderstanding" outstanding definitional issues in international investment law, such as the legitimate expectation of investors or sustainable development, can be reduced by empirically based, nuanced rules underlying the relationship between the investor and host

163 Yoshimichi Murakami and Keijiro Otsuka, 'Governance, Information Spillovers, and Productivity of Local Firms: Toward an Integrated Approach to Foreign Direct Investment and Global Value Chains' (2020) 58 The Developing Economies 19–20.

164 Lise Johnson, 'Green Foreign Direct Investment in Developing Countries' (United Nations Environment Programme (UNEP) 2017) UNEP Inquiry 11.

165 Lars Jensen, 'Foreign Direct Investment and Growth in Fragile and Conflict Affected Countries: Role of Peacekeeping and Natural Resources' (United Nations Development Programme (UNDP) 2020) UNDP Global Policy Network 5–6.

166 Markus W Gehring and Marie-Claire Cordonier Segger, 'Overcoming Obstacles with Opportunities: Trade and Investment Agreements for Sustainable Development' [2015] International Investment Law and Development: Bridging the Gap 93, 105–8.

167 Markus W Gehring and Marie-Claire Cordonier Segger, 'Overcoming Obstacles with Opportunities: Trade and Investment Agreements for Sustainable Development' [2015] International Investment Law and Development: Bridging the Gap 104.

state.[168] There remain many challenges to empirical tools in analysing the interaction between sustainable development and international investment law, primarily the technical difficulty in attempting to construct an objective measure that was precise in its readings while being able to package a wide range of substantive concepts into the metric.[169] The use of empirical tools has, however, been able to draw insightful conclusions concerning broader trends in international investment law. For instance, arbitrator selection in terms of nationality and the outcome of investment treaty arbitrations appeared to have little correlation with the development status of a country,[170] pointing to an observation that asymmetries between developing and developed countries were not procedural in origin.

Research in the evolutionary view has also looked to international trade law in connection to the World Trade Organization (WTO) and its interactions with sustainable development—a literature broadly referred to as Trade and Development. While this literature is also not explored in depth, it is useful to examine some of its main premises as a departure point in understanding the evolutionary view.[171] The Trade and Development research largely identifies a broader gravitation of international economic law practice and interpretation towards facilitating sustainable development. This gravitation largely arises from the conflict between green industrial policies and WTO governance.[172]

Two distinct concerns within Trade and Development about the use of public policy measures are of special interest to this work. The first is the credibility of government motives in pursuing public policy objectives. Under the banner of the public interest, Member States may instead be pursuing means to nurture infant industries into national champions away from the purview of WTO law. The

168 Franck, 'Empiricism and International Law' (n 123) 800–1.

169 See Tom Ginsburg, 'Pitfalls of Measuring the Rule of Law' (2011) 3 Hague Journal on the Rule of Law 269.

170 See Susan D Franck, 'Development and Outcomes of Investment Treaty Arbitration' (2009) 50 Harvard International Law Journal 435.

171 In *United States—Import Prohibition of Certain Shrimp and Shrimp Products* (WT/DS58), for instance, the Appellate Body took up an "evolutionary interpretation" of GATT Article XX(g) that would include species facing extinction pressure into its remit of exhaustible natural resources (Cosette D Creamer and Zuzanna Godzimirska, '(De)Legitimation at the WTO Dispute Settlement Mechanism' (2016) 49 Vanderbilt Journal of Transnational Law 275, 299).

172 See, for instance, Caroline Henckels, 'Permission to Act: The Legal Character of General and Security Exceptions in International Trade and Investment Law' (2020) 69 International & Comparative Law Quarterly; Kjaer and others (n 95); Rolland, Santos and Trubek (n 45); Alvaro Santos, Chantal Thomas and David M Trubek (eds), *World Trade and Investment Law Reimagined: A Progressive Agenda for an Inclusive Globalization* (Anthem Press 2019); Tilman Altenburg and Claudia Assmann (eds), *Green Industrial Policy: Concept, Policies, Country Experiences* (United Nations Environment Programme (UNEP) 2017); Frank Ackerman and others, *Trade in the Balance: Reconciling Trade and Climate Policy: Report of the Working Group on Trade, Investment, and Climate Policy* (Boston University Frederick S Pardee Center for the Study of the Longer-Range Future 2016) <https://open.bu.edu/handle/2144/22909> accessed 26 February 2020; Gehring and Segger (n 166); Diane A Desierto, 'Development as an International Right: Investment in the New Trade-Based IIAs' (2011) 3 Trade, Law and Development 296.

second is promoting the type of international trade that creates "additional environmental benefits", such as through public policy measures.[173] In WTO law, this policy space finds direction through GATT Article XX among other means.[174] In the iconic *Canada–Renewable Energy/FIT Program* dispute, for example, the conflict between legitimate policy space and international trade law acted as a central point of contention.[175] More specifically, this conflict was shown to exist between consistency with WTO rules on subsidies, namely the *Subsidies and Countervailing Measures Agreement*, and the policies meant to advance a transition to sustainable energy.[176] The Appellate Body identified that the reservation of such a policy space was assessed in proportionality between the contended government measure and "any less trade-restrictive alternative measure(s) reasonably available that would make an equivalent contribution to [the] policy goal".[177] This fundamentally

173 Sadeq Z Bigdeli, 'Clash of Rationalities: Revisiting the Trade and Environment Debate in Light of WTO Disputes over Green Industrial Policy Special Issue: Trade & Climate Change' (2014) 6 Trade, Law and Development [i], 195.

174 See, for instance, Soo-hyun Lee, 'The Role of the WTO in Sustainable Development Governance, Revisited' (2018) 10 Trade, Law and Development 135.

175 Bigdeli (n 173) 184.

176 Ilaria Espa and Gracia Marín Durán, 'Renewable Energy Subsidies and WTO Law: Time to Rethink the Case for Reform Beyond Canada—Renewable Energy/Fit Program' (2018) 21 Journal of International Economic Law 621, 634–35. The contended policy was enacted by the Canadian province of Ontario, which was meant to promote more wind and solar energy generation that are locally sourced in the province as one part of a larger plan to promote sustainability. The policy involved establishing a feed-in tariff (FIT) and a micro FIT system. The Ontario FIT programme only allowed energy generated from renewable sources to be fed into the grid. In order to get more people involved in the programme, Ontario provided support measures that allowed participants or potential participants to scale up the amount of renewable energy that they were generating and then feeding into the grid. The amount of support received was based on priority points that were earned if the FIT participant contributed to other policy objectives of Ontario, such as creating local employment in the renewable energy sector (Ministry of Energy, Northern Development and Mines, Canada, 'Renewable Energy Development in Ontario: A Guide for Municipalities: 4.0 Feed-In Tariff Program' <www.ontario.ca/document/renewable-energy-development-ontario-guide-municipalities/40-feed-tariff-program> accessed 8 October 2020). Japan and the European Union filed three complaints the Ontario FIT programme as a specific subsidy. The first claimed that the FIT programme was a specific subsidy on the basis of the requirement to be locally based in Ontario in order to benefit. This meant that energy produced in Ontario would have an unfair advantage over energy that Japan or the EU could have sold to Canada because the government would be subsidizing Ontario producers. This complaint was raised against the imposition of domestic content requirements, by which the use of national components, resources, or workforce is required by the state and normally considered inconsistent with the GATT. The second complaint was that non-Canadian firms were receiving less favourable treatment by the government than Canadian firms, which would have easier access to benefiting from the FIT programme due to geographical advantages. The third complaint was that the FIT programme discouraged trade in energy generation, which contradicted the mandate to promote rather than restrict trade ('Canada—Certain Measures Affecting the Renewable Energy Generation Sector/Measures Relating to the Feed-in Tariff Program, Reports of the Panels, WT/DS412/DS426/R (19 December 2012)' paras 177–85).

177 Espa and Durán (n 176) 645.

arranged endeavours to advance sustainable development as antagonistic to the WTO principle of encouraging more global trade.

Yet perhaps the most doctrinal evolutionary account for international investment law and its contribution towards sustainable development is that the object and purpose of IIAs are by design and in principle geared towards sustainable development. In protecting investors and investments, host states are seeking to attract FDI in order to achieve their development objectives. If FDI does not serve towards that goal, then the very object and purpose of admitting the investment are challenged. In that manner, the protection of FDI can be viewed as an intermediary rather than the sole objective of IIAs, which includes the promotion of economic development of the host state.[178] In that regard, sustainability as a predominant qualification of economic development in turn influences both the interpretation of the object and purpose of IIAs within the national context and its protection through international investment law.[179] This expansive approach to interpreting the object and purpose of IIAs finds basis in the view towards treaty interpretation as circumstantial rather than singular and fixed.[180] More specifically, the interpretation of object and purpose also accounts for "subsequent agreements between the parties, relevant subsequent practice of the parties, and any relevant rules of international law" in its approach to treaty interpretation, which includes commitments of the home and/or host state arising from sustainable development–related agreements.[181]

Not limited to the object and purpose, framing specific terms in IIAs as conditioned by safeguards has been an increasingly regular means of incorporating sustainable development in investment law instruments.[182] For instance, legitimate expectations and FET in application to the investor as being conferred within this "further-reaching objective, namely to help the development of the host country" in connection to the meaning in the preamble of the IIA.[183] The rights and protections

178 Ilze Dubava, 'The Future of International Investment Protection Law: The Promotion of Sustainable (Economic) Development as a Public Good' in Ernst-Ulrich Petersmann and others (eds), *Reflections on the Constitutionalisation of International Economic Law: Liber Amicorum for Ernst-Ulrich Petersmann* (Martinus Nijhoff Publishers 2014) 392.

179 Ilze Dubava, 'The Future of International Investment Protection Law: The Promotion of Sustainable (Economic) Development as a Public Good' in Ernst-Ulrich Petersmann and others (eds), *Reflections on the Constitutionalisation of International Economic Law: Liber Amicorum for Ernst-Ulrich Petersmann* (Martinus Nijhoff Publishers 2014) 395.

180 See, for instance, Jan Klabbers, 'Some Problems Regarding the Object and Purpose of Treaties' (1997) 8 Finnish Yearbook of International Law 138. Klabbers rejects that object and purpose have any "single fixed meaning", rather "its precise meaning in any given context must be determined on a case by case basis, depending on the treaty concerned and the circumstances in which the notion is invoked", including in application to their substantive interpretation (Jan Klabbers, 'Some Problems Regarding the Object and Purpose of Treaties' (1997) 8 Finnish Yearbook of International Law 141–48).

181 David S Jonas and Thomas N Saunders, 'The Object and Purpose of a Treaty: Three Interpretive Methods' (2010) 43 Vanderbilt Journal of Transnational Law 565, 577–79.

182 VanDuzer (n 50) 7–8.

183 Schill, Tams and Hofmann (n 73) 27.

vested to the foreign investor are taken as conditional to protecting the public interest of the host state, such as its sustainable development.[184] Integrating sustainable development into the preambular language of IIAs advances this understanding of the object and purpose of the treaty, providing a basis upon which to interpret applicable standards, such as FET, as provided in the operative text of the treaty.[185]

The inclusion of development as a criterion of investment is widely associated with *Salini v Morocco*.[186] This is often framed in Article 25 of the Convention on the Settlement of Investment Disputes between States and Nations of Other States ("ICSID Convention"), which establishes the jurisdiction of the ICSID over the investor-State dispute for covered investments.[187] The criteria approach[188] sought to identify the definitive characteristics of a FDI, which would include a contribution to the host state's development.[189] This was largely in reference to the preamble the ICSID Convention, which identifies the "need for international cooperation for economic development, and the role of private international investment therein".[190] Following *Salini v Morocco*, the development contribution criterion was subject to varying interpretation in investment treaty arbitration. For instance, certain arbitration tribunals did not view a contribution to development as an independent criterion to investment, meaning that it could not alone satisfy the conditions of a covered investment.[191] Other arbitral tribunals have concluded that a separate

184 Yannick Radi, 'International Investment Law and Development: A History of Two Concepts' in Stephan Schill, Christian J Tams and Rainer Hofmann (eds), *International Investment Law and Development: Bridging the Gap* (Edward Elgar Publishing 2015) 78.

185 Dubava (n 178) 398.

186 Schill, Tams and Hofmann (n 73) 24.

187 Article 25 states that the "jurisdiction of the Centre shall extend to any legal dispute arising directly out of an investment" (Convention on the Settlement of Investment Disputes between States and Nations of Other States (2006), Art 25).

188 The criteria approach in the investment treaty arbitration context was first identified, however, in *Fedax NV v Venezuela*, CSID Case No ARB/96/3 and then again in *Ceskoslovenska Obchodni Banka, AS (CSOB) v The Slovak Republic,* ICSID Case No ARB/97/4.

189 As stated by the Tribunal: "The doctrine generally considers that investment infers: contributions, a certain duration of performance of the contract and a participation in the risks of the transaction. In reading the Convention's preamble, one may add the contribution to the economic development of the host State of the investment as an additional condition" (*Salini Costruttori SpA and Italstrade SpA v Kingdom of Morocco*, ICSID Case No ARB/00/4, Decision on Jurisdiction (23 July 2001) para 57).

190 Convention on the Settlement of Investment Disputes between States and Nations of Other States (2006) preamble.

191 For instance, the Tribunal in *Saba Fakes v Turkey* stated the following: "The Tribunal is not convinced, on the other hand, that a contribution to the host State's economic development constitutes a criterion of an investment within the framework of the ICSID Convention. Those tribunals that have considered this element as a separate requirement for the definition of an investment, such as the Salini Tribunal, have mainly relied on the preamble to the ICSID Convention to support their conclusions. The present Tribunal observes that while the preamble refers to the "need for international cooperation for economic development", it would be excessive to attribute to this reference a meaning and function that is not obviously apparent from its wording. In the Tribunal's opinion, while the economic development of a host State is one of the proclaimed objectives of the ICSID

contribution to economic development is not necessary as it is implicitly covered by the traditional conditions of investment.[192] By being included in the ambit of the public interest that can be claimed by host states in the context of international investment law, considerations such as the right to development and sustainable development were taken up by the discretion of investment treaty arbitration tribunals.[193]

One such alternative means, for instance, has been to consider the host state's level of development.[194] Considering economic, political, and/or social circumstances of the host state prior to the investment that may compromise the host state's capacity to provide such minimum standards of treatment have also served as grounds for assessing the extent to which a host state is reasonably expected to uphold such obligations.[195]

One limitation, however, is that there has yet to have been any systematic or harmonized effort in substantiating the normative substance of "development".[196] One major trend in uniting international investment law and sustainable development has also been through renegotiating IIAs. Known as new generation IIAs, these bilateral or multilateral agreements are more expansive in scope than traditional investment agreements, which focus on protecting and promoting investment rather than safeguarding public interest issues such as sustainable development.[197] The UN Commission on Trade and Development provides the following definition:

> Broadly, "new generation" investment policies are characterized by (i) a recognition of the role of investment as a primary driver of economic growth and development and consequent realization that investment policies are a central part of *development strategies*; and (ii) a desire to pursue sustainable development through *responsible investment*, placing social and environmental goals on the same footing as economic growth and development

Convention, this objective is not in and of itself an independent criterion for the definition of an investment. The promotion and protection of investments in host States is expected to contribute to their economic development. Such development is an expected consequence, not a separate requirement, of the investment projects carried out by a number of investors in the aggregate. Taken in isolation, certain individual investments might be useful to the State and to the investor itself; certain might not. Certain investments expected to be fruitful may turn out to be economic disasters. They do not fall, for that reason alone, outside the ambit of the concept of investment" (*Saba Fakes v Republic of Turkey*, ICSID Case No ARB/07/20, Award (14 July 2010) para 111).

192 *Consortium Groupement LESI-DIPENTA v République Algérienne Démocratique et Populaire*, ICSID Case No ARB/03/08, Award (10 January 2005) para II.13(iv).

193 Radi (n 184) 79.

194 Dai Tamada, 'Must Investments Contribute to the Development of the Host State? The Salini Test Scrutinised' in Piotr Szwedo, Richard Peltz-Steele and Dai Tamada (eds), *Law and Development: Balancing Principles and Values* (Springer 2019) 111.

195 Schill, Tams and Hofmann (n 73) 26.

196 Nitish Monebhurrun, 'The Political Use of the Economic Development Criterion in Defining Investments in International Investment Arbitration' (2012) 29 Journal of International Arbitration 567, 569.

197 Sornarajah, *The International Law on Foreign Investment* (n 45) 172–73.

> objectives. Furthermore, (iii) a shared recognition of the need to *improve the effectiveness* of policies to promote and facilitate investment.[198]

New generation IIAs attempt to preserve both policy spaces for states to regulate on matters of the public interest and predictability to encourage investor confidence.[199] These policy spaces facilitated the exercise of regulatory power for legitimate objectives, such as sustainable development. In such spaces, the adequate exhaustion of local remedies before initiating international arbitration increased deference in standards of review. In doing so, such requirements represent a positive trend in empowering local judiciaries to contribute to larger public policy goals.[200] Deference helps to establish a balance between observing international standards, such as those that arise out of international investment law, and domestic judicial sovereignty. It does this by permitting foreign investors to access investment treaty arbitration while preventing national judicial systems from being eclipsed entirely. Investment treaty arbitration would then serve as a second forum for the settlement of disputes on the basis of treaty law through a fork-in-the-road clause while helping to preclude parallel submissions or forum shopping.[201]

This trend that has been observable in new generation IIAs that reference sustainable development in their preambular text as "purposive" under Article 31 of the Vienna Convention on the Law of Treaties.[202] Article 31(1) provides that "where the ordinary meaning of a treaty provision is vague", which in this case may be seen as the purpose of investment, "using the object and purpose will make the meaning of the provision more precise".[203] Thus in referencing sustainable development under the purpose of an investment agreement, new generation IIAs provide a further lens of interpreting "investment", which remains vague in its lack of specific definition.[204] Furthermore, one may argue that in referencing sustainable development, these new generation agreements confer to a broader nexus of multilateral instruments on sustainable development.[205] In doing so, these instruments may be

198 United Nations Trade and Development (UNCTAD), 'Investment Policy Framework for Sustainable Development' (United Nations 2015) UNCTAD/DIAE/PCB/2015/5 17.

199 Brauch and others (n 71) 20–22.

200 Caroline Henckels, 'Balancing Investment Protection and the Public Interest: The Role of the Standard of Review and the Importance of Deference in Investor—State Arbitration' (2013) 4 Journal of International Dispute Settlement 197, 199.

201 See George Foster, 'Striking a Balance Between Investor Protections and National Sovereignty: The Relevance of Local Remedies in Investment Treaty Arbitration' (2011) 49 Columbia Journal of Transnational Law.

202 Gehring and Segger (n 166) 110.

203 Ulf Linderfalk, *On the Interpretation of Treaties: The Modern International Law as Expressed in the 1969 Vienna Convention on the Law of Treaties* (Springer 2007) 203.

204 This was explored in Chapter 1, the problematization of which is explored in Pillar Four of the Conceptual Framework (Section 2.5). See, most recently, Roberto Castro de Figueiredo, 'The ICSID Convention and the VCLT: Interpreting the Term "Investment"' in Esmé Shirlow and Kiran Nasir Gore (eds), *The Vienna Convention on the Law of Treaties in Investor-State Disputes: History, Evolution and Future* (Kluwer Law International 2022) 76–77.

205 Such as those described later in Pillar One of the conceptual framework (Section 2.2).

viewed as alluding to a broader contextual understanding wherein the purpose of an investment need not be restricted to the interpretation of a single instrument, namely the IIA, but rather any number of instruments that may contextualize[206] the relationship between investment and sustainable development. One may go even further to argue that omitting considerations of sustainable development, having specifically been identified in new generation IIAs, would in fact be contrary to the general rule of interpretation in the Vienna Convention.[207]

Through a combination of interpretative statements and general exceptions in both operative and preambular provisions, new generation investment agreements more openly confront issues of sustainable development. In doing so, arbitral tribunals can more systematically encounter the challenge of balancing investment promotion and "non-investment policy objectives".[208] The increasing frequency and deeper integration of these features in investment agreements recognize that the promotion and protection of FDI is not the ends but the means to a longer run objective, such as sustainable development.[209]

1.3 Significance

FDI trebled at a record of more than USD 2 trillion at the end of 2015—a dramatic increase from USD 200 billion in 1990. From 2019 to 2020, with the onset of a global pandemic, FDI was shown to recover in a year (2021) to pre-pandemic levels.[210] The continued growth and resilience of FDI make it more important to ensure that investment is compatible with the constantly changing needs of sustainable development. This invariably also applies to the systems that govern FDI. International investment law must thus remain adaptable to multilateral as well as private sector efforts to enshrine sustainable development into the expanding trend of international investment and overall economic integration. Failure to do so risks dooming the international investment law and sustainable development nexus to Rodrik's paradox of globalization: regulatory systems increasingly unable to function in a sustainable manner as globalization expands due to policy diversity despite regulatory systems becoming more important to ensure sustainable globalization.[211] This same paradox is present in sustainable finance. Powerful private sector interests controlling enormous values of assets have been taking the lead in

206 Linderfalk (n 203) 103–5.

207 Castro de Figueiredo (n 204) 62.

208 Suzanne A Spears, 'The Quest for Policy Space in a New Generation of International Investment Agreements' (2010) 13 Journal of International Economic Law 1037, 1071.

209 Suzanne A Spears, 'The Quest for Policy Space in a New Generation of International Investment Agreements' (2010) 13 Journal of International Economic Law 1066–67.

210 United Nations Trade and Development (UNCTAD), 'Global Foreign Direct Investment Flows Over the Last 30 Years' (*World Investment Report*) <https://unctad.org/topic/investment/world-investment-report/fdi-flows-2022> accessed 22 June 2022.

211 For a summary of Rodrik's *The Globalization Paradox: Democracy and the Future of the World Economy*, see Dani Rodrik, 'The Paradox of Globalisation Is That Pushing It Too Far Undermines Its Own Institutional Foundations' (*LSE European Institute*, 2 January 2014) <https://blogs.lse.ac.uk/

designing ways to govern sustainable finance.[212] Governments have been slow to keep up,[213] though significant achievements have been made in establishing regulatory systems that can regulate but not stifle sustainable finance.[214] Meanwhile, in international investment law, there have been signs of change, yet a more marked systemic transformation remains far from sight. One area that has been particularly lacking is regulatory assessment of investment contributions to sustainable development.[215]

Within the broader research on international investment law, sustainable development, and Sustainable Investment, this work is placed in a smaller subset of scholarship that brings these fields together at the cross-disciplinary nexus that binds them together.[216] The outcome of this cross-disciplinary nexus is the Consolidated Method, which is one of the key contributions of this book. This project

---

europpblog/2014/01/02/the-paradox-of-globalisation-is-that-pushing-it-too-far-undermines-its-own-institutional-foundations-2/> accessed 17 August 2020.

212 See, for instance, International Institute for Sustainable Development (IISD), 'GISD Alliance Issues Recommendations to Scale up SDG Financing' (*SDG Knowledge Hub*, 11 August 2020) <http://sdg.iisd.org/news/gisd-alliance-issues-recommendations-to-scale-up-sdg-financing/> accessed 17 August 2020; Wal van Lierop, 'Most ESG Investing Makes a Charade of Fighting Climate Change' *Forbes* (2020) <www.forbes.com/sites/walvanlierop/2020/07/14/most-esg-investing-makes-a-charade-of-fighting-climate-change/> accessed 17 August 2020; Camilla Hodgson, 'Funds Branded "ESG" Are Laden with Technology Stocks' *Financial Times* (15 August 2020) <www.ft.com/content/ea295d51-d5c2-4916-8c63-017c352ea577> accessed 17 August 2020; 'Refinitiv Debuts ESG Scores' (*Finextra Research*, 7 July 2020) <www.finextra.com/pressarticle/83207/refinitiv-debuts-esg-scores> accessed 17 August 2020; Annie Massa, 'BlackRock's Green Dreams Got Complicated Fast' *Bloomberg* (6 June 2020) <www.bloomberg.com/news/articles/2020-06-06/larry-fink-s-green-dreams-for-blackrock-got-complicated-fast> accessed 17 August 2020.

213 The United States Department of Labor, for instance, proposed rules to exclude ESG considerations from pension investments. See Mark Schoeff Jr, 'SEC, DOL Take Different Approaches to Regulating ESG Investing' (*The Washington Insider: Investment*, 27 July 2020) <www.investmentnews.com/sec-dol-take-different-approaches-regulating-esg-investing-195514> accessed 17 August 2020; Haynes and Boone LLP, 'DOL Issues Proposed Rule to Amend the Investment Duties Regulation' (*Lexology*, 15 July 2020) <www.lexology.com/library/detail.aspx?g=fc6f1386-5394-47c3-83f5-ba9b12213dbe> accessed 17 August 2020; Ted Godbout, 'DOL's ESG Proposal Blasted by Commenters' (*National Association of Plan Advisors*, 5 August 2020) <www.napa-net.org/news-info/daily-news/dols-esg-proposal-blasted-commenters> accessed 17 August 2020.

214 The European Union has been leading regulatory efforts in this regard. See Seema Chandaria and Anna Perry, 'New European Rules Underline the Fund Industry's Desire for Sustainable Investment' (*Lexology*, 28 July 2020) <www.lexology.com/library/detail.aspx?g=8256554f-4fab-46c0-ae40-ffb73b6b9953> accessed 17 August 2020; Christian Hald-Mortensen, 'EU Taxonomy on Sustainable Finance and Its Expected Impacts' (*Medium*, 15 June 2020) <https://medium.com/@christian-haldmortensen/eu-taxonomy-on-sustainable-finance-and-its-expected-impacts-d4efbe7afa0d> accessed 17 August 2020; Regulation (EU) 2019/2088 on sustainability-related disclosures in the financial services sector 2020.

215 The OECD, for instance, has been focusing its work on this interaction. See David Gaukrodger, 'Business Responsibilities and Investment Treaties' (Organisation for Economic Cooperation and Development (OECD) 2020) Consultation paper by the OECD Secretariat.

216 Related research finds more thorough scoping in Chapter 2.

investigates and draws from that nexus through a single yet central tenet and mechanism in international investment law: the right to regulate for the public interest of sustainable development. In doing so, the right to regulate is viewed as a mechanism in international investment law that safeguards actions that result in verifiable sustainable development contributions, whether those actions are government measures or international investments (these referred to together as "Actions"). This view is further substantiated in Chapter 5, which synthesizes the approaches mounted throughout this work into the Consolidated Method.

The first of these approaches, the Framework, is explored in Chapter 3, which continues from efforts to rebalance the role of international investment and the regulatory space of the host state. This efforts have been captured in both the practice of and scholarship on investment treaty arbitration, where the activities of investors and TNCs through their investments promote "certain aspects of sustainable development" while also frustrating sustainable development in other ways.[217] Despite the pronounced role of investment in sustainable development in both the UN system and international investment law literature, there has been little cross-referencing at a procedurally and substantively operative level.

The second of these approaches, the Notion, adds to the research on the use of the right to regulate for the public interest of sustainable development by constructing a cross-sectional analysis with Sustainable Investment. In doing so, Chapter 4 identifies correlational elements that can be carried into both diverse scholarship as well as international development and investment law practice. However, one obstacle, as Chapter 4 identifies, is that the role of investment in sustainable development has largely been addressed separately within financial, legal, and development scholarship mostly in isolation from one another. Cross-sectional and correlational research and application of this kind has been of recent interest at the level of multilateral institutions, which signals a pertinent moment in both practice and scholarship to further pursue this connection. Chapter 5 combines these two approaches to shape a complementary and interdisciplinary synthesis, the Consolidated Method, in application to right to regulate for sustainable development. The implications of the Consolidated Method are explored further in application to key stakeholders in Chapter 6. Namely, those stakeholding interests most vulnerable to the consequences of an obdurate international investment law regime that continues to insulate itself from the new realities posed by a planetary and socioeconomic system in flux with only one true constant: the relentlessly growing costs of sustainability.

References

Ackerman F and others, *Trade in the Balance: Reconciling Trade and Climate Policy: Report of the Working Group on Trade, Investment, and Climate Policy* (Boston University Frederick S Pardee Center for the Study of the Longer-Range Future 2016) <https://open.bu.edu/handle/2144/22909> accessed 26 February 2020

217 Gehring and Segger (n 166) 95.

ADC Affiliate Limited and ADC & ADMC Management Limited v The Republic of Hungary, ICSID Case No ARB/03/16

Agreement Between the Government of Canada and the Government of the Republic of Benin for the Promotion and Reciprocal Protection of Investments (2013)

Alfaro L and others, 'Does Foreign Direct Investment Promote Growth? Exploring the Role of Financial Markets on Linkages' (2010) 91 Journal of Development Economics 242

Allee T and Peinhardt C, 'Contingent Credibility: The Impact of Investment Treaty Violations on Foreign Direct Investment' (2011) 65 International Organization 401

Altenburg T and Assmann C (eds), *Green Industrial Policy: Concept, Policies, Country Experiences* (United Nations Environment Programme (UNEP) 2017)

Baumgartner J, *Treaty Shopping in International Investment Law* (OUP 2016)

Bear Creek Mining Corporation v Republic of Peru, ICSID Case No ARB/14/21, Partial Dissenting Opinion of Professor Phillipe Sands QC (30 November 2017)

Behn D, 'Legitimacy, Evolution, and Growth in Investment Treaty Arbitration: Empirically Evaluating the State-of-the-Art' (2014) 46 Georgetown Journal of International Law 363

Berkowitz AC, Berkowitz BE and Berkowitz TB, *(Formerly Spence International Investments and Others) v Republic of Costa Rica*, ICSID Case No UNCT/13/2, Notice of Arbitration and Statement of Claim (10 June 2013)

Berkowitz AC, Berkowitz BE and Berkowitz TB, *(Formerly Spence International Investments and Others) v Republic of Costa Rica*, ICSID Case No UNCT/13/2, Respondent Response to Notice of Arbitration (26 July 2013)

Berkowitz AC, Berkowitz BE and Berkowitz TB, *(Formerly Spence International Investments and Others) v Republic of Costa Rica*, ICSID Case No UNCT/13/2, Interim Award (Corrected) (30 May 2017)

Bigdeli SZ, 'Clash of Rationalities: Revisiting the Trade and Environment Debate in Light of WTO Disputes Over Green Industrial Policy Special Issue: Trade & Climate Change' (2014) 6 Trade, Law and Development I

Bjorklund AK, 'The Emerging Civilization of Investment Arbitration' (2009) 113 Penn State Law Review 1269

Bonnitcha J, Poulsen LNS and Waibel M, *The Political Economy of the Investment Treaty Regime* (OUP 2017)

Branson WH, Guerrero I and Gunter BG, *Patterns of Development 1970–1994* (The World Bank 1998) 19670 <http://documents.worldbank.org/curated/en/675081468739202610/Patterns-of-development-1970-1994> accessed 18 February 2020

Brassett J and Tsingou E, 'The Politics of Legitimate Global Governance' (2011) 18 Review of International Political Economy 1

Brauch MD and others, 'Treaty on Sustainable Investment for Climate Change Mitigation and Adaptation: Aligning International Investment Law with the Urgent Need for Climate Change Action' (2019) 36 Journal of International Arbitration 7

Brown C and Miles K (eds), *Evolution in Investment Treaty Law and Arbitration* (CUP 2011)

Buchanan A and Keohane RO, 'The Legitimacy of Global Governance Institutions' (2006) 20 Ethics & International Affairs 405

'Canada-Certain Measures Affecting the Renewable Energy Generation Sector/Measures Relating to the Feed-in Tariff Program' Reports of the Panels, WT/DS412/DS426/R (19 December 2012)

'The Case for Simplifying Sustainable Investment Terminology' (Institute of International Finance 2019) IIF Sustainable Finance Working Group Report

Castro de Figueiredo R, 'The ICSID Convention and the VCLT: Interpreting the Term "Investment"' in Esmé Shirlow and Kiran Nasir Gore (eds), *The Vienna Convention on the Law of Treaties in Investor-State Disputes: History, Evolution and Future* (Kluwer Law International 2022)

'CETA Chapter by Chapter: Chapter Eight-Investment' (*Trade-European Commission*, 24 August 2018) <https://ec.europa.eu/trade/policy/in-focus/ceta/ceta-chapter-by-chapter/index_en.htm> accessed 20 August 2020

Chandaria S and Perry A, 'New European Rules Underline the Fund Industry's Desire for Sustainable Investment' (*Lexology*, 28 July 2020) <www.lexology.com/library/detail.aspx?g=8256554f-4fab-46c0-ae40-ffb73b6b9953> accessed 17 August 2020

Charanne and Construction Investments v Spain, SCC Case No V 062/2012

Charlotin D, 'Analysis: Tribunal Majority in Lone Star v Korea Decides That Financial Regulator Acted in Its Own Self-Interest by Covertly Lowering the Investor's Exit Payment; Dissenter Doubts This Finding on the Facts, and Sees No Wrongful Conduct or Causality' (*Investment Arbitration Reporter*, 10 October 2022) <www.iareporter.com/articles/analysis-tribunal-majority-in-lone-star-v-korea-decides-that-financial-regulator-acted-in-its-own-self-interest-by-covertly-lowering-the-investors-exit-payment-dissenter-doubts-this-findin/> accessed 20 October 2022

Choudhury B, 'International Investment Law as a Global Public Good Business Law Forum: Balancing Investor Protections, the Environment, and Human Rights' (2013) 17 Lewis & Clark Law Review 481

Consortium Groupement LESI-DIPENTA v République Algérienne Démocratique et Populaire, ICSID Case No ARB/03/08, Award (10 January 2005)

Convention on the Recognition and Enforcement of Foreign Arbitral Awards (1958)

Convention on the Settlement of Investment Disputes Between States and Nations of Other States (2006)

Cordonier Segger M-C, Gehring MW and Newcombe AP (eds), *Sustainable Development in World Investment Law* (Kluwer Law International 2011)

Creamer CD and Godzimirska Z, '(De)Legitimation at the WTO Dispute Settlement Mechanism' (2016) 49 Vanderbilt Journal of Transnational Law 275

Daniels RJ, *Defecting on Development: Bilateral Investment Treaties and the Subversion of the Rule of Law in the Developing World* (U of Toronto P, Faculty of Law 2004)

Danzman SB, 'The Political Economy of Bilateral Investment Treaties' in Markus Krajewski and Rhea Tamara Hoffmann (eds), *Research Handbook on Foreign Direct Investment* (Edward Elgar Publishing 2019)

Davitti D, *Investment and Human Rights in Armed Conflict: Charting an Elusive Intersection* (Bloomsbury Publishing 2019)

Delaney J and Magraw DB, 'Procedural Transparency' in *The Oxford Handbook of International Investment Law* (OUP 2008)

Desierto DA, 'Development as an International Right: Investment in the New Trade-Based IIAs' (2011) 3 Trade, Law and Development 296

Dolzer R and Schreuer C, *Principles of International Investment Law* (2nd edn, OUP 2012)

Dubava I, 'The Future of International Investment Protection Law: The Promotion of Sustainable (Economic) Development as a Public Good' in Ernst-Ulrich Petersmann and others (eds), *Reflections on the Constitutionalisation of International Economic Law: Liber Amicorum for Ernst-Ulrich Petersmann* (Martinus Nijhoff Publishers 2014)

EDF (Services) Limited v Romania, ICSID Case No ARB/05/13, Award (8 October 2009)

El Paso Energy International Company v The Argentine Republic, ICSID Case No ARB/03/15, Award (22 September 2014)

Espa I and Durán GM, 'Renewable Energy Subsidies and WTO Law: Time to Rethink the Case for Reform Beyond Canada—Renewable Energy/Fit Program' (2018) 21 Journal of International Economic Law 621

Faundez J, 'International Economic Law and Development: Before and After Neo-Liberalism' in Julio Faundez and Celine Tan (eds), *IEL, Globalization and Developing Countries* (Edward Elgar Publishing 2010)

Foster G, 'Striking a Balance Between Investor Protections and National Sovereignty: The Relevance of Local Remedies in Investment Treaty Arbitration' (2011) 49 Columbia Journal of Transnational Law

Franck SD, 'The Legitimacy Crisis in Investment Treaty Arbitration: Privatizing Public International Law Through Inconsistent Decisions' (2005) 73 Fordham Law Review 1521

Franck SD, 'Empiricism and International Law: Insights for Investment Treaty Dispute Resolution' (2008) 48 Virginia Journal of International Law

Franck SD, 'Development and Outcomes of Investment Treaty Arbitration' (2009) 50 Harvard International Law Journal 435

Free Trade Agreement Between Central America, the Dominican Republic and the United States of America (2004)

Freeman NW, 'Domestic Institutions, Capacity Limitations, and Compliance Costs: Host Country Determinants of Investment Treaty Arbitrations, 1987–2007' (2013) 39 International Interactions 54

The Future We Want: Outcome document of the United Nations Conference on Sustainable Development 2012 (UN Document A/RES/66/288)

Gaukrodger D, 'Business Responsibilities and Investment Treaties' Organisation for Economic Cooperation and Development (OECD) (2020) Consultation paper by the OECD Secretariat

Gehring MW and Segger M-CC, 'Overcoming Obstacles with Opportunities: Trade and Investment Agreements for Sustainable Development' [2015] International Investment Law and Development: Bridging the Gap 93

Ginsburg T, 'Pitfalls of Measuring the Rule of Law' (2011) 3 Hague Journal on the Rule of Law 269

Godbout T, 'DOL's ESG Proposal Blasted by Commenters' (*National Association of Plan Advisors*, 5 August 2020) <www.napa-net.org/news-info/daily-news/dols-esg-proposal-blasted-commenters> accessed 17 August 2020

Hald-Mortensen C, 'EU Taxonomy on Sustainable Finance and Its Expected Impacts' (*Medium*, 15 June 2020) <https://medium.com/@christianhaldmortensen/eu-taxonomy-on-sustainable-finance-and-its-expected-impacts-d4efbe7afa0d> accessed 17 August 2020

Hallward-Driemeier M, *Do Bilateral Investment Treaties Attract FDI? Only a Bit . . . and They Could Bite* (OUP 2009)

Hatchard J and Perry-Kessaris A, *Law and Development: Facing Complexity in the 21st Century* (Routledge-Cavendish 2012)

Havranek T and Irsova Z, 'Estimating Vertical Spillovers from FDI: Why Results Vary and What the True Effect Is' (2011) 85 Journal of International Economics 234

Haynes and Boone LLP, 'DOL Issues Proposed Rule to Amend the Investment Duties Regulation' (*Lexology*, 15 July 2020) <www.lexology.com/library/detail.aspx?g=fc6f1386-5394-47c3-83f5-ba9b12213dbe> accessed 17 August 2020

Henckels C, 'Balancing Investment Protection and the Public Interest: The Role of the Standard of Review and the Importance of Deference in Investor—State Arbitration' (2013) 4 Journal of International Dispute Settlement 197

Henckels C, 'Permission to Act: The Legal Character of General and Security Exceptions in International Trade and Investment Law' (2020) 69 International & Comparative Law Quarterly

Hindelang S and Krajewski M (eds), *Shifting Paradigms in International Investment Law: More Balanced, Less Isolated, Increasingly Diversified* (OUP 2016)

Hippolyte AR, 'Foreign Investment Law and Developing Countries' in Markus Krajewski and Rhea Tamara Hoffmann (eds), *Research Handbook on Foreign Direct Investment* (Edward Elgar Publishing 2019)

Hodgson C, 'Funds Branded "ESG" Are Laden with Technology Stocks' *Financial Times* (15 August 2020) <www.ft.com/content/ea295d51-d5c2-4916-8c63-017c352ea577> accessed 17 August 2020

Hollander-Blumoff R and Tyler TR, 'Procedural Justice and the Rule of Law: Fostering Legitimacy in Alternative Dispute Resolution' (2011) 2011 Journal of Dispute Resolution 1

International Institute for Sustainable Development (IISD), 'GISD Alliance Issues Recommendations to Scale up SDG Financing' (*SDG Knowledge Hub*, 11 August 2020) <http://

sdg.iisd.org/news/gisd-alliance-issues-recommendations-to-scale-up-sdg-financing/> accessed 17 August 2020

International Law Commission (ILC), 'Fragmentation of International Law: Difficulties Arising from the Diversification and Expansion of International Law' (2006) A/CN.4/L.702

Jang H, 'Government-Lone Star ISD, Final Hearing Concluded . . . If Recognized, Decision This Year ("Jeongbu-Lonseuta ISD, Choejong Byeonlon Mamuli . . . Ileumyeon Olhae Nae Gyeollon")' *Law Times* (7 June 2016)

Jensen L, 'Foreign Direct Investment and Growth in Fragile and Conflict Affected Countries: Role of Peacekeeping and Natural Resources' (United Nations Development Programme (UNDP) 2020) UNDP Global Policy Network

Johnson L, 'Green Foreign Direct Investment in Developing Countries' (United Nations Environment Programme (UNEP) 2017) UNEP Inquiry

Johnson L, Sachs L and Lobel N, 'Aligning International Investment Agreements with the Sustainable Development Goals' (Columbia Center on Sustainable Investment 2019) <http://ccsi.columbia.edu/work/projects/aligning-investment-treaties-with-sustainable-development/> accessed 25 February 2020

Jonas DS and Saunders TN, 'The Object and Purpose of a Treaty: Three Interpretive Methods' (2010) 43 Vanderbilt Journal of Transnational Law 565

Joseph Charles Lemire v Ukraine, ICSID Case No ARB/06/18, Award (8 July 2013)

Kalicki J and Raouf MA, *Evolution and Adaptation: The Future of International Arbitration* (Kluwer Law International BV 2019)

Kennedy D and Stiglitz JE (eds), *Law and Economics with Chinese Characteristics: Institutions for Promoting Development in the Twenty-First Century* (OUP 2013)

Kerner A, 'Why Should I Believe You? The Costs and Consequences of Bilateral Investment Treaties' (2009) 53 International Studies Quarterly 73

Kethireddy SR, 'Still the Law of Nations: Legitimate Expectations and the Sovereigntist Turn in International Investment Law' (2019) 44 Yale Journal of International Law 315

Kim HJ, 'A Study of Core Issues in Investor-State Dispute (Lone Star Funds vs. the Republic of Korea) ("Lone Star-Hangook Jeongbugan ISDui Juyo Naeyong-Gwa Jaengjeom")' (2012) 36 Dankook University Law Review 855

Kjaer PF and others (eds), 'The End of Trade and Investment Law as We Know It: From Singularity to Pluralism' in *World Trade and Investment Law Reimagined: A Progressive Agenda for an Inclusive Globalization* (CUP 2019)

Klabbers J, 'Some Problems Regarding the Object and Purpose of Treaties' (1997) 8 Finnish Yearbook of International Law 138

Knaus C, 'Philip Morris Cigarettes Charged Millions after Losing Plain Packaging Case against Australia' *The Guardian* (10 July 2017) <www.theguardian.com/business/2017/jul/10/philip-morris-cigarettes-charged-millions-after-losing-plain-packaging-case-against-australia> accessed 20 March 2020

Krugman P, 'Increasing Returns and Economic Geography' (1991) 99 Journal of Political Economy 483

Lang A, 'Heterodox Market Orders in the Global Trade System' in Alvaro Santos, Thomas Chantal and David M Trubek (eds), *World Trade and Investment Law Reimagined: A Progressive Agenda for an Inclusive Globalization* (CUP 2019)

Lee E, 'Treaty Shopping in International Investment Arbitration: How Often Has It Occurred and How Has It Been Perceived by Tribunals?' (London School of Economics and Political Science 2015) Department of International Development Working Paper Series No 15–167

Lee S, 'The Role of the WTO in Sustainable Development Governance, Revisited' (2018) 10 Trade, Law and Development 135

Lee S, 'In the Habit of Giants: Fair and Equitable Treatment and Structural Risk Factors in Conglomerate-Led Newly Industrialized Countries' in Junji Nakagawa (ed), *Asian Perspectives on International Investment Law* (Routledge 2019)

Levashova Y, *The Right of States to Regulate in International Investment Law: The Search for Balance Between Public Interest and Fair and Equitable Treatment* (Kluwer Law International BV 2019)

Linderfalk U, *On the Interpretation of Treaties: The Modern International Law as Expressed in the 1969 Vienna Convention on the Law of Treaties* (Springer 2007)

Love I and Klapper LF, *Corporate Governance, Investor Protection, and Performance in Emerging Markets* (The World Bank 2002)

LSF-KEB Holdings SCA and Others v Republic of Korea, ICSID Case No ARB/12/37, Award (30 August 2022)

LSF-KEB Holdings SCA and Others v Republic of Korea, ICSID Case No ARB/12/37, Concurring Opinion of Judge Charles N. Brower (30 August 2022)

LSF-KEB Holdings SCA and Others v Republic of Korea, ICSID Case No ARB/12/37, Dissenting Opinion of Professor Brigitte Stern (30 August 2022)

Massa A, 'BlackRock's Green Dreams Got Complicated Fast' *Bloomberg* (6 June 2020) <www.bloomberg.com/news/articles/2020-06-06/larry-fink-s-green-dreams-for-black rock-got-complicated-fast> accessed 17 August 2020

Massoud MF, 'International Arbitration and Judicial Politics in Authoritarian States' (2014) 39 Law & Social Inquiry 1

Meuer J, Koelbel J and Hoffmann VH, 'On the Nature of Corporate Sustainability' (2020) 33 Organization & Environment 319

Miles K (ed), *Research Handbook on Environment and Investment Law* (Edward Elgar Publishing 2019)

Ministry of Energy, Northern Development and Mines, Canada, 'Renewable Energy Development in Ontario: A Guide for Municipalities: 4.0 Feed-In Tariff Program' <www.ontario.ca/document/renewable-energy-development-ontario-guide-municipalities/40-feed-tariff-program> accessed 8 October 2020

Moehlecke C, 'The Chilling Effect of International Investment Disputes: Limited Challenges to State Sovereignty' (2020) 64 International Studies Quarterly 1

Mollestad C, 'See No Evil? Procedural Transparency in International Investment Law and Dispute Settlement' (PluriCourts 2014) PluriCourts Research Paper No 14-20

Monebhurrun N, 'The Political Use of the Economic Development Criterion in Defining Investments in International Investment Arbitration' (2012) 29 Journal of International Arbitration 567

Montt S, *State Liability in Investment Treaty Arbitration: Global Constitutional and Administrative Law in the BIT Generation* (Bloomsbury Publishing 2009)

Morosini F and Sanchez MR (eds), *Reconceptualizing International Investment Law from the Global South* (CUP 2017)

Mouyal LW, *International Investment Law and the Right to Regulate: A Human Rights Perspective* (Routledge 2016)

Muchlinski P, 'Caveat Investor? The Relevance of the Conduct of the Investor Under the Fair and Equitable Treatment Standard' (2006) 55 International & Comparative Law Quarterly 527

Murakami Y and Otsuka K, 'Governance, Information Spillovers, and Productivity of Local Firms: Toward an Integrated Approach to Foreign Direct Investment and Global Value Chains' (2020) 58 The Developing Economies

Newton S, 'The Dialectics of Law and Development' in David M Trubek and Alvaro Santos (eds), *The New Law and Economic Development: A Critical Appraisal* (CUP 2005)

Olmedo JG, 'Recalibrating the International Investment Regime Through Narrowed Jurisdiction' (2020) 69 International & Comparative Law Quarterly 301

Pauwelyn J, 'At the Edge of Chaos? Foreign Investment Law as a Complex Adaptive System, How It Emerged and How It Can Be Reformed' (2014) 29 ICSID Review—Foreign Investment Law Journal 372

Philip Morris Asia Ltd v Australia, PCA Case No 2012-12, Award on Jurisdiction and Admissibility (17 December 2015)

Plama Consortium Limited v Republic of Bulgaria, ICSID Case No ARB/03/24, Award (27 August 2008)
Puig S and Shaffer G, 'Imperfect Alternatives: Institutional Choice and the Reform of Investment Law' (2018) 112 American Journal of International Law 361
Radi Y, 'International Investment Law and Development: A History of Two Concepts' in Stephan Schill, Christian J Tams and Rainer Hofmann (eds), *International Investment Law and Development: Bridging the Gap* (Edward Elgar Publishing 2015)
'Refinitiv Debuts ESG Scores' (*Finextra Research*, 7 July 2020) <www.finextra.com/pressarticle/83207/refinitiv-debuts-esg-scores> accessed 17 August 2020
Regulation (EU) 2019/2088 on Sustainability-Related Disclosures in the Financial Services Sector 2020
Robbins J, 'The Emergence of Positive Obligations in Bilateral Investment Treaties' (2005) 13 University of Miami International & Comparative Law Review 403
Rodrik D, 'The Paradox of Globalisation Is That Pushing It too Far Undermines Its Own Institutional Foundations' (*LSE European Institute*, 2 January 2014) <https://blogs.lse.ac.uk/europpblog/2014/01/02/the-paradox-of-globalisation-is-that-pushing-it-too-far-undermines-its-own-institutional-foundations-2/> accessed 17 August 2020
Rolland S, Santos A and Trubek D (eds), 'Embedded Neoliberalism and Its Discontents: The Uncertain Future of Trade and Investment Law' in *World Trade and Investment Law Reimagined: A Progressive Agenda for an Inclusive Globalization* (CUP 2019)
Rostow WW, *The Stages of Economic Growth: A Non-Communist Manifesto* (CUP 1990)
Saba Fakes v Republic of Turkey, ICSID Case No ARB/07/20, Award (14 July 2010)
Salini Costruttori SpA and Italstrade SpA v Kingdom of Morocco, ICSID Case No ARB/00/4, Decision on Jurisdiction (23 July 2001)
Saluka Investments BV v The Czech Republic, UNCITRAL, Partial Award (17 March 2006)
Santos A, Thomas C and Trubek DM (eds), *World Trade and Investment Law Reimagined: A Progressive Agenda for an Inclusive Globalization* (Anthem Press 2019)
Schill SW and Gülay K, 'Approaches to Foreign Direct Investment in Legal Research' in Markus Krajewski and Rhea Tamara Hoffmann (eds), *Research Handbook on Foreign Direct Investment* (Edward Elgar Publishing 2019)
Schill SW, Tams CJ and Hofmann R, 'International Investment Law and Development: Friends or Foes?' in *International Investment Law and Development: Bridging the Gap* (Edward Elgar Publishing 2015)
Schoeff M Jr, 'SEC, DOL Take Different Approaches to Regulating ESG Investing' (*The Washington Insider: Investment*, 27 July 2020) <www.investmentnews.com/sec-dol-take-different-approaches-regulating-esg-investing-195514> accessed 17 August 2020
Schram A and others, 'Internalisation of International Investment Agreements in Public Policymaking: Developing a Conceptual Framework of Regulatory Chill' (2018) 9 Global Policy 193
Schreuer C, 'Nationality of Investors: Legitimate Restrictions vs. Business Interests' (2009) 24 ICSID Review—Foreign Investment Law Journal 521
Schultz T and Dupont C, 'Investment Arbitration: Promoting the Rule of Law or Over-Empowering Investors? A Quantitative Empirical Study' (2015) 25 European Journal of International Law 1147
Smarzynska Javorcik B, 'Does Foreign Direct Investment Increase the Productivity of Domestic Firms? In Search of Spillovers Through Backward Linkages' (2004) 94 American Economic Review 605
SolEs Badajoz GmbH v Kingdom of Spain, ICSID Case No ARB/15/38, Award (31 July 2019)
Sornarajah M, 'Power and Justice: Third World Resistance in International Law' (2006) 10 Singapore Year Book of International Law 19
Sornarajah M, 'Developing Countries in the Investment Treaty System: A Law for Need or a Law for Greed?' in Stephan W Schill, Christian J Tams and Hofmann Rainer (eds), *International Investment Law and Development: Bridging the Gap* (Edward Elgar Publishing 2015)

Sornarajah M, *Resistance and Change in the International Law on Foreign Investment* (CUP 2015)

Sornarajah M, 'An International Investment Court: Panacea or Purgatory?' (Columbia Center on Sustainable Investment 2016) Columbia FDI Perspectives 180

Sornarajah M, 'International Investment Law as Development Law: The Obsolescence of a Fraudulent System' (2016) 7 European Yearbook of International Economic Law 209

Sornarajah M, *The International Law on Foreign Investment* (4th edn, CUP 2017)

Sornarajah M, Linarelli J and Salomon ME, *The Misery of International Law: Confrontations with Injustice in the Global Economy* (OUP 2018)

Spears SA, 'The Quest for Policy Space in a New Generation of International Investment Agreements' (2010) 13 Journal of International Economic Law 1037

Stiglitz JE, 'Whither Reform: Ten Years of the Transition' (Annual World Bank Conference on Development Economics, Washington, DC, 28 April 1999)

St John T, *The Rise of Investor-State Arbitration: Politics, Law, and Unintended Consequences* (OUP 2018)

Tamada D, 'Must Investments Contribute to the Development of the Host State? The Salini Test Scrutinised' in Piotr Szwedo, Richard Peltz-Steele and Dai Tamada (eds), *Law and Development: Balancing Principles and Values* (Springer 2019)

Tan C, 'Reviving the Emperor's Old Clothes: The Good Governance Agenda, Development and International Investment Law' in Stephan W Schill, Christian J Tams and Rainer Hofmann (eds), *International Investment Law and Development Bridging the Gap* (Edward Elgar Publishing 2015)

Tan C, 'Beyond the "Moments" of Law and Development: Critical Reflections on Law and Development Scholarship in a Globalized Economy' (2019) 12 Law and Development Review 285

Thomas MD, 'Memorandum Required by Article 8.1 of the Agreement Between the Government of the Republic of Korea and the Belgium-Luxembourg Economic Union for the Reciprocal Promotion and Protection of Investments with Respect to the Dispute Between Lone Star and the Republic of Korea' (21 May 2012)

Tienhaara K, 'Regulatory Chill and the Threat of Arbitration: A View from Political Science' in Chester Brown and Kate Miles (eds), *Evolution in Investment Treaty Law and Arbitration* (CUP 2011)

Tienhaara K, 'Regulatory Chill in a Warming World: The Threat to Climate Policy Posed by Investor-State Dispute Settlement' (2018) 7 Transnational Environmental Law 229

Tokios Tokelės v Ukraine, ICSID Case No ARB/02/18, Award (26 July 2007)

Total SA v Argentine Republic, ICSID Case No ARB/04/01, Decision on Liability (27 December 2010)

Transforming Our World: The 2030 Agenda for Sustainable Development 2015 (UN Document A/RES/70/1)

Tulip Real Estate Investment and Development Netherlands BV v Republic of Turkey, ICSID Case No ARB/11/28, Decisions on Annulment (30 December 2015)

United Nations, 'Promote Inclusive and Sustainable Economic Growth, Employment and Decent Work for All' (*Sustainable Development Goals*) <www.un.org/sustainabledevelopment/economic-growth/> accessed 27 February 2020

United Nations Trade and Development (UNCTAD), 'Investment Policy Framework for Sustainable Development' (United Nations 2015) UNCTAD/DIAE/PCB/2015/5

United Nations Trade and Development (UNCTAD), 'Global Foreign Direct Investment Flows Over the Last 30 Years' (*World Investment Report*) <https://unctad.org/topic/investment/world-investment-report/fdi-flows-2022> accessed 22 June 2022

United Nations Trade and Development (UNCTAD), 'Goal 8: Decent Work and Economic Growth' (*SDG Pulse*) <https://sdgpulse.unctad.org/sdgs/goal-8-decent-work-and-economic-growth/> accessed 27 February 2020

Urbaser SA and Consorcio de Aguas Bilbao Bizkaia, Bilbao Biskaia Ur Partzuergoa v The Argentine Republic, ICSID Case No ARB/07/26, Award (8 December 2016)

VanDuzer JA, 'Can International Investment Agreements Be Instruments of Sustainable Development? Systemic Capacity Challenges for Developing Countries' in Joost Pauwelyn and Mengyi Wang (eds), *Building Legal Capacity for a More Inclusive Globalization: Barriers to and Best Practices for Integrating Developing Countries into The Maze of Global Economic Regulation* (Georgetown Law and The Graduate Institute 2019)

Van Harten G, *Investment Treaty Arbitration and Public Law* (OUP 2008)

Van Harten G, 'Investment Treaty Arbitration, Procedural Fairness, and the Rule of Law' in Stephan W Schill (ed), *International Investment Law and Comparative Public Law* (OUP 2010)

Van Harten G and Loughlin M, 'Investment Treaty Arbitration as a Species of Global Administrative Law' (2006) 17 European Journal of International Law 121

Van Harten G and Scott DN, 'Investment Treaties and the Internal Vetting of Regulatory Proposals: A Case Study from Canada' (2016) 7 Journal of International Dispute Settlement 92

van Lierop W, 'Most ESG Investing Makes a Charade of Fighting Climate Change' *Forbes* (2020) <www.forbes.com/sites/walvanlierop/2020/07/14/most-esg-investing-makes-a-charade-of-fighting-climate-change/> accessed 17 August 2020

Vastardis AY, 'Chapter 7: Evaluation of Responses to Nationality Shopping and the Way Forward' in *The Nationality of Corporate Investors Under International Investment Law* (Hart Publishing 2020)

Waibel M, *The Backlash Against Investment Arbitration: Perceptions and Reality* (Kluwer Law International BV 2010)

Williamson J, *A Short History of the Washington Consensus* (OUP 2008)

Yannaca-Small K (ed), *Arbitration under International Investment Agreements: A Guide to the Key Issues* (OUP 2010)

Zagha R and Nankani GT, *Economic Growth in the 1990s: Learning from a Decade of Reform* (World Bank 2005)

2 Four-pillar interdisciplinary analysis

2.1 Background and scope

This work posits that sustainable development should be understood in international investment law within the context of other obligations, such as multilateral agreements concerning sustainable development, as well as the sustainable development impact of international investment. Building from the evolutionary approach to international investment research discussed in the previous chapter, this chapter presents the four conceptual pillars of the interdisciplinary analysis featured in this text.

The first pillar is a definitional framework concerning sustainable development as it is addressed in this chapter. The second pillar concerns the notion of Sustainable Investment. The third pillar is the specific mechanism in international investment law at the centre of this work: the right to regulate. The fourth and final pillar examines the idea of an incomplete assessment, was which was raised in the research questions.

These four pillars come together to form the conceptual foundation in the shape of two synthesizing statements, upon which this work is built. These statements help to tie the constructed methodology to the existing research as well as the conceptual backdrop provided in this chapter.

2.2 Pillar One: international investment and sustainable development

A central theme in this work is investigating the balance between guaranteeing minimum standards of treatment to investors and maintaining the capacity of the state hosting the investment to enumerate those standards for matters concerning sustainable development. On the one hand, granting rights and protections to the foreign investor typically in exchange for some of the host state's policy space.[1]

1 Stephan W Schill, Christian J Tams and Rainer Hofmann, 'International Investment Law and Development: Friends or Foes?' in *International Investment Law and Development: Bridging the Gap* (Edward Elgar Publishing 2015) 9.

DOI: 10.4324/9781003495871-2

On the other hand, reserving[2] dynamic policy capacities for the host state comes at the cost of regulatory predictability, which can undermine investor confidence.[3] In international investment law, these dynamic policy capacities are usually reserved to the host state in order to regulate on matters concerning "reasons of internal security, the economic well-being of the nation, public order, health and morality or to secure respect for the rights and freedoms of others".[4] Efforts to achieve sustainable development fall into that remit.[5]

Starting from this point of departure, this chapter begins with a working definition of the role of international investment in sustainable development. In continuing from the argument presented in this work, which sought to embrace a multilaterally agreed conceptualization of sustainable development, the working definition is assembled by tracing the relationship between investment and sustainable development as identified by through the UN system.

While a comprehensive treatment of the theoretical origins of sustainable development as a concept is beyond the scope of this writing,[6] Table 2.1 presents the way in which the operative descriptors of sustainable development and the role of investment in sustainable development were conceptualized based on an analysis of major multilateral instruments and agreements by the UN from 1972 until 2021. These descriptors, taken together, help identify key ideational and correlational elements in a working definition of sustainable development employed by and within the UN system. The following table is a summary of the key findings of the analysis presented later in this chapter.

In searching for a working definition to be used throughout this book, the above documents were analysed by first identifying the content that broach the topic of

2 As an "inalienable right", see Srinath Reddy Kethireddy, 'Still the Law of Nations: Legitimate Expectations and the Sovereigntist Turn in International Investment Law' (2019) 44 Yale Journal of International Law 315, 319.

3 Rudolf Dolzer and Christoph Schreuer, *Principles of International Investment Law* (2nd edn, OUP 2012) 9.

4 Ian Brownlie, *Principles of Public International Law* (7th edn, OUP 2008) 527.

5 Markus W Gehring and Andrew Paul Newcombe, 'Chapter 1: An Introduction to Sustainable Development in World Investment Law' in Marie-Claire Cordonier Segger, Markus W Gehring and Andrew Paul Newcombe (eds), *Sustainable Development in World Investment Law* (Kluwer Law International 2011) 2.

6 A comprehensive literature review and accompanying meta-analysis can be found in Justice Mensah and Sandra Ricart Casadevall, 'Sustainable Development: Meaning, History, Principles, Pillars, and Implications for Human Action: Literature Review' (2019) 5 Cogent Social Sciences 1653531. Contrasts have been drawn between sustainability and sustainable development, as in Rob Gray, 'Is Accounting for Sustainability Actually Accounting for Sustainability . . . and How Would We Know? An Exploration of Narratives of Organisations and the Planet' (2010) 35 Accounting, Organizations and Society 47. More relevant to this project, however, is sustainable development as it is understood from the perspective of governance, referring here to John C Dernbach, 'Sustainable Development as a Framework for National Governance' (1998) 49 Case Western Reserve Law Review 1. A recent and comprehensive treatment of sustainable development as a both a principle of governance and law is found in the seminal work, Hans Christian Bugge and Christina Voigt (eds), *Sustainable Development in International and National Law* (Europa Law Publishing 2008).

Table 2.1 Operational definition of sustainable development and the role of investment

Instrument (Year)	*Operative descriptor of sustainable development*	*Role of investment in sustainable development*
Stockholm Declaration (1972)	Human-centric prosperity balanced with due diligence and liability for environmental harm	Included into private sector actions held liable for environmental harm arising from economic processes
Declaration on the Right to Development (1986)	Collective responsibility for minimum standard of living conditions and human rights	Included into the sovereign right over and to exploit natural resources As a means of international cooperation towards collective responsibility
Agenda 21 (1992)	Improve welfare of populations, meet their basic needs without deteriorating or depleting the resource base that underpins development	As having a significantly elevated role in achieving domestic sustainable development: welfare, technology, and infrastructure As part of conduct of transnational corporations supportive of sustainable development As needing to be facilitated through partnerships with government and the UN
United Nations Framework Convention on Climate Change (1994) and Kyoto Protocol (1998)	Precautionary principles to climate change with common but differentiated responsibilities as embodying intergenerational development	As a means of private sector finance eligible for certified emissions reductions under the clean development mechanism
Monterrey Consensus (2002)	Pursuit of international agreed development goals and objectives, e.g., the Millennium Development Goals	As one dimension of the Financing for Development framework (investment, trade, official development assistance, and debt) As promoting a stable and predictable system of economic governance and integration
Doha Declaration (2009)	National ownership and implementation of Financing for Development while encouraging more investment with maximum development impact	As a means of encouraging responsible corporate behaviour As a means to promote a stable and predictable investment climate
Rio+20 (2009)	Three dimensions of sustainable development: economic, social and environmental Green economy principles	As "green investment", or a means towards achieving the green economy concept, balancing the three dimensions of sustainable development
Addis Ababa Action Agenda (2015)	Strengthened presence of environmental dimension in Financing for Development framework from Rio+20	As being held accountable through environmental, social, and governance (ESG) reporting
2030 Agenda (2015)	Sustainable Development Goals as cohesive framework both integrating and balancing the three dimensions of sustainable development	As part of a "trade-investment nexus" connecting multilateral agreements with the three dimensions of sustainable development
Paris Agreement (2015)	Integrate climate change resilience (mitigation and adaptation) into national development policy	As a means of scaling up "climate finance" that balances adaptation and mitigation

international investment and then extracting the way in which international investment is conceived to contribute to sustainable development. The table above is an outline of this analysis, which provides the basis upon which the following working definition is synthesized:

The role of investment in sustainable development is defined by the extent to which it meets three fundamental criteria:

1 It is high-quality and positive, which in turn is measured by its observation of the precautionary principle[7];
2 It coheres with national development planning of the host state especially in developing economies and in respecting national ownership and sovereignty over natural resources; and
3 It remains an engine of sustained growth that is supportive of the host state's promotion and maintenance of a stable and predictable regulatory climate in its financing for development.

This definition is employed centrally at different stages throughout this book. First, in the present chapter, it is presented as a set of nucleic elements in providing a definition of sustainable development tailored to the needs of this project. Second, in Chapter 3, it is examined in its operationalization by the United Nations and

7 The precautionary principle here refers the general principle in international environmental law. McIntyre and Mosedale trace the origins and applications of the precautionary principle from the assimilative capacity approach ("assumption that science could accurately determine the assimilative capacity of the environment") to a more general principle that bends towards safety, caution and excess environmental protections based on "an entirely new set of assumptions, including: the vulnerability of the environment; the limitations of science to accurately predict threats to the environment; and, the availability of alternative, less harmful processes and products" (Owen McIntyre and Thomas Mosedale, 'The Precautionary Principle as a Norm of Customary International Law' (1997) 9 Journal of Environmental Law 221–22). Foster, in her text on the application of the precautionary principle in international adjudication as bearing the burden of proof, observed that the "precautionary principle is understood to involve a move away from the 'primacy of scientific proof'. The emphasis falls instead on the limitations of scientific prediction, and the need for decision-making that errs on the side of allowing for worst-case scenarios. . . . While preventive action involves intervention prior to the occurrence of damage in relation to known risks, precaution involves a preparedness by public authorities to intervene in advance in relation to potential, uncertain or hypothetical threats. If the risk is sufficiently serious in character, precaution may posit intervention even where a risk is simply suspected, conjectured, or feared" (Caroline E Foster, *Science and the Precautionary Principle in International Courts and Tribunals: Expert Evidence, Burden of Proof and Finality* (CUP 2011) 18). On matters of responsibility, Brownlie, for instance, identified that the "taking of precautions does not preclude responsibility if the risks are foreseeably high at the outset and damage is in fact caused. . . . [C]ertain standards of environmental conservation come to be regarded as binding *erga omnes* . . . certain forms of threat to the environment, in particular those which are known to cause intolerable risk, including irreversible forms of degradation, and waste, may be assimilated to the category *delicta juris gentium*" (Ian Brownlie, 'A Survey of International Customary Rules of Environmental Protection' (1973) 13 Natural Resources Journal 179, 182–83).

applications in the private sector. Finally, in Chapter 4, it is studied in the context of investment in sustainable development, a key theme of this research.

Beyond the definition presented above, however, one of the most fundamental, if not the most ubiquitous, concepts[8] in defining sustainable development is intergenerational development. Tracing the origins and legacy of this concept, especially in connection to investment, is helpful in determining whether the working definition provided above is compatible with a more generalized understanding of sustainable development.

Intergenerational development was identified by the Brundtland Report as seeking to "meet the needs and aspirations of the present without compromising the ability to meet those of the future".[9] The Report identified sustainable development to be a right that should also be reserved for future generations, or an intergenerational right, but also a means to realize human rights. Development has also been further conceptualized as a right to, or the removal of the constraints to, economic, social, cultural, and political development.[10] Sen, for instance, articulated development as a freedom and as a way to the full realization of a person's capabilities. He identified the achievement of such freedom to develop as the primary ends and principal means of development.[11] This then required what Sen identified as the capabilities approach:

> The primary claim is that in evaluating well-being, the value-objects are the functionings and capabilities. That claim neither entails that all types of capabilities are equally valuable, nor indicates that any capability whatsoever—even if totally remote from the person's life—must have some value in assessing that person's well-being. It is in asserting the need to examine the value of functionings and capabilities as opposed to confining attention to the means to these achievements and freedoms (such as resources or primary

8 Insofar as it served a common starting point adopted multilaterally through the United Nations (Andrew Steer and Will Wade-Gery, 'Sustainable Development: Theory and Practice for a Sustainable Future' (1993) 1 Sustainable Development 23).

9 United Nations General Assembly, 'Report of the World Commission on Environment and Development: "Our Common Future"' (1987) UNEP/GC/14/13 ch 1, para 49 <http://digitallibrary.un.org/record/133790> accessed 18 February 2020. The Brundtland Commission Report was produced by 22 members from 21 nations representing all regions and a wide variety of professions in the effort to be independent and unanimous, representing thousands of views from institutions and individuals around the world. The report sought to emphasize different qualities of growth based on balanced economic expansion and environmental protection through critical objectives related to jobs, population, natural resources and technology Hans Christian Bugge, '1987–2007: "Our Common Future" Revisited' in Christina Voigt (ed), *Sustainable Development in International and National Law* (Europa Law Publishing 2008) 4–9.

10 The reframing of sustainable development into the context of the Global South was a key factor behind this. See, generally, Sakiko Fukuda-Parr and Bhumika Muchhala, 'The Southern Origins of Sustainable Development Goals: Ideas, Actors, Aspirations' (2020) 126 World Development.

11 Amartya Sen, *Development as Freedom* (OUP 2001) 35–38.

> goods or incomes) that the capability approach has something to offer. The relative valuation of different functionings and capabilities has to be an integral part of the exercise.[12]

Developing capabilities then defines the extent to which one can achieve well-being, which Sen identified as "well-being freedom"[13]:

> Importance may well be attached to checking whether one person did have the opportunity of achieving the functioning vector that another actually achieved. This involves comparison of actual opportunities that different persons have. If one person could have achieved all the relevant functioning vectors that the other could, then in some important sense the first person had at least as much freedom to live well. The general idea of the freedom to achieve well-being can be called well-being freedom.[14]

Sen's work was fundamental to what was later taken up by the UN as the human development approach as seen in the report "Towards a Common Understanding among UN Agencies", which sought to redirect the object and purpose of development agendas towards the achievement of the Universal Declaration of Human Rights.[15] Sustainable development became increasingly enshrined in UN treaty text as attention shifted to applying sustainability as a qualifier to development, facilitated by an expansion of the concept of development to increasingly include socio-political dimensions.[16]

Moving closer to investment, in connection to transnational corporations (TNCs), De Schutter, former UN Special Rapporteur on the right to food and

12 Amartya Sen, *Inequality Reexamined* (OUP 1995) 45–46.

13 Though as Nussbaum identified, this was incomplete in its aim to "reorient the development and policy debate, rather than to advance a systematic economic or political theory" (Martha Craven Nussbaum, *Creating Capabilities: The Human Development Approach* (Harvard UP 2011) 17). She offers a contrasting notion of freedom in connection to capabilities that diverges from what she identified as a utilitarianism in Sen's notion: "Capabilities such as health, bodily integrity, practical reason, and religious liberty are on the list precisely because they are valuable in pursuit of many different life plans. But it does not take a stand on each and every freedom to pursue each and every element in all the conceptions of the good, nor does it guarantee every citizen an opportunity to pursue every such element. Some conceptions of good, for example, require expensive resources that would compromise the state's ability to protect its citizens in fundamental matters" (Martha Craven Nussbaum, *Creating Capabilities: The Human Development Approach* (Harvard UP 2011) 201).

14 Amartya Sen, 'Well-Being, Agency and Freedom: The Dewey Lectures 1984' (1985) 82 The Journal of Philosophy 169, 201.

15 United Nations Sustainable Development Group (UNSDG), 'The Human Rights Based Approach to Development Cooperation Towards a Common Understanding Among UN Agencies' <https://unsdg.un.org/resources/human-rights-based-approach-development-cooperation-towards-common-understanding-among-un> accessed 18 February 2020.

16 Christina Voigt, *Sustainable Development as a Principle of International Law: Resolving Conflicts Between Climate Measures and WTO Law* (Martinus Nijhoff Publishers 2009) 13.

current Special Rapporteur on extreme poverty and human rights, identified the responsibility of business enterprises to address business-related constraints, such as those abusive towards the right to food[17] and human rights.[18] Due diligence in relation to that responsibility can be observed, for instance, by the corporation adopting "horizontal policy coherence" that coordinates "across different policy areas and levels of governance" with the state maintaining an "adequate domestic policy space"[19] to protect its public interests such as human rights. That role of the state includes finding a balance between economic growth and the interests of sustainable development, which continues to be a central theme in the UN system.[20]

2.2.1 Institutional history of the role of investment in sustainable development from within the UN system

The centrality of private sector investment in advancing sustainable development began with a human-centric approach adopted in the 1972 *Declaration of the UN Conference on the Human Environment* (the "Stockholm Declaration"), described as an "instrumentalist approach to the environment".[21] This instrumentalism highlighted an incompatibility in and following the Stockholm Convention, between a state's obligation to carry out due diligence to prevent damage to the environment and the state's right to exploit its natural resources for development purposes. While international law mechanisms were designed to address the balance between environmental due diligence and a state's right to exploit "its" environment, states "tended to shy away from addressing the matter head-on or comprehensively, preferring instead to establish so-called private law regimes that focus on liability, while mostly excluding consideration of States' accountability".[22]

17 Olivier De Schutter, 'Promotion and Protection of All Human Rights, Civil, Political, Economic, Social and Cultural Rights, Including the Right to Development: Report of the Special Rapporteur on the Right to Food, Mr Olivier De Schutter' (United Nations Human Rights Council (HRC) 2009) A/HRC/10/5 <https://www2.ohchr.org/english/bodies/hrcouncil/docs/10session/A.HRC.10.5.pdf>.

18 Olivier De Schutter, 'Towards a New Treaty on Business and Human Rights' (2016) 1 Business and Human Rights Journal 41–42.

19 Olivier De Schutter, 'Towards a New Treaty on Business and Human Rights' (2016) 1 Business and Human Rights Journal 57.

20 Olivier De Schutter, 'Chapter 4. Generalized Systems of Preferences: The "Conditional Preferences" Approach' in *Trade in the Service of Sustainable Development: Linking Trade to Labour Rights and Environmental Standards* (Hart Publishing 2015) 114.

21 Günther Handl, 'Declaration of the United Nations Conference on the Human Environment (Stockholm Declaration), 1972 and the Rio Declaration on Environment and Development, 1992' (United Nations 2012) Introductory Note 3 <https://legal.un.org/avl/ha/dunche/dunche.html> accessed 1 July 2020.

22 Günther Handl, 'Declaration of the United Nations Conference on the Human Environment (Stockholm Declaration), 1972 and the Rio Declaration on Environment and Development, 1992' (United Nations 2012) Introductory Note 8 <https://legal.un.org/avl/ha/dunche/dunche.html> accessed 1 July 2020.

Following the recognition of the right to exploit natural resources came the recognition of the "right to development"[23] that was identified in 1968 as a "collective responsibility of the international community to ensure the attainment of the minimum standard of living necessary for the enjoyment of human rights and fundamental freedoms by all persons throughout the world".[24] In doing so, the *Declaration on the Right to Development*[25] placed international investment policy within the state's "right and duty to formulate appropriate national development policies"[26] that would serve the interest of the population.[27] The Declaration goes on to describe the right to development as also embodying a responsibility "for the creation of national and international conditions favourable to the realization of the right to development",[28] which would also include the state's policy approach to international investment. The Declaration further concluded that "steps should be taken to ensure the full exercise and progressive enhancement of the right to development, including the formulation, adoption and implementation of policy, legislative and other measures at the national and international levels".[29] The Right to Development attained legal applicability with the African Commission on Human and Peoples' Rights, which recognized both its procedural and substantive implications.[30] Some scholars have also conceptualized it as a "structural principle in international law" that "serves first to postulate orientation marks that are legally relevant for the more concrete structure of the international legal system".[31]

23 The "right to development" originated from a work by Senegalese jurist Keba M'baye in 1972 (Keba M'baye, 'Le Droit Du Developpement Comme Un Droit de l'Homme' (1972) 5 Revue des Droits de l'Homme 503).

24 United Nations Office of the High Commissioner for Human Rights (OHCHR), 'Background on the Right to Development' (*Development Is a Human Right*) <www.ohchr.org/EN/Issues/Development/Pages/Backgroundrtd.aspx> accessed 1 July 2020.

25 Declaration on the Right to Development 1986 (UN Document A/RES/41/128).

26 Declaration on the Right to Development 1986 (UN Document A/RES/41/128) Art 2(3). It is also notable that with the exception of Art (1)2, which reaffirms the "inalienable right to full sovereignty over all their natural wealth and resources", the due diligence and responsibility to prevent environmental harm is not mentioned in either the preambulatory or operational text.

27 Building from the first United Nations Development Decade in the 1960s, the "Declaration further defined the concept of development as a process based on the principles of non-discrimination, equality, social justice and solidarity in which the human person, individually and collective, is the central subject, rather than the object, the active participant and beneficiary" United Nations Office of the High Commissioner for Human Rights (OHCHR), *Realizing the Right to Development: Essays in Commemoration of 25 Years of the United Nations Declaration on the Right to Development* (United Nations 2013) 24.

28 Declaration on the Right to Development Art 3(1).

29 Declaration on the Right to Development Art 10.

30 Christian Tietje, 'The Right to Development within the International Economic Legal Order' in Ernst-Ulrich Petersmann and others (eds), *Reflections on the Constitutionalisation of International Economic Law: Liber Amicorum for Ernst-Ulrich Petersmann* (Martinus Nijhoff Publishers 2014) 547–49.

31 Christian Tietje, 'The Right to Development within the International Economic Legal Order' in Ernst-Ulrich Petersmann and others (eds), *Reflections on the Constitutionalisation of International*

In this latter formulation, the Right to Development has been especially significant in defining the nexus between international investment and development by clarifying the role of international investment in the process of development, and by addressing that role as part of a state's sovereign right over natural resources. The Right to Development, in fact, defined investment as one facet of the international cooperation and partnership that it sought to promote.[32] This becomes clearer in the work of the UN Office of the Commissioner for Human Rights (OHCHR), according to which one of the "added value[s] of the Right to Development" is to "foster friendly relations between states, international solidarity, cooperation" in areas such as, for instance, technology transfer and international trade.[33] Herein, investment takes on its instrumental role as a means of international cooperation to advance sustainable development. The OHCHR, in referring to the *Declaration on Permanent Sovereignty over Natural Resources*,[34] clarified that the "sovereign and permanent control of every State over its natural resources, wealth and economic activities" also meant that "every State has the sovereign right to rule and exercise effective control over foreign investment".[35] This would set the undercurrent that continues to define the position of the UN system concerning the role of investment in sustainable development.

To provide historical context, this role of investment and the primacy of development sought to address the vicious cycle of commodity poverty traps and innovation crowding out effects into which systems like international investment were observed to bound developing economies, especially the least developed countries. Bedjaoui described this further in the context of the New International Economic Order (NIEO)[36]:

> The sovereign right to choose their economic, political, social and cultural system, to exercise complete and lasting sovereignty over all their riches, to

---

Economic Law: Liber Amicorum for Ernst-Ulrich Petersmann (Martinus Nijhoff Publishers 2014) 555.

32 United Nations Office of the High Commissioner for Human Rights (OHCHR), *Realizing the Right to Development* (n 27) 63.

33 United Nations Office of the High Commissioner for Human Rights (OHCHR), 'The Right to Development at a Glance' (Development and Economic and Social Issues Branch (DESIB), Research and Right to Development Division (RRDD)) <www.un.org/en/events/righttodevelopment/pdf/rtd_at_a_glance.pdf>.

34 Permanent Sovereignty Over Natural Resources 1963 (UN Document A/RES/1803(XVII)).

35 United Nations Office of the High Commissioner for Human Rights (OHCHR), *Realizing the Right to Development* (n 27) 12.

36 NIEO set off an extensive scholarship in its challenge of justice as established by international law in a period of neoliberalism (see, generally, (Margot E Salomon, 'From NIEO to Now and the Unfinishable Story of Economic Justice' (2013) 62 The International and Comparative Law Quarterly 31). A major theme in this literature that is the most pertinent to this study is sovereignty over natural resources, over which "[n]orms relating to property protection and contractual sanctity came back with vigour dressed up in neoliberal garbs as a package of legal institutions essential for economic development" (John Linarelli, Margot E Salomon and Muthucumaraswamy Sornarajah, 'The End of Empire and the Search for Justice' in *The End of Empire and the Search for Justice:*

> regulate the activities of transnational firms and foreign investment, to suffer no discrimination in international trade within the framework of international cooperation, to form any producers' association with other States, to participate in technological progress and benefit from it.[37]

He poignantly observed that on the merits of the *Charter of Economic Rights and Duties of States*,[38] rights come with a responsibility to "respect the legitimate interests of other States in the exploitation of common natural resources" as well as a "duty to contribute to the development of world trade and to favour the progress not only of their own peoples but of others also".[39]

In 1992, the UN Conference on Environment and Development (the "Earth Summit") produced *Agenda 21*, which expanded further on the role of private sector investment and TNCs in sustainable development. The document clearly stated that investment and TNCs had a "crucial role in the social and economic development of a country" in terms of increasing prosperity, a "major goal in the development process", and transitioning to sustainable means of operations and technological innovation.[40] *Agenda 21* not only continued to place investment within the international cooperation element of sustainable development, but also identified market access and economic integration "in conjunction with sound macroeconomic and environmental policies" as having a "positive environmental impact and therefore mak[ing] an important contribution towards sustainable development".[41]

Notably, the role of investment in sustainable development is considerably elevated in *Agenda 21*:[42]

> Investment is critical to the ability of developing countries to achieve needed economic growth to improve the welfare of their populations and to meet

NIEO and Beyond (OUP 2018) 99). The shortcomings of the NIEO have largely been associated with the increasing centrality of the private sector and investment in the economic development of the Global South (Ingo Venzke, 'Possibilities of the Past: Histories of the NIEO and the Travails of Critique' (2018) 20 Journal of the History of International Law/Revue d'histoire du droit international 263).

37 Mohammed Bedjaoui, *Towards a New International Economic Order* (UNESCO 1979) 233–34.

38 Charter of Economic Rights and Duties of States 1974 (UN Document A/RES/29/3281).

39 Bedjaoui (n 37) 234.

40 United Nations Conference on Environment and Development (UNCED), 'Agenda 21: Programme of Action for Sustainable Development: Rio Declaration on Environment and Development' (United Nations 1994) para 2.37, 30.1–30.3.

41 United Nations Conference on Environment and Development (UNCED), 'Agenda 21: Programme of Action for Sustainable Development: Rio Declaration on Environment and Development' (United Nations 1994) 2.5.

42 *Agenda 21* was met with criticism in its identification of economic growth as a prerequisite for human development, which was argued to exacerbate disparities between the Global North and South in such areas as the environmental costs of industrialization and the elevation of big business to usher in the new, technology-centred economy (Timothy Doyle, 'Sustainable Development and Agenda 21: The Secular Bible of Global Free Markets and Pluralist Democracy' (1998) 19 Third

> their basic needs in a sustainable manner, all without deteriorating or depleting the resource base that underpins development. Sustainable development requires increased investment, for which domestic and external financial resources are needed. Foreign private investment and the return of flight capital, which depend on a healthy investment climate, are an important source of financial resources.[43]

The promotion of foreign direct investment (FDI) was therefore identified by *Agenda 21* as an objective of sustainable development, to be achieved through strengthening the "policies to attract direct investment".[44] In doing so, *Agenda 21* also shifted the UN system's views in part towards investment and trade liberalization by calling for the removal of "sources of distortion in the area of trade and investment"[45] and "biases against exports and in favour of inefficient import substitution" in order to "establish policies that allow [host states] to benefit fully from the flows of foreign investment".[46] The document goes on to identify more specific ways to mobilize investment and create suitable infrastructure to achieve sustainable economic growth and diversification on an environmentally sound and sustainable basis.[47]

A final unique contribution of *Agenda 21* was providing prescriptions concerning the conduct of TNCs and enterprises as investors for the "social and economic development of a country" through "reducing impacts on resource use and the environment" while providing "major trading, employment and livelihood opportunities" as well as "technological innovations, development, applications, transfer".[48] In doing so, *Agenda 21* clarified how the TNC can advance sustainable development through two "programme areas": (1) promoting cleaner production and (2) responsible entrepreneurship.[49] Table 2.2 highlights three key aspects of that relationship: corporate responsibility, extended stakeholderism, and added value creation. These aspects of the two programme areas, as shown in Chapters 3 and 4, continue to remain central elements of the role of investment in sustainable development.

World Quarterly 771). Meanwhile, the elevated role of development finance in *Agenda 21* drew more attention to the activities of international financial institutions like the World Bank, particularly to its environmental impact (World Bank Group (WBG), *Advancing Sustainable Development: The World Bank and Agenda 21* (WBG 1997) 19).

43 United Nations Conference on Environment and Development (UNCED) (n 40) para 2.23.

44 United Nations Conference on Environment and Development (UNCED) (n 40) para 2.27(e).

45 United Nations Conference on Environment and Development (UNCED) (n 40) para 2.34.

46 United Nations Conference on Environment and Development (UNCED) (n 40) para 2.37(h).

47 United Nations Conference on Environment and Development (UNCED) (n 40) para 2.37(d).

48 United Nations Conference on Environment and Development (UNCED) (n 40) para 30.1–30.2.

49 United Nations Conference on Environment and Development (UNCED) (n 40) para 30.4.

Table 2.2 Transnational corporations in sustainable development

Corporate Responsibility
(Paragraph 30.3) • Recognize environmental management as among the highest corporate priorities and as a key determinant to sustainable development • Implement "responsible care" and product stewardship policies and programmes, fostering openness and dialogue with employees and the public and carrying out environmental audits and assessments of compliance • Take voluntary initiatives, promoting and implementing self-regulations and greater responsibilities in ensuring their activities have minimal impacts on human health and the environment
(Paragraph 30.10) • Report annually on their environmental records, as well as on their use of energy and natural resources • Adopt and report on the implementation of codes of conduct promoting the best environmental practice
(Paragraph 30.26) • Ensure responsible and ethical management of products and processes from the point of view of health, safety and environmental aspects • Increase self-regulation, guided by appropriate codes, charters and initiatives integrated into all elements of business planning and decision-making, and fostering openness and dialogue with employees and the public
Extended Stakeholderism
(Paragraph 30.12) Incorporate cleaner production policies in its operations and investments, taking also into account its influence on *suppliers and consumers*
(Paragraph 30.22) • Arrange for environmentally sound technologies to be available to affiliates owned substantially by their parent company in *developing countries* without extra external charges • Encourage *overseas affiliates* to modify procedures in order to reflect local ecological conditions and share experiences with local authorities
(Paragraph 30.23) Consider establishing partnership schemes with *small and medium-sized enterprises* to help facilitate the exchange of experience in managerial skills, market development and technological know-how
Added Value Creation
(Paragraph 30.24) Establish national councils for sustainable development and help *promote entrepreneurship* in the formal and informal sectors. The inclusion of women entrepreneurs should be facilitated
(Paragraph 30.25) Increase *research and development* of environmentally sound technologies and environmental management systems

Source: Agenda 21.[50]

50 United Nations Conference on Environment and Development (UNCED) (n 40) para 21.

Thus, in a marked departure from the hands-off approach of the Stockholm Convention, *Agenda 21* called for a more integrated relationship between the state, international organizations and the private sector. Paragraph 30.19, for instance, calls on governments to employ "regulatory measures, economic incentives and streamlining of administrative procedures [that] facilitate investment decisions". Paragraph 30.28 follows by designating a role of UN organizations and agencies as improving "mechanisms for business and industry inputs, policy and strategy formulation processes, to ensure that environmental aspects are strengthened in foreign investment". The latter is of particular salience as it refines the role of the UN system as not only facilitating progress towards sustainable development, but also private sector investment towards that purpose.

These mechanisms materialized as the UN Framework Convention on Climate Change (UNFCCC) came into effect in 1994, with the Kyoto Protocol to the UN Framework Convention on Climate Change (1998). Together they further addressed the balance between economic development and the environment, particularly in connection to greenhouse gas (GHG) emissions and country capacities. Climate change, which embodied the concerns of intergenerationality of sustainable development phrased in the Brundtland Commission Report, required that states exercise precaution to "anticipate, prevent or minimize the causes of climate change and mitigate adverse effects" while observing the common but differentiated responsibility and respective capabilities of developing country parties.[51]

Two notable features arose from the UNFCCC that sought to help establish that balance: emissions reporting and market-based mechanisms. The former marked the importance of transparent and objective compliance through reporting[52] in accordance with the "best available scientific information and assessment on climate change and its impact".[53] Measurement, reporting, and verification (MRV) became and remain central to the role of investment in sustainable development, which is later highlighted in Chapter 4. At this early stage, however, the UNFCCC provided guidance primarily on the differentiation between developed (Annex I Parties) and developing (Non-Annex I Parties) countries.[54]

Three market-based mechanisms are identified in the UNFCCC: (1) emissions trading, (2) the clean development mechanism, and (3) joint implementation. Of these, the clean development mechanism[55] identified the role of private sector finance, such as FDI,[56] as eligible for certified emissions reductions under the

51 United Nations Framework Convention on Climate Change 1992 Arts 1–3.

52 United Nations Framework Convention on Climate Change 1992 Arts 4(1).

53 United Nations Framework Convention on Climate Change 1992 Arts 4(2)(c).

54 United Nations Framework Convention on Climate Change (UNFCCC), 'What Is Transparency and Reporting?' (*Transparency and Reporting*) <https://unfccc.int/process-and-meetings/transparency-and-reporting/the-big-picture/what-is-transparency-and-reporting> accessed 15 July 2020.

55 Defined as assisting developing countries achieve sustainable development in Kyoto Protocol to the United Nations Framework Convention on Climate Change 1998 Art 12(2).

56 As financial resources through 'bilateral, regional and other multilateral channels' in Kyoto Protocol to the United Nations Framework Convention on Climate Change 1998 Art 11(3).

existing regime.[57] This was one of the first acts in the UN system's newfound position of facilitating both sustainable development and investment.

Leading up to the Earth Summit in 1992, the UN Environment Programme established the Finance Initiative (UNEP FI), which sought to integrate "environmental considerations into all aspects of the financial sector's operations and services".[58] As per the UNEP's commitments to the Finance Initiative, these operations and services include international investment.[59] The Finance Initiative continues to play a central role in the notion of Sustainable Investment ("Notion") today, as will be further expounded upon in Chapter 4. It also signalled the advent of the Financing for Development framework, which would forever set the tone of the UN system's approach towards investment and sustainable development.

2.2.2 The emergence of financing for development

In 2002, with the Monterrey Consensus of the International Conference on Financing for Development (hereinafter "Monterrey Consensus"), the narrative on sustainable development and the role of investment to achieve it shifted to one of multilaterally set goals and the subsequent financing gaps in accomplishing them over a set period of time with eight Millennium Development Goals by 2015.[60] Furthermore, the Monterrey Consensus further reoriented the UN system in facilitating investment and sustainable development towards one within an "increasingly globalizing interdependent world economy", thereby calling for the "common pursuit of growth, poverty eradication and sustainable development". This common pursuit specifically called for productive investment[61] at adequate levels,[62] emphasizing in particular the crucial role to be played by FDI:

> Private international capital flows, particularly foreign direct investment, along with international financial stability, are vital complements to national

57 Kyoto Protocol to the United Nations Framework Convention on Climate Change 1998 Art 12(9).

58 United Nations Environment Programme Finance Initiative (UNEP FI), 'Background' <www.unepfi.org/about/background/> accessed 24 February 2021.

59 UNEP Statement of Commitment by Financial Institutions (FI) on Sustainable Development 1992, 1.5.

60 United Nations, 'Background' (*United Nations Millennium Development Goals and Beyond 2015*) <www.un.org/millenniumgoals/bkgd.shtml> accessed 3 July 2020.

61 Productive investments are those that produce new capacities, such as jobs, as opposed to relying on existing capacities. The UN Commission on Trade and Development adds that productive investments are those that are value-added in a manner that results in long-term, sustained growth (United Nations Trade and Development (UNCTAD), 'Trade and Development Report, 2013: Adjusting to the Changing Dynamics of the World Economy' (United Nations 2013) UNCTAD/TDR/2013 48). Productive investments have later been linked to development given their long-term nature and emphasis on value-added, as opposed to short-term credit that can drive economies further into debt (United Nations Trade and Development (UNCTAD), 'Making the International Financial Architecture Work for Development' (United Nations 2015) UNCTAD/TDR/2015 47).

62 United Nations Department of Economic and Social Affairs (DESA), 'Monterrey Consensus on Financing for Development' (United Nations 2003) Report of the International Conference on Financing for Development, Monterrey, Mexico, 18–22 March 2002 paras 8–10.

> and international development efforts. Foreign direct investment contributes toward financing sustained economic growth over the long term. It is especially important for its potential to transfer knowledge and technology, create jobs, boost overall productivity, enhance competitiveness and entrepreneurship, and ultimately eradicate poverty through economic growth and development. A central challenge, therefore, is to create the necessary domestic and international conditions to facilitate direct investment flows, conducive to achieving national development priorities.[63]

Thus, the Monterrey Consensus did not simply call for more flows of FDI, but rather for "development-oriented investments" with "maximum development impact" such as those that result in infrastructure development[64] or employment.[65]

Notably, the Monterrey Consensus also tied investment and trade together into a single programme of Financing for Development by committing to the Doha Ministerial Declaration (2001) in an effort to bring investment into a "multilateral framework to secure transparent, stable and predictable conditions".[66] In doing so, the United Nations development framework engaged the legal dimensions of FDI in connection to sustainable development, particularly on the issue of balance between a state's right to regulate for the public interest and the need to attract investment:

> Any framework should reflect in a balanced manner the interests of home and host countries, and take due account of the development policies and objectives of host governments as well as their right to regulate for the public interest. The special development, trade and financial needs of developing and least-developed countries should be taken into account as an integral part of any framework, which should enable members to undertake obligations and commitments commensurate with their individual needs and circumstances.[67]

The theme of balancing the right to regulate for the public interest and facilitating investment through "international rules and commitments" continued in the Doha Declaration on Financing for Development (2008):

> The increasing interdependence of national economies in a globalizing world and the emergence of rules-based regimes for international economic

63 United Nations Department of Economic and Social Affairs (DESA), 'Monterrey Consensus on Financing for Development' (United Nations 2003) Report of the International Conference on Financing for Development, Monterrey, Mexico, 18–22 March 2002 para 20.

64 United Nations Department of Economic and Social Affairs (DESA), 'Monterrey Consensus on Financing for Development' (United Nations 2003) Report of the International Conference on Financing for Development, Monterrey, Mexico, 18–22 March 2002 para 21.

65 United Nations Department of Economic and Social Affairs (DESA), 'Monterrey Consensus on Financing for Development' (United Nations 2003) Report of the International Conference on Financing for Development, Monterrey, Mexico, 18–22 March 2002 para 27.

66 Doha Ministerial Declaration 2001 (WT/MIN(01)/DEC/1) para 20.

67 Doha Ministerial Declaration 2001 (WT/MIN(01)/DEC/1) para 22.

> relations have meant that the space for national economic policy, that is, the scope for domestic policies, especially in the areas of trade, investment and international development, is now often framed by international disciplines, commitments and global market considerations. It is for each Government to evaluate the trade-off between the benefits of accepting international rules and commitments and the constraints posed by the loss of policy space.[68]

Two significant developments accompanied the Doha Declaration. The first is that it encouraged a socially responsible private sector[69] and the promotion of corporate social responsibility (CSR).[70] The second is that it promoted "programmes, mechanisms and instruments at the disposal of multilateral development agencies" and bilateral investment treaties (BITs) that help to encourage investment by "contributing to mitigating some of the risks faced by private investors in critical sectors".[71] In doing so, the Doha Declaration shifted some of the responsibilities of the host state, and for that matter the UN system, in governing investment and its impact on sustainable development to the investor.

This did not, however, connote an enervated role of the state. The Doha Declaration reiterated that while a "stable and predictable investment climate, with proper contract enforcement and respect for property rights" remains fundamental to investment,[72] "every State has, and shall freely exercise permanent sovereignty over all its wealth, natural resources and economic activity".[73] It further identified the need for an "integrated treatment of financing for development issues in national development plans . . . in enhancing national ownership and implementation".[74]

Rio+20 sought to return the focus of the discussion to the environment by introducing the concept of a green economy into the UN system's approach to investment in sustainable development. Green economy was defined as "eradicating

68 Doha Declaration on Financing for Development: Outcome Document of the Follow-Up International Conference on Financing for Development to Review the Implementation of the Monterrey Consensus, 2008–2009 para 14.

69 Doha Declaration on Financing for Development: Outcome Document of the Follow-Up International Conference on Financing for Development to Review the Implementation of the Monterrey Consensus, 2008–2009 para 10.

70 Doha Declaration on Financing for Development: Outcome Document of the Follow-Up International Conference on Financing for Development to Review the Implementation of the Monterrey Consensus, 2008–2009 para 25.

71 Doha Declaration on Financing for Development: Outcome Document of the Follow-Up International Conference on Financing for Development to Review the Implementation of the Monterrey Consensus, 2008–2009 para 24.

72 Doha Declaration on Financing for Development: Outcome Document of the Follow-Up International Conference on Financing for Development to Review the Implementation of the Monterrey Consensus, 2008–2009 para 25.

73 Doha Declaration on Financing for Development: Outcome Document of the Follow-Up International Conference on Financing for Development to Review the Implementation of the Monterrey Consensus, 2008–2009 para 27.

74 Doha Declaration on Financing for Development: Outcome Document of the Follow-Up International Conference on Financing for Development to Review the Implementation of the Monterrey Consensus, 2008–2009 para 88.

poverty as well as sustained economic growth, enhancing social inclusion, improving human welfare and creating opportunities for employment and decent work for all, while maintaining the healthy functioning of the Earth's ecosystems".[75] The UNEP added that private investment "into such economic activities, infrastructure and assets" that embody the three principles of the green economy—low carbon, resource efficient and socially inclusive—were "green investments [that] need to be enabled and supported through public expenditure, policy reforms and changes in taxation and regulation".[76] This was an important accomplishment as it provided greater insight into the characteristics of an investment that could qualify as sustainable or contributing to sustainable development.

Rio+20 thus reoriented the Financing for Development discussion towards three dimensions of sustainable development: economic, social, and environmental.[77] The role of the private sector and investment was then reframed within these three dimensions and the green economy principles, which meant more refined targets such as energy transitions, infrastructure investment, environmentally sound technology transfer and innovation, and technology for sustainable development.[78] Furthermore, a "science-policy interface" was encouraged as a means to provide "inclusive, evidence-based and transparent scientific assessment".[79] This would later transform into the "real-life" and "science-based" assessments of investment that is central to the UN system's approach to sustainable finance as defined in Chapter 4.

After the world failed to achieve the Millennium Development Goals, the Addis Ababa Action Agenda sought to form a cohesive, synergistic[80] post-2015 Financing for Development framework. One notable manifestation of the approach pursued by the Addis Ababa Action Agenda in relation to the private sector and investment is "reporting on environmental, social and governance impacts, to help ensure transparency and accountability".[81] This turn to strengthened monitoring, reporting, and verification was a logical response to falling short in meeting the Millennium Development Goals. Meanwhile, it continued to reflect the concerns of

75 The Future We Want: Outcome Document of the United Nations Conference on Sustainable Development 2012 (UN Document A/RES/66/288) para 56.

76 United Nations Environment Programme (UNEP), 'Green Economy' (*Regional Initiatives*) <www.unenvironment.org/regions/asia-and-pacific/regional-initiatives/supporting-resource-efficiency/green-economy> accessed 23 July 2020. This is further explored in the set of 11 "most common green economy principles" in Cameron Allen, *A Guidebook to the Green Economy—Issue 2: Exploring Green Economy Principles* (United Nations Division for Sustainable Development (UNDESA) 2012) 12.

77 The Future We Want: Outcome Document of the United Nations Conference on Sustainable Development para 58(b).

78 The Future We Want: Outcome Document of the United Nations Conference on Sustainable Development paras 127, 149, 154, 271.

79 The Future We Want: Outcome Document of the United Nations Conference on Sustainable Development para 76(g).

80 Addis Ababa Action Agenda of the Third International Conference on Financing for Development 2015 (A/RES/69/313) para 11.

81 Addis Ababa Action Agenda of the Third International Conference on Financing for Development 2015 (A/RES/69/313) para 17, 37.

national ownership that were prevalent in Monterrey and Doha[82] while being more openly cognizant of the environmental dimension of sustainable development.[83] In doing so, the Addis Ababa Action Agenda made clear the UN position on the balance to be struck between investment and public policy objectives:

> The goal of protecting and encouraging investment should not affect our ability to pursue public policy objectives. We will endeavour to craft trade and investment agreements with appropriate safeguards so as not to constrain domestic policies and regulation in the public interest.[84]

The Addis Ababa Action Agenda went further to state that "private business activity, investment and innovation are major drivers of productivity, inclusive economic growth and job creation", identifying a diversity of businesses "from micro-enterprises to cooperatives to multinationals" as "partners in the development process, to invest in areas critical to sustainable development".[85] In doing so, it generated the final of the three criteria identified in the working definition formed at the beginning of this chapter.[86] In the relationship between the state and TNCs, governments would "strengthen regulatory frameworks to better align private sector incentives with public goals, including incentivizing the private sector to adopt sustainable practices, and foster long-term quality investments".[87] While these strategies are more fully explored in Chapter 3, they include screening FDIs more stringently at the level of admissions, prioritizing investments that promote "full and productive employment and decent work for all, sustainable patterns of production and consumption, structural transformation and sustainable industrialization, productive diversification and agriculture".[88]

The UN Sustainable Development Goals (SDGs) further complemented this narrative on sustainable development–oriented investment in 2015, viewing international investment as an engine of growth as well as a means of financing sustainable

82 Addis Ababa Action Agenda of the Third International Conference on Financing for Development 2015 (A/RES/69/313) para 9, 26.

83 Addis Ababa Action Agenda of the Third International Conference on Financing for Development 2015 (A/RES/69/313) para 5.

84 Addis Ababa Action Agenda of the Third International Conference on Financing for Development 2015 (A/RES/69/313) para 91.

85 Addis Ababa Action Agenda of the Third International Conference on Financing for Development 2015 (A/RES/69/313) para 35.

86 The role of investment in sustainable development was defined by the extent to which it meets three fundamental criteria: (1) it is high-quality and positive, which in turn is measured by its observation of the precautionary principle; (2) it coheres with national development planning of the host state especially in developing economies and in respecting national ownership and sovereignty over natural resources; and (3) it remains an engine of sustained growth that is supportive of the host state's promotion and maintenance of a stable and predictable regulatory climate in its financing for development.

87 Addis Ababa Action Agenda of the Third International Conference on Financing for Development 36.

88 Addis Ababa Action Agenda of the Third International Conference on Financing for Development 45.

development in its three dimensions (economic, social, and environmental). They also served to continue the three criteria of the working definition into the consolidated approach of the UN system towards sustainable development into 2030. This 2030 Agenda sought to emphasize an integrated, balanced relationship between the three dimensions of sustainable development while "taking into account different national realities, capacities and levels of development".[89] The 2030 Agenda foregrounds international investment as a principal means of implementing the SDGs,[90] predominantly in relation to advancing technology, innovation, and infrastructure as specifically stated in SDGs 2.a, 7.a, and 9.5.[91] This is further corroborated by Goal 8 (decent work and economic growth), which seeks to recouple economic growth with social and environmental objectives through the "trade-investment nexus"[92] that includes "relevant international standards and agreements and other ongoing initiatives".[93] In this document, one can identify the ongoing emphasis on sustainable development–oriented investment, or as was defined in three criteria definition of investment in sustainable development, highly value-added productive or high-quality investments in specific areas (technology, innovation, and infrastructure). The SDGs continue a subscription to the green growth paradigm and in doing so seek to return balance between the three dimensions of sustainable development. The trade-investment nexus continues to emphasize the centrality of trade and investment governance standards, while simultaneously reaffirming the inseparability of trade and investment from its implications to sustainable development.

A conjoined accomplishment in 2015 was the passing of the Paris Agreement under the UNFCCC, which called for "finance flows with a pathway towards low greenhouse gas emissions and climate-resilient development".[94] The Paris Agreement sought to integrate MRV at the level of national development policy through nationally determined contributions (NDCs), which were commitments to limit "warming to 1.5 to 2 degrees C above pre-industrial levels" through reducing and/or removing anthropogenic GHG emissions.[95] Through MRV and the NDCs, the UNFCCC reemphasized the centrality of ensuring that contributions to the process of sustainable development should be assessed in a way that is science-based and quantifiable. The role of investment is also clearly addressed in this framework with an emphasis on the importance of climate finance, which seeks a "balance between

89 Transforming Our World: The 2030 Agenda for Sustainable Development 2015 (UN Document A/RES/70/1) para 5.

90 Transforming Our World: The 2030 Agenda for Sustainable Development 2015 (UN Document A/RES/70/1) para 28, 39, 41, 43, 60, 62, 67.

91 Transforming Our World: The 2030 Agenda for Sustainable Development 2015 (UN Document A/RES/70/1) paras 16, 19–20.

92 United Nations Trade and Development (UNCTAD), 'Goal 8: Decent Work and Economic Growth' (*SDG Pulse*) <https://sdgpulse.unctad.org/sdgs/goal-8-decent-work-and-economic-growth/> accessed 27 February 2020.

93 Transforming Our World: The 2030 Agenda for Sustainable Development para 67.

94 Paris Agreement 2015 Art 2(1)(c).

95 United Nations Framework Convention on Climate Change (UNFCCC), 'Nationally Determined Contributions (NDCs)' <https://unfccc.int/process-and-meetings/the-paris-agreement/the-paris-agreement/nationally-determined-contributions-ndcs> accessed 15 July 2020.

adaptation and mitigation, taking into account country-driven strategies, and the priorities and needs of developing country Parties".[96] While bestowed a different title, climate investment is largely a continuation of Financing for Development but with an emphasis on equity and the best available science in advancing the combination of sustainable development and national development goals. Perhaps a clear testament to a renewed commitment to MRV was the "global stocktake", which was a form of review to ensure alignment with the attributes of sustainable development solicited through the UN system.[97]

2.2.3 *Criticisms of the UN system's sustainable development framework*

As illustrated over the institutional history examined in the previous sections, the UN system consistently identified international investment as a means of cross-border cooperation amidst a "mutual suspicion of asymmetric bargaining power" between TNCs and "small, poor, developing countries"[98] and a central means to sustainable development. The UN system also calls for multilateral economic governance over all forms of Financing for Development: trade, investment, and development finance. However, as was discussed in Chapter 1, international investment law has been the cause of much contention, such as triggering regulatory chill amongst host states against implementing the necessary measures to advance matters of public interest.[99] While the UN General Assembly recognized these as the "unintended consequence" of international investment agreements (IIAs),[100] various UN agencies continue to attribute a central role to international private sector investment in advancing sustainable development and subsequently the governance of international investment. The challenges facing the international investment law regime and its conflicts with the expected role of investment in sustainable development continue to be matters of central interest to the UN system.[101]

96 Paris Agreement Art 9(4).

97 Paris Agreement Art 14.

98 United Nations General Assembly, 'Report of the World Commission on Environment and Development' (n 9) paras 28, 80.

99 Muthucumaraswamy Sornarajah, 'Developing Countries in the Investment Treaty System: A Law for Need or a Law for Greed?' in Stephan W Schill, Christian J Tams and Hofmann Rainer (eds), *International Investment Law and Development: Bridging the Gap* (Edward Elgar Publishing 2015) 45.

100 United Nations General Assembly, 'Seventy-Third Session Item 18 (b) of the Provisional Agenda, Macroeconomic Policy Questions, International Financial System and Development, Report of the Secretary-General' (2018) A/73/280 para 62 <www.un.org/ga/search/view_doc.asp?symbol=A/73/280> accessed 2 March 2020.

101 From 2015, UNCTAD began an ambitious initiative to reform international investment agreements. This initiative included updated or revoking old generational IIAs, which is further explored in United Nations Trade and Development (UNCTAD), 'Reform Package for the International Investment Regime' (United Nations 2018). The UNCITRAL turned the focus of its Working Group III to reforming the system of investor-state dispute settlement. Reform options arising from those discussions can be found in United Nations Commission on International Trade Law (UNCITRAL), 'Reform Options (Tabular Presentation)' (2019) A/CN.9/WG.III/WP.166/

Considerable scholarship points to the limitations of the sustainable development concept encapsulated by the UN system. In addition to lacking accountability due to their voluntary and political nature, the SDGs have also been criticized for not addressing the contentious issue of causal responsibility[102] associated to a thin cosmopolitanism.[103] These refer to the culpability of global economic structures in causing high levels of indebtedness and unsustainable consumption and production, levels which have left vulnerable populations more exposed to harm. Despite their roles in nurturing the conditions of these challenges to sustainable development, international financial institutions and instruments, such as international investment law, retain their authority and legitimacy in multilateral fora.[104] One reason behind this outcome has been that "disempowered populations whose full political, civil, economic, social, cultural, and developmental rights have not been the central focus of any grand ambitious global strategy such as the SDGs under Agenda 2030".[105]

Another poignant criticism of the UN development framework relates to the centrality of economic growth through such concepts as green growth and economy. Research on degrowth, for instance, identifies this economic growth-centric imperative as arising from historical inequalities across the North-South divide,

---

Add.1 <https://uncitral.un.org/en/reformoptions> accessed 14 May 2020. The OHCHR released the *Guiding Principles on Business and Human Rights* in 2011 under a mandate of "protect, respect and remedy" in application to the role of business in respecting human rights, see Office of the High Commissioner on Human Rights (OHCHR), 'Guiding Principles on Business and Human Rights' (United Nations 2011) HR/PUB/11/04. Based on that mandate, the UN Working Group on Business and Human Rights has centred its focus on a three pillar approach in specific application IIAs in the preservation of a regulatory space for the respect of human rights, see Office of the High Commissioner on Human Rights (OHCHR), 'International Investment Agreements (IIAs) and Human Rights' <www.ohchr.org/EN/Issues/Business/Pages/IIAs.aspx> accessed 14 May 2020.

102 Referring here to the responsibilities arising from historical relations, such as colonialism, resulting in different outcomes arising from globalization. Pogge identifies that this historical conception of social justice is necessary to identify "radical inequalities" that both aggravate and perpetuate inequality between rich and poor countries (Thomas Pogge, 'Real World Justice' (2005) 9 The Journal of Ethics 29, 37). For an overview of literature, see, for example, Andrew Peterson, 'Global Justice and Educating for Globally Oriented Citizenship' in Andrew Peterson and others (eds), *The Palgrave International Handbook of Education for Citizenship and Social Justice* (Palgrave Macmillan 2016).

103 Linklater defines thin cosmopolitanism as "compassion for the vulnerable [while leaving] asymmetries of power and wealth intact", opposite to which "thick conceptions of cosmopolitan citizenship [that] attempt to influence the structure conditions faced by vulnerable groups" (Andrew Linklater, *The Transformation of Political Community: Ethical Foundations of the Post-Westphalian Era* (U of South Carolina P 1998) 206).

104 See generally, Magdalena Bexell and Kristina Jönsson, 'Responsibility and the United Nations' Sustainable Development Goals' (2017) 44 Forum for Development Studies 13.

105 Diane Desierto, 'SDG Report 2020: The Civil, Political, Economic, Social, Cultural, and Development Rights Crises Deepening in the Global South' (*EJIL: Talk!* 15 July 2020) <www.ejiltalk.org/sdg-report-2020-the-civil-political-economic-social-cultural-and-development-rights-crises-deepening-in-the-global-south/> accessed 3 August 2020.

and as continuing and institutionalizing these inequalities on issues as the distribution of environmental burdens and ecological debt in a manner that does not sufficiently account for a wide spectrum of vulnerability in populations.[106] Another criticism highlights the extent to which economic dimensions of sustainable development, such as inclusive growth, enjoy significantly greater representation in the SDGs. Milante and Jang, for instance, identify comparatively weak coverage of contentious issues in the SDGs, such as political participation, independent judiciaries, refugees, and displacement.[107] There also has been work pointing to the SDGs and their wide acceptance acting as a smokescreen for a lack of evidence between the SDGs and actual sustainable development impact. Zeng et al. identify a gap between the changing conditions on the earth's surface and the prescriptions provided by the SDGs to as much as only a 7% correlation "between [Sustainable Development Goals] indicators and external indicators of biodiversity and environmental protection being significantly positive ($P < 0.05$)". They find that in fact there is a higher negative correlation at 14% between the SDGs and external indicators measuring environmental protection.[108]

Furthermore, FDI and the maintenance of stable and predictable regulatory climates are seen as important means of cross-border cooperation in the Financing for Development framing. This is despite the fact that the relationship between the investor and host state in international investment law are regularly exploitative, preying on power asymmetries.[109] One aspect of this polarization originates in firm-level behaviour, with the tendency of TNCs to consider one[110] rather than three bottom lines,[111] thereby seeking to maximize economic profit irrespective of the economic, social, and/or environmental costs passed on to the society of the host state. The lack of accountability of the private sector, especially within their role of leading the development of paradigm-shifting technologies that are taking increasingly central roles in society, was identified by the former UN Special Rapporteur on extreme poverty and human rights as enabling them to operate in "almost human rights-free zones".[112]

106 See generally Bengi Akbulut and others, 'Who Promotes Sustainability? Five Theses on the Relationships Between the Degrowth and the Environmental Justice Movements' (2019) 165 Ecological Economics 106418; Jason Hickel and Giorgos Kallis, 'Is Green Growth Possible?' (2020) 25 New Political Economy 469.

107 Gary Milante and Suyoun Jang, 'Measuring Peacebuilding and Statebuilding in the New SDG Framework' (2016) 11 Journal of Peacebuilding & Development 110.

108 Yiwen Zeng and others, 'Environmental Destruction Not Avoided with the Sustainable Development Goals' [2020] Nature Sustainability 1.

109 Sornarajah, 'Developing Countries in the Investment Treaty System' (n 100) 44–45.

110 For example, resource-based multinational corporations, see Sornarajah, 'Developing Countries in the Investment Treaty System' (n 100) 46.

111 Business, and the relationship between business and government, is pressured not to limit the economic, social and environmental options of future generations. This is later discussed in reference to John Elkington, *Cannibals with Forks: The Triple Bottom Line of 21st Century Business* (CapStone Press 1999).

112 Alston Philip, 'Extreme Poverty and Human Rights: Note/by the Secretary-General' (United Nations 2019) Report of the Special Rapporteur on Extreme Poverty and Human Rights A/74/493 para 72.

This first pillar of the conceptual framework narrated the institutional history of the UN system on the evolving role of international investment in sustainable development. The three-criteria definition provided in the beginning of this pillar does well to summarize the key attributes arising from this definition. While cognizant of the many challenges raised against this role of international investment in sustainable development, as was stated in Chapter 1, this book aligns with the view that investment remains pivotal to financing sustainable development.

2.3 Pillar Two: sustainable investment

The second pillar of the conceptual framework examines Sustainable Investment as a means to clarify normative aspects of international investment and its role in advancing sustainable development, both described within the UN system as well as the three-criteria definition synthesized in the previous chapter.[113] Within the Financing for Development framework, two conceptions of investment that contribute to sustainable development were identified. The UN system sought to promote these two conceptions not only with states hosting investment, but also with a broad spectrum of private sector stakeholders, such as TNCs and institutional investors. This pillar serves as a foundation for the notion of Sustainable Investment ("Notion") that is presented in Chapter 4. The Notion is constructed through the activities of the main initiatives within the UN system concerning Sustainable Investment.

A central theme to Sustainable Investment is the idea of "quality direct investments", which was identified in the UN system as productive investments to the extent that they have added value. The UN Inter-agency Task Force on Financing for Development defines quality investments as those that "incorporate consideration of important social, environmental and cross-cutting issues" thereby adding value to "SDG-promoting sectors".[114] The second conception incorporates environmental, social, and governance (ESG) factors in the management of investment and its strategies.[115] This broadly involves minimizing negative externalities that are counteractive to the SDG-additive effect of investment, or a "sustainability factor"; maximizing positive externalities towards a sustainability factor; and

113 As identified in the previous chapter, the role of investment in sustainable development was defined by the extent to which it meets three fundamental criteria: (1) it is high-quality and positive, which in turn is measured by its observation of the precautionary principle; (2) it coheres with national development planning of the host state especially in developing economies and in respecting national ownership and sovereignty over natural resources; and (3) it remains an engine of sustained growth that is supportive of the host state's promotion and maintenance of a stable and predictable regulatory climate in its financing for development.

114 United Nations Inter-Agency Task Force on Financing for Development, 'Encouraging Quality Direct Investments' (*United Nations*) <https://developmentfinance.un.org/encouraging-quality-direct-investment> accessed 7 July 2020.

115 United Nations Inter-Agency Task Force on Financing for Development, 'Private Sector Efforts and Initiatives on Environmental, Social and Governance (ESG) Factors' (*United Nations*) <https://developmentfinance.un.org/private-sector-efforts-and-initiatives-environmental-social-and-governance-esg-factors> accessed 7 July 2020.

operating along an explicit investment objective aligned with a particular sustainability factor.[116] In other words, sustainability factors that, for instance, promote a certain SDG or Paris Agreement target are seen as fundamental components of Sustainable Investment as they embody the key performance indication of an investment. A straightforward example would include the extent to which certain sectors that can be classified as working against the SDGs, such as indecent working conditions along a given supply chain, are flagged and excluded from being considered a Sustainable Investment.[117]

As is also further examined in Chapter 5, introducing aspects of Sustainable Investment into international investment law can in part substantiate its otherwise unrefined dimensions. As this work will identify as the "incomplete assessment", which is explored in the fourth pillar, matters related to sustainable development within the practice of international investment law remain largely unrefined, lacking a clear definition and approach to assessment. In shaping this second analytical pillar, this chapter continues the broader emphasis on the multilateral. The importance of this emphasis in connection to Sustainable Investment is particularly pronounced, as Chapter 4 details, due to the rapid growth in the number of Sustainable Investment scopes and metrics, but the lack of harmonization between metrics and transparency on how such metrics were monitored, reported, and verified. There is a diverse set of institutional approaches in the UN system concerning Sustainable Investment. While their substance is explored in greater depth in Chapter 4, this section provides an overview of the main institutions.

The UN Global Compact and the UNEP FI established the Principles for Responsible Investment (PRI) in 2006, calling for the active implementation, monitoring, reporting, expansion, and development of ESG factors in private sector investment. Promoted by Kofi Annan and institutional investors, the PRI are supported by the UN, while remaining independent from the UN, and are advanced by almost 3,000 private sector signatories.[118] In its *Blueprint for Responsible Investment*, the PRI identify that Sustainable Investment cannot be operationalized in its full potential without active policy actions that "remove barriers to a sustainable financial system".[119]

In working with exchanges as the platforms of investment, the United Nations Sustainable Stock Exchanges (SSE) initiative was established by the UN Conference on Trade and Development, the UN Global Compact, the UN Environment Finance Initiative, and the Principles on Responsible Investment in 2009.[120] The

116 United Nations Inter-Agency Task Force on Financing for Development, 'Financing for Sustainable Development Report 2019' (United Nations 2019) Report of the Inter-Agency Task Force on Financing for Development E/FFDF/2019 55.

117 See, for instance, in the broader context of ESG, Simon Rawson, 'Decent Work Is in Crisis, Investors Could Start by Driving Corporate Disclosure' (*Responsible Investor*, 7 October 2020).

118 Principles on Responsible Investment, 'About the PRI' (*PRI*) <www.unpri.org/pri/about-the-pri> accessed 1 April 2020.

119 Principles for Responsible Investment (PRI), *A Blueprint for Responsible Investment: Genesis, Assumptions and Process* (PRI 2017) 10.

120 United Nations Sustainable Stock Exchanges (SSE) Initiative, 'About the SSE Initiative' <https://sseinitiative.org/about/>.

SSE promotes and holds accountable the efforts by exchanges to improve the disclosure and performance of Sustainable Investments.[121] One way to do so has been to provide uniform guidance on issuing ESG investments for member exchanges.[122]

The UN Secretary-General established the Global Investors for Sustainable Development (GISD) Alliance in 2019 with a group of 30 private sector CEOs to mobilize long-term investment through institutional investors, banks, and financial institutions; scale up long-term investment through financing platforms that remove barriers to investment; and align business and investment with sustainable development.[123] The last of these, which is most pertinent to this study, includes objectives such as integrating long-term performance outlooks that recognize the importance of sustainable long-term value creation, fostering the harmonization of standards for sustainability reporting to enhance the impact of investment for all stakeholders, and supporting the quality of data and information related to Sustainable Investment.[124] The GISD seeks to expand Sustainable Investment to include philanthropy, impact investment, sustainable and responsible investment, and Sustainable Investment,[125] and proposes the term "Sustainable Development Investment" to address concerns of merely cosmetic applications of Sustainable Investment.[126]

Finally, in 2019, the UNEP FI and UN-backed PRI alongside 12 institutional investors began a commitment to transitioning their investment portfolios to net-zero GHG emissions by 2050. Having reached 33 institutional investor members as of the beginning of 2021, the UN-Convened Net-Zero Asset Owner Alliance (NZAOA) also committed to taking into account the best available scientific knowledge, regularly reporting on their progress, and establishing five-year intermediate goals.[127]

While the above initiatives function as partnerships with the private sector, they form the crux of the UN system's engagement in Sustainable Investment and as such the foundation of the Notion of Sustainable Investment ("Notion").

121 Tiffany Grabski and Anthony Miller, *10 Years of Impact and Progress* (United Nations Sustainable Stock Exchange (SSE) 2019) 3.

122 Tiffany Grabski and Anthony Miller, *10 Years of Impact and Progress* (United Nations Sustainable Stock Exchange (SSE) 2019) 26.

123 United Nations Department of Economic and Social Affairs (DESA), 'Our Work' (*Global Investors for Sustainable Development Alliance*) <www.gisdalliance.org/our-work> accessed 27 February 2021.

124 Global Investors for Sustainable Development Alliance (GISD), 'Joint Statement by Global Investors for Sustainable Development Alliance (GISD)' 2 <https://www.gisdalliance.org/sites/default/files/2022-10/GISD%20Alliance%20Joint%20Statement%202022.pdf>.

125 United Nations Inter-Agency Task Force on Financing for Development, 'Financing for Sustainable Development Report 2020' (United Nations 2020) Report of the Inter-Agency Task Force on Financing for Development E/FFDF/2020 73.

126 United Nations Department of Economic and Social Affairs (DESA), 'How Can Investors Move from Greenwashing to SDG-Enabling?' (2020) UN/DESA Policy Brief #77 <www.un.org/development/desa/dpad/publication/un-desa-policy-brief-77-how-can-investors-move-from-greenwashing-to-sdg-enabling/> accessed 7 July 2020.

127 United Nations Environment Programme Finance Initiative (UNEP FI), 'United Nations-Convened Net-Zero Asset Owner Alliance' <www.unepfi.org/net-zero-alliance/> accessed 3 March 2021.

Formulated in Chapter 4, the Notion is one of the two approaches of the Consolidated Method that this book advances as a response to the incomplete assessment of sustainable development in international investment law.

2.3.1 Sustainable investment: theoretical foundations and scholarship

Sustainable Investment as a general concept in sustainable finance begins with a partial rejection of the so-called Friedman doctrine that business interests, such as the performance of an investment, best contribute to public interest in the long run by maximizing freedom of choice. This fuelled a shareholder-centric business model (also known as "shareholder primacy"), focused on maximizing profitability as a single bottom line. According to this mode, integrating social responsibility into business practices would expose it to deceptive and fraudulent activity while asserting certain values on stakeholders who may not share in those moral consideration.[128] Decades of consistent application resulted in this classical or conventional shareholder primacy weaving itself into the very fabric of corporate law, leading to the following observation by Hansmann and Kraakman in their famous "End of History" essay on an ideological convergence:

> As a consequence of both logic and experience, there is convergence on a consensus that the best means to this end (that is, the pursuit of aggregate social welfare) is to make corporate managers strongly accountable to shareholder interests and, at least in direct terms, only to those interests.[129] . . . The developing consensus on the standard model will have important implications for the convergence of practice and law over the long run.[130]

The stronghold of shareholder primacy on corporate law, at least in the United States, can be confirmed as recently as in the middle of 2020. Amidst the rapidly rising interest in ESG investment in the country, as well as calls by individual and institutional investors for clarity concerning Sustainable Investment regulation, the United States Department of Labor proposed, on the matter of "investment duties" of national pension schemes in the Employee Retirement Income Security Act of 1974, that "fiduciaries may never subordinate the interest of plan participants and beneficiaries in their retirement income to non-pecuniary goals" and that the "evaluation of an investment must be focused only on pecuniary factors [making it] unlawful for a fiduciary to sacrifice return or accept additional risk to promote a public policy, political, or any other non-pecuniary goal".[131]

128 Milton Friedman, 'The Social Responsibility of Business Is to Increase Its Profits' *The New York Times Magazine* (1970).

129 Henry Hansmann and Reinier Kraakman, 'The End of History for Corporate Law Essay' (2000) 89 Georgetown Law Journal 439, 441.

130 Henry Hansmann and Reinier Kraakman, 'The End of History for Corporate Law Essay' (2000) 89 Georgetown Law Journal 455.

131 Employee Benefits Security Administration, Department of Labor, 'Financial Factors in Selecting Plan Investments: A Proposed Rule by the Employee Benefits Security Administration on 06/30/2020' paras 52–54.

In investment, the Friedman doctrine found its counterpart in modern portfolio theory by Markowitz, who in 1959 identified that optimal portfolio selection began with an analysis of past and projected future performance of the individual securities[132] that sought to minimize uncertainty.[133] Modern portfolio theory identified two "salient features" of investment that would serve as the principles to portfolio selection: uncertainty and correlation. Uncertainty involved non-economic factors, such as geopolitical intrigue or climate change, and applies to the future performance of securities. As such, optimal portfolio selection should focus primarily on "reasonable opinions" based on past performance, such as capital gains and dividend payoffs,[134] rather than considerations that were extra-financial like sustainable development impact. The second salient feature, correlation, involved an assumption that securities within the same industry would perform with greater resemblance than those in unrelated industries, forming the basis of portfolio diversification as a core investment strategy throughout the 20th century.[135]

The rejection of the core motive of modern portfolio theory, which was to diversify away from non-economic risk arising from uncertainty, has generally been placed in the theory of the firm and shareholder value creation. Commonly associated with Jensen and Meckling,[136] the firm was portrayed as not an individual with unified "motivations or intentions" but rather a "complex process in which the conflicting objectives of individuals . . . are brought into equilibrium within a framework of contractual relations".[137] As a composite of shareholders and their interests, the firm attempts to achieve an equilibrium state by balancing expenditures to not only pecuniary, but also non-pecuniary benefits. Given the diversity of interests represented by shareholders, both pecuniary and non-pecuniary, the firm is presented with multiple equilibria scenarios, meaning that it can pursue a range of strategies that are indifferent from one another as long as the firm is able to achieve at least one of the equilibrium points at profit maximization and thus surpassing a scenario wherein the firm experiences loss.[138]

132 Harry M Markowitz, *Portfolio Selection: Efficient Diversification of Investments* (Yale UP 1959) 3.

133 Harry M Markowitz, *Portfolio Selection: Efficient Diversification of Investments* (Yale UP 1959) 6.

134 Harry M Markowitz, *Portfolio Selection: Efficient Diversification of Investments* (Yale UP 1959) 4.

135 Harry M Markowitz, *Portfolio Selection: Efficient Diversification of Investments* (Yale UP 1959) 5.

136 Michael C Jensen and William H Meckling, 'Theory of the Firm: Managerial Behavior, Agency Costs and Ownership Structure' (1976) 3 Journal of Financial Economics 305, 305–6.

137 Michael C Jensen and William H Meckling, 'Theory of the Firm: Managerial Behavior, Agency Costs and Ownership Structure' (1976) 3 Journal of Financial Economics 311.

138 Jensen and Meckling equated the value of a firm (V) as including the level of non-pecuniary benefit (F) consumed in different ownership settings, $(1-\alpha)V$, over the indifference between wealth and non-pecuniary benefits, (U_J), with J as any slope (sensitivity) in the relationship $F=(1-\alpha)V/U_J$ (Michael C Jensen and William H Meckling, 'Theory of the Firm: Managerial Behavior, Agency Costs and Ownership Structure' (1976) 3 Journal of Financial Economics 316).

Building on this rejection of modern portfolio theory, Stout observed that given the diverse interests of shareholders, a "relentless focus" on shareholder primacy as a "monolith" that focuses exclusively on pecuniary profit left shareholders worse off as it was unable to capture disparate motivations for equity investment.[139] Stout identified alternatives to classical shareholder primacy, including that of the prosocial shareholder or investor as those who are "willing to sacrifice at least some corporate profits in order to benefit, or at least avoid harming, employees, consumers, society or the environment".[140] The prosocial investor provided an alternative depiction to that offered by conventional shareholder primacy, which tended to reduce the investor to a homogenous agent, or monolith, that functioned at the "lowest common human denominator, implicitly assuming they are uniformly short-sighted, impecunious, opportunistic, self-destructive, and psychopathically indifferent to the fates of others, future generations, and the planet".[141]

Yet one limitation to the prosocial investor concept is that while they may own equity, they do not command sufficient corporate ownership that prevents the firm from undergoing "amoral drift", such as permitting a hostile bidder to take control over the company and engage in activities that are contrary to the predilections of the prosocial investor.[142] Instead, investors must feel "responsible for the action in question":

> a consumer does not object to holding shares in a dirty company if he had no role in choosing the dirty action—indeed he will pay full price for such shares. If the consumer is asked to vote on a clean action rather than a dirty action, however, he may be prepared to vote for the former.[143]

In order to leverage the benefits brought on by prosocial investors, which can perhaps be best understood as the opposite of a conventional shareholder primacy monolith investor, Hart and Zingales argue that prosocial investors must be permitted to "vote on the broad outlines of corporate policy".[144]

The rise of institutional and proxy investors that control large margins of equity at scales influential enough to affect corporate ownership further invigorated the debate on the prosocial investor. Hawley and Williams were influential in their observations on the "universal owner", which were the owners of assets—investors,

139 Lynn A Stout, *The Shareholder Value Myth: How Putting Shareholders First Harms Investors, Corporations, and the Public* (Berrett-Koehler Publishers 2012) 9.

140 Lynn A Stout, 'New Thinking on Shareholder Primacy' (2012) 2 Accounting, Economics, and Law: A Convivium 16.

141 Lynn A Stout, 'New Thinking on Shareholder Primacy' (2012) 2 Accounting, Economics, and Law: A Convivium 18.

142 Oliver Hart and Luigi Zingales, 'Companies Should Maximize Shareholder Welfare Not Market Value' (2017) 2 Journal of Law, Finance, and Accounting 247, 256.

143 Oliver Hart and Luigi Zingales, 'Companies Should Maximize Shareholder Welfare Not Market Value' (2017) 2 Journal of Law, Finance, and Accounting 253.

144 Oliver Hart and Luigi Zingales, 'Companies Should Maximize Shareholder Welfare Not Market Value' (2017) 2 Journal of Law, Finance, and Accounting 270.

shareholders, etc.—who would take into account the "impact of current decisions not only on other actors on the current economic scene, but on future generations as well" in connection to the intergenerationality development concept associated to the Brundtland Commission.[145] Universal owners were those with widely diversified portfolios that were broad enough to depend "more on the overall health of the economy than on the fortunes of any particular company".[146] As such, universal owners would need to "identify important sources of positive and negative externalities" such as the "negative externality of adverse climate change [that] would likely force major costs onto portfolio companies".[147] One prominent example of a universal owner that clearly embodies the responsibility to account for externalities are public investment vehicles like sovereign wealth funds, which must balance their fiduciary duties to shareholders as well as ethical considerations in the distribution of assets.[148] This balancing of duties can be understood as that between sacrificing pecuniary profitability, namely the expansion of wealth, and addressing a certain externality, whether that is preventing its exacerbation, such as investments in fossil fuels, or promoting a positive externality, such as job creation.[149]

Meanwhile, stakeholderism, another fundamental pillar of the Notion, has been gaining traction from its formulation[150] in Freeman's much-cited text, *Strategic Management: A Stakeholder Approach*:

> When enough external changes have occurred so that our current theory no longer gives us valid answers then we must abandon the theory and turn to a new set of concepts which explains both external and internal change. . . .

145 James P Hawley and Andrew T Williams, 'The Universal Owner's Role in Sustainable Economic Development' (2002) 9 Corporate Environmental Strategy 284, 287.

146 James P Hawley and Andrew T Williams, 'The Universal Owner's Role in Sustainable Economic Development' (2002) 9 Corporate Environmental Strategy 286.

147 James P Hawley and Andrew T Williams, 'The Universal Owner's Role in Sustainable Economic Development' (2002) 9 Corporate Environmental Strategy 287–88.

148 See, for instance, Xenia Karametaxas, 'Sovereign Wealth Funds as Socially Responsible Investors' in Giovanna Adinolfi and others (eds), *International Economic Law: Contemporary Issues* (Springer International Publishing 2017).

149 John Hill, 'Chapter 3—Theory of the Firm' in *Environmental, Social, and Governance (ESG) Investing: A Balanced Analysis of the Theory and Practice of a Sustainable Portfolio* (Academic Press 2020).

150 Though challenging conventional shareholder primacy from the viewpoint of serving diverse interests, or "stockholders", debuted much earlier: "If, however, as much recent writing suggests, we are undergoing a substantial change in our public opinion of business to the community, it is natural to expect that this change of opinion will have some effect upon the attitude of those who manage business. If, therefore, the managers of modern businesses were also its owners, the development of a public opinion to the effect that business has responsibilities to its employees and its customers would, quite apart from any legal compulsion, tend to affect the conduct of the better type of business man. . . . Business might then become a profession of public service, not primarily because the law had made it such but because a public opinion shared in by businessmen themselves had brought about a professional attitude" (E Merrick Jr Dodd, 'For Whom Are Corporate Managers Trustees' (1931) 45 Harvard Law Review 1145, 1153).

> Many of these changes have been around for some time, yet we have been quite slow to incorporate them into our framework for managing the firm.[151]

Freeman proposed "stakeholder management" as a means to account for a broad range of stakeholders, defined as "any group or individual who can affect or is affected by the achievement of the firm's objectives", which includes, for instance, environmentalists and local community organizations.[152] CSR, Freeman writes, is "applying the stakeholder concept to non-traditional stakeholder groups who are usually thought of as having adversarial relationships with the firm" yet serve as a "catalyst for rethinking the role of the business enterprise in society".[153] Successful stakeholder management attempts to "integrate the perspective of all stakeholders rather than offsetting one against another", further adding that:

> All stakeholders will not benefit all the time. Obviously, even with a detailed understanding of concrete stakeholder relationships, most strategies will distribute both benefits and harms between different groups of stakeholders. Win-win situations are not guaranteed. Indeed, it is just as important for management to develop strategies that distribute harms in a way that ensures the long-term support of all the stakeholders. Yet over time, stakeholder interests must be managed in the same direction.[154]

The stakeholder approach, or stakeholderism, materialized into the ideological contender to shareholderism and was led by enterprises with prosocial inclinations to portfolio management. Bebchuk and Tallarita trace this process and classify two conceptually distinct versions of stakeholderism. The first is instrumental stakeholderism, in which an "enlightened shareholder value" approach acknowledges the "effects of the company's operations on stakeholders" by maximizing long-run shareholder value.[155] The second, pluralistic stakeholderism, "treats stakeholder welfare as an end in itself rather than a mere means".[156] Concurrently, some have questioned whether the split between stakeholderism and shareholderism is any longer meaningful, since these views are built on the presumption that such widely shared ideological camps still exist. Mayer, for instance, poses that the sheer diversity of corporate entities, leadership and purposes make that presumption unlikely because the "accountability of management [would become] hopelessly imprecise".[157]

151 R Edward Freeman, *Strategic Management: A Stakeholder Approach* (CUP 2010) 7.

152 R Edward Freeman, *Strategic Management: A Stakeholder Approach* (CUP 2010) 25.

153 R Edward Freeman, *Strategic Management: A Stakeholder Approach* (CUP 2010) 38.

154 R Edward Freeman and John McVea, 'A Stakeholder Approach to Strategic Management' in Michael A Hitt, R Edward Freeman and Jeffrey S Harrison (eds), *The Blackwell Handbook of Strategic Management* (3rd edn, Blackwell Publishing 2008) 189.

155 Lucian A Bebchuk and Roberto Tallarita, 'The Illusory Promise of Stakeholder Governance' (2020) 105 Cornell Law Review 11.

156 Lucian A Bebchuk and Roberto Tallarita, 'The Illusory Promise of Stakeholder Governance' (2020) 105 Cornell Law Review 15.

157 Colin Mayer, 'Shareholderism Versus Stakeholderism—A Misconceived Contradiction. A Comment on "The Illusory Promise of Stakeholder Governance" by Lucian Bebchuk and Roberto Tallarita' (European Corporate Governance Institute 2020) No 522/2020 10.

Nevertheless, the stakeholder approach to asset management, particularly pluralistic stakeholderism, left deep impressions on corporate governance,[158] the role of the corporate enterprise, and on Sustainable Investment as it pertains to this project. Multilateral organizations have advanced various initiatives, such as those introduced earlier in this section and explored in more depth in Chapter 4, seeing to improve unity in approach. Multistakeholderism as multistakeholder governance was also embraced by the UN system through the Global Compact and the UN Guiding Principles on Business and Human Rights as the preferred means of engaging in new governance theory which, rather than pursuing a "legally binding treaty prescribing applicable norms and policies", sought a polycentric governance approach that involved "multistakeholder processes of public-private partnerships and informal cooperation".[159]

The connection between multistakeholderism as pluralistic stakeholderism and multistakeholder governance can be understood as part of a continuum. As Gleckman identifies, multistakeholder governance is a product of dissatisfaction with the efforts of government, the UN system, and a drive towards pragmatic action.[160] In response, a "small, powerful sub-group of actors" such as TNCs, banded together as "representatives" of a "conceptually defined social community" to convene initiatives in response to existing governance gaps,[161] such as standard-setting in Sustainable Investment. A governance gap, in this context, is understood as "the political and economic space created by non-action of the multilateral system".[162] The combination of these corporate enclaves and governance gaps would be rallying themes in the views that are critical to Sustainable Investment.

2.3.2 Sustainable investment: criticisms

The lack of a uniform definition and measurement of Sustainable Investment resulted in criticisms concerning "SDG-washing", which is the "risk that financial products and strategies are presented as sustainable without making a meaningful

158 Stakeholderism, for instance, was clearly affirmed in the "Davos Manifesto" for 2020 arising out of the World Economic Forum (WEF). The first line of the Manifesto reads: "The purpose of a company is to engage all its stakeholders in shared and sustained value creation. In creating such value, a company serves not only its shareholders, but all its stakeholders—employees, customers, suppliers, local communities and society at large" (Klaus Schwab, 'Davos Manifesto 2020: The Universal Purpose of a Company in the Fourth Industrial Revolution' <www.weforum.org/agenda/2019/12/davos-manifesto-2020-the-universal-purpose-of-a-company-in-the-fourth-industrial-revolution/>).

159 Daria Davitti, 'Regulating Multinational Corporations' in Koen De Feyter, Stéphanie De Moerloose and Gamze Erdem Türkelli (eds), *Law and Development Encyclopedia* (Edward Elgar 2020) 3–4.

160 Harris Gleckman, *Multistakeholder Governance and Democracy: A Global Challenge* (Routledge 2018) 1–2.

161 Harris Gleckman, *Multistakeholder Governance and Democracy: A Global Challenge* (Routledge 2018) 7–8.

162 Harris Gleckman, *Multistakeholder Governance and Democracy: A Global Challenge* (Routledge 2018) 19.

contribution to the achievement of the [Sustainable Development Goals]".[163] From the latter half of 2019, portfolio investments in funds that value in the magnitude of billions of US dollars have been enjoying the benefits of the ESG label only to later be revealed to have included investments in firearms manufacturers[164] and deep-water drilling for hydrocarbon resources.[165] Meanwhile, despite active environmental disclosures for investment, without uniformity of standards in definition and scope, the identification and accounting of emissions reductions remain difficult. For instance, the emissions that occur from the supply and production of energy, such as scope 2 emissions (produced by companies supplying energy), account for 14% to 23% from energy generation, and scope 3 emissions (resulting from the sale of non-renewable energy sources, such as oil, between energy companies) can account for up to 84% of the total carbon footprint.[166] Research shows that scope 2 and 3 emissions are not regularly included in the environmental disclosures of investment in energy projects.[167] Meanwhile, private sector entities in the energy sector, especially those in hydrocarbons, are producing in-house ESG benchmarks, further complicating coherence in the emissions accounting process.[168] Bebchuk and Tallarita identified this as the largest challenge to stakeholderism:

> Stakeholderists have largely avoided offering answers for these questions [concerning the implementation of pluralistic stakeholderism], or even a

163 United Nations Inter-Agency Task Force on Financing for Development, 'Financing for Sustainable Development Report 2020' (United Nations 2020) Report of the Inter-Agency Task Force on Financing for Development E/FFDF/2020 73. The OECD identified this as, "businesses that use the Sustainable Development Goals to market their positive contribution to some SDGs while ignoring their negative impact on others" (Development Matters, 'Ever Heard of SDG Washing? The Urgency of SDG Due Diligence' (*Development Matters*, 25 September 2017) <https://oecd-development-matters.org/2017/09/25/ever-heard-of-sdg-washing-the-urgency-of-sdg-due-diligence/> accessed 21 September 2020). This definition has largely corresponded with corporate monitoring by institutions, which find that a majority of corporations have done little more than plan for contributions to the SDGs, do not measure actual impact, or fail to view the value of SDG commitments (International Institute for Sustainable Development (IISD), 'Responsible Business Report Finds High Risk of "SDG Washing"' (*SDG Knowledge Hub*, 29 May 2018) <http://sdg.iisd.org/news/responsible-business-report-finds-high-risk-of-sdg-washing/> accessed 21 September 2020).

164 Billy Nauman, 'Vanguard Ditches Over Two Dozen Stocks from ESG Funds' *Financial Times* (12 August 2019) <www.ft.com/content/5b6caa5e-bd4f-11e9-89e2-41e555e96722> accessed 7 July 2020.

165 Billy Nauman, 'Investors Balk at Green Bond from Group Specialising in Oil Tankers' *Financial Times* (18 October 2019) <www.ft.com/content/b1d4201c-f142-11e9-bfa4-b25f11f42901> accessed 7 July 2020.

166 'How Much Can Financiers Do About Climate Change?' *The Economist* (2020) <www.economist.com/briefing/2020/06/20/how-much-can-financiers-do-about-climate-change> accessed 9 December 2020.

167 'Green Investing Is Red Hot but Its Impact Is Underwhelming' *The Economist* (2020) <www.economist.com/graphic-detail/2020/06/22/green-investing-is-red-hot-but-its-impact-is-underwhelming> accessed 13 July 2020.

168 Leen Pressman, 'Shell's Dutch Scheme Introduces Own ESG Benchmark' (*IPE*, 18 May 2020) <www.ipe.com/news/shells-dutch-scheme-introduces-own-esg-benchmark/10045688.article> accessed 13 July 2020.

> methodology for reaching such answers. Instead, supporters of pluralistic stakeholderism have largely dealt with these questions by assigning them to corporate leaders to resolve at their discretion. Similarly, state constituency statutes have chosen to delegate to directors a broad discretion to identify the relevant stakeholders. Thus, on this matter, . . . stakeholderism critically relies on the discretion of corporate leaders.[169]

Identifying and countering SDG-washing is challenging due to the sheer diversity of the SDGs, which attempt to address multivariate targets across the three dimensions of sustainable development while lacking a means to aggregate key performance indicators across them.[170] A more far-reaching contestation to Sustainable Investment, irrespective of indicator limitations, is whether the corporation can have real long-term impacts on advancing sustainable development[171] given conflicting structural factors such as the threat of bankruptcy.[172] Furthermore, expanding the range of factors considered in corporate leadership in the way that Sustainable Investment encourages may ensnare decision-making by introducing division between potentially conflicting views on nonpecuniary factors. This can ultimately reduce the efficacy of corporate leadership as a result of having "too many masters",[173] which can result in consequences such as noncyclical unemployment during the transitory periods between shifting investment strategies.

Trouble involving Banca Generali, which is a signatory[174] to both the Principles on Responsible Investment (PRI) and the UN-convened Net-Zero Asset Owner Alliance,[175] is demonstrative of a tested correlation between Sustainable Investment

169 Bebchuk and Tallarita (n 156) 19.

170 An overview of methodologies is provided in Ria Sinha and Manipadma Datta, 'Institutional Investments and Responsible Investing' in Magdalena Ziolo and Bruno S Sergi (eds), *Financing Sustainable Development: Key Challenges and Prospects* (Springer International Publishing 2019).

171 For instance, on the effects of inequality, as observed as part of a broad scoping of challenges to pluralistic stakeholderism in Matteo Gatti and Chrystin D Ondersma, 'Can a Broader Corporate Purpose Redress Inequality? The Stakeholder Approach Chimera' (2020) 46 Journal of Corporation Law. The past, present and future of stakeholderism is more thoroughly examined in the 'A New Deal Conference Papers' (Institute for Corporate Governance and Finance and Rock Center for Corporate Governance 2019) <www.law.nyu.edu/centers/icgf/events/new-deal-new-century>.

172 Refer to the "shrinking pie" argument concerning the nature of corporate duties under the threat of bankruptcy in Stephen Bainbridge, 'Much Ado About Little? Directors' Fiduciary Duties in the Vicinity of Insolvency' (2007) 1 Journal of Business & Technology Law 336. Simultaneously, dismissing corporate leadership as unable to adapt to changing circumstances as criticized in Alex Edmans, *Grow the Pie: How Great Companies Deliver Both Purpose and Profit* (CUP 2020). Edmans argues that the concerns raised in stakeholderism are becoming impossible to dismiss at the daily operations level of corporations, such as the impacts of climate change (Alex Edmans, *Grow the Pie: How Great Companies Deliver Both Purpose and Profit* (CUP 2020) 53).

173 See, for instance, Sanjai Bhagat and R Glenn Hubbard, *Should the Modern Corporation Maximize Shareholder Value?* (American Enterprise Institute 2020).

174 Banco Generali, 'SRI Network' (*Generali Network*) <www.generali.com/our-responsibilities/responsible-investments/sri-network> accessed 8 July 2020.

175 The UN-Convened Net-Zero Asset Owner Alliance is a group of institutional investors seeking to transition their "investment portfolios to net-zero GHG emissions by 2050 consistent with a

and its actual impact on sustainable development. Banca Generali may have very well advanced its environmental targets through negative screening of its investments—only to discover that it had invested in an asset that is diminutive towards relevant social and governance factors.[176]

Banca Generali purchased bonds from CFE Finance, an investment bank based in Geneva, which included outstanding debt of a commercial entity connected to a mafia group that then benefited from a guaranteed penalty interest rate under the EU's Late Payment Directive. This in turn mitigated some of the credit-based risk of that debt, which was then included as one part of an asset-backed security, which are types of bonds that are collateralized by a pool of assets, such as loans. The asset-backed security was issued by Chiron, a special purpose vehicle established in Italy for securitization purposes. The asset-backed security was then arranged into a bond by CFE, which was then cleared by financial supervisory authorities for money laundering concerns and then purchased by Banca Generali for distribution to global investors.[177] The Banca Generali case demonstrates some of the complexities facing Sustainable Investment when involving multiple financial intermediaries and the type of risk analysis conducted at each transaction.

Due diligence to disclose social risk (which mafia assets would clearly raise), or the S in ESG, was not observed either at the level of securitization by the special purpose vehicle, or at the point of the investment agreement between CFE and Banca Generali despite having involved financial supervisory agencies. This demonstrates an ongoing methodological challenge facing Sustainable Investment. The failure to disclose social risk in this scenario can be identified at the origination stage, i.e. in providing debt financing to the mafia-linked commercial entity, as well as the underwriting process, when the special purpose vehicle included that debt into an asset-backed security—or perhaps even at the stage when the debt had benefited from EU guaranteed penalty interest rates. Ultimately, this is not surprising as asset-backed securities look primarily at factors that determine creditworthiness to balance the different risk levels of each asset,[178] such as outstanding debt or wealth holdings. This adds a further level of complexity in ESG disclosures: calculating the value of an investment that addresses a particular type

maximum temperature rise of 1.5°C above pre-industrial temperatures, taking into account the best available scientific knowledge including the findings of the IPCC, and regularly reporting on progress, including establishing intermediate targets every five years in line with Paris Agreement Article 4.9" (United Nations-Convened Net-Zero Asset Owner Alliance, 'Collective Commitment Document' <www.unepfi.org/wordpress/wp-content/uploads/2019/09/AOACollectiveCommitment.pdf>).

176 Miles Johnson, 'Italian Mafia Bonds Sold to Global Investors' *Financial Times* (7 July 2020) <www.ft.com/content/bcebd77c-057b-4fd0-bd99-b97e0e559455> accessed 8 July 2020.

177 As explained with greater detail in Cristian Angeloni, 'Investment Bank Hits Back at "Mafia Bond" Allegations' (*International Adviser*, 13 July 2020) <https://international-adviser.com/investment-bank-hits-back-at-mafia-bond-allegations/> accessed 24 July 2020.

178 A more thorough explanation found in Andrew Lennox, 'Spectrum—ABS Analysis: Through the ESG Lens' *Hermes Credit Newsletter Q3* (Hermes Investment Management 2019) <www.hermes-investment.com/se/wp-content/uploads/2019/10/hermes-spectrum-q3-2019.pdf>.

of risk, such as credit risk for an asset-backed security, and how that risk interacts with another mechanism of risk reduction, such as the mitigated risk arising from ESG disclosures.[179]

As this section attempted to elucidate, a "common and more granular" definition of Sustainable Investment is crucial to its governing principles, such as those espoused by the Principles on Responsible Investment. This includes, for instance, clarifying matters of fiduciary duty of investment managers, particularly those in the public realm such as national pension schemes.[180] This also impacts the approaches that are available to investors when engaging in Sustainable Investments, such as being made aware of the assets included into a portfolio and then providing excusal rights, which permit investors to identify certain sectors that they would like to exclude from their portfolio.[181] However, without a uniform and comprehensive understanding of Sustainable Investments, methods made available to investors engaging in ESG remain blunt instruments. This was seen in the controversy surrounding the World Bank Group financing the fossil fuel industry of Guyana in an attempt to help fund its transition into renewable energies: a part of that financing would invariably fund the business-as-usual operations of the fossil fuel industry, though perhaps as part of a larger effort to transform the industry while minimizing job destruction.[182]

2.4 Pillar Three: right to regulate for the public interest in international investment law

The third pillar to this interdisciplinary analysis involves the right to regulate, which in international investment law permits flexibilities for host states to implement government measures on behalf of the public interest that may at times or to some extent be contrary to minimum standards of treatment defined in the IIA(s) to which they are party.[183] This customary international legal principle "signifies freedom to engage in political, economic, legislative and other regulatory activity as the state sees fit".[184] In international investment law, this right to regulate is typically reserved through the applicable IIA in reference to the promotion and

179 These relationships are further explored in Christoph Stellner, Christian Klein and Bernhard Zwergel, 'Corporate Social Responsibility and Eurozone Corporate Bonds: The Moderating Role of Country Sustainability' (2015) 59 Journal of Banking & Finance 538.

180 Zabel Lovell, 'ESG Investing: Growing and Evolving' (Schulte Roth & Zabel LLP) <www.lexology.com/library/detail.aspx?g=85d6def4-6cce-4694-85a9-bfe37b33a056> accessed 8 July 2020.

181 Zabel Lovell, 'ESG Investing: Growing and Evolving' (Schulte Roth & Zabel LLP) <www.lexology.com/library/detail.aspx?g=85d6def4-6cce-4694-85a9-bfe37b33a056> accessed 8 July 2020.

182 Jasper Jolly, 'Anger Over World Bank's $55m Pledge to Guyana's Fossil Fuel Industry' *The Guardian* (27 February 2020) <www.theguardian.com/business/2020/feb/27/world-bank-guyana-fossil-fuel-industry-climate> accessed 8 July 2020.

183 See, for instance, Yulia Levashova, *The Right of States to Regulate in International Investment Law: The Search for Balance Between Public Interest and Fair and Equitable Treatment* (Kluwer Law International BV 2019) 4.

184 Aikaterini Titi, *The Right to Regulate in International Investment Law* (Nomos 2014) 32.

protection of investment,[185] often in retaining the "freedom to revise its laws on admission after the investment treaty has entered into force . . . allow[ing] the adoption of measures that are more restrictive than those existing at the time of the signature of the treaty".[186] In principle, the state retains its right to regulate as a matter of sovereignty:

> While maximal regulatory flexibility exists where a state does not enter into an investment treaty in the first place, circumscribing this freedom by means of an [international investment agreement or IIA] is itself a manifestation of the state's regulatory capacity. After assuming an international obligation, a state retains its ability to regulate, to terminate a treaty, or simply to renege on its international obligations. This capacity, or general state freedom to regulate, assumes *de facto* existence and coincides with a *lato sensu* right to regulate.[187]

Reserving the right to regulate has been interpreted by investment treaty arbitration tribunals in line with such treaty provisions, as was demonstrated, for instance, in *Aguas del Tunari v Bolivia*, where the tribunal recognized the "State's duty to admit investments not to the laws and regulations of Bolivia, but rather to the 'right to exercise powers' conferred by such laws or regulations".[188]

However, in the context of international investment law, the right to regulate is not absolute in the way that it is applied within the terms of an IIA. Usually, it is regulated in accordance with customary understandings of minimum standards of treatment towards investors, such as fair and equitable treatment (FET). While the right to regulate is applied at the level of interpretation, as discussed later in this section, it remains different from discretion:

> [T]he right to regulate is a *right* with a concrete legal basis, such as an investment treaty or general international law, and it connotes state entitlement

185 The international investment agreement between the United Kingdom and Turkey, for instance, reads: "Each Contracting Party shall encourage and create favourable conditions for investments of nationals or companies of the other Contracting Party in its territory and subject to its right to exercise powers conferred by its laws or regulations, each Contracting Party shall admit investments of nationals or companies of the other Contracting Party" (Agreement between the Government of the United Kingdom of Great Britain and Northern Ireland and the Government of the Republic of Turkey for the Promotion and Protection of Investments 1991, Art 2[1]). While the specific language surrounding this clause varies, they are operatively similar. See, for instance, the Netherlands-Uzbekistan BIT (Agreement on Encouragement and Reciprocal Protection of Investments between the Kingdom of the Netherlands and the Republic of Uzbekistan 1996, Art 2). Pollan provides a survey of these articles in Thomas Pollan, *Legal Framework for the Admission of FDI* (Eleven International Publishing 2006) 276–79.

186 Dolzer and Schreuer (n 3) 89.

187 Titi (n 185) 32.

188 Aguas Del Tunari, *SA v Republic of Bolivia*, ICSID Case No ARB/02/3, Decision on Respondent's Objections to Jurisdiction (21 October 2005) para 147.

> to act as it does. Deference, on the other hand, has no legal basis; it is an approach to interpretation relying on judicial restraint—or activism.[189]

Nevertheless, the right to regulate remains an important means for the host state to retain a policy space for government measures within the operative terms of the treaty obligations that bind the state to observe certain minimum standards of treatment to the investor *stricto sensu*. On a substantive level, the right to regulate has often served as the basis to address the balance between public and private interests as they apply to international investment law.[190] In an overview of the elements of the right to regulate for the public interest, Levashova identifies two dimensions of application:

> (1) [F]rom the perspective of investors, in some cases where the state exercises its regulatory authority, e.g. through the enactment or amendment of legislation, this may undermine the stability of the investment climate and generate adverse effects for investment. Consequently, as may be argued by an investor, the state's measures constitute unfair treatment and are hence in violation of the FET standard.
> (2) [F]rom the perspective of the state, however, in addition to fulfilling its obligations under the applicable IIA, the state has a prerogative to ensure public welfare for its population through the exercise of its regulatory authority. As such, a state's exercise of its right to regulate for the public interest may interfere with the right of the investor to obtain FET.[191]

As per the former, investors may raise claim against or request compensation for direct or indirect expropriation of lost assets resulting from the government measure.[192] In such cases, the host state is expected to compensate the investor a value commensurate to the importance of the public policy objective in relation to the damages incurred by the investor.[193] In this sense, assessments of compensation for

189 Titi (n 185) 40.
190 Titi (n 185) 75.
191 Levashova (n 184) 41.
192 Differences between nationalization, expropriation and indirect expropriation are defined as: "Direct expropriation means a mandatory legal transfer of the title to the property or its outright physical seizure. Normally, the expropriation benefits the State itself or a State-mandated third party. . . . Indirect expropriation involves total or near-total deprivation of an investment but without a formal transfer of title or outright seizure ('Expropriation: A Sequel' (United Nations 2012) UNCTAD/DIAE/IA/2011/7 6–7). Subcategories of indirect expropriation also include "de facto, creeping, constructive, disguised, consequential, regulatory or virtual expropriation" ('Expropriation: A Sequel' (United Nations 2012) UNCTAD/DIAE/IA/2011/7 11). For a more comprehensive classification of indirect expropriation and its procedural and normative meaning within the practice of investment treaty arbitration, see Jonathan Bonnitcha, 'Indirect Expropriation' in *Substantive Protection Under Investment Treaties: A Legal and Economic Analysis* (CUP 2014).
193 Yannick Radi, 'International Investment Law and Development: A History of Two Concepts' in Stephan Schill, Christian J Tams and Rainer Hofmann (eds), *International Investment Law and Development: Bridging the Gap* (Edward Elgar Publishing 2015) 81–82.

the losses incurred by the investor arising from a government public interest measure, such as public health or environmental protection, are important to understanding how those public interest policies are evaluated within international investment law.[194] In determining whether a government measure is lawful insofar as it falls within the remit of the right to regulate for international investment law, customary interpretation derived from practice identifies certain "classical requirements":

1 The measure must serve a public purpose;
2 The measure must not be arbitrary and discriminatory within the generally accepted meaning of the term;
3 The procedure of expropriation must follow principles of due process;
4 Expropriatory measures must be accompanied by "prompt, adequate, and effective compensation".431F[195]

Should a government measure not satisfy these classical requirements, the losses incurred by the investor as a result of the state employing its right to regulate are viewed as having been expropriated.[196] Conversely, measures that are legitimate but result in the regulatory taking of a foreign asset have been identified as nationalization, and whether they require compensation or not remains a controversial point.[197] Different approaches taken by investment treaty arbitration tribunals to testing for expropriation or nationalization are organized into Table 2.3. As shown in the table, it is possible to identify three overall approaches which represent a certain continuum along the spectrum for evaluating the legitimacy of a measure: the sole effect test, the purpose test, and the balancing test.

194 Compensation for a regulatory taking was the grounds for dispute in *Funnekotter v Zimbabwe*, which involved indirect investments in large commercial farms in Zimbabwe protected under the Netherlands-Zimbabwe BIT. The claimants contended that over a process between 1997 and 2005 involving law reform, near constitutional amendment and violence concerning the acquisition of farmland for agricultural settlement purposes in a state of necessity or emergency, they "were deprived of their investments by Respondent by actions that were tantamount to expropriation" to which no compensation was offered (*Bernardus Henricus Funnekotter and Others v Republic of Zimbabwe*, ICSID Case No ARB/05/6, Award (22 April 2009) para 40).

195 Dolzer and Schreuer (n 3) 99. Compensation for expropriation following the so-called Hull formula, which calls for prompt, adequate and effective compensation of expropriated alien property, has been viewed as a common feature of fair and equitable treatment. An overview of the contention surrounding "prompt, adequate, and effective" compensation as a standard can be found in, generally, R Rajesh Babu, 'Standard of Compensation for Expropriation of Foreign Investment' in Julien Chaisse, Leïla Choukroune and Sufian Jusoh (eds), *Handbook of International Investment Law and Policy* (Springer 2020).

196 UNCTAD identified that "an expropriation must be made for a public purpose is recognized by most legal systems and is a rule of international law. The taking of property must be motivated by the pursuance of a legitimate welfare objective, as opposed to a purely private gain or an illicit end. This condition is reflected in most domestic legal systems as well, which indicates a convergence of approaches among States in various regions with different legal cultures" ('Expropriation: A Sequel' (n 193) 29).

197 In *Feldman v Mexico*, however, the tribunal finds that compensation is required irrespective of the legitimacy of the regulatory taking (*Marvin Roy Feldman Karpa v United Mexican States*, ICSID Case No ARB(AF)/99/1, Award (16 December 2002) para 99).

Table 2.3 Testing for expropriation

Approach	*Description*
Sole effect test	Whether the government measure constituted an expropriation arising from a regulatory measure that is "sufficiently restrictive" to the investor, rather than a "valid police power regulation . . . that does not have a sufficiently restrictive effect on property rights". The "police powers doctrine" serves as the ideological opposite of the sole effect doctrine, turning the focus from the investor to the state, e.g. restrictive to expansive public policy space.
Purpose test	Whether the objective or purpose of the measure is of a legitimate public interest, rather than *malas fides* or discriminatory, rendering the measure as a "normal exercise of police powers" as an arm's length assessment (the measure would have been conducted in similar circumstances elsewhere, such as in situations of international public policy as discussed later).
Balancing test	Whether the purpose and resulting benefit of the government measure towards the public interest is proportional in scale to the "level of investment interference" that occurs in effect, considering "all of the circumstances surrounding the measure".[198]

Source: Fortier and Drymer (2004).[199]

In considering the public interest within the view of applying the right to regulate, an important aspect of evaluating the legitimacy of a government measure will therefore rely on the interpretation of the object and purpose of IIAs. At one end, the agreement seeks to promote FDI by maintaining a regulatory environment that is conducive to foreign capital, such as a predictable and stable regulatory climate. This commonly refers to FET, which has become a prominent and well-established minimum standard in international investment law.[200] On the other end, IIAs clarify the relationship of rights and obligations between the host state and the foreign investor, striking "an appropriate balance between various legitimate interests involved".[201] These concepts are more fully explored in the following subsections.

2.4.1 Public interest

This work refers to the "public interest" as a concept generally referred to in IIAs, though its exact wording shows some variation such as public purpose, public

198 The tribunal in *Feldman v Mexico*, for instance, recognizes here that, in line with customary international law, "reasonable governmental regulation of this type cannot be achieved if any business that is adversely affected may seek compensation" (*Marvin Roy Feldman Karpa v United Mexican States*, ICSID Case No ARB(AF)/99/1, Award (16 December 2002) para 103).

199 L Yves Fortier and Stephen L Drymer, 'Indirect Expropriation in the Law of International Investment: I Know It When I See It, or Caveat Investor' (2004) 19 ICSID Review—Foreign Investment Law Journal 293, 300.

200 Dolzer and Schreuer (n 3) 130; Bonnitcha (n 193) 144.

201 United Nations Trade and Development (UNCTAD), *Fair and Equitable Treatment* (United Nations 1999) 77.

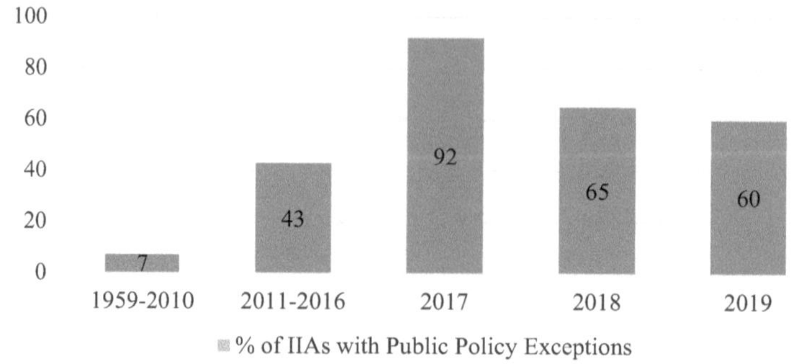

Figure 2.1 Percentage of international investment agreements (IIAs) with public policy exceptions

policy, national interest, public necessity, and so forth. UN Trade and Development (UNCTAD), in a review of these variations, observed that they are "equivalent in their scope and may be a result of different legal cultures and languages".[202] In a comparison between 2,432 BITs concluded between 1959 and 2010 and 110 BITs concluded between 2011 and 2016, UNCTAD found a 36% increase in references to public policy, amounting to 43% of the IIAs examined.[203] Figure 2.1 shows the percentage of IIAs featuring public interest.[204]

While the public interest within the context of international dispute settlement finds usage in other forms of international law and dispute settlement,[205] this work

202 "IIAs generally refer to "public purpose", although some treaties use other formulations such as "public benefit" (Germany-Pakistan BIT (2009)), "public interest" (China-Peru FTA (2009)), "public order and social interest" (Canada-Colombia FTA (2008)), "internal needs" (Hong Kong, China-Thailand BIT (2006) and Israel-Slovakia BIT (2001)), "legal ends" (Malaysia-Uruguay BIT (1996)), "national interest" (Chile-Philippines BIT (1997) and Malaysia-United Arab Emirates BIT (1992)), "public necessity" (Peru-Singapore FTA (2008)) and "public purpose related to internal needs" (Angola-United Kingdom BIT (2000)" ('Expropriation: A Sequel' [n 193] 29).

203 United Nations Trade and Development (UNCTAD), 'World Investment Report 2017: Investment and the Digital Economy' (United Nations 2017) UNCTAD/WIR/2017 122.

204 12 out of 13 international investment agreements concluded in 2017 included public interest exceptions (United Nations Trade and Development (UNCTAD), 'World Investment Report 2018: Investment and New Industrial Policies' (United Nations 2018) UNCTAD/WIR/2018 96); 19 out of 29 in 2018 (United Nations Trade and Development (UNCTAD), 'World Investment Report 2019: Special Economic Zones' (United Nations 2019) UNCTAD/WIR/2019 105); and 9 out of 15 in 2019 (United Nations Trade and Development (UNCTAD), 'World Investment Report 2020: International Production Beyond the Pandemic' (United Nations 2020) UNCTAD/WIR/2020 112).

205 One of the most quoted cases that bears the closest relevance to international economic law, for instance, was heard at the European Court of Human Rights in *James and others v The United Kingdom*, where the concept of "social justice" was evoked and deliberated upon in detail (*James and others v United Kingdom* (1986) European Court of Human Rights 8793/79). The ruling introduced the nationalization of foreign assets *pour cause d'utilité publique*, which extended beyond generality of interest or public utility and into matters of social justice (*James and others v*

looks specifically to its manifestation within the practice and scholarship of international economic law. By referring to the public interest, states seek to provide flexibilities in investment treaties, such as in the interpretation of FET and national treatment or through carving out police powers, general and security exceptions, and reservations.

For instance, an important iteration of the public interest can be found in the Convention on the Recognition and Enforcement of Foreign Arbitral Awards ("New York Convention"), whose Article V(2)(b) reads as follows:

> 2. Recognition and enforcement of an arbitral award may also be refused if the competent authority in the country where recognition and enforcement is sought finds that:
>
>   (a) The subject matter of the difference is not capable of settlement by arbitration under the law of that country; or
>   (b) The recognition or enforcement of the award would be contrary to the public policy of that country.[206]

While Article V(2)(b) has been interpreted parsimoniously enough not to include general concerns of the public interest, it remains a widely adopted instrument that identifies the exceptional nature of public interest concerns. In doing so, Article V(2)(b) recognizes the discretion of the dispute settlement authority in determining a public policy exception for the enforcement of an arbitral award.[207] In making that determination, in addition to the substantive elements of public policy,[208] procedural public policy is also considered, which concerns "procedural exceptions such as the impartiality of arbitrators, lack of reasons in the award and irregularities in the arbitral procedure".[209]

United Kingdom (1986) European Court of Human Rights 40–45). The Court made the important decision that should a regulatory taking be "pursued in measures of economic reform or measures designed to achieve greater social justice", the full market value of the expropriated property is not required to be compensated (*James and others v United Kingdom* (1986) European Court of Human Rights 54–57).

206 Convention on the Recognition and Enforcement of Foreign Arbitral Awards 1958 Art V(2)(b).

207 The debate surrounding the concept of the "public interest" as it relates to arbitral proceedings, however, reveals a strong resistance to permit matters of international politics influencing procedural matters. See, for instance, Shearman & Sterling, Columbia Law School, and United Nations Commission on International Trade Law (UNCITRAL), 'Article V—Guide—NYCG 1958' (*1958 New York Convention Guide*) para 5 <http://newyorkconvention1958.org/index.php?lvl=cmspage&pageid=10&menu=730&opac_view=-1> accessed 7 August 2020.

208 However, it should be noted that the New York Convention has been viewed to promote a narrow rather than expansive substantive interpretation of Article V(2)(b) based on its *travail préparatoire* and overall purpose, which is procedural harmonization. See, for instance, Anton G Maurer (ed), *The Public Policy Exception Under the New York Convention: History, Interpretation and Application* (Rev edn, Juris Publishing Inc 2013) 64–67.

209 Fifi Junita, 'Public Policy Exception in International Commercial Arbitration—Promoting Uniform Model Norms' (2012) 5 Contemporary Asia Arbitration Journal 45, 54.

In terms of the substantive elements of public policy, there have been varying levels of narrow and expansive interpretations of public policy, the latter perhaps best embodied by the idea of an international public policy.[210] One of the most well-known international public policy frameworks of substantive public policy or interest is the chapeau of general exceptions in the General Agreement on Tariffs and Trade (GATT).[211]

Other references to the public interest can be found in connection to significant economic reform during times of extraordinary financial conditions, such as the investment treaty arbitrations that took place involving Argentina, such as *Sempra Energy International v Argentine Republic*.[212] Beyond this, the concept of the public interest finds diverse form in investment treaty arbitration practice. For instance, it may broadly be represented as non-economic public goods that are safeguarded either for ecological concerns or their "environmental effect and impact on the site and surrounding communities".[213] The public interest may also constitute an intention to serve a public purpose, such as environmental interests,[214] irrespective of contested scientific bases insofar as regulation can be established with due process and in a non-discriminatory manner.[215]

As affirmed by both practice and scholarship, sustainable development has not only been recognized as a legitimate public interest, but also as having achieved a "normative status within the framework of 'traditional' international law, binding states and constraining their behaviour".[216] Sustainable development, in fact, has been found to represent an "element of the process of judicial reasoning" affecting other primary norms, and in this sense, holding "interstitial normativity"[217] as a "modifying norm".[218] This interpretation of sustainable development as a modifying

210 Fifi Junita, 'Public Policy Exception in International Commercial Arbitration—Promoting Uniform Model Norms' (2012) 5 Contemporary Asia Arbitration Journal 58–59. Investment treaty arbitration that refer to an international public policy include *Inceysa Vallisoletana SL v Republic of El Salvador*, ICSID Case No ARB/03/26, Award (2 August 2006); Fraport AG Frankfurt Airport Services Worldwide v The Republic of the Philippines, ICSID Case No ARB/03/25, Award (16 August 2007); World Duty Free Company v Republic of Kenya, ICSID Case No Arb/00/7, Award (4 October 2006).

211 General Agreement on Tariffs and Trade 1947 Art XX.

212 *Sempra Energy International v Argentine Republic*, ICSID Case No ARB/02/16, Award (28 September 2007).

213 *Metalclad Corporation v the United Mexican States*, ICSID Case No ARB (AF)/97/1, Award (30 August 2000) para 92.

214 *Methanex v United States*, UNCITRAL (NAFTA), Final Award (3 August 2005) Part IV(E), para 20.

215 *Methanex v United States*, UNCITRAL (NAFTA), Final Award (3 August 2005) Part IV(D), para 7.

216 Vaughan Lowe, 'Sustainable Development and Unsustainable Arguments' in Alan Boyle and David Freestone (eds), *International Law and Sustainable Development: Past Achievements and Future Challenges* (OUP 1999) 21.

217 Vaughan Lowe, 'Sustainable Development and Unsustainable Arguments' in Alan Boyle and David Freestone (eds), *International Law and Sustainable Development: Past Achievements and Future Challenges* (OUP 1999) 31.

218 Vaughan Lowe, 'Sustainable Development and Unsustainable Arguments' in Alan Boyle and David Freestone (eds), *International Law and Sustainable Development: Past Achievements and Future Challenges* (OUP 1999) 35.

norm allocates its application to judicial discretion, based on the extensive range of legal instruments concerning sustainable development,[219] in the case of conflicting norms, e.g., FET, such as in the warranting of exception or derogation.[220]

Sustainable development as a concept with procedural merit in international law was invoked within an international court setting in the *Gabčíkovo-Nagymaros Project*, a dispute between Hungary and (now) Slovakia that was brought to the International Court of Justice (ICJ) in 1993 concerning Hungary's termination of a contract on environmental grounds. Hungary and Slovakia appealed to sustainable development, but with different means to achieve it,[221] thereby elevating the interpretation of sustainable development to a central contention in the dispute.[222] The ICJ judgement identified that "new norms and standards have been developed" on the "need to reconcile economic development with the protection of the environment [as] aptly expressed in the concept of sustainable development" that must be taken into consideration and "given proper weight".[223] As the first time that the ICJ addressed sustainable development as a concept, the *Gabčíkovo-Nagymaros* case "balance[d] two interests . . . first, the interests in enforceable rules of conduct guiding relations among nations and, second, the interest in protecting the common heritage of mankind against ill-conceived development".[224] The Court attempted to achieve this balance by applying the precautionary principle,[225] albeit in a manner that inadequately sought technical solutions, to the state's invocation of the defence of necessity.[226] Importantly, however, the *Gabčíkovo-Nagymaros Project* case

219 Sustainable development in this context has been identified in both preambulatory and normative text of international treaties (Virginie Barral, 'Sustainable Development in International Law: Nature and Operation of an Evolutive Legal Norm' (2012) 23 European Journal of International Law 377, 383–85).

220 Lowe (n 218) 35.

221 The parties submitted conflicting scientific studies concerning the existence of an ecological state of necessity (*Case Concerning Gabčíkovo-Nagymaros Project (Hungary/Slovakia)* (1997) International Court of Justice Judgement (44)).

222 Philippe Sands, 'International Courts and the Application of the Concept of "Sustainable Development"' (1999) 3 Max Planck Yearbook of United Nations Law Online 389, 393.

223 *Case Concerning Gabčíkovo-Nagymaros Project (Hungary/Slovakia)* (n 223) para 140.

224 Stephen Stec and Gabriel Eckstein, 'Of Solemn Oaths and Obligations: The Environmental Impact of the ICJ's Decision in the Case of the Gabcikovo-Nagymaros Project' (1998) 8 Yearbook of International Environmental Law 41–42.

225 See, for instance, *Certain Activities Carried Out by Nicaragua in the Border Area* (*Costa Rica v Nicaragua*), where the Court ruled against Costa Rica having found that it did not comply with an "obligation under general international law to carry out an environmental impact assessment", in turn resulting in a "breach of substantive obligations, beginning with the obligation to exercise due diligence to avoid causing significant transboundary harm" (International Court of Justice (ICJ), 'Certain Activities Carried Out by Nicaragua in the Border Area (*Costa Rica v Nicaragua*)' (*Latest Developments*) <www.icj-cij.org/en/case/150> accessed 9 December 2020).

226 The Court responded to the conflicting scientific material as follows: "Both Parties have placed on record an impressive amount of scientific material aimed at reinforcing their respective arguments. The Court has given most careful attention to this material, in which the Parties have developed their opposing views as to the ecological consequences of the Project. It concludes, however, that, as will be shown below, it is not necessary in order to respond to the questions put to it in the Special Agreement for it to determine which of those points of view is scientifically better founded" (*Case Concerning Gabčíkovo-Nagymaros Project (Hungary/Slovakia)* (n 223) para 54).

raised sustainable development to a level of legal principle and legitimate interest "rather than a mere policy or moral invocation" with possible *erga omnes* characteristics in connection to Rio 1992,[227] and therein the larger purview of sustainable development offered by the UN. The *Gabčíkovo-Nagymaros Project* case, as well as a wider range of instruments in international trade law, extended the far reach of sustainable development as a legal concept to challenge "some basic tenets of traditional international law", such as those in international investment law.[228]

According to the critics of these developments, one illustration of the conflict between public policy and FET is the difference between the sole effect doctrine, which views government measures as automatically resulting in indirect expropriation, and the police powers doctrine, which recognizes legitimate uses of the right to regulate.[229] Interpretive uncertainty arising from public interest exceptions has also been noted as having both normative and practical implications for international investment law.[230] Two interpretations of public interest exceptions have been identified:

1 *Permissive*: Measures that would otherwise be limited in a normal reading of treaty provisions (and in that sense unlawful) are permitted within the scope of legitimate interests. In this sense, they "limit the scope of investment protections in the treaty", reserving the application of investment protection from specific areas such as tax policy.467F[231]
2 *Affirmative*: Recognition of government measures that are contrary to the prohibitive lens of the treaty, though the extent to which they are authorized and therefore legitimate are decided post-fact by the dispute settlement mechanism, e.g. investment treaty arbitration tribunal.468F[232]

At the multilateral level, UNCTAD advocates a "nexus" approach to general exceptions, which seeks to "lower the threshold for the use of exceptions by States" by linking "the measure and the alleged policy objective pursued by this measure".[233] Identifying public interest exceptions in IIAs for the preservation of regulatory space has been the primary means of orientating international investment law with

Stec and Eckstein offered the interpretation that the "absence of scientific consideration in the Court's decision further suggests that the Court did not regard environmental concerns as being sufficiently important to override or modify treaty obligations" (Stec and Eckstein (n 226) 46).

227 Alan E Boyle, 'The Gabcíkovo-Nagymaros Case: New Law in Old Bottles' (1998) 8 Yearbook of International Environmental Law 13, 18–19.

228 Sands (n 224) 404.

229 See, for instance, Chapter 2.3.3 of August Reinisch, *Advanced Introduction to International Investment Law* (Edward Elgar Publishing 2020).

230 Caroline Henckels, 'Should Investment Treaties Contain Public Policy Exceptions Essays: Substantive and Procedural Reforms' (2018) 59 Boston College Law Review 2825, 2829.

231 Caroline Henckels, 'Should Investment Treaties Contain Public Policy Exceptions Essays: Substantive and Procedural Reforms' (2018) 59 Boston College Law Review 2832–34.

232 Caroline Henckels, 'Should Investment Treaties Contain Public Policy Exceptions Essays: Substantive and Procedural Reforms' (2018) 59 Boston College Law Review 2830.

233 United Nations Trade and Development (UNCTAD), 'Investment Policy Framework for Sustainable Development' (United Nations 2015) UNCTAD/DIAE/PCB/2015/5 103.

the achievement of sustainable development,[234] in which safeguarding the right to regulate for legitimate public interest objective is a core mechanism.[235]

A concern surrounding this reliance on public interest exceptions[236] has been its perpetuation of a system that moves public interest policy beyond the scope of IIAs. When investors as claimant parties submit materials to be considered in the deliberation of disputes concerning public interest regulation,[237] investment treaty arbitration tribunals on this issue invariably constructs dichotomous incompatibilities between investment protection and the right to regulate; whether a public interest measure is legitimate when viewed on a scale of investment protection. Yet as there is no clear consensus on the normative standards for assessing application of government measures for the public interest, said measures are taken in good faith to applicable agreements. The claimant's burden of proof lies in challenging whether the host state, as the respondent party, implemented the government measure in good faith with the applicable IIA. Unfortunately, this also meant that the measure is assessed by an investment treaty arbitration tribunal on grounds of whether its application is non-discriminatory and reasonable on strictly procedural grounds ("in relation to the risk identified and the avenues chosen to address it"), rather than whether the policy goal in itself is legitimate.[238]

An alternative has been to include public interest regulation as a substantive obligation rather than general exception, thereby permitting the host state a more effective regulatory space on matters of the public interest rather than relinquishing the public interest to an incidental exception.[239] For instance, on matters of environmental regulation, formulating substantive obligations in identifying legitimate public policy objectives can better serve the public interest of environmental protection by examining "the primary objective of the [government] measure [within the] whole regulatory and factual context".[240] A consequence of an incidental, exception-based approach to public interest provisions is that interpretation lacks consistency across ad hoc investment treaty arbitration tribunals. Research shows that while states adopt a police power doctrine in the application of environmental regulation, "they have adopted different approaches as to the threshold of states'

234 United Nations Trade and Development (UNCTAD), 'Reform Package for the International Investment Regime' (n 102) 38.

235 United Nations Trade and Development (UNCTAD), 'Reform Package for the International Investment Regime' (n 102) 33.

236 See, generally, Pierre Mayer and Audley Sheppard, 'Final ILA Report on Public Policy as a Bar to Enforcement of International Arbitral Awards' (2003) 19 Arbitration International 249; Charles Brower, 'Obstacles and Pathways to Consideration of the Public Interest in Investment Treaty Disputes' in Karl P Sauvant (ed), *Yearbook on International Investment Law & Policy* (OUP 2009).

237 Bradly J Condon, 'Treaty Structure and Public Interest Regulation in International Economic Law' (2014) 17 Journal of International Economic Law 333, 341–42.

238 Todd J Grierson-Weiler and Ian A Laird, 'Part II Substantive Issues, Ch.8 Standards of Treatment' in Peter Muchlinski, Federico Ortino and Christoph Schreuer (eds), *The Oxford Handbook of International Investment Law* (OUP 2008) 296.

239 Condon (n 239) 352–53.

240 Ying Zhu, 'Do Clarified Indirect Expropriation Clauses in International Investment Treaties Preserve Environmental Regulatory Space' (2020) 60 Harvard International Law Journal 377, 411.

legitimate exercise of police powers".[241] As a result, a state may have no specific limitations to a right to environmental regulation in one setting, as in *Crystallex v Venezuela*,[242] and face stricter limitations in another setting, such as in *Tecmed v Mexico*, as is discussed later in this chapter.

2.4.2 *Fair and equitable treatment*

Investors are provided fair and equitable treatment (FET) as promissory guarantees by recipient, or host, states that admit FDI contingent on an IIA. The source of FET is also widely established in both multilateral and BITs, as well as in arbitral practice.[243] The provisions therein prevail over the relationship between the investor and the host state, shaping the notion of mutuality and reciprocity in international investment law, which unlike reciprocity between states in a "classical agreement", focus instead on the "mutual benefit of the host state and the investor and on the complementarity of interest flowing from the long-term commitment of resources"[244] that constitutes FDI.

Despite FET serving as a core principle in defining the minimum standard of treatment granted to covered investments, there remains no multilateral consensus on its procedural and normative substance. In drawing the threshold of standards of treatment from the perspective of the investor, the "fair and equitable component establishes an important fixed reference point because it provides an apparently definite standard that will not vary according to external considerations—its content turns solely on what is fair and reasonable in the circumstances".[245] FET as a threshold enjoys near ubiquity in IIAs and has been identified, by some scholars, as demonstrating the characteristics of international customary law.[246] The investment treaty arbitration tribunal in *LG&E v Argentina*, for instance, defined FET as consisting of the "host State's consistent and transparent behaviour, free of ambiguity that involves the obligation to grant and maintain a stable and predictable legal

241 Ying Zhu, 'Do Clarified Indirect Expropriation Clauses in International Investment Treaties Preserve Environmental Regulatory Space' (2020) 60 Harvard International Law Journal 401.

242 The investment treaty arbitration tribunal in *Crystallex v Venezuela* identified that "States are afforded a wide margin of appreciation in determining whether an expropriation serves a public purpose" (*Crystallex International Corporation v Bolivarian Republic of Venezuela*, ICSID Case No ARB(AF)/11/2, Award (4 April 2016) para 712). The tribunal in this sense continued the reasoning in the stronger wording found in the Iran-United States Claims Tribunal in 1981: "no system of law are private interests permitted to prevail over duty established public interest, making impossible actions required for the public good. Rather private parties who contract with a government are only entitled to fair compensation when measures of public policy are implemented at the expense of their contract rights" (*Amoco International Finance Corp v Government of the Islamic Republic of Iran*, Iran-US Claims Tribunal, Partial Award No 310-56-3 (14 July 1987) para 178).

243 An overview of treaties and arbitration establishing this fact can be found in, for example, Matthias Herdegen, *Principles of International Economic Law* (2nd edn, OUP 2016) 456–67.

244 Dolzer and Schreuer (n 3) 22–23.

245 Jeswald W Salacuse, *The Law of Investment Treaties* (2nd edn, OUP 2015) 244.

246 See, for instance, Part III Chapter 7(C), paras 7.73–7.81 in Campbell McLachlan, Laurence Shore and Matthew Weiniger, *International Investment Arbitration: Substantive Principles* (2nd edn, OUP 2017).

framework necessary to fulfil the justified expectations of the foreign investor".[247] Schill observed seven features of FET:[248]

1 Stability and predictability in legal and business environment for business planning and investment, consistency in applying domestic regulation;
2 Domestic actors, such as the judiciary and other administrative agencies, do not violate domestic law;
3 Protection of confidence and legitimate expectations in actions taken by the government as they pertain to the foreign national and their investment;
4 Administrative due process guaranteed to foreign nationals in any claims in relation to their investment;
5 Protection against arbitrariness and discrimination in government measures;
6 Transparency in the rules and regulations, policies and administrative practices governing the foreign national and their investment; and
7 Reasonableness and proportionality in interventions made by the government into the investment.

While the normative content of FET, such as the seven features above, and its place in international investment law remain contentious issues in international investment law, a more comprehensive coverage of that debate remains beyond the scope of these present purposes.

Broadly, there are generally two prevailing views in the debate concerning FET. The first views the standard as falling under the minimum standards of treatment premised in international law, stipulating that FET needs to be interpreted within the broader purview of international law.[249] The second views FET as an

247 *LG&E Energy Corp, LG&E Capital Corp, and LG&E International, Inc v Argentine Republic*, ICSID Case No ARB/02/1, Decision on Liability (3 October 2006).

248 See Stephan W Schill, 'Fair and Equitable Treatment under Investment Treaties as an Embodiment of the Rule of Law' (Institute for International Law and Justice 2006) Global Administrative Law Series IILJ Working Paper 2006/6 <www.iilj.org/publications/fair-and-equitable-treatment-under-investment-treaties-as-an-embodiment-of-the-rule-of-law/> accessed 8 March 2020.

249 The OECD finds that when viewing the fair and equitable treatment standard as being incorporated into international customary law, decisions arising from disputes showed a trend towards prioritizing the rights of the state over those of the investor (David Gaukrodger, 'Addressing the Balance of Interests in Investment Treaties: The Limitation of Fair and Equitable Treatment Provisions to the Minimum Standard of Treatment Under Customary International Law' (OECD 2017) No 2017/3 9 <www.oecd-ilibrary.org/finance-and-investment/addressing-the-balance-of-interests-in-investment-treaties_0a62034b-en> accessed 8 March 2020). One illustrative trend has been the inclusion of a so-called Calvo clause in international investment agreements that rejected "any right of the investor's state to exercise diplomatic protection" and to "formulate international law rules applicable to the relations among sovereign states" (Ibrahim FI Shihata, 'Toward a Greater Depoliticization of Investment Disputes: The Roles of ICSID and MIGA' in Gero Verheyen, Srilal M Perera and Kevin W Lu (eds), *Investing with Confidence: Understanding Political Risk Management in the 21st Century* (World Bank Group 2009) 3). Efforts like the Calvo clause seek to secure the margin of appreciation for the host state, thereby providing national courts "certain leeway in deciding how to apply certain rules" (Meinhard Hilf and Tim R Salomon, 'Margin of Appreciation Revisited: The Balancing Pole of Multilevel Governance' in Marise Cremona and others (eds), *Reflections on the Constitutionalisation of International Economic Law: Liber*

autonomous standard applicable specifically to international investments, thereby requiring an independent interpretation from the wider body of international law.[250]

For the purposes of this writing, however, it is important to note that FET has been widely recognized in the literature as a "flexible, elastic standard, whose normative content is being constantly expanded to include new elements" that are "determined by reference to specific circumstances of application".[251] The vagueness of the normative standard set by FET, in turn, has been seen as intentional, thereby leaving room for investment treaty arbitration tribunals to employ their judicial discretion.[252] This resulted in the interpretation of FET falling within the discretion of "ad hoc tribunals with no effective appellate review [opening] the standard to inconsistent interpretations resulting in the uncertainty regarding its meaning".[253] Furthermore, the lack of transparency in judicial discretion, with disproportionate weight applied to investor interests, has been a consistent point of contention when FET is considered in investment treaty arbitration.[254]

Amicorum for Ernst-Ulrich Petersmann (Martinus Nijhoff Publishers 2014) 40). Such efforts have been employed by the European Court of Human Rights (*Handyside v The United Kingdom* (1976) European Court of Human Rights 5493/72) in assessing necessity insofar as it expresses social need, and has since been a means to provide leeway in judging "state actions on the basis of ambiguous rules" (Meinhard Hilf and Tim R Salomon, 'Margin of Appreciation Revisited: The Balancing Pole of Multilevel Governance' in Marise Cremona and others (eds), *Reflections on the Constitutionalisation of International Economic Law: Liber Amicorum for Ernst-Ulrich Petersmann* (Martinus Nijhoff Publishers 2014) 84).

250 Viewing fair and equitable treatment as an autonomous standard shaped around the rights and protections of the investor tended to constrain the regulatory powers of the state (Muthucumaraswamy Sornarajah, *The International Law on Foreign Investment* (4th edn, CUP 2017) 349). Interpretation of fair and equitable treatment as an autonomous standard in international law epitomizes a "fundamental assumption underlying the investment treaty regime", which is that an investor appeals for standards of treatment "based upon the vindication of its own rights rather than those of its national state", thus placing it outside of the scope of diplomatic protections (Zachary Douglas, *The International Law of Investment Claims* (CUP 2009) 32). This interpretation garners rights and protections to the investor arising from a "special regime for foreign investment established by bilateral and multilateral investment treaties . . . determinable by an international arbitration tribunal", therefore characterizing a *lex specialis* configuration in relation to the responsibility of states (John Dugard, 'Fourth Report on Diplomatic Protection' (United Nations) UN Doc A/CN.4/530 para 116). This was provided for in the judgment by the International Court of Justice in *Barcelona Traction, Light and Power Company, Limited (Belgium v Spain)*, which viewed the circumstances of the case concerning the rights and protections afforded to corporate entities as needing to "viewed as distinctive processes, arising out of circumstances peculiar to the respective situations" (*Barcelona Traction, Light and Power Company, Limited*, International Court of Justice Second Phase, Judgment of 5 February 1970 61–63).

251 Catherine Yannaca-Small, 'Fair and Equitable Treatment Standard: Recent Developments' in August Reinisch (ed), *Standards of Investment Protection* (OUP 2008) 111. Salacuse further adds that in addition to the elasticity of fair and equitable treatment, there lacks guidance on the application of the standard in international investment agreements as well as the limitations of scholarship due to the fact that when fair and equitable treatment is raised, it relies so heavily on the specific circumstances of each case "as to limit the utility of the arbitral decisions and doctrinal analysis" (Salacuse (n 247) 244).

252 Yannaca-Small (n 253) 118.

253 United Nations Trade and Development (UNCTAD), *Fair and Equitable Treatment* (n 203) 6.

254 The lack of transparency and a larger weight given to investment protections have been major criticisms of the legitimacy of arbitral discretion concerning the balancing of fair and equitable

2.4.3 Applying the right to regulate for the public interest

While both the public interest and FET have become prominent dimensions of international investment law, they remain, as the previous subsection attempted to demonstrate, interpretively vague in both their normative and procedural substance and merits. The right to regulate functions, within the circumstances it is housed, on that uncertainty, evaluating the balance between the public interest and investor rights in identifying a "public policy space" within which a government can enact relevant measures and meet public policy objectives such as progressing toward sustainable development.[255] In its application, the right to regulate for the public interest differs from the right to regulate for other purposes, such as in states of necessity, national security, or maintaining public order.[256]

In practice, examining the right to regulate for the public interest can take place either (1) as it is drafted into the IIA or (2) with post facto determination of legitimacy by an investment treaty arbitration tribunal. As the first application has already been discussed earlier in this section, the final segment of this subsection examines the latter: implementation of government measures that are claimed to be inconsistent with the IIA and thus whose legitimacy must be determined by the investment treaty arbitration tribunal.

In assessing the legitimate use of the right to regulate for the public interest, investment treaty arbitration tribunals turn to standards of review for the use of government measures in the public interest,[257] namely those of proportionality, reasonableness, deference, and margin of appreciation.[258] The application of these principles within international investment law are addressed in Table 2.4.

---

treatment, see Christopher Campbell, 'House of Cards: The Relevance of Legitimate Expectations Under Fair and Equitable Treatment Provisions in Investment Treaty Law' (2013) 30 Journal of International Arbitration 361–62.

255 Mouyal refers to this public policy space in her characterization of the right to regulate: "From a conceptual perspective, the *right to regulate* is an affirmation of states' authority to act as sovereigns on behalf of the will of the people. . . . The right to regulate thus covers the authority of states to adopt regulation, i.e. to make deliberate changes (e.g. through legislation and administrative orders). . . . [T] he right to regulate is the affirmation of the sovereign right for states to choose their political, social and economic priorities—within certain limits—through the adoption of legislation and administrative practices without violating international rules protecting foreign investments. The scope of which states may regulate without violating international law, the regulatory space of manoeuvre, is also referred to as the *public policy space* of host states, the *regulatory scope of manoeuvre* or in connection with expropriation, the *police power* of the host state". Lone Wandahl Mouyal, *International Investment Law and the Right to Regulate: A Human Rights Perspective* (Routledge 2016) 8–9.

256 An overview of these types of regulatory interests for which the right to regulate is applied can be found in, for example, Titi (n 185) 76–99.

257 In the context of international investment law, Henckels describes such methods of review as proportionality as "trade-off devices that operate as aids to problem solving and to express the reasoning processes of adjudicators" that can "rationalize decision-making by restricting reasoning and argumentation to a pre-determined analytical structure". Though she further adds that a "criticism that has particular resonance beyond the human rights context is that proportionality analysis involves balancing incommensurable values—values that do not share a common measure and therefore cannot be ranked in terms of importance" (Caroline Henckels, *Proportionality and Deference in Investor-State Arbitration: Balancing Investment Protection and Regulatory Autonomy* (CUP 2015) 26–27).

258 Levashova (n 184) 98–99.

Table 2.4 General principles of international law and their application to international investment law as standards of review for measures used in the right to regulate for the public interest

Principle	*Application in international investment law*
Proportionality	Proportionality analysis thus facilitates balancing between interests of foreign investors, or more generally property rights, and conflicting public interests. . . . Proportionality analysis is a method of legal interpretation and decision-making in situations of collisions or conflicts of different principles and legitimate public policy objectives. It is characteristic of this approach to distinguish principles on the basis that they do not work in an "all-or-nothing fashion" but allow for a "more or less".[259]
Reasonableness	Reasonableness had to be analysed with the help of two elements—the existence of a rational policy and the reasonableness of the act in question. . . . A rational policy is taken by a state following a logical (good sense) explanation and with the aim of addressing a public interest matter. . . . A rational policy is taken by a state following a logical (good sense) explanation and with the aim of addressing a public interest matter.[260]
Deference	The greater the degree of deference afforded by investment tribunals, the greater the degree of regulatory flexibility will be enjoyed by host states. Conversely the stricter the standard of review, the greater the risk of state liability, including for measures adopted in pursuit of public welfare objectives. . . . "Deference" refers to the degree of scrutiny of the judgement of a primary decision-maker by an adjudicator in relation to the evaluation of factual and legal issues including factual determinations, substantive policy choices and legal interpretations. Deference involves an adjudicator exercising restraint where the adjudicator's judgment is different from that of the primary decision-maker, where there is uncertainty as to what the right conclusion should be, or where there is no objectively correct answer to an issue.[261]
Margin of appreciation	[T]he margin of appreciation allows a tribunal to set an appropriate space within which national authorities are able to take regulatory action without a tribunal second-guessing those decisions or acting in a legislative capacity. Again, national authorities are generally better positioned, both in terms of expertise and embeddedness within the domestic polity to engage in an explicit balancing between rights and interests at stake than is an international arbitral tribunal.[262]

259 Benedict Kingsbury and Stephan W Schill, 'Public Law Concepts to Balance Investors' Rights with State Regulatory Actions in the Public Interest—the Concept of Proportionality' in *International Investment Law and Comparative Public Law* (OUP 2010) 78–79.

260 Dolzer and Schreuer (n 3) 193.

261 Caroline Henckels, 'Balancing Investment Protection and the Public Interest: The Role of the Standard of Review and the Importance of Deference in Investor—State Arbitration' (2013) 4 Journal of International Dispute Settlement 197, 200.

262 William W Burke-White and Andreas von Staden, 'Private Litigation in a Public Sphere: The Standard of Review in Investor-State Arbitrations' (2010) 35 Yale Journal of International Law 283, 337.

Addressing the balance between regulatory capacity and investor protections, however, relates specifically to proportionality and is thus highly relevant to the objectives of this work. The principle of proportionality is regularly invoked when government measures result in claims of expropriation.[263] A proportionality assessment employed to test the legitimacy of the government measure usually includes the following criteria:

1 The extent to which the desired policy objective is achieved;
2 Whether the effects of the government measure are proportional to the extent to which the policy objective is achieved;
3 The necessity of the government measure in the circumstances in which they were applied; and
4 The availability of a less treaty-inconsistent, e.g. less-invasive, alternative.[264]

In respect to the first two criteria, one approach to assessing policy and regulation through the use of proportionality has been the "Tecmed standard", which arose from the *Tecmed v Mexico* award:

> The Arbitral Tribunal considers that this provision of the Agreement, in light of the good faith principle established by international law, requires the Contracting Parties to provide to international investments treatment that does

263 This test was employed in the public health and cigarette branding arbitrations. In *Philip Morris v Uruguay*, for instance, the host state of Uruguay adopted a "single presentation requirement precluding tobacco manufacturers from marketing more than one variant of cigarette per brand family and increase in the size of graphic health warnings appearing on cigarette packages" (*Philip Morris Brand Sàrl (Switzerland), Philip Morris Products SA (Switzerland) and Abal Hermanos SA (Uruguay) v Oriental Republic of Uruguay*, ICSID Case No ARB/10/7, Award (8 July 2016) para 9). Uruguay held that the measures were "in compliance with Uruguay's international obligations, including the BIT, for the single purpose of protecting public health . . . a reasonable, good faith exercise of Uruguay's sovereign prerogatives" (*Philip Morris Brand Sàrl (Switzerland), Philip Morris Products SA (Switzerland) and Abal Hermanos SA (Uruguay) v Oriental Republic of Uruguay*, ICSID Case No ARB/10/7, Award (8 July 2016) para 13). The claimants contended that the government measure did not "fall within the police powers doctrines on the basis that: The government measures were not in fact 'designed and applied to achieve' reduced tobacco consumption' . . . Respondent had not conducted a 'serious, objective and scientific' assessment of whether the Challenged Measures were justified. Moreover, the measures have been ineffective in practice and are not 'proportional to the public interest the Respondent alleges they serve given the severe harm they inflict" (*Philip Morris Brand Sàrl (Switzerland), Philip Morris Products SA (Switzerland) and Abal Hermanos SA (Uruguay) v Oriental Republic of Uruguay*, ICSID Case No ARB/10/7, Award (8 July 2016) para 199). The tribunal assessed Uruguay's usage of the right to regulate for the public interest as legitimate following a separate technical evaluation by the World Health Organisation (*Philip Morris Brand Sàrl (Switzerland), Philip Morris Products SA (Switzerland) and Abal Hermanos SA (Uruguay) v Oriental Republic of Uruguay*, ICSID Case No ARB/10/7, Award (8 July 2016) para 305–7). Other decisions include *Methanex v United States*, UNCITRAL (NAFTA), Final Award (3 August 2005) para 298; *Crompton (Chemtura) Corp v Government of Canada*, UNCITRAL, Award (2 August 2010) para 299.

264 Levashova (n 184) 100.

> not affect the basic expectations that were taken into account by the foreign investor to make the investment. The foreign investor expects the host State to act in a consistent manner, free from ambiguity and totally transparently in its relations with the foreign investor, so that it may know beforehand any and all rules and regulations that will govern its investments, as well as the goals of the relevant policies and administrative practices or directives, to be able to plan its investment and comply with such regulations.[265]

The Tecmed standard thus attempts to determine whether the implemented government measures "were reasonable with respect to their goals" in relation to the "deprivation of economic rights and the legitimate expectations of those who suffered such deprivation" in assessing whether the measure resulted in expropriation and therefore requires compensation equal to the resulting material injury. In doing so, the principle of proportionality seeks to "protect regulatory measures enacted in good faith and aimed at the public interest and to identify malicious and fictitious public interest measures".[266] However, while the Tecmed standard recognized public policy measures as within the host state's eminent domain, its rendition of proportionality testing "first and foremost proceduralizes the principle of fair and equitable treatment and infers from it the obligation to accord specific procedural rights and guarantees to a foreign investor in administrative proceedings".[267] In doing, the Tecmed standard sought to reduce the extent to which the right to regulate would be assessed circumstantially on a case-by-case basis.

As per the latter, two criteria for determining proportionality (i.e. necessity and the availability of less intrusive measures), a common means to determine the necessity of a government measure has been to turn to the International Law Commission in its 53rd session on state responsibility.[268] In addition to Article 51, which places limits on the intensity of countermeasures a state may apply, Article 25 provides further conditions based on which a state can evoke circumstances of necessity to "preclude the wrongfulness of an act not in conformity with an international obligation of that State":

> (a) is the only way for the State to safeguard an essential interest against a grave and imminent peril; and
> (b) does not seriously impair an essential interest of the State or States towards which the obligation exists, or of the international community as a whole.[269]

265 *Técnicas Medioambientales Tecmed SA v The United Mexican States*, ICSID Case No ARB (AF)/00/2, Award (29 May 2003) para 154.

266 Xiuli Han, 'The Application of the Principle of Proportionality in *Tecmed v Mexico*' (2007) 6 Chinese Journal of International Law 635, 642.

267 Stephan W Schill, 'Revisiting a Landmark: Indirect Expropriation and Fair and Equitable Treatment in the ICSID Case Tecmed' (2006) 3 Transnational Dispute Management 2.

268 See, for instance, *Bernardus Henricus Funnekotter and Others v Republic of Zimbabwe*, ICSID Case No ARB/05/6, Award (22 April 2009) para 278 and *Deutsche Telekom v India*, PCA Case No 2014-10, Judgment of the Swiss Federal Tribunal (11 December 2018) para 3.2.3.3.3.

269 'Yearbook of the International Law Commission 2001, Volume 2 (Part 2)' (United Nations 2007) A/CN.4/SER.A/2001/Add.1 (Part 2) 80.

Evoking questions of necessity on the basis of general international law, such as Article 25, however, can be procedurally difficult. This is due to a reluctance by investment treaty arbitration tribunals to accept the preclusion of substantive elements of an IIA, e.g. minimum standards of treatment for investors, for a general principle of international law. This is mainly due to the *lex specialis* nature of international investment law and a lack of specific mention, not only textually but also structurally, of necessity in applicable IIAs.[270] As stated in the commentary of Article 25, the necessity defence was drafted to "operate as a shield rather than a sword".[271]

In investment treaty arbitration, the test for necessity finds its most cited application in the investor-State dispute settlement cases against Argentina following its use of government measures during the economic crisis between 1998 and 2002.[272] Argentina has repeatedly put forward that the claims against such measures were non-justiciable and therefore beyond the jurisdiction of the International Centre for the Settlement of Investment Disputes.[273] However, jurisdiction was claimed insofar as the investment treaty arbitration tribunal retained competence over legal aspects of the use of necessity as a principle of customary international law and its interaction with an applicable BIT, such as that between Argentina and the United States.[274] Reinisch cogently summarized this contention in his work:

> Beneath the legal issue whether investment tribunals have jurisdiction to assess questions of economic emergencies, of course, a difficult policy issue whether investment arbitrators should be deemed sufficiently competent—not in a formal jurisdictional sense, but in a substantive one regarding their suitability to review complex macro-economic policy decisions—to sit in

270 As was seen in application to Argentine economic crisis in 2001/2002 in Diane A Desierto, 'Necessity and Supplementary Means of Interpretation for Non-Precluded Measures in Bilateral Investment Treaties' (2009) 31 University of Pennsylvania Journal of International Law 827, 876–82.

271 'Yearbook of the International Law Commission 2001, Volume 2 (Part 2)' (n 271) 71.

272 A background of which can be found in the evaluation document for IMF engagement in Argentina (Independent Evaluation Office (IEO), 'The Role of the IMF in Argentina, 1991–2002' (International Monetary Fund (IMF) 2003) Issues Paper <www.imf.org/External/NP/ieo/2003/arg/index.htm> accessed 28 August 2020).

273 August Reinisch, 'Necessity in Investment Arbitration' in IF Dekker and E Hey (eds), *Netherlands Yearbook of International Law Volume 41, 2010: Necessity Across International Law* (TMC Asser Press 2011) 139–40.

274 See, for instance, *CMS Gas Transmission Company v Republic of Argentina*, ICSID Case No ARB/01/8, Award (12 May 2005) paras 353–57; *LG&E Energy Corp, LG&E Capital Corp., and LG&E International, Inc v Argentine Republic* (n 249) paras 245–58; *Enron Creditors Recovery Corporation (Formerly Enron Corporation) and Ponderosa Assets, LP v Argentine Republic*, ICSID Case No ARB/01/3, Award (22 May 2007) 303–11; *Sempra Energy International v Argentine Republic*, ICSID Case No ARB/02/16, Award (28 September 2007) paras 344–53; *BG Group Plc v Republic of Argentina*, UNCITRAL, Award (24 December 2007) paras 407–12; *Continental Casualty Company v Argentine Republic*, ICSID Case No ARB/03/9, Award (5 September 2008) paras 165–68; *National Grid PLC v Argentina Republic*, UNCITRAL, Award (3 November 2008) paras 255–62; *Suez, Sociedad General de Aguas de Barcelona SA and Interagua Servicios Integrales de Agua SA v Argentine Republic*, ICSID Case No ARB/03/17, Decision on Liability (30 July 2010) paras 229–37.

> judgement over economic emergency situations and in particular over the measures adopted by States facing such situations.[275]

Despite the consistent approach concerning competence of the tribunal taken up by investment treaty arbitration tribunals, particularly in connection to the Argentine economic crisis disputes, the issue and role of necessity as a circumstance precluding wrongfulness remain contentious. At times tribunals may refer to broader instruments in international law, such as Article 25, while in other circumstances the conditions leading to claims of necessity are dismissed as beyond the competence of the tribunal. For the purposes of understanding the implications of this debate in application to proportionality as part of the methodology of this project, it suffices to recall the conclusion drawn by Paparinskis on this point:

> Treaty and arbitral practice on circumstances precluding wrongfulness demonstrate the messy reality of making and developing international law, drawing in its delightfully decentralized manner upon various sources, categories, regimes and institutions, all mixed together by the tactical considerations of particular disputing parties.[276]

At the same time, the Argentine arbitrations referred to the right to regulate for the public interest as self-judgement, which gives "host States room to address and react to events within the core of their police powers, or its 'sovereignty, security, public policy—or more generally—its essential interest'. . . . [A]ny analysis of 'self-judging' non-precluded measure clauses . . . highlights that there is not a uniform standard or a uniform treaty provision that forms the baseline for interpretation".[277] Self-judgement allows one to locate the right to regulate for the public interest as an instrument of judicial discretion.[278] The tribunal would need to consider self-judgement in the context of the "specific risk situation" and not as a "blunt exculpatory tool to be used by host states at their complete discretion"[279] unsympathetic to the treatment of investors.[280] Providing authorities of the host

275 Reinisch (n 231) 142.

276 Martins Paparinskis, 'Circumstances Precluding Wrongfulness in International Investment Law' (2016) 31 ICSID Review—Foreign Investment Law Journal 484, 502.

277 Michael D Nolan and Frederic G Sourgens, 'The Limits of Discretion? Self-Judging Emergency Clauses in International Investment Agreements' (2011) 362 Yearbook of International Investment Law and Policy 2–3.

278 Stephan Schill and Robyn Briese, '"If the State Considers": Self-Judging Clauses in International Dispute Settlement' (2009) 13 Max Planck Yearbook of United Nations Law Online 61, 92. This point was also made in Mohammad-Ali Bahmaei and Habib Sabzevari, 'Self-Judging Security Exception Clause as a Kind of Carte Blanche in Investment Treaties: Nature, Effect and Proper Standard of Review' (2023) 13 Asian Journal of International Law 97, 99.

279 Nolan and Sourgens (n 279) 5.

280 One may recall here the decision in *Certain Questions of Mutual Assistance in Criminal Matters (Djibouti v France)*, where in responding to France's claim of self-judgement on behalf of French essential security interests in the transmission of secret documents as a means of denying a request

state with blanket preclusion of wrongfulness could facilitate abusive practices that can have long-term legal and development implications for the host state. Arbitrary violations of legitimate expectation, for instance, could result in both hostile litigation as well as sour the climate for future investments. In an effort to balance self-judgement as a principle, and as a means to help neutralize the threat of abusive regulatory practices, the "nexus requirement" arose in international investment law practice, which was to assess the "link between measure and public policy is one of 'reasonable' or 'rational' relationship".[281]

In contrast to international trade law,[282] investment treaty arbitration tribunals have "taken a considerably softer approach [to appropriate standards of review for public policy] than the 'necessity test' under many GATT Article XX exceptions, looking only for a 'reasonable' or 'rational' nexus between the measure and the policy pursued".[283] Determining whether this nexus is reasonable or rational returns one to the balancing test offered through proportionality between the rights of the investor and the policy space of the host state to pursue public interest objectives.

Public interest considerations are not relinquished to purely circumstantial deliberations. One means in appealing to the right to regulate for the public interest has been to re-examine the very definition of investment within the context of applicable IIAs. This was identified earlier in Chapter 1 as the "criteria approach", which attempts to identify the qualifying criteria of an investment rather than subjecting that definition to a "party autonomy approach", which leaves the definition purely to circumstantial interpretations.

by Djibouti involving the investigation of a crime, the ICJ decided that claims of self-judgement can also be assessed by good faith ('Case Concerning Certain Questions of Mutual Assistance in Criminal Matters (*Djibouti v France*), Judgment, 4 June 2008').

281 Nicholas DiMascio and Joost Pauwelyn, 'Nondiscrimination in Trade and Investment Treaties: Worlds Apart or Two Sides of the Same Coin' (2008) 102 American Journal of International Law 48, 80. Nolan and Sourgens provide a survey of different non-precluded measures related to self-judgement in different countries and nexus requirements in international investment agreements (Nolan and Sourgens (n 279) 36).

282 For a comparison of proportionality in international trade law and international investment law, see Elizabeth Trujillo, 'Balancing Sustainability, the Right to Regulate, and the Need for Investor Protection: Lessons from the Trade Regime' (2018) 59 Boston College Law Review 2735. She identifies similar jurisprudential trends in international investment law without the regulatory machinery provided through the WTO for international trade law.

283 DiMascio and Pauwelyn (n 283) 76. The nexus requirement was also identified in *Pope & Talbot v Canada* in relation to national treatment: "In evaluating the implications of the legal context, the Tribunal believes that, as a first step, the treatment accorded a foreign owned investment protected by Article 1102(2) should be compared with that accorded domestic investments in the same business or economic sector. However, that first step is not the last one. Differences in treatment will presumptively violate Article 1102(2), unless they have a reasonable nexus to rational government policies that (1) do not distinguish, on their face or de facto, between foreign-owned and domestic companies, and (2) do not otherwise unduly undermine the investment liberalizing objectives of NAFTA" (*Pope & Talbot Inc v Government of Canada*, UNCITRAL, Award on the Merits of Phase 2 (10 April 2001) para 78).

As was explained in greater detail previously, the criteria approach involves setting out a positive list of criteria for covered investments and is widely associated with the *Salini v Morocco* decision in 2001.[284] This list resulted in four widely accepted criteria to investment:

1 Substantial commitment;
2 Certain duration;
3 Assumption of risk; and
4 Significance for the host state's development.

Resistance to the *Salini* criteria is commonly associated with the *Biwater Gauff v Tanzania* (2008) award, which advanced the position that "investment" did not come with a fixed set of criteria rather is left intentionally open.[285] Nevertheless, the fourth criterion, the extent to which the investment is significant for the host state's development, has been especially contentious, not only normatively, but also in practice.[286] Failing the fourth criterion of this "Salini test", for instance, influenced the determination that no investment had taken place in *Mitchell v DR Congo* and *Malaysian Historical Salvors v Malaysia*, thereby depriving the legal personality or *ratione personae* of the claimants.[287] One source of contention centres on whether investment treaty arbitration "as a judicial forum has no mandate to promote general policy" such as economic development.[288] In recalling the Broches concept of international investment law, "a tribunal would be on safer ground by making reference to the principle of estoppel or legitimate expectations" since the "tribunal is not equipped to assess whether a particular interpretation" will achieve the policy referenced by the respondent host state.[289]

284 *Salini Costruttori SpA and Italstrade SpA v Kingdom of Morocco*, ICSID Case No ARB/00/4, Award (31 July 2001).
285 Dolzer and Schreuer (n 3) 68–69.
286 Christoph Schreuer, *The ICSID Convention: A Commentary* (2nd edn, CUP 2009) 131.
287 Christoph Schreuer, *The ICSID Convention: A Commentary* (2nd edn, CUP 2009) 130.
288 Douglas (n 252) 82–83. Douglas in *The International Law of Investment Claims* (2009) endeavours to elucidate "rules governing the jurisdiction of international tribunals established pursuant to investment treaties, the admissibility of investment claims presented to them, and the laws applicable to the various legal issues arising out of such claims" (Douglas (n 252) xxii). In his 23rd rule, he writes: "The economic materialization of an investment requires the commitment of resources to the economy of the host state by the claimant entailing the assumption of risk in expectation of a commercial return" (Douglas (n 252) 189). In accordance to this rule he identifies in international investment law materials, his view is that "only three of the *Salini* characteristics of an investment in modified form" fit under Rule 23: "namely (i) commitment of resources to the economy of the host state, (ii) assumption of risk, and (iii) expectation of a commercial return. It is these elements that are capable of generating an objective test and the necessary level of certainty for putative investors" (Douglas (n 252) 191). Douglas borrows from Dworkin (1977) in distinguishing principles and policies: "Arguments of principles are arguments intended to establish an individual right; arguments of policy are arguments intended to establish a collective goal. Principles are propositions that describe rights; policies are propositions that describe goals" (Ronald Dworkin, *Taking Rights Seriously* (Harvard UP 1977) 22.).
289 Douglas (n 252) 84.

Criticisms concerning the right to regulate has also focused around broader concerns of a judicialization or juridification resulting from the expansion in the number and jurisdiction of international courts.[290] In application to international investment law, Alec Stone-Sweet identifies the important role of precedence as judicialization,[291] or the act of "building jurisprudence: a judge-made, precedent-grounded, law of investment arbitration, created in order to stabilize (potentially explosive) strategic environments, to entrench specific frameworks of argumentations, and to legitimize their own lawmaking".[292] This judicialization in international investment law resulted in "each investment treaty, in effect, establish[ing] a closed legal system—and gestures towards the networking of treaties and tribunals, progressive arbitral lawmaking, and constitutionalization . . . scholars have begun to consider linkages between the investment, trade, environmental protection, and human rights regimes, while tribunals now routinely cite to other international courts, not least, to borrow doctrinal solutions to common problems".[293] He took particular issue with the use of proportionality by investment treaty arbitration tribunals as a means to assess a balance between FET and public interest measures because it "allows the arbitrator to 'see' the entire contextual field and to narrow or expand their intervention as required".[294] In narrowing this scope by inter alia limiting the *ratione materiae* to exclude a tribunal's competence on issues involving the public interest, tribunals, in effect, deny access to dispute settlement to those issues when they are contended.

Furthermore, before even reaching the tribunal, another challenge that comes with judicialization involves whether it can be assumed that the host state is willing to engage meaningfully in an investment treaty arbitration on behalf of public interest issues. Francioni identifies three problematic assumptions involving the host state viewed in a "paternalistic model of governmental espousal of private claims":[295]

1 "The host state is willing to take up the claims of individuals and social groups against the investor";

290 The origins of this idea in international relations is provided in Erlend M Leonhardsen, 'Looking for Legitimacy: Exploring Proportionality Analysis in Investment Treaty Arbitration' (2012) 3 Journal of International Dispute Settlement 95, 96–97.

291 Defined as the "gradual entrenchment of investment arbitration as a stable system of governance in the field of foreign direct investment" Alec Stone-Sweet, 'Investor-State Arbitration: Proportionality's New Frontier' (2010) 4 Law & Ethics of Human Rights 48, 61.

292 Alec Stone-Sweet, 'Investor-State Arbitration: Proportionality's New Frontier' (2010) 4 Law & Ethics of Human Rights 60.

293 Alec Stone-Sweet and Florian Grisel, *The Evolution of International Arbitration: Judicialization, Governance, Legitimacy* (OUP 2017) 75.

294 Alec Stone-Sweet and Florian Grisel, *The Evolution of International Arbitration: Judicialization, Governance, Legitimacy* (OUP 2017) 62.

295 Francesco Francioni, 'Access to Justice, Denial of Justice and International Investment Law' (2009) 20 European Journal of International Law 729, 738.

2 The host state is interested in "bringing health, environmental, or social concerns to bear on the arbitration process", especially when the investment had already been admitted by the state; and
3 The host state provides the investor treaty arbitration tribunal with sufficient information to be able to consider "counterclaims brought on behalf and in the interest of the local population".

If these assumptions do not hold true, then the judicialization of investment treaty arbitration may result in a series of awards and decisions that have been influenced by the exogenous factor of a host state as a respondent party simply unwilling to fully participate in the process. This is problematic in the context where questions of public interest, whether they are better served by the host state government measure or private sector investment, can be advanced and/or protected through the use of third-party dispute settlement like investment treaty arbitration, but remains handicapped by an unwilling participant.

Last, the Tecmed standard has also been subject to extensive criticism. Schill identifies that the problematic nature of the Tecmed standard is in that the authority to apply proportionality in relation to government measures is not "backed by the wording of the [applicable international investment agreement] which, like most other investment treaties, neither contained a reference to the principle of proportionality" and that a "unilateral overemphasis of the rights of foreign investors . . . restricts the legitimate regulatory interests of state too vigorously".[296] The Tecmed standard has since been identified as a key criticism to the right to regulate for international investment law. Douglas in his oft quoted commentary viewed the introduction of the Tecmed standard as having a disquieting impact on the use of precedence. The public policy measure that the Tecmed standard seems to be legitimizing is one that is able to accomplish its public interest objective while respecting the full value of the foreign investment. To this, Douglas wrote that the "Tecmed 'standard' is actually not a standard at all; it is rather a description of perfect public regulation in a perfect world, to which all states should aspire but very few (if any) will ever attain".[297]

2.5 Pillar Four: incomplete assessments

Claims in response to government measures related to sustainable development constitute a considerable share of investment treaty arbitrations. For instance, between 1987 and 2021, at least 175 investment treaty arbitrations involved measures taken to protect the environment, which amounts to 15% of disputes in that period.[298] Of specific interest to this work are those investment treaty arbitrations

296 Schill (n 269) 12.

297 Zachary Douglas, 'Nothing If Not Critical for Investment Treaty Arbitration: Occidental, Eureko and Methanex' (2006) 22 Arbitration International 27–28.

298 United Nations Trade and Development (UNCTAD), 'Treaty-Based Investor—State Dispute Settlement Cases and Climate Action' (United Nations 2022) Issue 4 2.

that have rendered an "incomplete" assessment of sustainable development impact. The fourth and final pillar of the conceptual framework is the premise of an "incomplete assessment". An "incomplete assessment" refers to the approach taken in international investment law, particularly investment treaty arbitration, in assessing the sustainable development contribution of either international investment or government measures implemented in the right to regulate for the public interest ("Actions").

One way of understanding the idea of an "incomplete" assessment can be through a similar observation made by the WTO Appellate Body in *Canada—Certain Measures Affecting the Renewable Energy Generation Sector/Measures Relating to the Feed-in Tariffs*[299] regarding the assessment of a trade restrictive public policy measure in relation to its circumstantial nature.[300] By circumstantial, the Appellate Body was referring to a notion of incomparability or "indeterminacy" of public policy measures when taken out of their native context and the absence of a "globally agreed list" of policies that could be considered ideal interventions.[301] The tremendous diversity of natural, economic, socio-political, and technological settings calls for specifically responsive policy measures.[302] As such, in evaluating such public policy measures, "the relevant inquiry is not which of these measures are 'better', but, which combination of measures is more likely to work (or not) under what circumstances".[303] In connection to matters that fall within the global

299 'Canada—Certain Measures Affecting the Renewable Energy Generation Sector/Measures Relating to the Feed-in Tariff Program, WTO Appellate Body Report, WT/DS412/DS426/AB/R (24 May 2013)'.

300 The Appellate Body identified an "incomplete test" in assessing the government measure and its inconsistency with WTO rules. The Appellate Body overturned some of the reasoning by the Dispute Settlement Body on the basis that the thresholds and standards between conventional energy and renewable energy were not perfectly comparable, not only in terms of additional fixed costs unique to renewable energy generation, but also in relation to the added nonpecuniary value of renewable energy infrastructure, namely its contributions to legitimate public policy interests as sustainable development. By not factoring this into its investigation of the Canadian government measure, the Appellate Body determined that the assessment was incomplete and should be viewed as such as determining the measure's inconsistency with WTO provisions ('Canada—Certain Measures Affecting the Renewable Energy Generation Sector/Measures Relating to the Feed-in Tariff Program, WTO Appellate Body Report, WT/DS412/DS426/AB/R (24 May 2013)' 177–85).

301 On this indeterminacy, Rodrik writes: "Each Pareto-efficient outcome can be sustained by a different set of rules. And conversely, each set of rules has the potential to generate a different Pareto-efficient outcome. . . . It is precisely this indeterminacy that makes the choice among alternative institutions a difficult one, best left to political communities themselves" (Dani Rodrik, *Straight Talk on Trade* (Princeton UP 2018) 33).

302 The Intergovernmental Panel on Climate Change (IPCC), for instance, describes the social, economic and environmental obstacles to the deployment of renewable energy infrastructure as being technology-specific, whether solar, geothermal, hydropower, ocean or wind energy (Ottmar Edenhofer, Ramón Pichs Madruga and Youba Sokona (eds), *Renewable Energy Sources and Climate Change Mitigation: Special Report of the Intergovernmental Panel on Climate Change* (CUP 2012) 13).

303 Sadeq Z Bigdeli, 'Clash of Rationalities: Revisiting the Trade and Environment Debate in Light of WTO Disputes Over Green Industrial Policy Special Issue: Trade & Climate Change' (2014) 6 Trade, Law and Development I, 198–99.

public good,[304] such as those related to climate change and inequality,[305] a functional policy space can require a "thinner set of rules that recognizes the diversity of national circumstances".[306]

The WTO Appellate Body's interpretation of an incomplete test is a useful illustration of why this book engages the legal science approach defined in Pillar One. Within this context, an incomplete legal assessment occurs when it confronts limitations arising from uncertain norms, which can be seen as being near synonymous with indeterminacy. Furthermore, the Appellate Body's interpretation of incomplete also serves to illustrate the importance of a nexus approach to interpreting regulatory or policy space reserved in right to regulate for the public interest claims.[307]

The following review of arbitral proceedings and disputes identifies three forms of incomplete assessment demonstrated by investment treaty arbitration tribunals. This analysis is based on an examination of investment treaty arbitration awards in which sustainable development, across its constituent dimensions of economic, social, and environmental, is broached as an issued in the dispute.[308] From this

304 Policies that contribute to global public goods are those that "provide aa global benefit [that are] non-rival and from which individual countries cannot be excluded" (Dani Rodrik, 'Putting Global Governance in Its Place' (2020) 35 The World Bank Research Observer 1, 4). The opposing circumstance is what Rodrik identified as "beggar-thy-neighbour" policies, which negative-sum policies that "provide benefits at home only to the extent that they harm other countries. Additionally, they generate global inefficiency, a deadweight loss" (Dani Rodrik, 'Putting Global Governance in Its Place' (2020) 35 The World Bank Research Observer 6). An example of a beggar-thy-neighbour policy would be one that promotes a monopoly for a particular good that is traded in global markets, such as a rare metal, which can be subject to constraints like production quotas and price manipulation (Dani Rodrik, 'Putting Global Governance in Its Place' (2020) 35 The World Bank Research Observer 3).

305 Rodrik, *Straight Talk on Trade* (n 303) 236.

306 Rodrik, *Straight Talk on Trade* (n 303) 219–20.

307 On the application of international trade law in international investment law, Crawford and Baetens identified, for instance, that "[a]lthough investment tribunals are usually prevented from directly applying international trade law in disputes of which they are seized, they use trade rules in the process of interpreting investment provisions proper" (James Crawford and Freya Baetens, 'The Influence of International Trade Law on International Law' in Daniel Bethlehem and others (eds), *The Oxford Handbook of International Trade Law* (2nd edn, OUP 2022) 171).

308 This does not include, however, instances of investment treaty arbitration where challenges made on the grounds of issues related to sustainable development were not considered or dismissed without substantive deliberation by the arbitration tribunal. For instance, such cases would include *Antoine Biloune and Marine Drive Complex v Ghana*, where the *ratione materiae* of complaints related to the violation of the human rights of the investor after arbitrary detention and deportation were dismissed from the Tribunal's competence (Jarrod Hepburn, 'Looking Back: UNCITRAL Tribunal in *Biloune v Ghana* Found Creeping Expropriation of Resort Complex, but Declined Jurisdiction Over Denial of Justice and Human Rights Claims' [*Investment Arbitration Reporter*, 6 November 2020] <www.iareporter.com/articles/looking-back-uncitral-tribunal-in-biloune-v-ghana-found-creeping-expropriation-of-resort-complex-but-declined-jurisdiction-over-denial-of-justice-and-human-rights-claims/> accessed 17 November 2020). Another example includes *Pac Rim v El Salvador*, where the claimant advanced an argument in defence of the positive contribution of its presence in an area where it received a mining concession as a result of "hosting

broad undertaking, the cases examined in greater detail here are those in which claims submitted by the claimant (the investor) and the respondent (the host state) not only pertain to sustainable development, but also are opposing in that the claims submitted by both parties contend to have contributed to the host state's development while contesting the extent to which the opposing party has done the same. An analysis of this sample of investment treaty arbitrations resulted in the three forms of incomplete assessments:

1 Amalgamating financial contribution of an investment and an extra-financial contribution to the host state's development in a way in which the former could substitute or necessarily satisfy the latter;
2 Limiting the host state's right to regulate for the public interest of sustainable development; and
3 Misappropriating the value of science-based assessment when used in the context of evaluating contributions to host state development.

While these three forms are examined separately, the cases that populate them share certain characteristics in that they feature opposing claims on Actions in the context of the right to regulate for the public interest of sustainable development. This can include, for instance, the host state, on the grounds of considerations for sustainable development, reneging on a government measure that provided favourable conditions for the foreign investor, such as a subsidy or tax incentive. As a result, the claimant party, which is the investor, would at some point contend that the best interests of sustainable development were better serviced through the

hundreds of information meetings, arranging tours of its mining facilities and sponsoring educational programs, medical clinics and community sporting events. Pac Rim also sought tangibly to improve the standard of living of the local inhabitants in Cabañas by building roads, digging water supply wells and planting over 40,000 trees" (*Pac Rim Cayman LLC v Republic of El Salvador*, ICSID Case No ARB/09/12 para 3.8). They went on to add that its environmental impact study "contained a comprehensive assessment of all the other impacts that the planned mining operations could be predicted to have on the surrounding environment" and that this study was never rejected but rather "received favourable opinion" by the authorities and that the "experts engaged by the Respondent to assess the [environmental impact study] for the purposes of this arbitration never challenged the study's principal conclusion that all the impacts of the Project could in fact be satisfactorily avoided, controlled or mitigated" (*Pac Rim Cayman LLC v Republic of El Salvador*, ICSID Case No ARB/09/12 para 7.15). El Salvador, the respondent, defended a government measure that effectively terminated the investment based on the report of a mining expert that concluded that "El Salvador required substantial reforms to the practice of mining and granting of mining licenses, especially as regards environmental and social protections" (*Pac Rim Cayman LLC v Republic of El Salvador*, ICSID Case No ARB/09/12 para 6.82). The Tribunal later accepted that the Claimant "genuinely believed, in good faith, that their proposed underground mining activities would *not* adversely affect any owners or occupiers of the surface area of the requested concession area" and that it "should not be overlooked that the Claimant's officers and employees included mining specialists of long experience and great expertise" (*Pac Rim Cayman LLC v Republic of El Salvador*, ICSID Case No ARB/09/12 para 8.28). However, unsatisfyingly, the Tribunal does not further explore the merits of this aspect of the dispute in its decisions.

investment rather than the government measure that adversely affected the investment. This would in turn challenge the public interest basis of the government measure, rendering the damages incurred by the investor illegitimate.[309] Identifying these forms through the practice of investment treaty arbitration illuminates the procedural and substantive approaches in existing arbitral practice as well as how these approaches remain wanting in their capacities to assess both contributions to and issues concerning sustainable development.

2.5.1 First form: amalgamating contributions

The first form of incomplete assessment arises from amalgamating financial and extra-financial contributions, which in its broadest form refers to the performance of a firm or investment based on "criteria other than traditional financial performance" including ESG factors or practices and policies in CSR.[310] Amalgamating contributions refers to instances when the investment treaty arbitration tribunals do not distinguish between financial and extra-financial contributions to the host state's development and in doing so, decide that the achievement of one, usually the former, is seen to be advancing or somehow substituting the other.[311]

A financial contribution indicates profitability for the contracting parties whereas a contribution to the host state's development remains a separate criterion of a covered investment. This form subsumes these criteria into a single mould, assuming that profitability would necessarily result in contributions to development while dismissing the value of non-financial contributions, even if they may be more impactful to the development process. Alternatively, there has also been in investment treaty arbitration practice decisions to reject the need to consider extra-financial development contribution, revise the meaning of a contribution to the host state's development, or simply overlook this fourth criterion.[312] A common approach, for instance, has been subscribing to the belief that strictly "legal" considerations should be permitted into arbitral considerations. For instance, in *LESI-DIPENTA v Algeria*, the Tribunal observed that "it is not necessary that the investment contribute more specifically to the host country's economic

309 Illegitimate in a right to regulate assessment as defined the previous pillar.

310 Claudia Champagne, Frank Coggins and Amos Sodjahin, 'Can Extra-Financial Ratings Serve as an Indicator of ESG Risk?' [2021] Global Finance Journal 100638, 2.

311 Another way to read this first form is provided in *Fakes v Turkey*, wherein the Tribunal observed: "[T]he suggested characteristics need not be satisfied cumulatively and any number of elements may suffice to characterize an economic operation as an investment in a given case. Pursuant to this approach, the addition of new characteristics is meant to facilitate the recognition of an investment in a given case, as this approach accepts that investment be recognized on the basis of some, but not all, of the said characteristics" (*Saba Fakes v Republic of Turkey*, ICSID Case No ARB/07/20, Award (14 July 2010) paras 99–100).

312 See, for instance, case analysis in Alex Grabowski, 'The Definition of Investment Under the ICSID Convention: A Defense of Salini' (2014) 15 Chicago Journal of International Law Article 13, 298.

development, something that is difficult to ascertain and that is implicitly covered by the other three criteria".[313]

Yet there have been more expansive ruminations on contributions to the host state's development that have extended to the extra-financial. In *Bayindir v Pakistan*,[314] despite the claimants appealing for investor privileges in application to the contribution requirement from a purely financial understanding of contribution, the investment arbitration tribunal took a wider interpretation of contributions to the host state's development than a restrictively pecuniary reading. Bayindir's argument that it had provided training and knowledge transfers to the host state economy was recognized as having development value by the Tribunal. The Tribunal recognized the contribution criterion of investment under the Salini test[315] and concluded that "Bayindir did contribute 'assets' within the meaning of the general definition of investment set forth in Article 1(2) of the BIT"[316] as well as under the general meaning of investment under the preamble of the ICSID Convention.[317]

Appeals to extra-financial contributions to the host state's development have also been made by the investor. In *PNGSDP v PNG*, the claimant, Papua New Guinea Sustainable Development Program (PNGSDP), was formed through the transfer of shares by an Australian minerals TNC, BHP Minerals Holdings, in a mining company based in Papua New Guinea (PNG), Ok Tedi. PNGSDP was created to "promote sustainable development within PNG and to advance the general welfare

313 *Consortium Groupement LESI-DIPENTA v République Algérienne Démocratique et Populaire*, ICSID Case No ARB/03/08, Award (10 January 2005) para 13. In this case, Algeria claimed that the group of Italian construction companies (LESI-DIPENTA) that won a public procurement for the construction of the Koudiat-Acerdoune dam had not qualified as an investment under Article 25 of the ICSID Convention because inter alia it did not produce a substantial contribution to Algeria following several years of delays that resulted in the cancellation of the contract (*Consortium Groupement LESI-DIPENTA v République Algérienne Démocratique et Populaire*, ICSID Case No ARB/03/08, Award (10 January 2005) para 11).

314 In April 2001, the Turkish company Bayindir Insaat Turizm Ticaret Ve Sanayi AŞ ("Bayindir") received notice that its contract with the Pakistani government had been terminated. Citing undue delays to the national Pakistan Islamabad-Peshawar Motorway, which Bayindir was contracted to build in 1993, the Pakistani army evacuated the company's employees from the premises during ongoing attempts at reconciliation. One of the arguments pursued by Pakistan was that "Bayindir did not make any significant injections of funds that could be considered as in investment" in an attempt to deny the existence of a protected investment and thus the jurisdiction of the ICSID to hear the Bayindir claim. To this, Bayindir identified that its investment had involved a significant contribution to the host state's economy by having "trained approximately 63 engineers, and provided significant equipment and personnel to the Motorway" and that the knowhow, equipment, and personnel provided had clear economic value (*Bayindir Insaat Ticaret Ve Sanayi AS v Islamic Republic of Pakistan*, ICSID Case No ARB/03/29, Award (27 August 2009) paras 115–18).

315 *Bayindir Insaat Ticaret Ve Sanayi AS v Islamic Republic of Pakistan*, ICSID Case No ARB/03/29, Decision on Jurisdiction (14 November 2005) para 130.

316 *Bayindir Insaat Ticaret Ve Sanayi AS v Islamic Republic of Pakistan*, ICSID Case No ARB/03/29, Award (27 August 2009) para 121.

317 *Bayindir Insaat Ticaret Ve Sanayi AS v Islamic Republic of Pakistan*, ICSID Case No ARB/03/29, Award (27 August 2009) para 137.

of the people of PNG, particularly of the Western Province where the Ok Tedi mine is located".[318] PNG had challenged whether PNGSDG qualified as a protected investor,[319] to which it responded that its contributions to the state "'involve[d] GDP-changing, long-term investments' . . . that is 'far removed from . . . simple sales transactions' which would not fall within the definition of 'investment' under the ICSID Convention".[320] The claimant continued that it "also satisfies the requirement that 'the investment make a contribution to the economic development of the host state' applied in some decisions, and contends that the requirement 'is not necessarily limited to measurable monetary contributions'".[321] Despite containing all the elements to have made an impression on the nexus between international investment law and sustainable development, the Tribunal had largely overlooked these submissions and focused instead exclusively on formalistic issues concerning treaty language and its interpretation.[322]

Appeals for an expansive reading of contributions to development, however, can also accentuate the startling lack of consideration given to understanding development. In *Helnan v Egypt*, the jurisdiction of the Tribunal was contested by Egypt, which dismissed the existence of a covered investment due to a lack of contribution to its development.[323] Egypt argued that the contractual agreement

318 *PNG Sustainable Development Program Ltd v Independent State of Papua New Guinea*, ICSID Case No ARB/13/33 para 32.

319 PNG adopted its Mining Act 2013 that exposed shares in the Ok Tedi mine held by PNGSDG to regulatory taking (*PNG Sustainable Development Program Ltd v Independent State of Papua New Guinea*, ICSID Case No ARB/13/33 paras 35–37). PNGSDG claimed that this breached its fair and equitable treatment protections, to which PNG refuted that PNGSDG did not qualify as a protected investor because the shares received from BHP were gifted and no investments were made by PNGSDG thereafter (*PNG Sustainable Development Program Ltd v Independent State of Papua New Guinea*, ICSID Case No ARB/13/33 para 68). PNGSDG advanced that there was a qualitative difference between *rationae personae* and *rationae materiae*: there was no legal requirement for an investor to be private and for all effects and purposes PNGSDG's contributions qualified under the Broches, Structural, and Functional test of investment (*PNG Sustainable Development Program Ltd v Independent State of Papua New Guinea*, ICSID Case No ARB/13/33 paras 122–24). The Tribunal recuses itself of jurisdiction in the case due to a technicality regarding choice of forum without exploring the substantive elements of the dispute (*PNG Sustainable Development Program Ltd v Independent State of Papua New Guinea*, ICSID Case No ARB/13/33 para 379).

320 *PNG Sustainable Development Program Ltd v Independent State of Papua New Guinea*, ICSID Case No ARB/13/33 para 137.

321 *PNG Sustainable Development Program Ltd v Independent State of Papua New Guinea*, ICSID Case No ARB/13/33 para 138.

322 *PNG Sustainable Development Program Ltd v Independent State of Papua New Guinea*, ICSID Case No ARB/13/33 para 250.

323 This dispute arose after Egyptian authorities had downgraded a hotel, the Shepheard, from a five-star to a four-star rating. The Shepheard is owned by the Egyptian Organization for Tourism and Hotels (EGOTH), wholly owned by the state, and managed by Helnan, a Danish company. EGOTH had terminated its management contract with Helnan following the downgrade pursuant to a court decision made in Cairo, after which Helnan had then filed for an investment treaty arbitration. Helnan claimed that its financial and nonfinancial stake in the Shepheard was expropriated by the termination of the contract given the discriminatory and unfair nature to which it

with Helnan represented little more than a commercial transaction, recalling *Joy Mining v Egypt*, rather than an investment that would qualify for protection under the Denmark-Egypt BIT.[324] Helnan decried an excessively narrow reading of contribution by Egypt, advancing that its contributions to development were to the host state's tourism industry as the "first company investing in the popular areas of Egypt" and that "by its marketing, it induced other companies to invest".[325] To this the Tribunal had agreed to the merit of the contribution requirement, but had then made the following qualification: "As for the contribution to the development of Egypt's development, the importance of the tourism industry in the Egyptian economy makes it obvious".[326] While the Tribunal's intention was to focus on the interpretation in the subsequent deliberations that sought to establish that every kind of asset would qualify as an investment under the BIT, its dealing with the contribution requirement typifies the incomplete assessment when involving issues of development.

Like in *Helnan v Egypt*, this form of incomplete assessment is typically found in circumstances when the Tribunal's jurisdiction is questioned by the respondent state on the basis that it rejects that covered investment exists—a rejection premised on the lack of contribution to the host state's development. In such instances, the Tribunal will be pressed to engage on the issue albeit with a nominal consideration and/or understanding of development. For example, in *Kardassopoulos v Georgia*, the Tribunal decides that "there is no question that Claimant's investment was intended to contribute to Georgia's economic development"[327] based on the fact that "[f]ollowing its independence in April 1991, Georgia actively sought foreign investments as a means of both developing its national energy infrastructure and securing new export markets to replace the preferential access it had lost to the former Soviet Union".[328] As a result, the Tribunal decided that the Claimant's investment constituted a contribution to the host state's development despite the fact that the investment was grandfathered in from previous administrations during

was stripped of its management contract, arguing that the downgrade, court case, and contract termination were all the results of an abuse of the state's sovereign power. Egypt had responded that it was acting within its sovereign rights, the Helnan contract did not represent an investment covered by the BIT, and that Helnan could not have recourse to investment treaty arbitration given the res judicata of the Cairo court decision (*Helnan International Hotels A/S v Arab Republic of Egypt*, ICSID Case No ARB/05/19, Award (3 July 2008) para 96).

324 Egypt had argued that "managing a hotel on behalf of its owner can hardly be said to contribute to the host state's development" (*Helnan International Hotels A/S v Arab Republic of Egypt*, ICSID Case No ARB/05/19, Decision of the Tribunal on Objection to Jurisdiction (17 October 2006) paras 60–61).

325 *Helnan International Hotels A/S v Arab Republic of Egypt*, ICSID Case No ARB/05/19, Decision of the Tribunal on Objection to Jurisdiction (17 October 2006) para 66.

326 *Helnan International Hotels A/S v Arab Republic of Egypt*, ICSID Case No ARB/05/19, Decision of the Tribunal on Objection to Jurisdiction (17 October 2006) para 77.

327 *Ioannis Kardassopoulos v The Republic of Georgia*, ICSID Case No ARB/05/18, Decision on Jurisdiction (6 July 2007) para 117.

328 *Ioannis Kardassopoulos v The Republic of Georgia*, ICSID Case No ARB/05/18, Decision on Jurisdiction (6 July 2007) para 14.

a period of political tumult[329] and was also found to be performing at a financial loss of USD 106.3 million (in 2003).[330]

In *Jan de Nul v Egypt*, the Tribunal equated significant contribution to the host state's development based on the "amount of work involved (including the mobilization of two heavy ships for a period of approximately 19 months), and the related compensation shows that the Claimants' contribution was substantial", equating the investment's contribution to Egypt's economy to that of the significance of the Suez Canal.[331] The Tribunal suggested here that the different criteria posed by the Salini test of investment "should be examined in their totality", but in doing so seemed to have reached the conclusion that a partial satisfaction of the prima facie test could in and of itself serve as the basis of satisfying the other conditions, even if such characteristics may not have been demonstrable in the performance of the project. Within this view, it would suggest that since the Tribunal recognized that the duration and financial contribution of the investment fulfilled the requirements of a covered investment, the investment would also result in a contribution to the host state's economic development. This strain of formalistic brevity in cursorily assessing the contribution requirement has also been a means to avoid the issue altogether. In *Millicom v Senegal*, for instance, the Tribunal affirmed its jurisdiction over the dispute by recalling the Salini investment criteria, though only as a means to promptly elude any substantive reading of the issue. They write after referencing the Salini test that "[t]his is also not the place for the Arbitral Tribunal to discuss the relevance of each of these conditions, since it appears obvious that, regardless of the list relied on, they are all fulfilled in the present case", which included an assessment that the investment resulted in "contributions [that] allowed for encouraging the economic development of Senegal through the concessionary company".[332]

As this section attempted to demonstrate, this first form of incomplete assessment originates from viewing the financial performance of a FDI as a contribution to the host state's development outright. In viewing development from this oversimplistic analytical lens, investment arbitration tribunals have also subsumed financial and extra-financial contributions to development as an indistinguishable whole. In doing so, the profitability of a firm formed through FDI is seen as substitutable with an investment that may have resulted in providing significant development impact to the host state. Conversely, an investment that remains profitable may be construed as contributing to the host state's development while having no clear development impact at all.

329 The Georgian Civil War took place between 1991 and 1993.

330 *Ioannis Kardassopoulos v Georgia*, ICSID Case No ARB/05/18, Award (3 March 2010) para 202.

331 *Jan de Nul NV and Dredging International NV v Arab Republic of Egypt*, ICSID Case No ARB/04/13, Decision on Jurisdiction (16 June 2006) para 92.

332 *Millicom International Operations BV and Sentel GSM SA v The Republic of Senegal*, ICSID Case No ARB/08/20, Decision on Jurisdiction of the Arbitral Tribunal (16 July 2010) para 80.

2.5.2 Second form: confining the right to regulate

The second form of incomplete assessment involves either the investor or the Tribunal viewing the host state's right to regulate for a way that confines its capacities to serve public interest objectives. This form involves making the host state's development secondary to standards that the Tribunal may consider as having greater primacy, and then employing that hierarchy to contest the means and/or purpose of a government measure in contributing to public interests such as advancing sustainable development. These standards may include contesting the proportionality of a measure, emphasizing the importance of predictability in international investment regimes, or claiming the primacy of a treaty-based obligation to provide compensation for direct or indirect (creeping) expropriation. Unlike the incomplete assessment in the first form, which is inspired by a limited understanding and/or engagement with sustainable development, the second form finds its basis in inconsistent views towards the right to regulate for the public interest.

The investment treaty arbitrations set against Argentina are iconic examples of this form.[333] In *Siemens v Argentina*, for instance, Siemens advanced three arguments in an effort to confine Argentina's right to regulate: (1) by inviting and admitting foreign investment, the state had "deliberately self-limited its public powers and prerogatives";[334] (2) there were no change in circumstances that would "justify a different assessment of the public interest as it was when the Contract was awarded";[335] and (3) that the "purpose of the measures is not a criterion to determine whether an expropriation has occurred"; rather "public purpose is a criterion for the expropriation's legality [while] proportionality and reasonableness may play a role in assessing whether the power to expropriate has been exercised properly".[336] Evidence of this second form can also be found in the Tribunal's considerations. It identifies that the host state's guarantee to provide full protection and security involve legal securities, which it defined as "certainty in norms and, consequently, their foreseeable application", as taking precedence over the stated public interest objective of the host state (which the Tribunal ultimately dismissed as qualifying as serving a public purpose).[337]

333 Analysis on these arbitral decisions remain divided. See for instance José Alvarez and Gustavo Topalian, 'The Paradoxical Argentina Cases' (2012) 6 World Arbitration & Mediation Review 491; David Schneiderman, 'Judicial Politics and International Investment Arbitration: Seeking an Explanation for Conflicting Outcomes' (2010) 30 Northwestern Journal of International Law & Business 383.

334 *Siemens AG v The Argentine Republic*, ICSID Case No ARB/02/8, Award (17 January 2007) para 156.

335 *Siemens AG v The Argentine Republic*, ICSID Case No ARB/02/8, Award (17 January 2007) para 157.

336 *Siemens AG v The Argentine Republic*, ICSID Case No ARB/02/8, Award (17 January 2007) para 238.

337 *Siemens AG v The Argentine Republic*, ICSID Case No ARB/02/8, Award (17 January 2007) paras 304–9.

At the same time, legal securities were shown to not necessarily preclude the state's right to regulate. The *LESI-ASTALDI v Algeria* Tribunal, for instance, found that such legal securities could be satisfied while exercising a state's right to regulate without necessarily breaching treaty obligations in the context of a national emergency if the government measure was non-discriminatory in its implementation.[338] The sole arbitrator in *Pantechniki v Albania* took this a step further by conditioning full protection and security with the host state's circumstances, capacities, and level of development, distinguishing between a breach of a treaty obligation to provide those minimum standards with the failure to do so, which in itself would not constitute a breach.[339] In *Urbaser v Argentina*, both conditions were present: an economic crisis resulting in a state of emergency recognized[340] and extraordinary development need at the level of fundamental human rights disproportionately affecting the poorest and most vulnerable segments of the population.[341] To this, the Tribunal clearly recognized that "viewed in isolation" measures taken in the right to regulate may "appear as hurting the standard of fair and equitable treatment" but that their "assessment must always be made in the light of the facts and circumstances of the particular investment".[342]

Elsewhere, such legal securities have also been seen to be circumstantial in their scope, such as in application to certain sectors. In *SolEs Badajoz v Spain*, for instance, the Tribunal defined the legitimate expectations of the claimant within the scope of investments in photovoltaic (PV) energy. In doing so, the Tribunal seemed to have applied a separate standard in limiting the host state's right to regulate[343] "taking into account the capital-intensity, long period of capital recovery and high leverage that is characteristic of investment in PV plants".[344]

338 *LESI SpA and ASTALDI SpA v République Algérienne Démocratique et Populaire*, ICSID Case No ARB/05/3, Award (12 November 2008) para 171.

339 *Pantechniki SA Contractors & Engineers (Greece) v The Republic of Albania*, ICSID Case No ARB/07/21, Award (30 July 2009) paras 81–84.

340 *Urbaser SA and Consorcio de Aguas Bilbao Bizkaia, Bilbao Biskaia Ur Partzuergoa v The Argentine Republic*, ICSID Case No ARB/07/26, Award (8 December 2016) para 533.

341 *Urbaser SA and Consorcio de Aguas Bilbao Bizkaia, Bilbao Biskaia Ur Partzuergoa v The Argentine Republic*, ICSID Case No ARB/07/26, Award (8 December 2016) para 66.

342 *Urbaser SA and Consorcio de Aguas Bilbao Bizkaia, Bilbao Biskaia Ur Partzuergoa v The Argentine Republic*, ICSID Case No ARB/07/26, Award (8 December 2016) para 680.

343 Spain had modified a feed-in tariff (FIT) system that SolEs Badajoz, an investment mechanism that focuses on PV projects, claimed had annihilated the regulatory environment that was central to the initial investment decision, which both breached its FET (*SolEs Badajoz GmbH v Kingdom of Spain*, ICSID Case No ARB/15/38, Award (31 July 2019) para 292). and was a disproportionate government measure that was not commensurate with economic rationale or the public interest that Spain sought to serve (*SolEs Badajoz GmbH v Kingdom of Spain*, ICSID Case No ARB/15/38, Award (31 July 2019) paras 281–82). Spain's response was to evoke its sovereign right to regulate for accordance with what it derived as the public interest, which was to resolve macroeconomic problems caused by the FIT value (*SolEs Badajoz GmbH v Kingdom of Spain*, ICSID Case No ARB/15/38, Award (31 July 2019) paras 285–85, 301).

344 *SolEs Badajoz GmbH v Kingdom of Spain*, ICSID Case No ARB/15/38, Award (31 July 2019) paras 443–44.

Perhaps one of the most troubling instances of this form of limited assessment was in the *Metalclad v Mexico* decision, where the Tribunal confined Mexico's right to regulate without fully considering the legitimacy of the measures it implemented insofar as they may have served public interest objectives.[345] Here, the Tribunal determined that Mexico expropriated Metalclad's investment while denying consideration of whether Mexico's policy measures had served a legitimate public interest objective. This effectively curtailed the Mexico's right to regulate, which it exercised based on its perception of ecological harm that would have arisen from the operation of Metalclad's investment, which was a landfill. Instead, the Tribunal ruled in favour of the investor, Metalclad, due to breaches of its legitimate expectations by Mexico, and as such it "need not decide or consider the motivation or intent of the adoption of the Ecological Decree".[346]

A thematically similar yet perhaps milder rendition of this interpretation can be found in *Quiborax v Bolivia*, where mining licenses granted to Quiborax were revoked following measures taken by Bolivia to address the environmental impact of scaling up mining activities.[347] In response to claims by Quiborax concerning Bolivia's violation of its FET, Bolivia responded that it had identified "breaches in matters of industrial safety, environment and labor" as legitimizing the nullification of licenses provided to the investor on the basis of a newly enacted law (the "Revocation Decree") that granted the executive branch of the Bolivian government the authority to revoke public mining concessions ex post. The Tribunal, after having

345 In *Metalclad v Mexico*, Guadalcázar, a municipality in Mexico, had implemented an ecological decree that would prevent the claimant from operating its investment, a landfill, after it had received host state authorization and completed construction (*Metalclad Corporation v the United Mexican States*, ICSID Case No ARB (AF)/97/1, Award (30 August 2000) paras 39–43). The decree mandated the creation of an ecological reserve, barring "any conduct that might involve the discharge of polluting agents on the reserve soil, subsoil, running water or water deposits and prohibits the undertaking of any potentially polluting activities" (*Metalclad Corporation v the United Mexican States*, ICSID Case No ARB (AF)/97/1, Award (30 August 2000) para 110). This effectively precluded Metalclad from operating its investment, which the it claimed was expropriation. The Tribunal ruled in favour of this claim, having determined that Guadalcázar acted outside of its authority (*Metalclad Corporation v the United Mexican States*, ICSID Case No ARB (AF)/97/1, Award (30 August 2000) para 106).

346 *Metalclad Corporation v the United Mexican States*, ICSID Case No ARB (AF)/97/1, Award (30 August 2000) para 106.

347 *Quiborax v Bolivia* arose from the termination of a public concession awarded to Quiborax S.A., a Chilean mining company, based on a newly issued Law 2.564, which "enabled the Executive Power to annul mining concessions ex post . . . after the evaluation of audits, technical, legal, economic, and financial, tax, social and labor legislation and environmental and ecological preservation" (*Quiborax SA and Non Metallic Minerals SA v Plurinational State of Bolivia*, ICSID Case No ARB/06/2, Award (16 September 2015) paras 20–21). In responding to the claim that the measure was unlawful, unreasonable, arbitrary and discriminatory, the Tribunal executed a three-pronged test that involved whether the Revocation Decree found basis in the existing legal framework of Bolivia, the proportionality of the measure within existing and applicable Bolivian law, and whether the Claimant was provided due process (*Quiborax SA and Non Metallic Minerals SA v Plurinational State of Bolivia*, ICSID Case No ARB/06/2, Award (16 September 2015) para 207).

reviewed the "technical audit report" to these effects, concluded that the "irregularities identified therein were minor breaches of law" and that they "could not have served as basis for the revocation of the concessions".[348] Puzzlingly, the Tribunal proceeded to conclude that irrespective of whether Bolivia had implemented the measure (revocation of concession) to protect a public or national interest, the Revocation Decree could only be evoked should the annulment of a contract be sanctioned by national law.[349] Yet the industrial safety, environment and labour audit that identified breaches of law by the claimant were of a scale minor enough to not have warranted revocation—an assessment that was left unaccompanied by an explanation on how this standard was set—certainly not sufficient to precede the investor's legitimate expectations.[350]

Another proceeding that embodied this form can be found in *Eco Oro v Colombia*,[351] where the environmental permit needed for a mining permit was rejected following a general prohibition of mining in paramo ecosystems in Colombia. A majority of the arbitral tribunal agreed that the government measure was non-discriminatory and non-arbitrary, therefore a legitimate exercise of the right to regulate for the public interest of protecting the environment and in accordance with the Rio Declaration (1992). However, the Tribunal found that Colombia breached Eco Oro's legitimate expectations due to the inconsistent approach employed by authorities in deciding the physical delimitations of paramos in determining whether the areas conceded to Eco Oro did in fact fall under the target area of the government measure. As a result, while a legitimate exercise of the right to regulate, the government measure did not recuse Colombia's duty for compensation given that it had failed to provide stable and predictable regulatory conditions. Thus, despite having established and recognized the legitimacy of the government measure as an exercise in the right to regulate for the public interest of environmental protection, the decision attributed greater weight to the legitimate expectations of the investor in rendering its award for compensation.

In other instances, the Tribunal may find itself at odds with the host state in its interpretation of contributions to development, and therein the scope of the host state's right to regulate. In *Bernhard von Pezold and others v Zimbabwe*, the host state had questioned the jurisdiction of the under ICSID Convention Article 25 because the

> [c]laimants never contributed anything to Zimbabwe. . . . Their only concern was to maximise their individual family's financial gain. As they never contributed anything positive to our country, in that sense, they did not make

348 *Quiborax SA and Non Metallic Minerals SA v Plurinational State of Bolivia*, ICSID Case No ARB/06/2, Award (16 September 2015) para 219.

349 *Quiborax SA and Non Metallic Minerals SA v Plurinational State of Bolivia*, ICSID Case No ARB/06/2, Award (16 September 2015) para 245(a).

350 *Quiborax SA and Non Metallic Minerals SA v Plurinational State of Bolivia*, ICSID Case No ARB/06/2, Award (16 September 2015) paras 258–59.

351 *Eco Oro Minerals Corp v Republic of Colombia*, ICSID Case No ARB/16/41.

> an investment which merits benefitting from the protections of a BIT in this arbitration.586F[352]

The claimants then refuted that they in fact did make contributions to the host state's development, recalling separate testimonial accounts of senior government officials recognizing the investment's contribution to Zimbabwe's development, not only in terms of employment and productive capacity, but also the "protection and preservation of indigenous forests [with the] properly administered exploitation of the exotic timber plantations [which] employs some 16,000 people [and] accounts for 3% of the GDP",[353] referring to the industry in general and data provided by a study from 2001 published by the Food and Agriculture Organization (FAO).[354] The Tribunal concluded:

> The jurisprudence is uncertain as to whether a contribution to economic development of the State is required as part of the investment criteria. However, given the employment provided, contribution to the economy and know-how involved in the investment, it is clear that any such criterion would also be satisfied in the present case.[355]

Zimbabwe had then challenged the Tribunal's authority to decide on such matters since in reserving its right to regulate, it was also entitled to a wide margin of appreciation as to what was in the public interest of the country.[356] To this, the Tribunal had resorted to making numerous narrow assessments that focused on establishing a legal scope of the right to regulate as opposed to appraising the legitimacy of the government measure in its contribution to sustainable development. The Tribunal decided in favour of the claimant, dismissing Zimbabwe's right to regulate for its sustainable development based on four tests that would undermine the legitimacy of the measures taken:[357]

1 The proportionality test rendered that the measures by Zimbabwe failed the *Tecmed* test, which was that there was no state of emergency or necessity to have warranted a violation of the applicable BITs;592F[358]

352 *Bernhard von Pezold and Others v Republic of Zimbabwe*, ICSID Case No ARB/10/15, Award (28 July 2015) paras 233–36.
353 *Bernhard von Pezold and Others v Republic of Zimbabwe*, ICSID Case No ARB/10/15, Award (28 July 2015) para 257.
354 EM Shumba, 'FOSA Country Report—Zimbabwe' (Food and Agriculture Organization (FAO) 2001) Section 3.2.1.
355 *Bernhard von Pezold and Others v Republic of Zimbabwe*, ICSID Case No ARB/10/15, Award (28 July 2015) para 286.
356 *Bernhard von Pezold and Others v Republic of Zimbabwe*, ICSID Case No ARB/10/15, Award (28 July 2015) paras 453–54.
357 *Bernhard von Pezold and Others v Republic of Zimbabwe*, ICSID Case No ARB/10/15, Award (28 July 2015) paras 1016–18.
358 *Bernhard von Pezold and Others v Republic of Zimbabwe*, ICSID Case No ARB/10/15, Award (28 July 2015) paras 460–63.

2 The reasonableness test rendered that between competing interests, namely those of human rights and international investment, were based on practices found in human rights law, which had no equivalent standard in international investment law;593F[359]
3 The deference test rendered that the lack of necessity meant that it was up to the "adjudicator to determine whether particular conduct by a State 'crosses the line' that separates valid regulatory activity from expropriation";594F[360]
4 The margin of appreciation test was dismissed in the denial to recognize the "margin of appreciation doctrine" as constituting customary status.595F[361]

While this four-pronged test certainly adds to the breadth of the analysis taken up by the Tribunal, it is notable that the extent to which they pose relevance to Zimbabwe's reasoning for implementing such measures remains tenable. In doing so, the Tribunal chose to curtail the scope in which Zimbabwe is able to exercise its right to regulate by basing its assessment on a four-pronged test that seeks to identify conventional determinants of the legitimate use of public policy measures. This in effect crowded out any capacity to evaluate the government measures implemented for the purpose that they were intended to achieve.[362]

This second form of incomplete assessment finds its origins in a Tribunal's decision to emphasize the weight of certain principles in international investment law over others. The Tribunal, for instance, may base its decision on its belief in the importance of a predictable order of investment law, denying what might have otherwise been a legitimate reason for the host state to exercise its right to regulate for the public interest of sustainable development.

2.5.3 Third form: evaluating science-based assessment

The centrality of science-based assessment in relation to whether a government measure or an investment contributes to sustainable development is clear, as established both in this and Chapter 4. In investment treaty arbitration, this third form of incomplete assessment is embodied by inconsistent treatment of science-based assessment, particularly in application to matters of sustainable development and broader public interest objectives involving the environment or public health. Investment treaty arbitration disputes in this form of incomplete assessment can be

359 *Bernhard von Pezold and Others v Republic of Zimbabwe*, ICSID Case No ARB/10/15, Award (28 July 2015) para 465.

360 *Bernhard von Pezold and Others v Republic of Zimbabwe*, ICSID Case No ARB/10/15, Award (28 July 2015) para 464.

361 *Bernhard von Pezold and Others v Republic of Zimbabwe*, ICSID Case No ARB/10/15, Award (28 July 2015) para 466.

362 Tzouvala also points out that "racialized forms of reasoning are of particular use to liberal and neoliberal actors" in the *von Pezold* decision to exclude indigenous populations from landownership (Ntina Tzouvala, 'Full Protection and Security (for Racial Capitalism)' (2022) 25 Journal of International Economic Law 224, 239).

seen as science-based either directly or indirectly. Directly science-based disputes involve opposing scientific claims or refutation regarding the rigour or meaning of science-based assessment. Indirectly science-based disputes are those that involve some level of incompatibility with applicable multilateral environmental agreements or commitments.

In regards to directly science-based disputes, perhaps the most famous of these cases is *Methanex v United States*, where the claimants refuted the scientific assessment conducted by the host state, in this case the State of California, contending that the assessment had in its design "militated" its results[363] in a "sham environmental protection in order to cater to local political interests or in order to protect a domestic industry".[364] The Tribunal ruled in favour of the host state, deciding that a disagreement in good faith between experts and scientists on methodology in an "open and informed debate" served in itself as the "best evidence" on the legitimacy of the public policy measure taken by the state.[365] This would suggest that the process rather than the rigour or substance of a science-based assessment is critical to evaluating an investment's impact on the host state's development.

An important variation of this theme is found in *Chemtura Corporation v Canada*, which involved the phaseout of the pesticide lindane, the Chemtura Corporation claimed that the Canadian government through its relevant regulatory authority, the Pest Management Regulatory Agency (PMRA), illegitimately restricted the use of lindane before a voluntary phaseout date agreed upon by a coalition of related agricultural organizations. While the PMRA had conducted a science-based assessment, it was, according to the claimant, not based on scientific evidence but rather a foregone conclusion.[366] This was based on the fact that the PMRA did not request from the Chemtura Corporation data that it believed to be necessary to one such a review and that it was not given an opportunity to discuss the review with the PMRA.[367] The Chemtura Corporation also claimed that the government measure to expedite the phaseout of lindane amounted to expropriation as it was not taken for a public purpose because the PRMA had "no new, pertinent or reasonable scientific rationale".[368]

The position of the PMRA was it employed a valid and legitimate use of its police powers to protect public health and the environment based on a scientific assessment.[369] The further added that it was fulfilling Canada's international commitments to the Stockholm Convention on Persistent Organic Pollutants, which lists

363 *Methanex v United States*, UNCITRAL (NAFTA), Final Award (3 August 2005) para 38.

364 *Methanex v United States*, UNCITRAL (NAFTA), Final Award (3 August 2005) para 41.

365 *Methanex v United States*, UNCITRAL (NAFTA), Final Award (3 August 2005) para 101.

366 *Crompton (Chemtura) Corp v Government of Canada*, UNCITRAL, Award (2 August 2010) para 93.

367 *Crompton (Chemtura) Corp v Government of Canada*, UNCITRAL, Award (2 August 2010) para 45.

368 *Crompton (Chemtura) Corp v Government of Canada*, UNCITRAL, Award (2 August 2010) para 251.

369 *Crompton (Chemtura) Corp v Government of Canada*, UNCITRAL, Award (2 August 2010) para 254.

lindane as a chemical designated for elimination, as well as due process requirements in the Aarhus Protocol to the Convention on Long-Range Transboundary Air Pollution on Persistent Organic Pollutants,[370] namely the launching of a special review. The Tribunal recognized the legitimacy behind this claim, dismissing any claims of wrongdoing by the PMRA and the state.[371] As to the scientific study itself, the Tribunal identified that it was beyond its competencies to "judge the correctness or adequacy of the scientific results", choosing instead of focus on issues of due process.[372] Nevertheless, the Tribunal concluded that the phaseout of lindane was a "valid exercise of Canada's police powers to protect public health and the environment" based on the reasoning that the measure was not arbitrary because it "respected due process and was based on valid science" and that the measure was made in good faith as part of the country's commitments to multilateral agreements that recognized the risks posed by lindane.[373]

While the science-based assessment in and of itself became secondary to the reasoning of the investment treaty arbitration tribunal, an important conclusion drawn from *Chemtura Corporation v Canada* is the fact that standards of scientific review and the public purpose of the measure itself when in reference to Canada's commitments to multilateral environmental agreements were paramount to tribunal's reasoning on this point. A similar variation to this theme can be found in *Philip Morris v Uruguay*,[374] wherein the Tribunal dismissed claims that Uruguay's measures were arbitrary and unnecessary based on amicus curiae submissions by the World Health Organization and the Pan American Health Organization attesting to effective measures in tobacco control.[375]

However, unlike cases such as *Methanex v United States* and *Chemtura v Canada*, where the processes and results of scientific assessment are undervalued in comparison to an effort to establish and/or satisfy broader principles (such as best

370 *Crompton (Chemtura) Corp v Government of Canada*, UNCITRAL, Award (2 August 2010) paras 136–37.

371 *Crompton (Chemtura) Corp v Government of Canada*, UNCITRAL, Award (2 August 2010) paras 137–38.

372 *Crompton (Chemtura) Corp v Government of Canada*, UNCITRAL, Award (2 August 2010) para 153.

373 *Crompton (Chemtura) Corp v Government of Canada*, UNCITRAL, Award (2 August 2010) para 254.

374 Philip Morris had contested Uruguay's single presentation requirement that precluded tobacco manufacturers from "marketing more than one variant of cigarette per brand family" in an effort to protect public health (*Philip Morris Brand Sàrl (Switzerland), Philip Morris Products SA (Switzerland) and Abal Hermanos SA (Uruguay) v Oriental Republic of Uruguay*, ICSID Case No ARB/10/7, Award (8 July 2016) paras 9, 13). Philip Morris had contested the act as violating proportionality (for the expropriation of intellectual property) and that the measure was not based on a "serious, objective and scientific" assessment (*Philip Morris Brand Sàrl (Switzerland), Philip Morris Products SA (Switzerland) and Abal Hermanos SA (Uruguay) v Oriental Republic of Uruguay*, ICSID Case No ARB/10/7, Award (8 July 2016) para 199).

375 *Philip Morris Brand Sàrl (Switzerland), Philip Morris Products SA (Switzerland) and Abal Hermanos SA (Uruguay) v Oriental Republic of Uruguay*, ICSID Case No ARB/10/7, Award (8 July 2016) paras 305–7.

effort in *Methanex* and the primacy of multilateral environmental agreements in *Chemtura*), there have been cases that involve a more robust assessment of the scientific facts. Such cases involve conflicting scientific evidence seeking to support one of two conclusions: whether (in)action(s) of the host state have/had a detrimental impact or if the detrimental impact occurred regardless of (in)action(s) of the host state. This was the case in *Berkowitz v Costa Rica*[376] and in *Allard v Barbados*.[377] In the latter, the Tribunal was presented with conflicting expert testimony on each of the claims presented in the proceedings, such as water salinity and biodiversity, each of which was assessed in turn within its own right to identify whether liability can be attributed to the host state.[378]

Indirectly science-based disputes are those that refer to multilateral or national environmental commitments made by the host or home state. Perhaps the most common of these are net-zero commitments, which involve the phasing out of new fossil fuel production capacity and investments.[379] Despite these commitments, foreign investment projects find broad protections, such as access to investment treaty arbitration. The, for instance, Energy Charter Treaty applies to "19% of all treaty-protected oil and gas projects",[380] the implications for net zero commitments remaining yet to be seen. In *RWE v Netherlands*[381] and *Uniper v Netherlands*,[382] in observing its commitments to the Paris Agreement, the Netherlands implemented a law in 2019 that would prohibit the use of coal by power plants to generate electricity through a steady phaseout between 2020 and 2030. The claimants to have been affected by this measure then initiated investment treaty arbitration based on

376 Aaron C Berkowitz, Brett E Berkowitz and Trevor B Berkowitz, *(Formerly Spence International Investments and Others) v Republic of Costa Rica*, ICSID Case No UNCT/13/2, Interim Award (Corrected) (30 May 2017) para 171.

377 In this case, the claimant requested compensation from the host state for the environmental degradation of a mangrove that was purchased to turn into an eco-park. In addition to allegations of neglectful environmental management, the claimant asserted that zoning changes in neighbouring estates had resulted in further contamination and subsequent violation of full protection and security (*Peter A Allard v Government of Barbados*, PCA Case No 2012-6 paras 56–60). Barbados advanced that not only were the conditions identified by the claimant artificially produced decades earlier, but also that the environmental conditions of the mangrove had in fact improved based on its own scientific assessment (*Peter A Allard v Government of Barbados*, PCA Case No 2012-06 para 235). The Tribunal dismissed the claims that the host state was liable for the transformations observed based on lacking scientific and factual evidence (*Peter A Allard v Government of Barbados*, PCA Case No 2012-06 para 139).

378 *Peter A Allard v Government of Barbados*, PCA Case No 2012-6 paras 235–42.

379 Catherine Higham and Joana Setzer, '"Investor-State Dispute Settlement" as a New Avenue for Climate Change Litigation' (*Grantham Research Institute on Climate Change and the Environment*, 2 June 2021) <www.lse.ac.uk/granthaminstitute/news/investor-state-dispute-settlement-as-a-new-avenue-for-climate-change-litigation/> accessed 11 July 2022.

380 Kyla Tienhaara and others, 'Investor-State Disputes Threaten the Global Green Energy Transition' (2022) 376 Science 701–2.

381 *RWE AG and RWE Eemshaven Holding II BV v Kingdom of the Netherlands*, ICSID Case No ARB/21/4.

382 *Uniper SE, Uniper Benelux Holding BV and Uniper Benelux NV v Kingdom of the Netherlands*, ICSID Case No ARB/21/22.

what was believed to be a breach of their FET (disproportional economic harm and a violation of legitimate expectations). The Netherlands claimed that it invoked the right to regulate for the public interest of climate change mitigation.[383] A crucial aspect of this dispute in connection to this third form of limited assessment whether the 2030 phaseout is viewed on the basis of the scientific determinations of the UNFCCC.[384]

Another investor-State dispute that can broadly be categorized under this theme is *Rockhopper v Italy*,[385] which has come to infamy in 2021 and directed significant criticism to investment treaty arbitration as a means for companies to obstruct policies meant to advance sustainable development.[386] Also pursued under the Energy Charter Treaty, the claimant, an oil exploration firm, submitted for arbitration after Italy had implemented a moratorium on new hydrocarbon withdrawal from its coastal areas through fracking. The firm received compensation for future monetary value (EUR 185 million) that it could have gained should it have permitted to continue with extraction based on the timeline it was awarded a license by the host state.

The Tribunal awarded the claimant compensation for a breach of their FET, reasoning that it was not the role of the arbitration to assess whether the drilling ban from an "environmental standpoint" but to instead turn its attention to the "legal issue at hand". In this manner, the Tribunal's decision embodied this form of incomplete assessment by refusing to recognize a science-based assessment in evaluating whether the government measure was a legitimate exercise of the right to regulate in a manner informed by, for instance, the 2030 decarbonization target dictated by the Paris Agreement.[387]

As this subsection attempted to show, science-based assessments are employed in investment treaty arbitration directly, which appeal to scientific methods to evaluate claims issued by opposing parties, or indirectly, which are those that appeal to standards that arise from scientific methods. While direct science-based

383 See more at Stan Putter, 'The Netherlands Coal Phase-Out and the Resulting (RWE and Uniper) ICSID Arbitrations' (*Kluwer Arbitration Blog*, 24 August 2021) <http://arbitrationblog.kluwerarbitration.com/2021/08/24/the-netherlands-coal-phase-out-and-the-resulting-rwe-and-uniper-icsid-arbitrations/> accessed 11 July 2022.

384 Based on the United Nations Environment Programme (UNEP), 'Emissions Gap Report 2019' (United Nations 2019) <https://www.unep.org/resources/emissions-gap-report-2019>.

385 *Rockhopper Italia SpA, Rockhopper Mediterranean Ltd, and Rockhopper Exploration Plc v Italian Republic*, ICSID Case No ARB/17/14.

386 See, for instance, Josephine Moulds, 'Outrage as Italy Faces Multimillion Pound Damages to UK Oil Firm' *The Guardian* (25 July 2021) <www.theguardian.com/business/2021/jul/25/outrage-as-italy-faces-multimillion-pound-damages-to-uk-oil-firm> accessed 11 July 2022.

387 An analysis and summary of the Award can be found in Lisa Bohmer, 'Analysis: Unpacking the *Rockhopper v Italy* Award, Including Tribunal's Reasons for Finding That Denial of Hydrocarbons Concession Amounted to an Unlawful Expropriation, and for Awarding 190 Million EUR to Claimants' (*Investment Arbitration Reporter*, 1 September 2022) <https://www-iareporter-com/articles/analysis-unpacking-the-rockhopper-v-italy-award-revealing-tribunals-reasons-for-finding-that-denial-of-hydrocarbons-concession-amounted-to-an-unlawful-expropriation-and-for-awarding-190-m/> accessed 27 October 2022.

assessments remain limited in practice and disputes involving indirect science-based assessments remain largely unresolved, illustrating that this third form of limited assessment is an important step in contextualizing the argument and methodology advanced in the following chapters of this book.

2.6 Concluding remarks

The conceptual framework presented in this chapter follows the thesis and research questions advanced in Chapter 1 on the importance of understanding the sustainable development impact of both the government measure and international investment to acquire a more comprehensive assessment, especially in the context of a dispute. The four pillars that constitute this conceptual framework substantiate each of the foundational ideas of this work. They include first the role of international investment policy in sustainable development, second the notion of an investment contributing to sustainable development, third the governance structures surrounding international investment, and fourth the use government measures to protect legitimate public interests.

This fourth pillar of the conceptual framework in particular attempted to substantiate the meaning of an "incomplete assessment" in connection to an Action and its sustainable development impact. In doing so, it indicated one way that international investment law, particularly investment treaty arbitration, remains limited in its capacity to facilitate international investments and/or government measures that may advance sustainable development.

The salience of this limitation is founded in the fact that issues of sustainable development have been raised throughout the international investment law regime, not only in the scholarship as was demonstrated in Chapter 1, but also within the UN system itself.[388] The more precise delineation of an incomplete assessment presented in this section helps to further emphasize the importance of the research question that guides this work. Assessments of an Action in the context of the right to regulate for sustainable development are not constrained by the introduction of extralegal challenges related to sustainable development that are unfamiliar to international investment law. Rather, the constraint comes from a reluctance to accept that these challenges have been present but simply circumvented and/or circumscribed by conventional views of international investment law.

The result has been that the international investment law regime has been left bereft of a consistent and comprehensive basis upon which both substantive and legal questions concerning sustainable development policies and investments can be assessed. This, in turn, has evoked a conservatism to mitigate procedural uncertainty, with only stand-alone instances of international investment policies, treaty provisions, and investment treaty arbitration decisions that embody a greater awareness towards the multidimensional needs of advancing sustainable development. A continuation of this regime has been shown in Chapter 1 and throughout

388 This is explored further in Chapter 3.

this chapter to only result in controversy, embodied by the growing disenchantment surrounding the increasingly irreconcilable gap between evolutionary and revolutionary thinking on international investment law.

Building upon the four pillars presented in this chapter, it is worthwhile to revisit this book's underlying argument to examine how these pillars interact with the objective of this work. These interactions can be expressed through two underlying statements.

2.6.1 Underlying statement one (Pillars One and Four)

> *Investment treaty arbitration tribunals in assessing the right to regulate for the public interest in relation to matters involving sustainable development are incomplete.*

The first underlying statement establishes the challenge that this book addressed in the beginning of the work, namely, in identifying how the approach of assessing government measures taken by the host state in its reservation of right to regulate for the public interest is incomplete. As was introduced Pillar Four, an incomplete assessment arises from the fact that such Actions are circumstantial and as such analytically incomparable to past investments and the government measures that confront them when extracted from their native contexts. A measure taken in the right to regulate for the public interest of sustainable development if viewed as legitimate in one country context does not necessarily mean that the same holds true in the development context of another country. The same holds true for an international investment and its contribution to the host state's sustainable development.

Pillar Three detailed how reverting to silo thinking or restrictive interpretations of the right to regulate for the public interest have resulted in investment treaty arbitration tribunals dismissing such claims as extralegal and therefore inadmissible as *ratione materiae*. In this manner, Pillar Three also identified why right to regulate assessments are incomplete. The next step in this logical procession would be to examine how the assessment is incomplete, which is left to the second statement.

2.6.2 Underlying statement two (Pillars Two and Three)

> *On matters pertaining to the public interest of sustainable development, engaging multilateral frameworks on the role of foreign investments in development can address issues of imbalance in assessments of the right to regulate.*

The second underlying statement identifies how issues of imbalance in assessments of the right to regulate is the cause of its incompletion. As identified in Chapter 1, the extent to which contributions to sustainable development are evaluated within the setting of a dispute wherein this is a contention tends to overlook the agency of the investor and/or investment insofar as they/it potentially contribute(d) to the host state's development. As further elaborated earlier in this chapter, tribunals may choose to defer such considerations to margin of appreciation *stricto sensu*. This ipso facto excludes investors and/or investment from such considerations of contributions to sustainable development. This in turn is the basis for the imbalance resulting in an incomplete assessment of the right to regulate for the public interest in applicable circumstances in investment treaty arbitration. The patchwork framework offered in the current state of international investment law and investment treaty arbitration offers an inconsistent standing on the role of the investor and/or investment as defined across the four pillars presented in this chapter. This inconsistency on whether assessments of the right to regulate for the public interest are complete or incomplete hinges entirely on the arbitral tribunal's discretion, tying into some of the more stringent revolutionary criticisms of investment treaty arbitration as the previous chapter explored. The second statement of the thesis suggests embracing multilateral frameworks on the role of investment in sustainable development as capable of addressing the issue of imbalance.

Pillars One and Two provide the foundation upon which the second underlying statement is built. Pillar One constructed a broad, definitional approach to identifying the role of international investment in sustainable development within the setting of UN agreements. This has broadly been identified within the UN system and encapsulated into a working definition for the purposes of this project in Pillar One. Pillar Two, through Sustainable Investment, identified how investments and investors can be assessed as embodying the role of international investment in sustainable development. Specific methodology in Sustainable Investment that meet these criteria, namely multilaterally recognized and in line with the Pillar One working definition, are explored in Chapter 4. These then find application in law, policy, and development through Chapters 5 and 6.

The approach mounted by this work, constructed across Chapters 3 and 4, is based on a multilateral, institutional approach that supplements the structural elements of the international investment law regime to better align it with the pressing concerns of sustainable development. It also seeks to reconcile the interpretative flexibility to buttress the right to regulate for sustainable development with a stable legal system that nurtures the rule of law. Without such a reconciliation, the trade-off between the risks and rewards of international investment will only become more severe, where international investment is increasingly demonized rather than emphasized as a powerful tool in the process of sustainable development.

References

Addis Ababa Action Agenda of the Third International Conference on Financing for Development 2015 (A/RES/69/313)

Agreement Between the Government of the United Kingdom of Great Britain and Northern Ireland and the Government of the Republic of Turkey for the Promotion and Protection of Investments 1991

Agreement on Encouragement and Reciprocal Protection of Investments Between the Kingdom of the Netherlands and the Republic of Uzbekistan 1996

Akbulut B and others, 'Who Promotes Sustainability? Five Theses on the Relationships between the Degrowth and the Environmental Justice Movements' (2019) 165 Ecological Economics 106418

Allen C, *A Guidebook to the Green Economy—Issue 2: Exploring Green Economy Principles* (United Nations Division for Sustainable Development (UNDESA) 2012)

Alvarez J and Topalian G, 'The Paradoxical Argentina Cases' (2012) 6 World Arbitration & Mediation Review 491

Amoco International Finance Corp v Government of the Islamic Republic of Iran, Iran-US Claims Tribunal, Partial Award No 310-56-3 (14 July 1987)

Angeloni C, 'Investment Bank Hits Back at "Mafia Bond" Allegations' (*International Adviser*, 13 July 2020) <https://international-adviser.com/investment-bank-hits-back-at-mafia-bond-allegations/> accessed 24 July 2020

Babu RR, 'Standard of Compensation for Expropriation of Foreign Investment' in Julien Chaisse, Leïla Choukroune and Sufian Jusoh (eds), *Handbook of International Investment Law and Policy* (Springer 2020)

Bahmaei M-A and Sabzevari H, 'Self-Judging Security Exception Clause as a Kind of Carte Blanche in Investment Treaties: Nature, Effect and Proper Standard of Review' (2023) 13 Asian Journal of International Law 97

Bainbridge S, 'Much Ado About Little? Directors' Fiduciary Duties in the Vicinity of Insolvency' (2007) 1 Journal of Business & Technology Law 336

Banco Generali, 'SRI Network' (*Generali Network*) <www.generali.com/our-responsibilities/responsible-investments/sri-network> accessed 8 July 2020

Barcelona Traction, Light and Power Company, Limited [1970] International Court of Justice Second Phase, Judgment of 5 February 1970

Barral V, 'Sustainable Development in International Law: Nature and Operation of an Evolutive Legal Norm' (2012) 23 European Journal of International Law 377

Bayindir Insaat Ticaret Ve Sanayi AS v Islamic Republic of Pakistan, ICSID Case No ARB/03/29, Award (27 August 2009)

Bayindir Insaat Ticaret Ve Sanayi AS v Islamic Republic of Pakistan, ICSID Case No ARB/03/29, Decision on Jurisdiction (14 November 2005)

Bebchuk LA and Tallarita R, 'The Illusory Promise of Stakeholder Governance' (2020) 105 Cornell Law Review

Bedjaoui M, *Towards a New International Economic Order* (UNESCO 1979)

Berkowitz AC, Berkowitz BE and Berkowitz TB, *(Formerly Spence International Investments and Others) v Republic of Costa Rica*, ICSID Case No UNCT/13/2, Interim Award (Corrected) (30 May 2017)

Bernardus Henricus Funnekotter and Others v Republic of Zimbabwe, ICSID Case No ARB/05/6, Award (22 April 2009)

Bernhard von Pezold and Others v Republic of Zimbabwe, ICSID Case No ARB/10/15, Award (28 July 2015)

Bexell M and Jönsson K, 'Responsibility and the United Nations' Sustainable Development Goals' (2017) 44 Forum for Development Studies 13

BG Group Plc v Republic of Argentina, UNCITRAL, Award (24 December 2007)

Bhagat S and Hubbard RG, *Should the Modern Corporation Maximize Shareholder Value?* (American Enterprise Institute 2020)

Bigdeli SZ, 'Clash of Rationalities: Revisiting the Trade and Environment Debate in Light of WTO Disputes Over Green Industrial Policy Special Issue: Trade & Climate Change' (2014) 6 Trade, Law and Development I

Bohmer L, 'Analysis: Unpacking the Rockhopper v Italy Award, Including Tribunal's Reasons for Finding That Denial of Hydrocarbons Concession Amounted to an Unlawful Expropriation, and for Awarding 190 Million EUR to Claimants' (*Investment Arbitration Reporter*, 1 September 2022) <https://www-iareporter-com/articles/analysis-unpacking-the-rockhopper-v-italy-award-revealing-tribunals-reasons-for-finding-that-denial-of-

hydrocarbons-concession-amounted-to-an-unlawful-expropriation-and-for-awarding-190-m/> accessed 27 October 2022

Bonnitcha J, 'Indirect Expropriation' in *Substantive Protection under Investment Treaties: A Legal and Economic Analysis* (CUP 2014)

Boyle AE, 'The Gabcíkovo-Nagymaros Case: New Law in Old Bottles' (1998) 8 Yearbook of International Environmental Law 13

Brower C, 'Obstacles and Pathways to Consideration of the Public Interest in Investment Treaty Disputes' in Karl P Sauvant (ed), *Yearbook on International Investment Law & Policy* (OUP 2009)

Brownlie I, 'A Survey of International Customary Rules of Environmental Protection' (1973) 13 Natural Resources Journal 179

Brownlie I, *Principles of Public International Law* (7th edn, OUP 2008)

Bugge HC and Voigt C (eds), *Sustainable Development in International and National Law* (Europa Law Publishing 2008)

Bugge HC, '1987–2007: "Our Common Future" Revisited' in Christina Voigt (ed), *Sustainable Development in International and National Law* (Europa Law Publishing 2008)

Burke-White WW and von Staden A, 'Private Litigation in a Public Sphere: The Standard of Review in Investor-State Arbitrations' (2010) 35 Yale Journal of International Law 283

Campbell C, 'House of Cards: The Relevance of Legitimate Expectations Under Fair and Equitable Treatment Provisions in Investment Treaty Law' (2013) 30 Journal of International Arbitration 361

'Canada—Certain Measures Affecting the Renewable Energy Generation Sector/Measures Relating to the Feed-in Tariff Program, WTO Appellate Body Report, WT/DS412/DS426/AB/R (24 May 2013)'

'Case Concerning Certain Questions of Mutual Assistance in Criminal Matters (*Djibouti v France*), Judgment, 4 June 2008'

Case Concerning Gabčíkovo-Nagymaros Project (Hungary/Slovakia) [1997] International Court of Justice Judgement

Champagne C, Coggins F and Sodjahin A, 'Can Extra-Financial Ratings Serve as an Indicator of ESG Risk?' [2021] Global Finance Journal 100638

Charter of Economic Rights and Duties of States 1974 (UN Document A/RES/29/3281)

CMS Gas Transmission Company v Republic of Argentina, ICSID Case No ARB/01/8, Award (12 May 2005)

Condon BJ, 'Treaty Structure and Public Interest Regulation in International Economic Law' (2014) 17 Journal of International Economic Law 333

Consortium Groupement LESI-DIPENTA v République Algérienne Démocratique et Populaire, ICSID Case No ARB/03/08, Award (10 January 2005)

Continental Casualty Company v Argentine Republic, ICSID Case No ARB/03/9, Award (5 September 2008)

Convention on the Recognition and Enforcement of Foreign Arbitral Awards (1958)

Crawford J and Baetens F, 'The Influence of International Trade Law on International Law' in Daniel Bethlehem and others (eds), *The Oxford Handbook of International Trade Law* (2nd edn, OUP 2022)

Crompton (Chemtura) Corp. v Government of Canada, UNCITRAL, Award (2 August 2010)

Crystallex International Corporation v Bolivarian Republic of Venezuela, ICSID Case No ARB(AF)/11/2, Award (4 April 2016)

Davitti D, 'Regulating Multinational Corporations' in Koen De Feyter, Stéphanie De Moerloose and Gamze Erdem Türkelli (eds), *Law and Development Encyclopedia* (Edward Elgar 2020)

De Schutter O, 'Chapter 4. Generalized Systems of Preferences: The "Conditional Preferences" Approach' in *Trade in the Service of Sustainable Development: Linking Trade to Labour Rights and Environmental Standards* (Hart Publishing 2015)

De Schutter O, 'Promotion and Protection of All Human Rights, Civil, Political, Economic, Social and Cultural Rights, Including the Right to Development: Report of the Special Rapporteur on the Right to Food, Mr. Olivier De Schutter' (United Nations Human Rights Council (HRC) 2009) A/HRC/10/5 <https://www2.ohchr.org/english/bodies/hrcouncil/docs/10session/A.HRC.10.5.pdf>

De Schutter O, 'Towards a New Treaty on Business and Human Rights' (2016) 1 Business and Human Rights Journal 41

Declaration on the Right to Development 1986 (UN Document A/RES/41/128)

Del Tunari A, *SA v Republic of Bolivia*, ICSID Case No ARB/02/3, Decision on Respondent's Objections to Jurisdiction (21 October 2005)

Dernbach JC, 'Sustainable Development as a Framework for National Governance' (1998) 49 Case Western Reserve Law Review 1

Desierto DA, 'Necessity and Supplementary Means of Interpretation for Non-Precluded Measures in Bilateral Investment Treaties' (2009) 31 University of Pennsylvania Journal of International Law 827

Desierto DA, 'SDG Report 2020: The Civil, Political, Economic, Social, Cultural, and Development Rights Crises Deepening in the Global South' (*EJIL: Talk!* 15 July 2020) <www.ejiltalk.org/sdg-report-2020-the-civil-political-economic-social-cultural-and-development-rights-crises-deepening-in-the-global-south/> accessed 3 August 2020

Deutsche Telekom v India, PCA Case No 2014-10, Judgment of the Swiss Federal Tribunal (11 December 2018)

DiMascio N and Pauwelyn J, 'Nondiscrimination in Trade and Investment Treaties: Worlds Apart or Two Sides of the Same Coin' (2008) 102 American Journal of International Law 48

Dodd EM Jr, 'For Whom Are Corporate Managers Trustees' (1931) 45 Harvard Law Review 1145

Doha Declaration on Financing for Development: Outcome Document of the Follow-Up International Conference on Financing for Development to Review the Implementation of the Monterrey Consensus, 2008–2009

Doha Ministerial Declaration 2001 (WT/MIN(01)/DEC/1)

Dolzer R and Schreuer C, *Principles of International Investment Law* (2nd edn, OUP 2012)

Douglas Z, 'Nothing If Not Critical for Investment Treaty Arbitration: Occidental, Eureko and Methanex' (2006) 22 Arbitration International 27

Douglas Z, *The International Law of Investment Claims* (CUP 2009)

Doyle T, 'Sustainable Development and Agenda 21: The Secular Bible of Global Free Markets and Pluralist Democracy' (1998) 19 Third World Quarterly 771

Dugard J, 'Fourth Report on Diplomatic Protection' (United Nations) UN Doc A/CN.4/530

Dworkin R, *Taking Rights Seriously* (Harvard UP 1977)

Eco Oro Minerals Corp v Republic of Colombia, ICSID Case No ARB/16/41

Edenhofer O, Pichs Madruga R and Sokona Y (eds), *Renewable Energy Sources and Climate Change Mitigation: Special Report of the Intergovernmental Panel on Climate Change* (CUP 2012)

Edmans A, *Grow the Pie: How Great Companies Deliver Both Purpose and Profit* (CUP 2020)

Elkington J, *Cannibals with Forks: The Triple Bottom Line of 21st Century Business* (Cap-Stone Press 1999)

Employee Benefits Security Administration, Department of Labor, 'Financial Factors in Selecting Plan Investments: A Proposed Rule by the Employee Benefits Security Administration on 30 June 2020' <https://www.federalregister.gov/documents/2020/11/13/2020-24515/financial-factors-in-selecting-plan-investments>

Enron Creditors Recovery Corporation (Formerly Enron Corporation) and Ponderosa Assets, LP v Argentine Republic, ICSID Case No ARB/01/3, Award (22 May 2007)

'Expropriation: A Sequel' (United Nations 2012) UNCTAD/DIAE/IA/2011/7

Fortier LY and Drymer SL, 'Indirect Expropriation in the Law of International Investment: I Know It When I See It, or Caveat Investor' (2004) 19 ICSID Review—Foreign Investment Law Journal 293

Foster CE, *Science and the Precautionary Principle in International Courts and Tribunals: Expert Evidence, Burden of Proof and Finality* (CUP 2011)

Francioni F, 'Access to Justice, Denial of Justice and International Investment Law' (2009) 20 European Journal of International Law 729

Fraport AG Frankfurt Airport Services Worldwide v The Republic of the Philippines, ICSID Case No ARB/03/25, Award (16 August 2007)

Freeman RE, *Strategic Management: A Stakeholder Approach* (CUP 2010)

Freeman RE and McVea J, 'A Stakeholder Approach to Strategic Management' in Michael A Hitt, R Edward Freeman and Jeffrey S Harrison (eds), *The Blackwell Handbook of Strategic Management* (3rd edn, Blackwell Publishing 2008)

Friedman M, 'The Social Responsibility of Business Is to Increase Its Profits' *The New York Times Magazine* (1970)

Fukuda-Parr S and Muchhala B, 'The Southern Origins of Sustainable Development Goals: Ideas, Actors, Aspirations' (2020) 126 World Development

The Future We Want: Outcome Document of the United Nations Conference on Sustainable Development 2012 (UN Document A/RES/66/288)

Gatti M and Ondersma CD, 'Can a Broader Corporate Purpose Redress Inequality? The Stakeholder Approach Chimera' (2020) 46 Journal of Corporation Law

Gaukrodger D, 'Addressing the Balance of Interests in Investment Treaties: The Limitation of Fair and Equitable Treatment Provisions to the Minimum Standard of Treatment under Customary International Law' (OECD 2017) No 2017/03 <www.oecd-ilibrary.org/finance-and-investment/addressing-the-balance-of-interests-in-investment-treaties_0a62034b-en> accessed 8 March 2020

Gehring MW and Newcombe AP, 'Chapter 1: An Introduction to Sustainable Development in World Investment Law' in Marie-Claire Cordonier Segger, Markus W Gehring and Andrew Paul Newcombe (eds), *Sustainable Development in World Investment Law* (Kluwer Law International 2011)

General Agreement on Tariffs and Trade 1947

Gleckman H, *Multistakeholder Governance and Democracy: A Global Challenge* (Routledge 2018)

Global Investors for Sustainable Development Alliance (GISD), 'Joint Statement by Global Investors for Sustainable Development Alliance (GISD)' <https://www.gisdalliance.org/sites/default/files/2022-10/GISD%20Alliance%20Joint%20Statement%202022.pdf>

Grabowski A, 'The Definition of Investment under the ICSID Convention: A Defense of Salini' (2014) 15 Chicago Journal of International Law Article 13

Grabski T and Miller A, *10 Years of Impact and Progress* (United Nations Sustainable Stock Exchange (SSE) 2019)

Gray R, 'Is Accounting for Sustainability Actually Accounting for Sustainability . . . and How Would We Know? An Exploration of Narratives of Organisations and the Planet' (2010) 35 Accounting, Organizations and Society 47

'Green Investing Is Red Hot but Its Impact Is Underwhelming' *The Economist* (2020) <www.economist.com/graphic-detail/2020/06/22/green-investing-is-red-hot-but-its-impact-is-underwhelming> accessed 13 July 2020

Grierson-Weiler TJ and Laird IA, 'Part II Substantive Issues, Ch 8 Standards of Treatment' in Peter Muchlinski, Federico Ortino and Christoph Schreuer (eds), *The Oxford Handbook of International Investment Law* (OUP 2008)

Han X, 'The Application of the Principle of Proportionality in *Tecmed v. Mexico*' (2007) 6 Chinese Journal of International Law 635

Handl G, 'Declaration of the United Nations Conference on the Human Environment (Stockholm Declaration), 1972 and the Rio Declaration on Environment and Development,

1992' (United Nations 2012) Introductory Note <https://legal.un.org/avl/ha/dunche/dunche.html> accessed 1 July 2020

Handyside v The United Kingdom [1976] European Court of Human Rights 5493/72

Hansmann H and Kraakman R, 'The End of History for Corporate Law Essay' (2000) 89 Georgetown Law Journal 439

Hart O and Zingales L, 'Companies Should Maximize Shareholder Welfare Not Market Value' (2017) 2 Journal of Law, Finance, and Accounting 247

Hawley JP and Williams AT, 'The Universal Owner's Role in Sustainable Economic Development' (2002) 9 Corporate Environmental Strategy 284

Helnan International Hotels A/S v Arab Republic of Egypt, ICSID Case No ARB/05/19, Award (3 July 2008)

Helnan International Hotels A/S v Arab Republic of Egypt, ICSID Case No ARB/05/19, Decision of the Tribunal on Objection to Jurisdiction (17 October 2006)

Henckels C, 'Balancing Investment Protection and the Public Interest: The Role of the Standard of Review and the Importance of Deference in Investor—State Arbitration' (2013) 4 Journal of International Dispute Settlement 197

Henckels C, *Proportionality and Deference in Investor-State Arbitration: Balancing Investment Protection and Regulatory Autonomy* (CUP 2015)

Henckels C, 'Should Investment Treaties Contain Public Policy Exceptions Essays: Substantive and Procedural Reforms' (2018) 59 Boston College Law Review 2825

Hepburn J, 'Looking Back: UNCITRAL Tribunal in *Biloune v Ghana* Found Creeping Expropriation of Resort Complex, but Declined Jurisdiction over Denial of Justice and Human Rights Claims' (*Investment Arbitration Reporter*, 6 November 2020) <www.iareporter.com/articles/looking-back-uncitral-tribunal-in-biloune-v-ghana-found-creeping-expropriation-of-resort-complex-but-declined-jurisdiction-over-denial-of-justice-and-human-rights-claims/> accessed 17 November 2020

Herdegen M, *Principles of International Economic Law* (2nd edn, OUP 2016)

Hickel J and Kallis G, 'Is Green Growth Possible?' (2020) 25 New Political Economy 469

Higham C and Setzer J, '"Investor-State Dispute Settlement" as a New Avenue for Climate Change Litigation' (*Grantham Research Institute on Climate Change and the Environment*, 2 June 2021) <www.lse.ac.uk/granthaminstitute/news/investor-state-dispute-settlement-as-a-new-avenue-for-climate-change-litigation/> accessed 11 July 2022

Hilf M and Salomon TR, 'Margin of Appreciation Revisited: The Balancing Pole of Multilevel Governance' in Marise Cremona and others (eds), *Reflections on the Constitutionalisation of International Economic Law: Liber Amicorum for Ernst-Ulrich Petersmann* (Martinus Nijhoff Publishers 2014)

Hill J, 'Chapter 3—Theory of the Firm' in *Environmental, Social, and Governance (ESG) Investing: A Balanced Analysis of the Theory and Practice of a Sustainable Portfolio* (Academic Press 2020)

'How Much Can Financiers Do About Climate Change?' *The Economist* (2020) <www.economist.com/briefing/2020/06/20/how-much-can-financiers-do-about-climate-change> accessed 9 December 2020

Inceysa Vallisoletana SL v Republic of El Salvador, ICSID Case No ARB/03/26, Award (2 August 2006)

Independent Evaluation Office (IEO), 'The Role of the IMF in Argentina, 1991–2002' (International Monetary Fund (IMF) 2003) Issues Paper <www.imf.org/External/NP/ieo/2003/arg/index.htm> accessed 28 August 2020

International Court of Justice (ICJ), 'Certain Activities Carried Out by Nicaragua in the Border Area (*Costa Rica v Nicaragua*)' (*Latest Developments*) <www.icj-cij.org/en/case/150> accessed 9 December 2020

International Institute for Sustainable Development (IISD), 'Responsible Business Report Finds High Risk of "SDG Washing"' (*SDG Knowledge Hub*, 29 May 2018) <http://sdg.iisd.org/news/responsible-business-report-finds-high-risk-of-sdg-washing/> accessed 21 September 2020

Ioannis Kardassopoulos v Georgia, ICSID Case No ARB/05/18, Award (3 March 2010)

Ioannis Kardassopoulos v The Republic of Georgia, ICSID Case No ARB/05/18, Decision on Jurisdiction (6 July 2007)

James and others v United Kingdom (1986) European Court of Human Rights 8793/79

Jan de Nul NV and Dredging International NV v Arab Republic of Egypt, ICSID Case No ARB/04/13, Decision on Jurisdiction (16 June 2006)

Jensen MC and Meckling WH, 'Theory of the Firm: Managerial Behavior, Agency Costs and Ownership Structure' (1976) 3 Journal of Financial Economics 305

Johnson M, 'Italian Mafia Bonds Sold to Global Investors' *Financial Times* (7 July 2020) <www.ft.com/content/bcebd77c-057b-4fd0-bd99-b97e0e559455> accessed 8 July 2020

Jolly J, 'Anger Over World Bank's $55m Pledge to Guyana's Fossil Fuel Industry' *The Guardian* (27 February 2020) <www.theguardian.com/business/2020/feb/27/world-bank-guyana-fossil-fuel-industry-climate> accessed 8 July 2020

Junita F, 'Public Policy Exception in International Commercial Arbitration—Promoting Uniform Model Norms' (2012) 5 Contemporary Asia Arbitration Journal 45

Karametaxas X, 'Sovereign Wealth Funds as Socially Responsible Investors' in Giovanna Adinolfi and others (eds), *International Economic Law: Contemporary Issues* (Springer International Publishing 2017)

Kethireddy SR, 'Still the Law of Nations: Legitimate Expectations and the Sovereigntist Turn in International Investment Law' (2019) 44 Yale Journal of International Law 315

Kingsbury B and Schill SW, 'Public Law Concepts to Balance Investors' Rights with State Regulatory Actions in the Public Interest—the Concept of Proportionality' in *International Investment Law and Comparative Public Law* (OUP 2010)

Kyoto Protocol to the United Nations Framework Convention on Climate Change 1998

Lennox A, 'Spectrum—ABS Analysis: Through the ESG Lens' *Hermes Credit Newsletter Q3* (Hermes Investment Management 2019) <www.hermes-investment.com/se/wp-content/uploads/2019/10/hermes-spectrum-q3-2019.pdf>

Leonhardsen EM, 'Looking for Legitimacy: Exploring Proportionality Analysis in Investment Treaty Arbitration' (2012) 3 Journal of International Dispute Settlement 95

LESI SpA and ASTALDI SpA v République Algérienne Démocratique et Populaire, ICSID Case No ARB/05/3, Award (12 November 2008)

Levashova Y, *The Right of States to Regulate in International Investment Law: The Search for Balance Between Public Interest and Fair and Equitable Treatment* (Kluwer Law International BV 2019)

LG&E Energy Corp, LG&E Capital Corp, and LG&E International, Inc v Argentine Republic, ICSID Case No ARB/02/1, Decision on Liability (3 October 2006)

Linarelli J, Salomon ME and Sornarajah M, 'The End of Empire and the Search for Justice' in *The End of Empire and the Search for Justice: NIEO and Beyond* (OUP 2018)

Linklater A, *The Transformation of Political Community: Ethical Foundations of the Post-Westphalian Era* (U of South Carolina P 1998)

Lovell Z, 'ESG Investing: Growing and Evolving' (Schulte Roth & Zabel LLP) <www.lexology.com/library/detail.aspx?g=85d6def4-6cce-4694-85a9-bfe37b33a056> accessed 8 July 2020

Lowe V, 'Sustainable Development and Unsustainable Arguments' in Alan Boyle and David Freestone (eds), *International Law and Sustainable Development: Past Achievements and Future Challenges* (OUP 1999)

Markowitz HM, *Portfolio Selection: Efficient Diversification of Investments* (Yale UP 1959)

Marvin Roy Feldman Karpa v United Mexican States, ICSID Case No ARB(AF)/99/1, Award (16 December 2002)

Matters D, 'Ever Heard of SDG Washing? The Urgency of SDG Due Diligence' (*Development Matters*, 25 September 2017) <https://oecd-development-matters.org/2017/09/25/ever-heard-of-sdg-washing-the-urgency-of-sdg-due-diligence/> accessed 21 September 2020

Maurer AG (ed), *The Public Policy Exception Under the New York Convention: History, Interpretation and Application* (Rev edn, Juris Publishing, Inc 2013)

Mayer C, 'Shareholderism Versus Stakeholderism—A Misconceived Contradiction: A Comment on "The Illusory Promise of Stakeholder Governance" by Lucian Bebchuk and Roberto Tallarita' (European Corporate Governance Institute 2020) N° 522/2020

Mayer P and Sheppard A, 'Final ILA Report on Public Policy as a Bar to Enforcement of International Arbitral Awards' (2003) 19 Arbitration International 249

M'baye K, 'Le Droit Du Developpement Comme Un Droit de l'Homme' (1972) 5 Revue des Droits de l'Homme 503

McIntyre O and Mosedale T, 'The Precautionary Principle as a Norm of Customary International Law' (1997) 9 Journal of Environmental Law 221

McLachlan C, Shore L and Weiniger M, *International Investment Arbitration: Substantive Principles* (2nd edn, OUP 2017)

Mensah J and Casadevall SR, 'Sustainable Development: Meaning, History, Principles, Pillars, and Implications for Human Action: Literature Review' (2019) 5 Cogent Social Sciences 1653531

Metalclad Corporation v the United Mexican States, ICSID Case No ARB (AF)/97/1, Award (30 August 2000)

Methanex v United States, UNCITRAL (NAFTA), Final Award (3 August 2005)

Milante G and Jang S, 'Measuring Peacebuilding and Statebuilding in the New SDG Framework' (2016) 11 Journal of Peacebuilding & Development 110

Millicom International Operations BV and Sentel GSM SA v The Republic of Senegal, ICSID Case No ARB/08/20, Decision on Jurisdiction of the Arbitral Tribunal (16 July 2010)

Moulds J, 'Outrage as Italy Faces Multimillion Pound Damages to UK Oil Firm' *The Guardian* (25 July 2021) <www.theguardian.com/business/2021/jul/25/outrage-as-italy-faces-multimillion-pound-damages-to-uk-oil-firm> accessed 11 July 2022

Mouyal LW, *International Investment Law and the Right to Regulate: A Human Rights Perspective* (Routledge 2016)

National Grid PLC v Argentina Republic, UNCITRAL, Award (3 November 2008)

Nauman B, 'Investors Balk at Green Bond from Group Specialising in Oil Tankers' *Financial Times* (18 October 2019) <www.ft.com/content/b1d4201c-f142-11e9-bfa4-b25f11f42901> accessed 7 July 2020

Nauman B, 'Vanguard Ditches Over Two Dozen Stocks from ESG Funds' *Financial Times* (12 August 2019) <www.ft.com/content/5b6caa5e-bd4f-11e9-89e2-41e555e96722> accessed 7 July 2020

'A New Deal Conference Papers' (*Institute for Corporate Governance and Finance and Rock Center for Corporate Governance* 2019) <www.law.nyu.edu/centers/icgf/events/new-deal-new-century>

Nolan MD and Sourgens FG, 'The Limits of Discretion? Self-Judging Emergency Clauses in International Investment Agreements' (2011) 362 Yearbook of International Investment Law and Policy

Nussbaum MC, *Creating Capabilities: The Human Development Approach* (Harvard UP 2011)

Office of the High Commissioner on Human Rights (OHCHR), 'Guiding Principles on Business and Human Rights' (United Nations 2011) HR/PUB/11/04

Office of the High Commissioner on Human Rights (OHCHR), 'International Investment Agreements (IIAs) and Human Rights' <www.ohchr.org/EN/Issues/Business/Pages/IIAs.aspx> accessed 14 May 2020

Pac Rim Cayman LLC v Republic of El Salvador, ICSID Case No ARB/09/12

Pantechniki SA Contractors & Engineers (Greece) v The Republic of Albania, ICSID Case No ARB/07/21, Award (30 July 2009)

Paparinskis M, 'Circumstances Precluding Wrongfulness in International Investment Law' (2016) 31 ICSID Review—Foreign Investment Law Journal 484

Paris Agreement 2015

Permanent Sovereignty Over Natural Resources 1963 (UN Document A/RES/1803(XVII))

Peter A Allard v Government of Barbados, PCA Case No 2012-06

Peterson A, 'Global Justice and Educating for Globally Oriented Citizenship' in Andrew Peterson and others (eds), *The Palgrave International Handbook of Education for Citizenship and Social Justice* (Palgrave Macmillan 2016)

Philip A, 'Extreme Poverty and Human Rights: Note/by the Secretary-General' (United Nations 2019) Report of the Special Rapporteur on Extreme Poverty and Human Rights A/74/493

Philip Morris Brand Sàrl (Switzerland), Philip Morris Products SA (Switzerland) and Abal Hermanos SA (Uruguay) v Oriental Republic of Uruguay, ICSID Case No ARB/10/7, Award (8 July 2016)

PNG Sustainable Development Program Ltd v Independent State of Papua New Guinea, ICSID Case No ARB/13/33

Pogge T, 'Real World Justice' (2005) 9 The Journal of Ethics 29

Pollan T, *Legal Framework for the Admission of FDI* (Eleven International Publishing 2006)

Pope & Talbot Inc v The Government of Canada, UNCITRAL, Award on the Merits of Phase 2 (10 April 2001)

Pressman L, 'Shell's Dutch Scheme Introduces Own ESG Benchmark' (*IPE*, 18 May 2020) <www.ipe.com/news/shells-dutch-scheme-introduces-own-esg-benchmark/10045688.article> accessed 13 July 2020

Principles for Responsible Investment (PRI), *A Blueprint for Responsible Investment: Genesis, Assumptions and Process* (PRI 2017)

Principles on Responsible Investment, 'About the PRI' (*PRI*) <www.unpri.org/pri/about-the-pri> accessed 1 April 2020

Putter S, 'The Netherlands Coal Phase-Out and the Resulting (RWE and Uniper) ICSID Arbitrations' (*Kluwer Arbitration Blog*, 24 August 2021) <http://arbitrationblog.kluwerarbitration.com/2021/08/24/the-netherlands-coal-phase-out-and-the-resulting-rwe-and-uniper-icsid-arbitrations/> accessed 11 July 2022

Quiborax SA and Non Metallic Minerals SA v Plurinational State of Bolivia, ICSID Case No ARB/06/2, Award (16 September 2015)

Radi Y, 'International Investment Law and Development: A History of Two Concepts' in Stephan Schill, Christian J Tams and Rainer Hofmann (eds), *International Investment Law and Development: Bridging the Gap* (Edward Elgar Publishing 2015)

Rawson S, 'Decent Work Is in Crisis, Investors Could Start by Driving Corporate Disclosure' (*Responsible Investor*, 7 October 2020)

Reinisch A, 'Necessity in Investment Arbitration' in IF Dekker and E Hey (eds), *Netherlands Yearbook of International Law Volume 41, 2010: Necessity Across International Law* (TMC Asser Press 2011)

Reinisch A, *Advanced Introduction to International Investment Law* (Edward Elgar Publishing 2020)

Rockhopper Italia SpA, Rockhopper Mediterranean Ltd, and Rockhopper Exploration Plc v Italian Republic, ICSID Case No ARB/17/14

Rodrik D, *Straight Talk on Trade* (Princeton UP 2018)

Rodrik D, 'Putting Global Governance in Its Place' (2020) 35 The World Bank Research Observer 1

RWE AG and RWE Eemshaven Holding II BV v Kingdom of the Netherlands, ICSID Case No ARB/21/4

Saba Fakes v Republic of Turkey, ICSID Case No ARB/07/20, Award (14 July 2010)

Salacuse JW, *The Law of Investment Treaties* (2nd edn, OUP 2015)

Salini Costruttori SpA and Italstrade SpA v Kingdom of Morocco, ICSID Case No ARB/00/4, Award (31 July 2001)

Salomon ME, 'From NIEO to Now and the Unfinishable Story of Economic Justice' (2013) 62 The International and Comparative Law Quarterly 31

Sands P, 'International Courts and the Application of the Concept of "Sustainable Development"' (1999) 3 Max Planck Yearbook of United Nations Law Online 389

Schill SW, 'Fair and Equitable Treatment under Investment Treaties as an Embodiment of the Rule of Law' (Institute for International Law and Justice 2006) Global Administrative Law Series IILJ Working Paper 2006/6 <www.iilj.org/publications/fair-and-equitable-treatment-under-investment-treaties-as-an-embodiment-of-the-rule-of-law/> accessed 8 March 2020

Schill SW, 'Revisiting a Landmark: Indirect Expropriation and Fair and Equitable Treatment in the ICSID Case Tecmed' (2006) 3 Transnational Dispute Management

Schill SW and Briese R, '"If the State Considers": Self-Judging Clauses in International Dispute Settlement' (2009) 13 Max Planck Yearbook of United Nations Law Online 61

Schill SW, Tams CJ and Hofmann R, 'International Investment Law and Development: Friends or Foes?' in *International Investment Law and Development: Bridging the Gap* (Edward Elgar Publishing 2015)

Schneiderman D, 'Judicial Politics and International Investment Arbitration: Seeking an Explanation for Conflicting Outcomes' (2010) 30 Northwestern Journal of International Law & Business 383

Schreuer C, *The ICSID Convention: A Commentary* (2nd edn, CUP 2009)

Schwab K, 'Davos Manifesto 2020: The Universal Purpose of a Company in the Fourth Industrial Revolution' <www.weforum.org/agenda/2019/12/davos-manifesto-2020-the-universal-purpose-of-a-company-in-the-fourth-industrial-revolution/>

Sempra Energy International v Argentine Republic, ICSID Case No ARB/02/16, Award (28 September 2007)

Sen A, 'Well-Being, Agency and Freedom: The Dewey Lectures 1984' (1985) 82 The Journal of Philosophy 169

Sen A, *Development as Freedom* (OUP 2001)

Sen A, *Inequality Reexamined* (OUP 1995)

Shearman & Sterling, Columbia Law School, and United Nations Commission on International Trade Law (UNCITRAL), 'Article V—Guide—NYCG 1958' (*1958 New York Convention Guide*) <http://newyorkconvention1958.org/index.php?lvl=cmspage&pageid=10&menu=730&opac_view=-1> accessed 7 August 2020

Shihata IF, 'Toward a Greater Depoliticization of Investment Disputes: The Roles of ICSID and MIGA' in Gero Verheyen, Srilal M Perera and Kevin W Lu (eds), *Investing with Confidence: Understanding Political Risk Management in the 21st Century* (World Bank Group 2009)

Shumba EM, *FOSA Country Report—Zimbabwe* (Food and Agriculture Organization (FAO) 2001)

Siemens AG v The Argentine Republic, ICSID Case No ARB/02/8, Award (17 January 2007)

Sinha R and Datta M, 'Institutional Investments and Responsible Investing' in Magdalena Ziolo and Bruno S Sergi (eds), *Financing Sustainable Development: Key Challenges and Prospects* (Springer International Publishing 2019)

SolEs Badajoz GmbH v Kingdom of Spain, ICSID Case No ARB/15/38, Award (31 July 2019)

Sornarajah M, 'Developing Countries in the Investment Treaty System: A Law for Need or a Law for Greed?' in Stephan W Schill, Christian J Tams and Hofmann Rainer (eds), *International Investment Law and Development: Bridging the Gap* (Edward Elgar Publishing 2015)

Sornarajah M, *The International Law on Foreign Investment* (4th edn, CUP 2017)

Stec S and Eckstein G, 'Of Solemn Oaths and Obligations: The Environmental Impact of the ICJ's Decision in the Case of the Gabcikovo-Nagymaros Project' (1998) 8 Yearbook of International Environmental Law 41

Steer A and Wade-Gery W, 'Sustainable Development: Theory and Practice for a Sustainable Future' (1993) 1 Sustainable Development 23

Stellner C, Klein C and Zwergel B, 'Corporate Social Responsibility and Eurozone Corporate Bonds: The Moderating Role of Country Sustainability' (2015) 59 Journal of Banking & Finance 538

Stone-Sweet A, 'Investor-State Arbitration: Proportionality's New Frontier' (2010) 4 Law & Ethics of Human Rights 48

Stone-Sweet A and Grisel F, *The Evolution of International Arbitration: Judicialization, Governance, Legitimacy* (OUP 2017)

Stout LA, 'New Thinking on Shareholder Primacy' (2012) 2 Accounting, Economics, and Law: A Convivium

Stout LA, *The Shareholder Value Myth: How Putting Shareholders First Harms Investors, Corporations, and the Public* (Berrett-Koehler Publishers 2012)

Suez, Sociedad General de Aguas de Barcelona SA and Interagua Servicios Integrales de Agua SA v Argentine Republic, ICSID Case No ARB/03/17, Decision on Liability (30 July 2010)

Técnicas Medioambientales Tecmed SA v The United Mexican States, ICSID Case No ARB (AF)/00/2, Award (29 May 2003)

Tienhaara K and others, 'Investor-State Disputes Threaten the Global Green Energy Transition' (2022) 376 Science 701

Tietje C, 'The Right to Development within the International Economic Legal Order' in Ernst-Ulrich Petersmann and others (eds), *Reflections on the Constitutionalisation of International Economic Law: Liber Amicorum for Ernst-Ulrich Petersmann* (Martinus Nijhoff Publishers 2014)

Titi A, *The Right to Regulate in International Investment Law* (Nomos 2014)

Transforming Our World: The 2030 Agenda for Sustainable Development 2015 (UN Document A/RES/70/1)

Trujillo E, 'Balancing Sustainability, the Right to Regulate, and the Need for Investor Protection: Lessons from the Trade Regime' (2018) 59 Boston College Law Review 2735

Tzouvala N, 'Full Protection and Security (for Racial Capitalism)' (2022) 25 Journal of International Economic Law 224

UNEP Statement of Commitment by Financial Institutions (FI) on Sustainable Development 1992

Uniper SE, *Uniper Benelux Holding BV and Uniper Benelux NV v Kingdom of the Netherlands*, ICSID Case No ARB/21/22

United Nations, 'Background' (*United Nations Millennium Development Goals and Beyond* 2015) <www.un.org/millenniumgoals/bkgd.shtml> accessed 3 July 2020

United Nations Commission on International Trade Law (UNCITRAL), 'Reform Options (Tabular Presentation)' (2019) A/CN.9/WG.III/WP.166/Add.1 <https://uncitral.un.org/en/reformoptions> accessed 14 May 2020

United Nations Conference on Environment and Development (UNCED), 'Agenda 21: Programme of Action for Sustainable Development: Rio Declaration on Environment and Development' (United Nations 1994)

United Nations Department of Economic and Social Affairs (DESA), 'Monterrey Consensus on Financing for Development' (United Nations 2003) Report of the International Conference on Financing for Development, Monterrey, Mexico, 18–22 March 2002

United Nations Department of Economic and Social Affairs (DESA), 'How Can Investors Move from Greenwashing to SDG-Enabling?' (2020) UN/DESA Policy Brief #77 <www.un.org/development/desa/dpad/publication/un-desa-policy-brief-77-how-can-investors-move-from-greenwashing-to-sdg-enabling/> accessed 7 July 2020

United Nations Department of Economic and Social Affairs (DESA), 'Our Work' (*Global Investors for Sustainable Development Alliance*) <www.gisdalliance.org/our-work> accessed 27 February 2021

United Nations Environment Programme (UNEP), 'Emissions Gap Report 2019' (United Nations 2019) <https://www.unep.org/resources/emissions-gap-report-2019>

United Nations Environment Programme (UNEP), 'Green Economy' (*Regional Initiatives*) <www.unenvironment.org/regions/asia-and-pacific/regional-initiatives/supporting-resource-efficiency/green-economy> accessed 23 July 2020

United Nations Environment Programme Finance Initiative (UNEP FI), 'Background' <www.unepfi.org/about/background/> accessed 24 February 2021

United Nations Environment Programme Finance Initiative (UNEP FI), 'United Nations-Convened Net-Zero Asset Owner Alliance' <www.unepfi.org/net-zero-alliance/> accessed 3 March 2021

United Nations Framework Convention on Climate Change (UNFCCC), 'Nationally Determined Contributions (NDCs)' <https://unfccc.int/process-and-meetings/the-paris-agreement/the-paris-agreement/nationally-determined-contributions-ndcs> accessed 15 July 2020

United Nations Framework Convention on Climate Change (UNFCCC), 'What Is Transparency and Reporting?' (*Transparency and Reporting*) <https://unfccc.int/process-and-meetings/transparency-and-reporting/the-big-picture/what-is-transparency-and-reporting> accessed 15 July 2020

United Nations Framework Convention on Climate Change 1992 <https://en.wikipedia.org/wiki/United_Nations_Framework_Convention_on_Climate_Change>

United Nations General Assembly, 'Report of the World Commission on Environment and Development: "Our Common Future"' (1987) UNEP/GC/14/13 <http://digitallibrary.un.org/record/133790> accessed 18 February 2020

United Nations General Assembly, 'Seventy-Third Session Item 18 (b) of the Provisional Agenda, Macroeconomic Policy Questions, International Financial System and Development, Report of the Secretary-General' (2018) A/73/280 <www.un.org/ga/search/view_doc.asp?symbol=A/73/280> accessed 2 March 2020

United Nations Inter-Agency Task Force on Financing for Development, 'Financing for Sustainable Development Report 2019' (United Nations 2019) Report of the Inter-agency Task Force on Financing for Development E/FFDF/2019

United Nations Inter-Agency Task Force on Financing for Development, 'Financing for Sustainable Development Report 2020' (United Nations 2020) Report of the Inter-agency Task Force on Financing for Development E/FFDF/2020

United Nations Inter-Agency Task Force on Financing for Development, 'Encouraging Quality Direct Investments' (United Nations) <https://developmentfinance.un.org/encouraging-quality-direct-investment> accessed 7 July 2020

United Nations Inter-Agency Task Force on Financing for Development, 'Private Sector Efforts and Initiatives on Environmental, Social and Governance (ESG) Factors' (United Nations) <https://developmentfinance.un.org/private-sector-efforts-and-initiatives-environmental-social-and-governance-esg-factors> accessed 7 July 2020

United Nations Office of the High Commissioner for Human Rights (OHCHR), *Realizing the Right to Development: Essays in Commemoration of 25 Years of the United Nations Declaration on the Right to Development* (United Nations 2013)

United Nations Office of the High Commissioner for Human Rights (OHCHR), 'Background on the Right to Development' (*Development Is a Human Right*) <www.ohchr.org/EN/Issues/Development/Pages/Backgroundrtd.aspx> accessed 1 July 2020

United Nations Office of the High Commissioner for Human Rights (OHCHR), 'The Right to Development at a Glance' (Development and Economic and Social Issues Branch (DESIB), Research and Right to Development Division (RRDD)) <www.un.org/en/events/righttodevelopment/pdf/rtd_at_a_glance.pdf>

United Nations Sustainable Development Group (UNSDG), 'The Human Rights Based Approach to Development Cooperation Towards a Common Understanding Among UN Agencies' <https://unsdg.un.org/resources/human-rights-based-approach-development-cooperation-towards-common-understanding-among-un> accessed 18 February 2020

United Nations Sustainable Stock Exchanges (SSE) Initiative, 'About the SSE Initiative' <https://sseinitiative.org/about/>

United Nations Trade and Development (UNCTAD), 'Trade and Development Report, 2013: Adjusting to the Changing Dynamics of the World Economy' (United Nations 2013) UNCTAD/TDR/2013

United Nations Trade and Development (UNCTAD), 'Investment Policy Framework for Sustainable Development' (United Nations 2015) UNCTAD/DIAE/PCB/2015/5

United Nations Trade and Development (UNCTAD), 'Making the International Financial Architecture Work for Development' (United Nations 2015) UNCTAD/TDR/2015

United Nations Trade and Development (UNCTAD), 'World Investment Report 2017: Investment and the Digital Economy' (United Nations 2017) UNCTAD/WIR/2017

United Nations Trade and Development (UNCTAD), 'Reform Package for the International Investment Regime' (United Nations 2018)

United Nations Trade and Development (UNCTAD), 'World Investment Report 2018: Investment and New Industrial Policies' (United Nations 2018) UNCTAD/WIR/2018

United Nations Trade and Development (UNCTAD), 'World Investment Report 2019: Special Economic Zones' (United Nations 2019) UNCTAD/WIR/2019

United Nations Trade and Development (UNCTAD), 'World Investment Report 2020: International Production Beyond the Pandemic' (United Nations 2020) UNCTAD/WIR/2020

United Nations Trade and Development (UNCTAD), 'Treaty-Based Investor—State Dispute Settlement Cases and Climate Action' (United Nations 2022) Issue 4

United Nations Trade and Development (UNCTAD), 'Goal 8: Decent Work and Economic Growth' (*SDG Pulse*) <https://sdgpulse.unctad.org/sdgs/goal-8-decent-work-and-economic-growth/> accessed 27 February 2020

United Nations Trade and Development (UNCTAD), *Fair and Equitable Treatment* (United Nations 1999)

United Nations-Convened Net-Zero Asset Owner Alliance, 'Collective Commitment Document' <www.unepfi.org/wordpress/wp-content/uploads/2019/09/AOACollectiveCommitment.pdf>

Urbaser SA and Consorcio de Aguas Bilbao Bizkaia, Bilbao Biskaia Ur Partzuergoa v The Argentine Republic, ICSID Case No ARB/07/26, Award (8 December 2016)

Venzke I, 'Possibilities of the Past: Histories of the NIEO and the Travails of Critique' (2018) 20 Journal of the History of International Law/Revue d'histoire du droit international 263

Voigt C, *Sustainable Development as a Principle of International Law: Resolving Conflicts between Climate Measures and WTO Law* (Martinus Nijhoff Publishers 2009)

World Bank Group (WBG), *Advancing Sustainable Development: The World Bank and Agenda 21* (WBG 1997) 19

World Duty Free Company v Republic of Kenya, ICSID Case No Arb/00/7, Award (4 October 2006)

Yannaca-Small C, 'Fair and Equitable Treatment Standard: Recent Developments' in August Reinisch (ed), *Standards of Investment Protection* (OUP 2008)

Yearbook of the International Law Commission 2001, Volume 2 (Part 2) (United Nations 2007) A/CN.4/SER.A/2001/Add.1 (Part 2)

Zeng Y and others, 'Environmental Destruction Not Avoided with the Sustainable Development Goals' [2020] Nature Sustainability 1

Zhu Y, 'Do Clarified Indirect Expropriation Clauses in International Investment Treaties Preserve Environmental Regulatory Space' (2020) 60 Harvard International Law Journal 377

3 International investment–sustainable development framework

The main strategies in the Framework can be divided into those that are implemented before the entry into an international investment agreement (IIA; pre-admission) and those following entry (post-admissions). At the pre-admissions stage, key strategies include the following:

1 Clear promissory terms of the investment in respect to the right and obligations of both the host state and investor(s);
2 Coherent rather than competing national policy framework that is cross-sectoral in its treatment of international investment, or special administrative zones with separate policy applications;
3 Screening and targeting investment(s) based on national circumstances and value-added in the domestic context; and
4 Harmonization and coordination between host states on best practices of both putative investors and host states in investment promotion activities.

Meanwhile, post-admission strategies include:

1 Maintaining supervisory, standard-setting, and control mechanisms to ensure dynamic policy adaptation to promote the public interest;
2 Reviewing in a timely and constant manner government policies that influence protected investments to ensure that they remain effective in contributing to national development;
3 Involving and encouraging transnational investors in promoting national public interests through self-regulation, corporate social responsibility (CSR), and encouraging vertical linkages; and
4 Installing and maintaining safeguards against abusive practices.

3.1 Background and scope

Despite the challenges beset against international investment, law, and their role in advancing sustainable development,[1] these issues are central to the UN approach

1 The United Nations Commission on Trade and Development openly recognize the risks of engaging in international investment agreements, such as a lack of mono-causality between investment

DOI: 10.4324/9781003495871-3

to development.[2] In the wording of the *Financing for Sustainable Development Report 2020*, private and public sector investment in infrastructure are the "basic building blocks that enable participation"[3] in a development agenda that pursues "sustained, more sustainable and resilient growth, decarbonization, and resource and energy efficiency".[4] Therein, international investment is viewed as a development pathway to "achieve rapid and sustained growth and structural transformation, by building domestic linkages" through global supply chains, providing an "escalator" to economic progress.[5]

While recognizing that international investment is "more than a flow of capital that can stimulate economic growth", there is a clear recognition within the UN that the positive development impacts of international investment "do not always materialize automatically".[6] Instead, international investment and its role in sustainable development represent "difficult policy choices among desired outcomes and significant trade-offs between objectives" that are economic and non-economic in nature.[7] These trade-offs can take place either pre- or post-admission of the foreign direct investment (FDI).[8] For example, pre-admission trade-offs include foreign investment laws and policies that contribute to "incentive wars",

---

agreements and foreign direct investment, asymmetries between the host state and the investor, neoliberal straightjacket effects on least development countries, and belligerent usages of investor-State dispute settlement (United Nations Commission on Trade and Development (UNCTAD), 'Investment Policy Framework for Sustainable Development' (2015) UNCTAD/DIAE/PCB/2015/5 74–75).

2 United Nations Economic and Social Commission for Asia and the Pacific (UNESCAP) very clearly substantiates this relationship: "[Foreign direct investment] can contribute to sustainable development in several important ways: through expanding access to markets, bringing in foreign exchange, contributing to skills development/human capital growth, technology transfer and increasing competition in local markets. It can also support indigenous industry upgrading in host economies and facilitate their enhanced participation in global value chains" (United Nations Economic and Social Commission for Asia and the Pacific (UNESCAP), 'Foreign Direct Investment and Sustainable Development in International Investment Governance' 90 <https://unescap.org/publications/studies-trade-investment-and-innovation-no-90-foreign-direct-investment-and-sustainable>).

3 United Nations Inter-Agency Task Force on Financing for Development, 'Financing for Sustainable Development Report 2020' (United Nations 2020) Report of the Inter-Agency Task Force on Financing for Development E/FFDF/2020 21.

4 United Nations Inter-Agency Task Force on Financing for Development, 'Financing for Sustainable Development Report 2020' (United Nations 2020) Report of the Inter-Agency Task Force on Financing for Development E/FFDF/2020 16.

5 United Nations Inter-Agency Task Force on Financing for Development, 'Financing for Sustainable Development Report 2020' (United Nations 2020) Report of the Inter-Agency Task Force on Financing for Development E/FFDF/2020 28.

6 United Nations Commission on Trade and Development (UNCTAD), 'World Investment Report 2012: Towards a New Generation of Investment Policies' (United Nations 2012) UNCTAD/WIR/2012 116.

7 United Nations Commission on Trade and Development (UNCTAD), 'World Investment Report 1998: Trends and Determinants' (United Nations 1998) 95.

8 United Nations Commission on Trade and Development (UNCTAD), 'World Investment Report 1999: Foreign Direct Investment and the Challenge of Development' (United Nations 1999) 154.

which refer to incentives offered by host governments seeking to attract foreign investment. As later explored in this chapter, these incentive wars can result in a "financial incentives–competition race towards the sky", which is when host states offer lucrative investment incentives that are untenable in the long-run, and/or a "policy-competition race towards the bottom", which is when host states overzealously liberalize governance structures that threaten the government's regulatory capacities.

Post-admission trade-offs refer to the harmful environmental, social, or economic consequences that can be directly or indirectly attributable to FDI. For instance, a greenfield FDI may result in the creation of hundreds of employment opportunities for nationals of the host state, but it may come at the cost of environmental degradation or crowding out domestic entrepreneurship. Elsewhere, the acquisition of a formerly state-owned power generation facility by a foreign investor may delay plans of transitioning the facility into generating renewable energy at the demand of shareholder interests.

Post-admissions measures to safeguard the public interest, primarily investment treaty arbitration, often results in unpredictable outcomes contingent on the arbitral tribunal and the extent to which they are willing to engage in a holistic analysis of government measures, foreign investments, and their impact on sustainable development. Yet as statement one in the previous chapter identified, these assessments remain incomplete. This chapter lays out the first half of this work's approach to supplementing that assessment, which is identified as the International Investment–Sustainable Development Framework (the "Framework"). Preceding this Framework is an institutional history of the evolving role of international investment in sustainable development within the UN system.

3.2 Institutional history of the framework

Continuing from the wider historical context was provided in Chapter 2, this section focuses on the normative content of the UN system's engagement of these issues. The significance of this endeavour is to demonstrate that while UN Trade and Development (UNCTAD) and the UN Commission on International Trade Law (UNCITRAL) spearhead the UN system's engagement on international investment and international investment law issues, they function within a conceptualization of development—and the role of investment in development—that extends throughout the entire system. Establishing this historical context identifies the basis upon which the Framework is constructed, leveraging the decades of evolutionary positioning that the UN system was able to refine over its history of engaging the nexus of international investment and sustainable development. This institutional history is divided into two parts: the first examines how the UN system has conceptualized the role of international investment in the process of development. The second turns to the UN system's engagement with issues of international investment law specifically.

3.2.1 UN system approach to international investment

Within the UN system, Financing for Development (FfD) is an important multilateral approach to defining the role of international investment in sustainable development.[9] FfD emphasized the centrality of international investment while also encouraging more stringent rules on investment governance and promotion. More specifically, it upheld a view that the performance and promotion of international investment should be evaluated on not only economic factors like job creation, but also all dimensions of sustainable development, such as its impact on social and environmental factors. Guiding that effort are central beliefs concerning the governance of FDI that can be identified in FfD, which include:

1 Assessments of the impacts of investment on sustainability are specific in their application to the host state;
2 Sectors connected to the Sustainable Development Goals (SDGs) key to the host state economy are prioritized for investment; and
3 Investment laws and policies are coherent with national sustainable development and innovation policies.[10]

Meanwhile, FfD recognized that overbearing conditions and administrative constraints can detract from potential investment inflows as investors are less inclined to commit. In doing so, FfD was an attempt to establish a balance between maximizing investment and ensuring the positive sustainable development impact of investment. This balance, which can be viewed as a "precautionary approach", is defined by three objectives that continue to guide the private sector engagement policy of the UN system.

1 The first objective is enhancing accountability by mandating sustainable development impact disclosures for shareholder-led corporate governance for both companies and foreign investment;
2 The second objective is incentivizing foreign investment and investors into aligning with sustainable development commitments of the host state through public policy and regulatory measures; and
3 The third objective is harmonizing the meaning, scope, and criteria of what qualifies as a Sustainable Investment.[11]

9 Financing for Development, now known as Financing for Sustainable Development, as described earlier in Chapter 2, is a process that follows up on the multilateral commitments on development finance made through the Monterrey Consensus (2002), Doha Declaration on Financing for Development (2008), and Addis Ababa Action Agenda (2015). While development finance includes a wide range of instruments, the Framework focuses specifically on international private finance.

10 United Nations Inter-Agency Task Force on Financing for Development, 'Financing for Sustainable Development Report 2020' (n 3) 66.

11 United Nations Inter-Agency Task Force on Financing for Development (n 3) 72–73. These are explored in greater depth in Chapter 4.

These three objectives help to identify the evolutionary positioning of the UN system,[12] where it is joined by other major international organizations such as the Organisation for Economic Cooperation and Development (OECD)[13] and the World Bank Group.[14]

UNCITRAL and UNCTAD predominately define the legal and policy stance of the UN system on FDI and international investment law. The evolutionary stance of the UN system, however, began earlier than UNCTAD and the UNCITRAL, originating in its efforts to enhance corporate governance within the realm of international law, state sovereignty in the right to regulate, and the pursuit of development. From that early stage, the UN system viewed the role of transnational corporations (TNCs) and international investment as paving development pathways, which were, however, conditional rather than automatic. To assist TNCs in fulfilling this function, the UN Centre on Transnational Corporations (UNCTC)[15] was established to administer the *Code of Conduct of Transnational Corporations* (1983).[16] Many of the core approaches of this ambitious document continue to

12 This evolutionary view was discussed in Chapter 2 of this work and generally refers to a perspective in the scholarship that promotes the role of international investment law in advancing sustainable development.

13 The OECD established its evolutionary stature early on in 1976 with its *Guidelines for Multinational Enterprises* that later was revised into the 2011 *Declaration on International Investment and Multinational Enterprises*. The preamble, for instance, begins the Declaration by making this view clear by recognizing that (1) international investment contributes to development of countries; (2) multinational enterprises play an important role in the process of international investment; (3) with an improved foreign investment climate, multinational enterprises can make positive contributions to sustainable development; and (4) the benefits of international investment are enhanced through international cooperation and a "balanced framework" (Organisation for Economic Cooperation and Development (OECD), *The OECD Declaration and Decisions on International Investment and Multinational Enterprises: Basic Texts* (OECD 2012) 4).

14 The World Bank Group in 1992 released the *Guidelines on the Treatment of Foreign Direct Investment*, which sought to "guide government behavior toward foreign investors" through a "general understanding of a desirable normative framework to guide future governmental conduct affecting foreign investment [such as] a sound legal framework, in terms of the availability of clear, stable and reasonable general rules as well as of honest and efficient mechanisms of implementation, enforcement and dispute settlement [as being] essential" (World Bank Group (WBG), 'Legal Framework for the Treatment of Foreign Investment, Volume II' (1992) Report to the Development Committee and Guidelines on the Treatment of Foreign Direct Investment 11).

15 For instance, the first edition of the World Investment Report, the flagship report of the UNCTC and later UNCTAD, identifies transnational corporations as "catalytic agents in the development of [least developed] countries" (United Nations Centre on Transnational Corporations (UNCTC), 'World Investment Report 1991: The Triad in Foreign Direct Investment' (United Nations 1991) ST/CTC/118 90). The interlinkages between FDI and its contribution to the development of the host state remains consistent: expanded trade, financing, and technology spillovers on top of domestic capital formation that can be channelled into improving capacities (United Nations Department of Economic and Social Development, 'World Investment Report 1992: Transnational Corporations as Engines of Growth' (United Nations 1992) ST/CTC/130 99).

16 UN engagement on transnational corporations began in the 1970s alongside the rising discontent towards the behaviour of transnational corporations from developed economies and the many controversies transnational corporations were found to be involved in, such as in South Africa. The

resonate in the evolutionary view taken up within the UN system. These include the right to regulate, which is featured prominently in the *Code of Conduct of Transnational Corporations*, such as in Articles 8 and 47:

> (8) Transnational corporations should/shall respect the right of each State to regulate and monitor accordingly the activities of their entities operating within its territory.
>
> (47) States have the right to regulate the entry and establishment of transnational corporations including determining the role that such corporations may play in economic and social development and prohibiting or limiting the extent of their presence in specific sectors.

A positive contribution to the host state as being a criterion of the conduct of TNCs was included in Article 9:

> Transnational corporations shall/should carry on their activities in conformity with the development policies, objectives and priorities set out by the Governments of the countries in which they operate and work seriously towards making a positive contribution to the achievement of such goals at the national and, as appropriate, the regional level, within the framework of regional integration programmes.

The World Investment Reports (WIRs), an annual flagship report by UNCTAD on global investment trends, policies, and laws, served, and in many ways continue to serve since its inaugural issue in the 1990s, as a means used to express the evolutionary stance of the UN system on the role of both international investment and international investment law in advancing sustainable development.[17] Broadly, this has and continues to be greater harmonization as a means to strengthen a "gradually emerging international legal framework for [foreign direct investment]", which can

---

UNCTC was established but they were ultimately unsuccessful, such as garnering consensus on the Code of Conduct. Many of the activities of the UNCTC were passed to UNCTAD. The comprehensive nature of the Code of Conduct was instead divided into issue-specific agreements and diluted. A more complete history and analysis can be found in Karl P Sauvant, 'The Negotiations of the United Nations Code of Conduct on Transnational Corporations: Experience and Lessons Learned' (2015) 16 The Journal of World Investment & Trade 11; Theodore H Moran, 'The United Nations and Transnational Corporations: A Review and a Perspective' (2009) 18 Transnational Corporations 91.

17 See, for instance, the front matter of World Investment Report 1993, which identifies the "objectives of the work programme [as including] to further the understanding of the nature of transnational corporations and of their economic, legal, political and social effects on home and host countries and in international relations, particularly between developed and developing countries" (United Nations Commission on Trade and Development (UNCTAD), 'World Investment Report 1993: Transnational Corporations and Integrated International Production' (United Nations 1993) ST/CTC/156 ii).

be seen as the starting point for the increased engagement by the UN system on issues of international investment law.[18] The WIRs together form the primary source of information in the construction of this Framework, not only for their multilateral scope, but also because they remain the most comprehensive treatment of international investment and international investment law in the context of sustainable development across the UN system.

The WIRs express policy positions regarding major issues in the international investment law–sustainable development nexus, which was discussed at greater length in the conceptual framework.[19] On the balance between investor rights and the state's right to regulate, the 1994 WIR identifies that:

> [T]he overall beneficial effects of the liberalization process depend, to a considerable extent, on the presence and, where necessary, the strengthening of controls aimed at ensuring the proper functioning of the market and promoting broader economic and social concerns. . . . In order to be beneficial, the liberalization of FDI policies should be accompanied by the kinds of legal and policy controls that are compatible with it, or indeed may be conditions for it.[20]

On standards of treatment towards the investor, which includes fair and equitable treatment (FET) and access to investment treaty arbitration, the UN system promotes a conditional affirmation of economic integration that is symbolic of the evolutionary view:

> [A] description or even an analysis of the liberalization process cannot involve a quest for perfection. It would be difficult to define in clear terms what constitutes a perfect investment regime, in terms of liberalization . . . from the viewpoint of a single investor . . . and the long-term interests of the countries concerned. Liberalization should, therefore, be introduced with care. Different industries may need to be approached differently, keeping in view the specific situation and objectives of a given country.[21]

Last, on matters concerning disputes between the international investor and host state, the WIRs advance the position that the settlement of such disputes must

18 United Nations Commission on Trade and Development (UNCTAD), 'World Investment Report 1993: Transnational Corporations and Integrated International Production' (United Nations 1993) ST/CTC/156 188.

19 Pillar One in Chapter 2.

20 United Nations Commission on Trade and Development (UNCTAD), 'World Investment Report 1994: Transnational Corporations, Employment and the Workplace' (United Nations 1994) UNCTAD/DTCI/10 287–88.

21 United Nations Commission on Trade and Development (UNCTAD), 'World Investment Report 1994: Transnational Corporations, Employment and the Workplace' (United Nations 1994) UNCTAD/DTCI/10 311.

equally consider both the actions of the host state and that of the TNC and/or investment in order to achieve "a more balanced appraisal of the facts of a dispute and of whether the [international investment agreement] has indeed been breached"[22]—a premise that inhabits a central tenet in the argument posited by this work.

This cautioned conviction in the centrality of international investment to the process of sustainable development claims an extensive presence, not only in the WIRs, but also throughout FfD. In that sense, rather than viewing international investment and its governance as solutions, the UN system views them as challenges to FfD that if addressed can then unlock the resources needed to achieve a sustainable future.

3.2.2 *UN system approach to international investment law*

The latter half of this institutional history of the UN system turns its focus to matters of international investment law. More specifically, this section examines the main attempts advanced within the UN system for addressing the nexus between sustainable development and international investment law. In doing so, this section tests how and to what extent the UN system has in practice interacted with the international investment law regime.

As identified in both Chapters 1 and 2, the nexus of sustainable development and international investment law and policy is a contentious one. The system of international investment governance currently in place does not systematically advance multilaterally negotiated international public interest objectives like the SDGs.

3.2.2.1 *Investment treaty arbitration reform*

As discussed in Chapter 2, the high costs of investment treaty arbitration, both financially and administrative for governments involved, particularly for developing economies, has been the target for enduring criticism. There have been efforts to address the prohibitive character of investment treaty arbitration by modifying the procedural and substantive elements of the practice, at the centre of which have been the negotiations taking place through the UNCITRAL. In 2017, the UNCITRAL identified reforming investor-State dispute settlement as a key element of their work plan with the start of Working Group III, summarizing many of the challenges to not only the practice of investment treaty arbitration, but international investment law in general.[23]

22 United Nations Commission on Trade and Development (UNCTAD), 'World Investment Report 2008: Transnational Corporations and the Infrastructure Challenge' (United Nations 2008) UNCTAD/WIR/2008 168.

23 These challenges are identified in United Nations Commission on International Trade Law (UNCITRAL), 'Possible Reform of Investor-State Dispute Settlement (ISDS)' (United Nations General Assembly 2019) A/CN.9/WG.III/WP.166, para 5. They include (1) a lack of consistency, coherence, predictability and correctness of arbitral decisions; (2) a lack of apparent lack of independence and impartiality of arbitrators and decision makers; (3) the cost, duration and allocation of costs; and (4)

Several reform options have been identified through Working Group III to better align the practice of investment treaty arbitration with the demands of development, within which improved oversight over and access to investor-State dispute settlement has been identified as two aspects of needed reform. The second of these has been particularly central to the discussion, where the UNCITRAL has called for the establishment of an advisory centre that would embody an expanded beneficiaries approach to investor-State dispute settlement that augments its capacities to cater to the needs of developing economies and small- and medium-sized enterprises.[24]

Other areas of reform include addressing concurrent or parallel proceedings as an abusive practice forcing a host state to "defend several claims in relation to the same measure, with possibly the same economic damage at stake, leading to a duplication of efforts, additional costs, procedural unfairness and potentially contradictory outcomes"[25]—a particularly egregious practice that can overburden the administrative capacities of development states.

Perhaps more remarkable reform measures considered by the UNCITRAL include the creation of stand-alone appellate mechanisms and a standing mechanism for the resolution of international investment disputes that would help replace the inconsistent discretion arising from ad hoc tribunals.[26] The grounds of appeal under discussion by the UNCITRAL Working Group are broad and widely capable of overturning an arbitral decision on "manifest errors" in the interpretation of the law and appreciation of the facts including domestic legislation.[27] These bodies would constitute a two-tier dispute settlement system, with the standing body as a dispute tribunal and an appellate body as an appeals tribunal.[28]

The UNCITRAL continues to address challenges facing the investment treaty arbitration system, a few of which were raised in Chapter 2, but procedural and substantive considerations of sustainable development remain limited.

---

the use and influence of third-party financing. The UNCITRAL has been addressing these concerns through multilateral and multistakeholder negotiations since the inception of Working Group III, engaging with much of the core debates surrounding investment treaty arbitration as a whole.

24 United Nations Commission on International Trade Law (UNCITRAL), 'Report of Working Group III (Investor-State Dispute Settlement Reform) on the Work of Its Thirty-Eighth Session' (United Nations General Assembly 2019) A/CN.9/1004 paras 28–39.

25 United Nations Commission on International Trade Law (UNCITRAL), 'Possible Future Work in the Field of Dispute Settlement: Concurrent Proceedings in International Arbitration' (United Nations General Assembly 2017) A/CN.9/915 para 7.

26 United Nations Commission on International Trade Law (UNCITRAL), 'Report of Working Group III (Investor-State Dispute Settlement Reform) on the Work of Its Thirty-Eighth Session' (n 24) paras 26–30.

27 United Nations Commission on International Trade Law (UNCITRAL), 'Possible Reform of Investor-State Dispute Settlement (ISDS): Draft Statute of a Standing Mechanism for the Resolution of International Investment Disputes' (United Nations General Assembly 2024) A/CN.9/WG.III/WP.239 Art 29.

28 United Nations Commission on International Trade Law (UNCITRAL), 'Possible Reform of Investor-State Dispute Settlement (ISDS): Annotations to the Draft Statute of a Standing Mechanism for the Resolution of International Investment Disputes' (United Nations General Assembly 2024) A/CN.9/WG.III/WP.240 Art 3.

3.2.2.2 Progressive international investment policy

A more direct encounters between the UN system and international investment law than its ongoing work on investment treaty arbitration reform involves its technical interventions on investment agreements and policy. One of the most notable accomplishments by the UN system in this regard is UNCTAD Investment Policy Framework for Sustainable Development, which was launched in 2012 "to serve as a point of reference for policymakers in formulating national investment policies, in negotiating or reviewing [international investment agreements], and in designing concrete policy initiatives to promote investment in priority sectors for sustainable development".[29] Representative of the UN systems' overall approach to the nexus of international investment and sustainable development,[30] the Investment Policy Framework for Sustainable Development embodies the iconic precautionary balancing between host state obligations and investor protections, between the benefits and responsibilities of investment liberalization for stakeholders, and between national rules and the expectations of the TNC as a foreign investor.[31]

The Investment Policy Framework is led by ten core principles that embody both provisions common to IIAs as well as the key normative features of the evolutionary stance of the UN system.[32] Common provisions include legitimate expectations and transparency concerning administrative procedures; minimum standards of treatment that includes non-discrimination towards foreign investors, full protection and security, access to third-party dispute settlement, and the free movement of capital; proportionality in regulatory measures that are the least restrictive option available; and an "openness" to investment. These are the investor rights and protections that UNCTAD identifies as fundamental to the international investment law regime.

While the inclusion of these principles essentially sidesteps many of the central contentions facing the international investment–sustainable development nexus identified in Chapters 1 and 2, the Investment Policy Framework also identifies modes of policy intervention wherein states may advance their sustainable development agendas.[33] These modes of policy intervention are closely aligned with the Framework constructed in this chapter, specifically in relation to:

1 *Policy coherent investment*

Development-centred policy that is coherent with national development planning and applies stakeholder-centric public and corporate governance that is

29 United Nations Commission on Trade and Development (UNCTAD), 'Investment Policy Framework for Sustainable Development' (n 1) 9.

30 The Investment Policy Framework is identified as seeking to "[foster] sustainable development and inclusive growth through investment [that] requires a balance of promotion [of foreign investment] and regulation" (United Nations Commission on Trade and Development (UNCTAD), 'Investment Policy Framework for Sustainable Development' (n 1) 47).

31 United Nations Commission on Trade and Development (UNCTAD), 'Investment Policy Framework for Sustainable Development' (n 1) 18–19.

32 United Nations Commission on Trade and Development (UNCTAD), 'Investment Policy Framework for Sustainable Development' (n 1) 30–36.

33 United Nations Commission on Trade and Development (UNCTAD), 'Investment Policy Framework for Sustainable Development' (n 1) 72–79.

adaptive and progressive. This involves shaping a coherent place for international investment policy within the larger nexus of national policies regarding the country's public interests. However, this can also mean being more selective in the types of investments admitted in either a positive or negative list approach,[34] such as those that may promote or protect key strategic sectors during a particular phase a state's development planning keeping in mind that entering into an IIA may result in unexpected domestic political and economic consequences.

2 *Reserving the right to regulate for the public interest*

Carving out policy spaces that reserve the right to regulate for the public interest when negotiating IIAs. This can involve clarifying stipulations concerning the conduct of the investor during operation and post-operation phases, such as observing national laws and regulation on socioeconomic activity and environmental responsibilities. Furthermore, enshrining the right to regulate whether through reservation or exception[35] in application to substantive obligations imbued in IIAs, such as FET, to provide the flexibility needed to respond to changing circumstances like global pandemics, financial crises or the threat thereof, and climate change. States may approach IIAs with a more selective approach to market liberalization, foregoing the more sweeping liberalization of the economy that can threaten national sustainable development planning.[36]

3 *Multilateral coordination and processes*

Engaging in multilateral fora that can facilitate international coordination and coordination such as in disputes, collective negotiations, and more generally issues of international investment law. Beyond engagement is to harmonize with existing multilateral fora and instruments that can help promote the universal adoption of key efforts that safeguard global progress towards sustainable development, such as the SDGs. Coordination and harmonization of this kind can take place at regional and/or superregional levels in connection to high sustainable development impact priority areas such as infrastructure. Examples of multilateral cooperation include enabling joint cross-border projects as well as interpretive mechanisms that clarify and bring greater certitude to investment agreement provisions.[37]

34 United Nations Commission on Trade and Development (UNCTAD), 'Investment Policy Framework for Sustainable Development' (n 1) 115–16.

35 United Nations Commission on Trade and Development (UNCTAD), 'Investment Policy Framework for Sustainable Development' (n 1) 117.

36 United Nations Commission on Trade and Development (UNCTAD), 'Investment Policy Framework for Sustainable Development' (n 1) 84–85.

37 United Nations Commission on Trade and Development (UNCTAD), 'Investment Policy Framework for Sustainable Development' (n 1) 130.

4 *Measuring development impact*

Using key indicators to measure "core development contributions of private investments".[38] While the methodologies are diverse, UNCTAD identifies the need for measurements through specific indicators under broad areas of development. For instance, an environmental impact indicator would include greenhouse gas emissions, carbon offset/credits, and carbon credit revenues. Such methodologies, including the creation of indicators and the use of data, closely resemble the assessment methodologies employed in portfolio investment, which Chapter 4 explores in further detail.

3.2.2.3 Comprehensive international investment agreements

By identifying that many of the most persistent issues facing IIAs were a product of outdated treaty provisions, UNCTAD began an ambitious push through the Reform Package for the International Investment Regime (hereinafter "Reform Package") to reform old generation investment agreements that were predominately skewed towards investor protections at the expense of safeguards for the host state.[39] By seeking to reform the way that IIAs were negotiated and implemented, the UN sought to align international investment treaty practice to align more closely with its broader approach towards international investment and sustainable development.

Broadly, the recommendations in the Reform Package address incompatibilities between the existing international investment treaty regime and many of the objectives identified in the Framework developed in this chapter. In doing so, the Reform Package configures systematic approaches to ensuring that future agreements would remain compatible.[40] For example, by revisiting or "stocktaking" existing IIAs, the Reform Package encouraged states to reconsider their obligations as hosts to international investment by revaluating which IIAs were policy coherent with the current national development agenda.[41]

After having identified which agreements needed to be addressed, the Reform Package encourages a bilateral or multilateral approach to negotiating revisions on such matters as phasing out old generation investment treaties that do not reflect the interests of sustainable development. This was to ensure that the termination and sunset provisions of treaties were based on common standards and encouraged rather than chilled economic relations. One recommended means to pursue this

38 United Nations Commission on Trade and Development (UNCTAD), 'Investment Policy Framework for Sustainable Development' (n 1) 53.

39 United Nations Commission on Trade and Development (UNCTAD), 'Reform Package for the International Investment Regime' (2018) 16–19.

40 United Nations Commission on Trade and Development (UNCTAD), 'Reform Package for the International Investment Regime' (2018) 26–29.

41 United Nations Commission on Trade and Development (UNCTAD), 'Reform Package for the International Investment Regime' (2018) 98.

strategy is through consolidated agreements or protocols that were progressive in their treatment of phenomena in flux like climate change as well as comprehensive in that provisions were expansive, dealing with matters that were not restricted to trade, but also the sustainable development-related impacts of investment.[42] To help guide these efforts, the Reform Package refers to the value of producing model IIAs that emphasize domestic needs in connection to FDI to garner stakeholder consensus on priority areas preceding treaty negotiations. Model treaties and subsequent changes to their provisions also serves as a signal of a state's investment policy priorities and objectives.[43]

Last, the Reform Package recommends following up on the (re)negotiation on IIAs with multilateral backstopping against the recurrence of issues addressed through national reform measures by harmonizing to multilaterally agreed standards on contentious aspects of IIAs.[44] For instance, one example would be aligning transparency rules regarding investment treaty arbitration proceedings with the UN Convention on Transparency in Treaty-based Investor-State Arbitration (2014). One means through which this is possible is joint interpretative mechanisms, which are bilaterally or multilaterally shared frameworks of interpreting provisions in IIAs.[45] The Reform Package advocates two overarching strategies when determining the scope of an IIA's application.

1 *Limitation*

In response to the most-favoured nation (MFN) clause as a means for investors to both treaty shop for the most favourable conditions as well as evade progressive reform measures by host states, the Reform Package recommends either omitting or limiting MFN in application to investment law and policy.[46] Legitimate expectations and stabilization clauses have had the effect of freezing the substantive protections offered to investor, thereby obstructing the effectiveness of reform. The Reform Package suggests qualifying the FET standard with a positive or negative list of applicability, through which the FET standard may not apply to certain areas of law and policy, such as sustainable development, or certain sectors that have high public interest impact.[47]

42 United Nations Commission on Trade and Development (UNCTAD), 'Reform Package for the International Investment Regime' (2018) 80.
43 United Nations Commission on Trade and Development (UNCTAD), 'Reform Package for the International Investment Regime' (2018) 96.
44 United Nations Commission on Trade and Development (UNCTAD), 'Reform Package for the International Investment Regime' (2018) 78.
45 United Nations Commission on Trade and Development (UNCTAD), 'Reform Package for the International Investment Regime' (2018) 33.
46 United Nations Commission on Trade and Development (UNCTAD), 'Reform Package for the International Investment Regime' (2018) 34.
47 United Nations Commission on Trade and Development (UNCTAD), 'Reform Package for the International Investment Regime' (2018) 36.

2 *Adaptation*

Indirect or creeping expropriation claims have been lodged against legitimate government measures, obstructing authorities from the dynamic policy powers they need to adjust national policymaking to fit changing circumstances or new ambitions, such as those in line with the SDGs. Providing for this adaptability includes clearly identifying legitimate public interest objectives in strong and hortatory language in a manner that reconciles potential conflict between public policy and IIA provisions.

For example, providing adaptability about the stringency of testing the legitimacy of exceptions from treaty obligations in instances involving public interest objectives like sustainable development by moving from a test of necessity (was the measure necessary to achieve the intended result) to one of good faith (measures or investments that were designed to achieve the intended result).[48] This adaptability can be in the form of the amount of compensation following nationalization of foreign asset(s) that is proportional to the public policy objective, such as sustainable development, pursuant by the measure.[49]

3 *Clarification*

In 2020, UNCTAD released the *International Investment Agreements Reform Accelerator*, further addressing the slow rate of reform citing the fact that all of the investor-State dispute settlement cases initiated in 2019 and 99% of the total number of known disputes have been on the basis of IIAs concluded before 2012.[50] While the Accelerator identifies numerous core challenges behind this lagging reform, many of which were identified in the Reform Package, it adds two crucial, largely unmentioned dimensions: (1) the definition of investment and (2) the definition of the investor.

Clarification of these definitions, which affect the scope of protected investments, responds to one of the most persistent dismissals of the materiality of sustainable development–related claims in investment treaty arbitration, as discussed throughout this chapter. Tribunals have regularly dismissed the jurisdiction of these claims within ICSID Convention Article 25 and thereby the general competencies of the Tribunal in contemplating extralegal questions. The Accelerator suggests a clarification of the requirements of a protected investment by more explicitly referencing sustainable development. By conditioning protected investments as those that can qualify as sustainable development–aligned investments, which are further defined in Chapter 4, the Accelerator

48 United Nations Commission on Trade and Development (UNCTAD), 'Reform Package for the International Investment Regime' (2018) 40.

49 United Nations Commission on Trade and Development (UNCTAD), 'Reform Package for the International Investment Regime' (2018) 37–38.

50 United Nations Commission on Trade and Development (UNCTAD), 'International Investment Agreements Reform Accelerator' (2020) UNCTAD/DIAE/PCB/INF/2020/8 2.

suggests that jurisdictional questions that involve sustainable development–related claims can be addressed through a denial-of-benefits process.[51]

3.2.2.4 Comprehensive and progressive instruments

The idea of "progressive" and "comprehensive" international investment law instruments is central to the evolutionary approach mounted by the UN system and thus the approach taken up by this work. To supplement the institutional history presented above, this section provides examples of investment agreements that embody these traits. While far from a comprehensive treatment of comprehensive and progressive IIAs, they sufficiently delineate the expansive language of new generation agreements.

Beginning with the Trans-Pacific Strategic Economic Partnership Agreement, the Trans-Pacific Partnership (TPP) took form after the United States expressed an interest in financial liberalization in 2008. While these negotiations quickly fell apart with the start of a new and less interested US administration, the TPP served to provide the basis of integrating the Association of Southeast Asian Nations (ASEAN) economies into a superregional economic agreement. Of particular interest was Viet Nam at that time was the involvement of Viet Nam, which was at the time had a very much state planned and controlled economy.[52] With the continued absence of the United States, the remaining parties to the TPP formed the CPTPP largely through the efforts of Japan. Those within the ASEAN who have sought an ASEAN-led agreement have pushed for the Regional Comprehensive Economic Partnership (RCEP). This aspect of the RCEP also presented a feasible option for China, Japan, and the Republic of Korea to enter into an economic agreement that was less hampered by political tensions.[53] The CPTPP entered in force in December 2018, though it did so without the United States, South Korea, and China.

Like the CETA, the CPTPP attempts to "to improve precision in substantive obligations and relevant norms and exercising more control over investment tribunals' interpretation" by expressing "explicit support for the right to regulate and clearer provisions on key concepts (e.g. FET, indirect expropriation)".[54] This is perhaps best illustrated by Article 9.6 (Minimum Standard of Treatment), which

51 United Nations Commission on Trade and Development (UNCTAD), 'International Investment Agreements Reform Accelerator' (2020) UNCTAD/DIAE/PCB/INF/2020/8 11–14.

52 For a more comprehensive background, see Chien-Huei Wu, 'ASEAN at the Crossroads: Trap and Track Between CPTPP and RCEP' (2020) 23 Journal of International Economic Law 97.

53 Chien-Huei Wu, 'ASEAN at the Crossroads: Trap and Track Between CPTPP and RCEP' (2020) 23 Journal of International Economic Law 114. However, one consequence is that the RCEP text is not expansive as the CETA or CPTPP and presents a more conventional focus on lowering trade barriers (Takako Gakuto, 'RCEP to Remove Tariffs on 86% of Japan's Exports to China' *Nikkei Asia* (15 November 2020) <https://asia.nikkei.com/Politics/International-relations/RCEP-to-remove-tariffs-on-86-of-Japan-s-exports-to-China> accessed 15 November 2020).

54 Heng Wang, 'The Future of Deep Free Trade Agreements: The Convergence of TPP (and CPTPP) and CETA?' (2019) 53 Journal of World Trade 325.

provides "greater certainty" in response to concerns of an overexpansive interpretation of FET.[55]

Legitimate public interest identified in the agreement are comprehensive based on a reading of the preamble. The object and purpose of the instrument, for instance, is identified as:

1 Promote economic integration;
2 Liberalize trade and investment;
3 Bring economic growth and social benefits;
4 Create new opportunities for workers and businesses;
5 Contribute to raising living standards;
6 Benefit consumers;
7 Reduce poverty; and
8 Promote sustainable growth.

Within these broad objectives, the preamble also identifies numerous concrete goals in a way that is unique to the CPTPP. They include:

1 Promoting the development and strengthening of regional supply chains;
2 Supporting the growth and development of micro, small, and medium-sized enterprises;
3 Establishing rules for state-owned enterprises that promote a level playing field with privately owned businesses, transparency, and sound business practices;
4 Promoting high levels of environmental protection;
5 Furthering the aims of sustainable development;
6 Promoting transparency, good governance, and the rule of law, and eliminating bribery and corruption in trade and investment;
7 Recognizing the importance of cultural identity and diversity among and within the Parties; and
8 Providing a catalyst to broader regional and international cooperation (further enhance regional economic integration and create the foundation of a Free Trade Area of the Asia Pacific).

55 Articles 9.6.2, 9.6.4, and 9.6.5, for instance, read as follows:

2. For greater certainty, . . . the customary international law minimum standard of treatment of aliens [is prescribed] as the standard of treatment to be afforded to covered investments. The concepts of "fair and equitable treatment" and "full protection and security" do not require treatment in addition to or beyond that which is required by that standard, and do not create additional substantive rights.
4. For greater certainty, the mere fact that a Party takes or fails to take an action that may be inconsistent with an investor's expectations does not constitute a breach of this Article, even if there is loss or damage to the covered investment as a result.
5. For greater certainty, the mere fact that a subsidy or grant has not been issued, renewed or maintained, or has been modified or reduced, by a Party, does not constitute a breach of this Article, even if there is loss or damage to the covered investment as a result.

The operative text also provides extensive protections for legitimate objectives. Article 19.4, for instance, identifies that "no Party shall waive or otherwise derogate from, or offer to waive or otherwise derogate from, its statutes or regulations" the labour protections under the *Declaration on Fundamental Principles and Rights at Work and its Follow-up* (1998). Article 20.3.2 recognizes the "sovereign right of each Party to establish its own levels of domestic environmental protection and its own environmental priorities, and to establish, adopt or modify its environmental laws and policies accordingly". This includes, as stated in Article 20.3.5, the "right to exercise discretion and to make decisions regarding: (a) investigatory, prosecutorial, regulatory and compliance matters; and (b) the allocation of environmental enforcement resources with respect to other environmental laws determined to have higher priorities".

In combination with Chapter 23 (Development), Chapter 20 (Environment) take a positive list approach to legitimate public interest objectives related to sustainable development.[56] They call for active participation in promoting certain activities and objectives such as "transparency, good governance and accountability" (Article 22.3.3); "enhancing the ability of women, including workers and business owners" (Article 23.4.2); and "joint development activities . . . to reinforce efforts to achieve sustainable development goals" (Article 23.2.5).

As per the safeguarding of public interests, the CPTPP reserves regulatory powers throughout the text.[57] Article 9.10 (Performance Requirements) provides standard protections against domestic performance requirements and technology transfer, but adds, for greater certainty, that the protections established in the provisions of the Article cannot be construed to "impose or enforc[e] a requirement, or

56 For instance, Chapter 20 (Environment) identifies protection and/or conservation of the ozone layer (Articles 20.5 and 20.15), marine environment from ship pollution (20.6), natural resources and local environment (Article 20.11.2(a)), biological diversity (Article 20.13.1), knowledge and practices of indigenous and local communities (Article 20.13.3), resilience against invasive alien species (Article 20.14), fisheries and marine ecosystems (Article 20.16), and endangered species (Article 20.17).

57 Articles 9.16 and 9.17, for instance, read as follows:

> Article 9.16: Investment and Environmental, Health and other Regulatory Objectives
>
> Nothing in this Chapter shall be construed to prevent a Party from adopting, maintaining or enforcing any measure otherwise consistent with this Chapter that it considers appropriate to ensure that investment activity in its territory is undertaken in a manner sensitive to environmental, health or other regulatory objectives.
>
> Article 9.17: Corporate Social Responsibility
>
> The Parties reaffirm the importance of each Party encouraging enterprises operating within its territory or subject to its jurisdiction to voluntarily incorporate into their internal policies those internationally recognised standards, guidelines and principles of corporate social responsibility that have been endorsed or are supported by that Party.

The inclusion of "otherwise consistent" in Article 9.16, however, has been viewed as making it unclear whether if the "host-state adopting, maintaining, or enforcing its self-judged regulatory measure would be able to avoid or mitigate liability for a breach of investment treaty standards" (Diane A Desierto, 'ASEAN Investment Treaties, RCEP, and CPTPP: Regional Strategies, Norms, Institutions, and Politics' (2017) 27 Washington International Law Journal 349, 374).

enforcing a commitment or undertaking, to employ or train workers in its territory". Article 23.9 takes these protections a step further in that "[n]o Party shall have recourse to dispute settlement" for matters that fall into the remit of Chapter 23 (Development).

Even in application to perhaps the most commonly established principles of international investment law, the CPTPP provides reservations on the right to regulate, which the instrument identifies in the preamble as an "inherent right to regulate and resolve to preserve the flexibility of Parties to set legislative and regulatory priorities". In connection to the national treatment and most-favoured nation principles, for instance, Article 9.12.7 provides that signatory states may make reservations.

Viet Nam, for instance, makes clear that it "reserves the right to adopt or maintain any measure conferring rights or privileges to socially, economically and geographically disadvantaged minorities and ethnic groups" (Annex II) in application to national treatment, most-favoured nation, and performance requirements for investments in all sectors. Annex 9-B.3(b) introduces the idea of "non-discriminatory regulatory actions", which are those that "are designed and applied to protect legitimate public welfare objectives, such as public health safety and the environment, do not constitute indirect expropriations, except in rare circumstances".

The CPTPP also showed to be widely responsive to other criticisms set against the investment treaty arbitration. For instance, Article 9.24 introduces public disclosure of proceedings and Article 9.29.4 permits tribunals to include legal fees into the quantum of arbitral awards should claims determined frivolous. As this section attempted to demonstrate, the CPTPP embodies and in many ways pioneers the new generation of investment agreement. However, having been borne of geopolitical origins has led to wide criticism that its thin institutionalization and attempts at regional megaregulation are contradictory and therefore ensnare attempts at meaningful progress in treaty negotiations.[58]

Another example of a comprehensive and progressive agreement includes the Comprehensive Economic and Trade Agreement (CETA) negotiations, which began after Canada and the European Union observed that at the provincial level, barriers to trade and investment continued to exist. This was largely seen to be a result of the strong subsidiarity impact at the Canadian provincial and individual EU state level.[59] The CETA has also noted for its explicit mention of sustainable development despite its trade and investment liberalizing design.[60] Simultaneously, the CETA has made more contentious recommendations such as the implementation

58 See, for instance, Benedict Kingsbury and others (eds), *Megaregulation Contested: Global Economic Ordering After TPP* (OUP 2019).

59 Günter Walzenbach, 'Procedure Over Substance? CETA and the Political Economy of Subsidiarity' (2019) 57 Commonwealth & Comparative Politics 153, 157–58.

60 See, for instance, Stefanie Schacherer, 'The CETA Investment Chapter and Sustainable Development: Interpretative Issues' in Makane Moïse Mbengue and Stefanie Schacherer (eds), *Foreign Investment Under the Comprehensive Economic and Trade Agreement (CETA)* (Springer International Publishing 2019).

of a Multilateral Investment Court as per Articles 8.27 and 8.29 in reference to the CETA Joint Committee. A permanent, multilateral investment court has been seen as one solution to the legitimacy issues facing international investment arbitration by providing "more substantive coherence and predictability as well as legal certainty for all concerned and thus lead to increased acceptance of decisions".[61] However, it has also been identified as embodying many of the most representative characteristics of new generation investment agreements, such at the right to regulate.[62] Accompanying the CETA is the joint interpretive instrument, which "in the sense of Article 31 of the Vienna Convention on the Law of Treaties, a clear and unambiguous statement of what Canada and the European Union".[63]

While the objective of the CETA is identified in Article 2.1 as the liberalization of trade in goods, the preambular statements identify the protection of investments and investors "without undermining the right of the Parties to regulate in the public interest within their territories". The joint interpretive instrument further identifies that the "principal purpose of trade is to increase the well-being of citizens, by supporting jobs and creating sustainable economic growth".[64] The development of trade and promotion of sustainable development as the object and purpose of the agreement are subject to contributing to the three dimensions of sustainable development.

On the right to regulate, the preamble of the CETA "preserve the right of the Parties to regulate within their territories and the Parties' flexibility to achieve legitimate policy objectives, such as public health, safety, environment, public morals and the promotion and protection of cultural diversity". It continues by identifying that implementation of the agreement must remain "consistent with the enforcement of their respective labour and environmental laws and that enhances their levels of labour and environmental protection and building upon their international commitments on labour and environmental matters". The comprehensive nature of the CETA means that the document covers both trade and investment, though the same principles found in preambulatory statement can also be identified in the

61 Marc Bungenberg and August Reinisch, *From Bilateral Arbitral Tribunals and Investment Courts to a Multilateral Investment Court: Options Regarding the Institutionalization of Investor-State Dispute Settlement* (Springer Nature 2020) 2. In addition to this volume, more on the process and debate surrounding the Multilateral Investment Court identified in the CETA can be found in Rob Howse, 'Designing a Multilateral Investment Court: Issues and Options' (2017) 36 Yearbook of European Law 209.

62 Catharine Titi, 'The Right to Regulate' in Makane Moïse Mbengue and Stefanie Schacherer (eds), *Foreign Investment Under the Comprehensive Economic and Trade Agreement (CETA)* (Springer International Publishing 2019).

63 Council of the European Union, 'Joint Interpretative Instrument on the Comprehensive Economic and Trade Agreement (CETA) Between Canada and the European Union and Its Member States' (2016) 13541/16 para 1(e) <https://data.consilium.europa.eu/doc/document/ST-13541-2016-INIT/en/pdf>.

64 Council of the European Union, 'Joint Interpretative Instrument on the Comprehensive Economic and Trade Agreement (CETA) Between Canada and the European Union and Its Member States' (2016) 13541/16 para 1(c) <https://data.consilium.europa.eu/doc/document/ST-13541-2016-INIT/en/pdf>.

operative text related to trade. For instance, Article 1.9 of the CETA reserves the right for parties to "protect and preserve its natural water resources". In relation to subsidies, Article 3.3 urges parties to consider whether pursuing a trade defence measure would "not be in the public interest". Furthermore, administrative barriers such as customs are permitted with proportionality for legitimate objectives as per Article 6.1.

Chapter 8 on investment begins with more conservative alignment by not including the contribution criterion to investment in Article 8.1, definitions, though it does include a diverse range of financial instruments such as bonds and equity shares. There are also common elements that are unchanged from conventional investment agreements, such as the observation of FET and full protection and security in Article 8.12. However, on reservations and exceptions, Article 8.15 and Article 13.10 inter alia deny protections and rights to investors based on Annex I, which subjects any new investments to review under domestic law, such as the *Investment Canada Act*. That determination is based on such factors as (1) "effect of the investment on the level and nature of economic activity in Canada" and (2) the "effect of the investment on productivity, industrial efficiency, technological development and product innovation".

Article 8.5 restricts any domestic requirements concerning technology transfer as well as eligibility to receive advantages from the state based on the "establishment, acquisition, expansion, management, conduct or operation of any investments". Further reservations are held in different circumstances. For instance, Article 8.16(b)(i) can deny protection to investments in connection to government measures that are related to the "maintenance of international peace and security". Article 13.16 reserve carve-outs for prudential measures in Article 13.16 to ensure the integrity and stability of the host state's financial system. Article 8.5, Paragraph 3, permits exceptions on admission of FDIs or the (continued) receipt of benefits by investors contingent on contributions made to the host state:

> Paragraph 2 [of Article 8.5] does not prevent a Party from conditioning the receipt or continued receipt of an advantage, in connection with an investment in its territory, on compliance with a requirement to locate production, provide a service, train or employ workers, construct or expand particular facilities, or carry out research and development in its territory.

Such measures include regulatory takings for public interest purposes. Article 8.12 on expropriation, for instance, excludes nationalization effected for a public purpose.

Beyond exceptions, Section D on investment protections reaffirms the state's right to regulate to achieve legitimate policy objectives in Article 8.9, Paragraph 1, identifying the "protection of public health, safety, the environment or public morals, social or consumer protection or the promotion and protection of cultural diversity". Paragraph 2 further corroborates this right to regulate for strong wording:

> For greater certainty, the mere fact that a Party regulates, including through a modification to its laws, in a manner which negatively affects an investment

> or interferes with an investor's expectations, including its expectations of profits, does not amount to a breach of an obligation under this Section.

For instance, in relation to environmental matters, CETA makes clear in Article 24.3:

> The Parties recognise the right of each Party to set its environmental priorities, to establish its levels of environmental protection, and to adopt or modify its laws and policies accordingly and in a manner consistent with the multilateral environmental agreements to which it is party and with this Agreement. Each Party shall seek to ensure that those laws and policies provide for and encourage high levels of environmental protection, and shall strive to continue to improve such laws and policies and their underlying levels of protection.

These are further corroborated in the joint interpretative instrument, which states in Paragraph 2:

> CETA preserves the ability of the European Union and its Member States and Canada to adopt and apply their own laws and regulations that regulate economic activity in the public interest, to achieve legitimate public policy objectives such as the protection and promotion of public health, social services, public education, safety, the environment, public morals, social or consumer protection, privacy and data protection and the promotion and protection of cultural diversity.[65]

The CPTPP and CETA are but two notable examples of IIAs, or treaties with investment provisions, that embody many of the evolutionary trends that are present from early in the institutional history of the UN system,[66] not only the precautionary stance taken in regard to the development impact of international investment, but also the international investment law issues that the UN system engages. Continuing from within this landscape of the institutional history of the UN system, the

65 Council of the European Union, 'Joint Interpretative Instrument on the Comprehensive Economic and Trade Agreement (CETA) Between Canada and the European Union and Its Member States' (2016) 13541/16 para 3 <https://data.consilium.europa.eu/doc/document/ST-13541-2016-INIT/en/pdf>.

66 In the *2021 Asia-Pacific Trade and Investment*, the UN Economic and Social Commission for Asia and the Pacific (UNESCAP) identified the growth of environmental provisions in regional trade agreements as a sign of its evolution, with 85% of regional trade agreements signed after 2005 involving an Asia-Pacific economy containing at least one climate-related provision (United Nations Economic and Social Commission for Asia and the Pacific (UNESCAP), United Nations Environment Programme (UNEP), and United Nations Commission on Trade and Development (UNCTAD), *Accelerating Climate-Smart Trade and Investment for Sustainable Development* (United Nations 2021) 76–77).

following section extracts the main lessons to be deposited into the approach taken up by this book.

3.3 The framework

The international investment–sustainable development framework ("Framework") presented in this section constructs the first half of the approach proposed by this book in aiding the assessment of Actions[67] in a manner that confronts the incomplete assessment[68] that Actions have and continue to be subjected. The Framework continues from the evolutionary approach identified in the institutional history of the UN system and is based on an analysis of the WIRs and multilateral instruments relevant to the nexus between international investment and sustainable development.[69]

The substantive policy recommendations woven into these materials are synthesized into this Framework, which are then paired with the initiatives advanced by the UN to promote unity in the standards of Sustainable Investment, as provided in Chapter 4. Together, in what this book identifies as the Consolidate Method, it shows that in order to surmount an incomplete assessment of Actions while remaining aligned to the multilateral values concerning sustainable development espoused through the UN system, Actions must be assessed to the extent to which they are adaptive, multistakeholder, and precautionary.

The means to achieve these broad ideals are identified in three tiers. First, there are objectives in aligning the laws and policies of international investment and sustainable development. Second, under each objective are policy strategies in reaching those objectives. Third are the specific government measures that constitute those policy strategies.

At the second tier, the main strategies in the Framework can be divided into those that are implemented before the entry into an IIA (pre-admission) and those following entry (post-admissions). At the pre-admissions stage, key strategies include the following:

1 Clear promissory terms of the investment in respect to the right and obligations of both the host state and investor(s);
2 Coherent rather than competing national policy framework that is cross-sectoral in its treatment of international investment, or special administrative zones with separate policy applications;
3 Screening and targeting investment(s) based on national circumstances and value-added in the domestic context; and
4 Harmonization and coordination between host states on best practices of both putative investors and host states in investment promotion activities.

67 As identified in Chapter 1, Actions refer to both foreign investments as well as government measures that affect foreign investments but are intended to advance sustainable development.

68 In reference to an "incomplete assessment" introduced in Chapter 1 and further substantiated in Chapter 2.

69 For easy referencing, a tabular version of these findings can be found in Appendix 1.

Meanwhile, post-admission strategies include:

1 Maintaining supervisory, standard-setting, and control mechanisms to ensure dynamic policy adaptation to promote the public interest;
2 Reviewing in a timely and constant manner government policies that influence protected investments to ensure that they remain effective in contributing to national development;
3 Involving and encouraging transnational investors in promoting national public interests through self-regulation, CSR, and encouraging vertical linkages; and
4 Installing and maintaining safeguards against abusive practices.

The third tier of the Framework provides specific government strategies that have been noted within the UN system as advancing second-tier strategies and in turn first-tier objectives.

Altogether, as mentioned in the institutional history of the UN system, the Framework presents international investment as a conditional (rather than automatic) pathway to sustainable development. In that regard, the objectives, strategies, and measures identified in the Framework come together to constitute a precautionary stance towards international investment rather than one that promotes international investment outright. This precautionary stance primarily seeks to safeguard the public interests of the host state, enabling policies that seek to benefit the most vulnerable stakeholders in society.[70] Simultaneously, this precautionary stance does not always empower the host state's regulatory powers, but can also serve to prevent widely accepted safeguards from being employed as "legal cover for investment protectionism or unjustified discrimination".[71]

The Framework is complemented by the latter half of the approach proposed by this work, the notion of Sustainable Investment ("Notion").[72] The Notion, like the Framework, employs concepts and methodologies from sustainable finance within the same multilateral scope of the UN system. In doing so, the Notion complements the Framework by providing a means to assess a foreign investment's contribution to the host state's sustainable development. Together, the Framework and Notion shape a unified approach to addressing the incomplete assessment of Actions,

70 The Action Plan for Private Sector Investment in the SDGs, for instance, identifies the centrality of balance in the "guiding principles for private sector investment in SDGs", which are (1) balancing liberalization and regulation, (2) balancing the need for attractive risk-return rates with the need for accessible and affordable services for all, (3) balancing a push for private funds with the push for public investment, and (4) balancing the global scope of the SDGs with the need to make a special effort in LDCs (United Nations Commission on Trade and Development (UNCTAD), 'World Investment Report 2014: Investing in the SDGs: An Action Plan' (United Nations 2014) UNCTAD/WIR/2014 186–87).

71 United Nations Commission on Trade and Development (UNCTAD), 'World Investment Report 2015: Reforming International Investment Governance' (United Nations 2015) UNCTAD/WIR/2015 128.

72 This Notion is presented in Chapter 4.

particularly when raised in the context of the right to regulate for the public interest.[73] The three tiers of the Framework (objectives, strategies, and measures) are designed in a manner to better assess the linkage between international investment and sustainable development both at the policy and state planning levels as well as that of appraising the role and impact of the investment.

3.3.1 Objective 1: Does the Action facilitate greater development impact?

The three strategies under the first objective seek to better align Actions (government measures and international investment), thereby amplifying their individual and combined sustainable development impact.

Strategy 1.1: Optimize development impact

The three government measures under Strategy 1.1 seek to optimize the development impact of international investment by optimizing their complementarity with SDGs and policies.

MEASURE 1.1.1: LINKAGE PROMOTION PROGRAMMES

Forming linkages between international investment and domestic economic actors by carving out special rules and preferential treatment ("linkages promotion programmes") can enhance domestic spillover effects and complementarities. This may include imposing domestic content requirements that focus on strengthening local supplier (and distributor) capabilities, induce technology diffusion, and/or discourage weak local linkage relationships such as those that involve a one-way transfer of capital. Effective linkage promotion programmes are those with clearly stated policy goals that complement the overarching development strategy of the host state, thereby establishing linkages that build on comparative advantages, benefit from matchmaking initiatives to encourage target linkages and/or develop low-carbon linkages. Another means of forming linkages with domestic actors is through public investment, which can signal to investors those areas or sectors being targeted for public policy objectives. Such signalling can generate financing multiplier effects in these targeted areas or sectors as foreign investors are more compelled to them, especially when public investment is matched with domestic investment and investment promotion schemes.

MEASURE 1.1.2: INTEGRATED INDUSTRIAL POLICY

Guiding investment policy through integrated industrial policy, which allocates industrial capital and output in a way that is grounded in a country's overall development strategy, can "mutually reinforce and create synergies among different

73 As defined in Pillar Three of Chapter 2.

sets of policies".[74] In this manner, industrial policies can integrate the objectives of environmental and/or social policies in the planning of an economy's productive capacities by setting environmental and/or social criteria in screening potential investment and trade. Effective integration between industrial and investment policy can create dynamic industry clusters, export processing zones, and other designated trade and investment liberalization spaces that can channel investment into areas with high development impact.

A common form of industrial policy is the designation of special economic zones, to which an integrated industrial policy approach may seek to optimize sustainable development impact by including "granular targets for aspects such as capital expenditures, skill levels, training and local content" as well as "safeguards to ensure that [special economic zones] remain aligned with development strategies".[75] For example, establishing special economic zones with government provisioned land and infrastructure to strategically shield domestic industry while promoting FDI to science parks that facilitate research and development (R&D) collaboration, best-in-class social and environmental standards, and domestic capacity building that promotes meaningful skill transfer.

In this way, the incentives offered through special economic zones can be paired with policies that aim to optimize development impact from foreign investments, such as mobilizing the injection of foreign capital to enhance human resources or create infrastructure to not only avoid regional disparities, but also locking disadvantaged regions into low-value-added traps. The presence of foreign investment in special economic zones can also push host governments to improve accountability in administrative procedures or in some cases act as "SDG model zones", which can provide incentives to foreign investors to enter "SDG-relevant activities", adopt the "highest level of ESG standards and compliance", and promote "inclusive growth through linkages and spillovers".[76] Overall, by applying forward-looking, progressively ambitious standards of Sustainable Investment, special economic zones can remain attractive to international investors while emboldening the host state's sustainable development agenda. These special economic zones may also be configured so that they can enable innovative, alternative, or more accessible forms of finance, such as through financial technologies.

MEASURE 1.1.3: SOUTH-SOUTH AND REGIONAL PREFERENCES

The final measure under this strategy is by agreeing on preferential treatment for foreign investments originating from developing economies within a global South-South development co-operative context, which tend to present greater

74 United Nations Commission on Trade and Development (UNCTAD), 'World Investment Report 2018: Investment and New Industrial Policies' (United Nations 2018) UNCTAD/WIR/2018 177.

75 United Nations Commission on Trade and Development (UNCTAD), 'World Investment Report 2019: Special Economic Zones' (United Nations 2019) UNCTAD/WIR/2019 198.

76 United Nations Commission on Trade and Development (UNCTAD), 'World Investment Report 2019: Special Economic Zones' (United Nations 2019) UNCTAD/WIR/2019 202.

gains, particularly in contexts where technological gaps are narrower, presenting more opportunities for productive investments on a level playing field. Collaboration and integration can help to create larger markets, especially regionally, that can promote inclusive growth opportunities based on comprehensive and progressive trade and investment agreements that shape clear positions on the role of international investment in sustainable development. Such agreements can become conduits for "harmonization, mutual recognition or approximation of regulatory standards and the consolidation of private standards on environmental, social and governance issues".[77]

Strategy 1.2: Enhance policy capacities

The three government measures under Strategy 1.2 seek to safeguard the policy space of the host state at the intersection between sustainable development and foreign investment law and policy.

MEASURE 1.2.1: MEASURABLE POLICY EFFECTS

Safeguarding the right to adjust policies based on measurable effects is important to ensuring both that policies remain effective and policy implementation is adaptive. This becomes particularly important for investment promotion policies, which are implemented in a manner that is responsive to such exogenous factors as policy or governmental changes and/or market disruption caused by, for example, the entry of a TNC. Given the multifaceted implementation difficulties of measuring policy effects, investment policy can be assessed based on objective, priorities, time frame, and support measures in place. For that reason, it is crucial to ensure that there are "efficient monitoring systems . . . in place to regularly the assess the effectiveness of existing investment promotion schemes for sustainable development" that are based on "reliable data to strengthen the credibility of sustainable financial products".[78]

MEASURE 1.2.2: DYNAMIC POLICYMAKING

Safeguarding the right for supervision, standard-setting, and control over international investment policies that are responsive to changing conditions, such as

77 United Nations Commission on Trade and Development (UNCTAD), 'World Investment Report 2013: Global Value Chains: Investment and Trade for Development' (United Nations 2013) UNCTAD/WIR/2013 196.

78 Lisa Bohmer, 'Analysis: In *Bahgat v Egypt*, Arbitrators Find That a Series of Measures, Including the Claimant's Arrest and the Freezing of His Assets, Amounted to a Violation of Two BITs' (*Investment Arbitration Reporter*, 18 August 2020) 225–26 <www.iareporter.com/articles/analysis-in-bahgat-v-egypt-arbitrators-find-that-a-series-of-measures-including-the-claimants-arrest-and-the-freezing-of-his-assets-amounted-to-a-violation-of-two-bits/> accessed 19 November 2020.

market conditions or broader public interest goals and different stages of development is important to ensuring that policies remain relevant and timely. One way to ensure this flexibility is by formulating implementation measures in a time-limited manner, such as by instituting sunset clauses and policy reviews based on performance monitoring. In times of crisis, it is important to consider both the "combined and cumulative effects"[79] of policy, such as their long-term and/or knock-on effects, particularly in relation to the most vulnerable economies. While a majority of reforms to IIAs deal with safeguarding broader policy goals such as sustainable development,[80] they have been limited in their effectiveness in part due to the long duration and automatic renewal (survival) of old generation IIAs.

MEASURE 1.2.3: PARALLEL POLICY

Designing FDI policies, particularly in relation to mergers and acquisitions, aware of the fact that they are "inextricably linked with policies in core areas of economic development".[81] This recognizes that investment is a means to an end (of advancing development), and as such investment policy should be parallel with overarching development strategy. Economic objectives behind FDI policies, and more broadly international investment policies, should be designed to complement rather than compete against policies meant to promote socioeconomic and environmentally responsible development.

For instance, policies seeking to increase business efficiency, secure quality capital for domestic firms to remain competitive, and reduce administrative barriers to attracted export-oriented FDI can complement policy efforts to enhance domestic technology, skill, and knowledge bases such as by forming linkages for local firms to foreign firms with high R&D potential; incubating domestic entrepreneurs who can benefit from an increased exposure to TNCs; and/or safeguarding government measures aimed to regulate against anticompetitive practices by firms. In assessing the viability of alternative policy solutions, policymakers can ensure that investment policy measures are "fit-for-purpose" or "parallel"[82] in relation to other policy objectives.

Strategy 1.3: Target high-impact investment

The three measures under Strategy 1.3 seek to target investments with high development impact, particularly in development priority areas.

79 United Nations Commission on Trade and Development (UNCTAD), 'World Investment Report 2020: International Production Beyond the Pandemic' (United Nations 2020) UNCTAD/WIR/2020 216.

80 United Nations Commission on Trade and Development (UNCTAD), 'World Investment Report 2023: Investing in Sustainable Energy for All' (United Nations 2023) 73–75.

81 United Nations Commission on Trade and Development (UNCTAD), 'World Investment Report 2019: Special Economic Zones' (n 75) 156.

82 United Nations Commission on Trade and Development (UNCTAD), 'World Investment Report 2016: Investor Nationality: Policy Challenges' (United Nations 2016) UNCTAD/WIR/2016 183–84.

MEASURE 1.3.1: PRODUCTIVE INVESTMENT

Targeting international investments that are "productive" to national development, such as investments that stand most to result in meaningful job or capacities creation and technology transfers. Certain types of investments are less productive than others, such as those that exclusively seek to boost efficiency, such as by reducing capital costs, or seek entry into target markets. These can include and investments in natural resources and extractive industries that are defined by a rentier attitude. Such investments do not account for the absorptive capacities of the host state or conduit noise,[83] which are important to determining the extent to which an investment can be anticipated to be productive.

Conversely, productive investments are "not only for economic growth as such, but for growth that benefits all".[84] They build on linkages identified within the host state, which in turn are based on inter alia revealed comparative advantage, by, for example, matching FDI with existing domestic factors of production and catalysing or crowding in further financial resources and investments in strategic areas.

MEASURE 1.3.2: CRITICAL NEED AREAS AND SUSTAINABLE DEVELOPMENT SECTORS

Directing investment to "specific priority sectors for sustainable development ('sustainable-development sectors')" based on a "thorough analysis of the country's competitive advantages and development challenges and opportunities can amplify the development impact. Such priority areas can include human resource development and financing, particularly in industries or regions that can "create employment for groups deserving affirmative action or to address poverty".[85] For example, focusing investment into an economy's productive capacities can be a priority area for lesser developed countries due to the relatively smaller number of such investments, the availability of alternative investment destinations, low insulation to external shocks, and the importance of manufacturing investment in ushering in structural change away from an exclusive reliance on natural resources. In such circumstances, non-equity modes of investment (NEMs)[86] may ease access

83 Defined as when a multinational enterprise "investing from home country A in host country B establishes an intermediate step through a third country C. The investment transits first from A to C, and only then, from C to B where it is deployed as productive investment" (Bruno Casella, 'Looking Through Conduit FDI in Search of Ultimate Investors—a Probabilistic Approach' (2019) 26 Transnational Corporations 109).

84 United Nations Commission on Trade and Development (UNCTAD), 'World Investment Report 2012: Towards a New Generation of Investment Policies' (n 6) 108.

85 United Nations Commission on Trade and Development (UNCTAD), 'World Investment Report 1999: Foreign Direct Investment and the Challenge of Development' (n 8) 279.

86 NEMs are investments that take place without the granting of equity, such as government grants or strategic alliances like contract farming. Equity options can entail "significant risk because it is limiting for the firm as it can cause conflicts over goals which interfere with the overall performance" especially for firms with social objectives (Luca Cacciolatti and others, 'Strategic Alliances and Firm Performance in Startups with a Social Mission' (2020) 106 Journal of Business Research 106).

to financial services, trigger crowd in additionality effects for other investments, and spillovers in training and technology for smaller producers.

MEASURE 1.3.3: PRE-FDI SCREENING OF TRANSNATIONAL CORPORATIONS

Screening foreign enterprises seeking admission of FDI for favourable characteristics such as high-level environmental, social, and governance standards, use of clean technology or uniform CSR standards can help attract high-quality, productive investments. An awareness of desirable characteristics of investment can be enhanced by active participation by domestic stakeholders. As further explored in Chapter 4, standards, rules, and regulations that are internationally harmonized can help to avoid conflicting interpretations of the qualifications of Sustainable Investment.

3.3.2 Objective 2: Does the Action encourage development cooperation?

Actions that strengthen development cooperation between the host state and foreign investor fit under the second objective of the Framework. The three strategies under this objective seek to facilitate partnership between the investor and the host state.

Strategy 2.1: Form robust relationships

The two measures under Strategy 2.1 seek to fortify the relationship between the foreign investor and both the host state and its stakeholders to ensure that it remains resilient under unexpected challenges.

MEASURE 2.1.1: CLEAR EXPECTATIONS

Establishing clear expectations from the investment relationship between the host state and TNCs based on concrete commitments in applicable agreements concerning sustainable development can forge reliable interactions between the foreign investor and host state. When these commitments are bottom-up rather than top-down, such investor-state relationships can become more efficient means of partnership-based development efforts. In the case of public-private partnerships, for instance, this may involve incentivizing R&D and innovation through financial options like low-interest grants that account for the host state's development needs and objectives or structuring public-private partnerships in ways that are conducive to technology transfer such as build-operate-transfer arrangements, which clearly define the expectations held by the parties before, during, and after the foreign investment is executed.

MEASURE 2.1.2: MULTISTAKEHOLDER CONSENSUS

If the liberalization of regulation in FDI is supported by strong political commitment, clear delineation of the lines of responsibility and authority, mindful of the need for technical viability and commercial profitability to retain foreign firms, and operated by "well-functioning institutions to channel" multistakeholder communication, then investment conditions offered to foreign investors are less likely to experience dramatic change in such circumstances as changes in government. This "participatory approach to policy development"[87] is also more likely to ensure inclusive gains from investment through an expanded involvement of stakeholders. This consensus is crucial in ensuring that the relationship between the TNC and domestic stakeholders are mutually beneficial and in line with the host state's long-run development goals and obligations to multilateral environmental agreements, especially in such sectors as extractive industries and ecosystem services. Engaging in international coalitions of like-minded stakeholders can also build resilience against market failures, particularly those that occur in periods of crisis.

Strategy 2.2: Reach a common understanding

The two measures under Strategy 2.2 seek to reach a common understanding on the conduct of both the host state and the foreign investor.

MEASURE 2.2.1: ADMINISTRATIVE PROCEDURES

Exchanging experience and knowledge between governments can increase procedural transparency and consistency in administrative processes involving TNCs through gaining an understanding of precedence. This can include such administrative processes as investment screening prior to admission of FDI with clear reporting requirements on extrafinancial performance such as environmental impact assessments preceding project implementation. These regulatory and institutional frameworks should be designed with both the host state and foreign investor being aware that the main responsibility of ensuring development impact remains with the host state to avoid a conflicting understanding of the host state's development priorities and the administrative processes leading to accomplishing those priorities.

MEASURE 2.2.2: GOOD CORPORATE CITIZENSHIP

The host state and foreign investor should reach a broader agreement on what CSR entails, forming commonly understood boundaries of international good corporate citizenship based on unambiguous standards of social and environmental policy. Such standards are most effective when adapted to international initiatives on corporate behaviour and disclosures such as inter alia the UN Global Compact, the Global Reporting Initiative, and International Labour Organization conventions in relation to labour standards. Permitting the foreign investor to execute its own corporate socially responsible directive irrespective of contextual factors of the

87 United Nations Commission on Trade and Development (UNCTAD), 'World Investment Report 2012: Towards a New Generation of Investment Policies' (n 6) 108.

host state can result in ineffectual interpretations of social and/or environmental responsibility in application to corporate behaviour.

Strategy 2.3: Establish equitable standards

The two measures under Strategy 2.3 seek to establish equitable standards of conduct between host and home countries rather than one-sided, exploitative relationships. By creating a level playing field in the negotiation of IIAs and the conditions upon which a foreign investment is admitted, the host state is further enabled to secure its public interests.

MEASURE 2.3.1: NO LESSER STANDARD

The no lesser standard clause requires foreign investors to follow the same standards in their home countries or specific intergovernmental policy documents and multilateral environmental agreements to which their home states are party in their activities in the host state. These efforts can be imposed on private sector entities based on an IIA between the home and host states, requiring compliance with investment-related national laws of the host state through a no lesser standard clause. TNCs then have the obligation to recognize those duties and obligations, especially those that are bound by subsidiarity and shareholderism in their corporate decision-making structures[88] recognizing the importance of local participation.

MEASURE 2.3.2: HOME COUNTRY MEASURES

Integrating home country measures (HCMs) into IIAs can range from hortatory policy declarations concerning sustainable development performance requirements to mandatory development assistance and cooperation obligations. HCMs based on strong policy commitments with binding obligations accompanied by detailed implementation plans and monitoring mechanisms can be effective tools to influence the conduct of foreign investors. For example, HCMs may influence companies to enrol into and implement international initiatives on corporate governance.

3.3.3 Objective 3: Does the Action advance mutual benefit in agreements?

Actions that improve mutual benefit by reducing harmful competitive positioning in agreements fit under the third objective of the Framework. The two strategies

88 Subsidiarity is understood as the exercise of public responsibility by the closest possible stakeholder. In application to transnational corporations and investors, their impact on the host state's economic affairs mean that have more capability and thus responsibility for self-regulation and corporate social responsibility within the context of their operations (United Nations Commission on Trade and Development (UNCTAD), 'World Investment Report 1994: Transnational Corporations, Employment and the Workplace' (n 20) 322).

under this objective seek to reorient approaches to agreements related to investment away from strategic competition and towards mutual gain.

Strategy 3.1: Harmonize investment incentives

The three measures under Strategy 3.1 seek to harmonize incentives for international investment in a way that progresses sustainable development, rather than compelling harmful competition in races to the bottom.

MEASURE 3.1.1: CONDITIONAL INCENTIVE-LIMITATION

IIAs may include conditional incentive-limitation clause (such as ceilings and limits), which would only grant incentives if a specific number or set of states adopt the same clause. The organizing condition can be based on a joint weighing of the costs and benefits of offering incentives. This sort of international coordination is particularly important for investment projects that are "too complex and expensive for one country alone" and rely instead of synergies such as public-private partnerships on infrastructure. As global value chains transform, competition for high-tech investments can result in a proliferation of favourable tax regimes that can risk "harmful tax competition between countries".[89]

MEASURE 3.1.2: DISCOURAGED INCENTIVES

Coordinating identification of objectionable investment promotion incentives in a negative list approach can help to avoid overlapping or conflicting national policy toolkits between states that were meant to achieve development objectives. This includes unnecessarily providing favourable treatment to foreign investors in areas where positive linkages would have formed regardless. In offering incentives, states should not lower regulatory standards on social or environmental issues that could compromise the SDGs. Lowering environmental, labour, and other regulatory standards in order to attract investment can result in a "regulatory race to the bottom".

MEASURE 3.1.3: ENCOURAGED INCENTIVES

Coordinating identification of investment promotion incentives that target FDI with universally beneficial development impact, such as linkages between FDI and domestic micro-, small- and medium-sized enterprises (MSMEs) can help alleviate harmful competition between states trying to incentivize investment. Governments can incentivize innovation through policy frameworks such as national innovation

89 United Nations Commission on Trade and Development (UNCTAD), 'World Investment Report 2018: Investment and New Industrial Policies' (n 74) 168.

systems that encourage and reward innovation by TNCs while strengthening the innovative capabilities of partner domestic enterprises and technology institutions.

To this end, bridging the gap between investment promotion and facilitation is important: not only incentivizing foreign investment, but also facilitating business and investment activities domestically via a government-wide approach to address obstacles such as administrative barriers as well as regulatory and policy transparency. One way to achieve this is through digitalization, whereby governments can improve access to administrative processes and information for both domestic firms and foreign investors at the level of IIAs.[90]

Incentives can also work as an alternative to more costly industrial policies, such as performance requirements, by offering cost-based tax incentives that are only granted when desired investment expenditures are made. Overall, investment promotion policies should "pay specific attention to those SDG sectors" that demonstrate the "biggest need for investment"[91] as well as identifying "lighthouse" projects that act as "steppingstones to attract subsequent investment in more ambitious projects".[92]

Strategy 3.2: Secure responsive contracts

The two measures under Strategy 3.2 seek to enhance private sector agreements so that they are more responsive to the changing development needs of the host state.

MEASURE 3.2.1: DURABLE RELATIONSHIPS

Establishing durable relationships through contracts that take into account changes in policies, demographics, wealth gaps, and technology; tendencies of actors to behave strategically and in their self-interest; careful allocation of risk that avoid overbearing contingent liabilities; and promoting the upgrading of domestic capacities. Such contractual relations can augment and, when necessary, overshadow general laws in the host state for certain categories of foreign investment that are particularly impactful to the domestic economy, such as natural resources, large infrastructure projects, and agriculture. Durable contracts become important when involving alternative means of investment, such as those that do not involve equity like strategic alliances or joint ventures, since they establish the main legal framework of the relationship between the TNC and the domestic entity.

90 United Nations Commission on Trade and Development (UNCTAD), 'World Investment Report 2024: Investment Facilitation and Digital Government' (United Nations 2024) UNCTAD/WIR/2024 129.

91 United Nations Commission on Trade and Development (UNCTAD), 'World Investment Report 2020: International Production Beyond the Pandemic' (n 79) 225.

92 United Nations Commission on Trade and Development (UNCTAD), 'World Investment Report 2021: Investing in Sustainable Recovery' (United Nations 2021) UNCTAD/WIR/2021 150.

MEASURE 3.2.2: CAPACITY BUILDING AND SUPPORT

Ensuring that domestic public and private sector entities have the "ability to conduct complex investment discussions and negotiate"[93] with the aim of boosting domestic firm competitiveness. For instance, establishing expert facilities in contract negotiations to ensure well-balanced, durable contracts for long-term projects and low-carbon investments. This is particularly true when involving low-income countries and TNCs or the agricultural sector, where the terms of contract are extremely important in retaining value in the host state and ensuring economic benefits for local farmers. Strengthening regulatory agencies in enforcing contracts can help counterweigh opportunistic investors who may attempt to shift risk to the host state and its public or leverage investment to manipulate negotiations to their favour, as can enabling collective bargaining associations to represent the interest of domestic entities.

3.3.4 *Objective 4: Are investment laws and policies harmonized with multilateral standards related to sustainable development?*

Actions that more closely align international investment to multilateral standards connected to sustainable development fit under the fourth objective of the Framework. The two strategies under this objective seek to redefine approaches to international investments, either through the agreements that govern them, or the means used to understand their performance.

Strategy 4.1: Reform approaches to investment agreements

The two measures under Strategy 4.1 reform approaches to IIAs that are more aligned with the needs and interest of sustainable development. This can occur either in the negotiation of the agreement itself or the interpretation of its provisions.

MEASURE 4.1.1: JOINT INTERPRETIVE STATEMENTS

Providing multilateral interpretative guidance for investment treaty arbitration tribunals on issues where a broad and unpredictable margin of discretion in the interpretation of IIAs may exist, such as climate change or FET. Joint interpretative statements can also take the form of joint committees for the interpretation of especially contentious issues in investment treaty arbitration, such as public policy exceptions. Joint interpretation can serve as a practical alternative to amending IIAs that does not require ratification while also helping (though with no guarantee) to refine the interpretive scope of arbitral tribunals.

93 United Nations Commission on Trade and Development (UNCTAD), 'World Investment Report 2019: Special Economic Zones' (n 75) 255.

MEASURE 4.1.2: NEW GENERATION INTERNATIONAL INVESTMENT AGREEMENTS

Mainstreaming sustainable development in IIAs by taking an active approach towards orienting international investment to the SDGs. An active approach would include establishing a national action plan for investment agreements ensuring that sustainable development is a dimension in treaty negotiations. One important aspect of this national plan should also include addressing older investment treaties that cause fragmentation: a lack of coordination with not only ongoing national investment law reform efforts, but also the larger universe of international law and legal governance.

Examples of sustainable development dimensions can include offering special and differential treatment for developing economies and carving out preferential treatment derogations for national and/or strategic investors/investments that contribute to sustainable development. Alternatively, provisions meant to protect the natural environment and confront other environmental issues can be embedded into international investment law and policy by specifically referencing intergovernmental policy documents, multilateral environmental agreements, and national environmental commitments. At the same time, intentionally leaving out certain traditional elements of IIAs can leave open policy spaces and room for firm-level negotiations in such areas that can have heightened development impact. For example, this can involve taking a flexible approach to performance requirements in order to best capitalize on potential technology transfers in priority areas like sustainable energy, or even removing them from new generation IIAs.

Strategy 4.2: Harmonize investment reporting standards

Pursuing an internationally harmonized approach to measuring and reporting on sustainable development-related factors affected by investment and investment-related activities, such as carbon leakages and pricing. Harmonized rules on corporate nationality and transparency standards, for example, can help address treaty shopping before it is given an opportunity to occur. Towards that end, it will be necessary to pursue a "harmonized approach to disclosure" that can help develop "sustainability assessment standards and reliable data" whether through a "global monitoring mechanism" or "SDG investment compacts".[94]

3.3.5 Objective 5: Do investment laws and policies sufficiently prevent abusive practices that hamper sustainable development?

Actions that bring international investment and sustainable development into a closer nexus by addressing obstructions founded in international investment law that hamper sustainable development progress fit under the fifth objective of the Framework. The two strategies under this objective seek to counteract practices that are inconsistent with advancing sustainable development.

94 United Nations Commission on Trade and Development (UNCTAD), 'World Investment Report 2020: International Production Beyond the Pandemic' (n 79) 225–26.

Strategy 5.1: Craft preventative arrangements before the admission of investment

The four measures under Strategy 5.1 seek to refine IIAs at the pre-admissions level to better service the public interests of the host state.

MEASURE 5.1.1: BACKSTOPPING

Establishing backstopping functions against abusive practices. Multilateral backstopping can include ensuring coherent and mutually beneficial exchange such as through information sharing. This can include establishing regional and subregional mechanisms that promote exchange of information on restrictive business practices as well as intellectual property rights systems that balance the interests of producers, consumers, and national partners and protects against the misappropriation of knowledge assets, such as, but not limited to, traditional knowledge and investments that involve large-scale land acquisitions and leases. Backstopping can also occur through domestic institutional readiness to respond to international investment-related issues raise by covered investors. This could include early warning systems, ombudsman-like institutions, and dispute prevention and alternative resolution mechanisms.

MEASURE 5.1.2: PROTECTIVE CARVE-OUTS FOR UNDERREPRESENTED INTERESTS

Carving out protections for domestic minority shareholders and stakeholders against power differentials against TNCs especially cognizant of the uneven regional and country distribution of FDI. When relationships between TNCs and local actors are defined by clear power differentials, such as when involving small producers, heightened power asymmetries can arise from over-dependencies and the crowding out of smallholders that cannot compete against capital-intensive producers competing in a more concentrated market.

MEASURE 5.1.3: CLARIFIED CONFLICT RULES BETWEEN PARALLEL INSTRUMENTS

Clarifying on and/or renegotiating treaty provisions or interpretation that may result in mixed approaches to negative and positive list FDI regulation in IIAs and trade-in-services agreements. Conflicting rules can result in unintended consequences, such as through the application of MFN in order to "cherry-pick"[95] or benefit from prior or subsequent agreements. When rules in IIAs conflict, such as between a bilateral and multilateral investment treaty, this can result in "parallelism"[96] that can facilitate a TNC to pursue multiple claims against the host

95 United Nations Commission on Trade and Development (UNCTAD), 'World Investment Report 2012: Towards a New Generation of Investment Policies' (n 6) 134.

96 United Nations Commission on Trade and Development (UNCTAD), 'World Investment Report 2013: Global Value Chains: Investment and Trade for Development' (n 77) 106.

state on the same complaint. The same conflict can take place between domestic law and obligations under IIAs as well as between older and newer investment agreements by prioritizing newer rules when there is conflict. Renegotiating inconsistent international agreements can help to prevent conflicting rules both at the national and international level in order to maximize the gains from international investment. For example, clarifying the legitimate use of regulatory powers by the state by defining "normal regulatory activities"[97] or that the MFN clause does not carry over substantive elements related to investment treaty arbitration from other, particularly older, treaties.

MEASURE 5.1.4: REFINED ELIGIBILITY THROUGH LINKING PROVISIONS

Confining the application of the rights and protections to genuine investors and excluding investments channelled through legal entities can limit or clarify the liability of the contracting parties, particularly in connection to contentious standards like FET. This may require revisiting the obligations woven into old IIAs to revise, replace, or terminate these instruments to better reflect and respond to existing realities. Restricting the range of covered investments and investors by refining the definition of covered investor through providing an "exhaustive list of covered investments"[98] and/or employing denial-of-benefits clauses, which permit the host state to deny the benefits of an applicable treaty to corporate entities or other contracting parties without substantial business activities, can help address nationality planning, round-tripping, and treaty shopping. One way that this can occur is through linking provisions, which conditions investor rights and protections on certain circumstances, such as compliance with domestic laws or level of host country development.

Strategy 5.2: Install post-admissions measures that safeguard against abusive practices

The two measures under Strategy 5.2 seek to install post-admissions protective measures that better equips the host state with the tools needed to ensure that they are able to regulate for the public interest, such as matters connected to sustainable development.

MEASURE 5.2.1: DEFERENCE, JURISDICTION, AND CORPORATE INFLUENCE RESERVATIONS

Reserving the right to counterclaim in investment treaty arbitration in connection to the investor's conduct in the host state during the performance of the investment,

97 United Nations Commission on Trade and Development (UNCTAD), 'World Investment Report 2015: Reforming International Investment Governance' (n 71) 139.

98 United Nations Commission on Trade and Development (UNCTAD), 'World Investment Report 2015: Reforming International Investment Governance' (n 71) 143.

such as the violation of domestic regulation or standards, can be made in connection to deference as a form of arbitral review and the exhaustion of local remedies in application to issues significant to the public interest. Alternatively, retaining "golden shares" to "enable [host states] to influence or even veto corporate decisions they consider undesirable",[99] such as asset-stripping by corporate raiders. Reservations at the project financing level, such as an infrastructure project, can target opportunistic contractors and investors who can shift the bargaining power away from the host state when the project is underway but meets obstacles, such as the need for refinancing, and attempt to escalate costs ex post or cut costs by reducing environmental or social standards.

MEASURE 5.2.2: NATIONAL POLICY SPACE AND RIGHT TO REGULATE CARVE-OUTS, SAFETY VALVE EXCEPTIONS

Host states can reserve enough flexibility to use a range of sustainable development policies and implement measures in the public interest appropriate to country-specific development strategies premised on their right to regulate as a sovereign prerogative. Such reservations afford policy space and regulatory flexibility to implement strategies that best fit national circumstances to pursue priorities important to sustainable development. These reservations can also come in the form of safety valves, which are exceptions from obligations to covered investors in situations deal with public policy, national security, and balance-of-payment crises. While such safety valves are crucial, it is also important to maintain the predictability of FDI screening. Identifying a list of sectors or industries that are of these special interests and thus are subject to review mechanisms can not only help to improve predictability, but also influence the conditions negotiated by the foreign investor. Sustainable energy transition, for instance, is a development priority area that can benefit from energy transition investment planning, taking into consideration the level of energy infrastructure in different country scenarios when deciding an appropriate energy mix and fossil fuel energy phaseout. Detailed transition planning and schedules can help to ensure that exceptions are not abused.

3.4 Concluding remarks

The Framework presented in this section undoubtedly takes a considerably expansive approach to international investment law on normative values threaded into the concept of sustainable development, which were introduced in relevance to this work in the first pillar introduced in Chapter 2. While there has been a proliferation of IIAs that at least partially feature such commitments,[100] host states have generally been reluctant to commit to such obligations, resulting in non-binding

99 United Nations Commission on Trade and Development (UNCTAD), 'World Investment Report 2000: Cross-Border Mergers and Acquisitions and Development' (United Nations 2000) 168.

100 These are explored in greater length in Chapter 5.

standards concerning the issues raised in these documents based on diverse hortatory language.[101] As traced earlier in this chapter, the institutional history of the UN system demonstrates remarkable progress in harmonizing this language through international consensus delivered through multilateral agreements. Viewing the same institutional history from a revolutionary lens, however, shows that there remains much progress to be made.

Of these many challenges, this work drew its focus on that of an incomplete assessment of Actions within international investment law. The Framework presented in this chapter extracted the main elements from within the UN system that are needed to addressing that challenge. The Framework alone, however, is not sufficient in achieving this task. While it broaches the issue in the fourth objective, the Framework provides little information concerning the means to assess the development contribution of international investment. Thus, to complement the Framework is the latter half of the Consolidated Method advanced by this work: the notion of Sustainable Investment.

References

Bohmer L, 'Analysis: In *Bahgat v Egypt*, Arbitrators Find That a Series of Measures, Including the Claimant's Arrest and the Freezing of His Assets, Amounted to a Violation of Two BITs' (*Investment Arbitration Reporter*, 18 August 2020) <www.iareporter.com/articles/analysis-in-bahgat-v-egypt-arbitrators-find-that-a-series-of-measures-including-the-claimants-arrest-and-the-freezing-of-his-assets-amounted-to-a-violation-of-two-bits/> accessed 19 November 2020

Bungenberg M and Reinisch A, *From Bilateral Arbitral Tribunals and Investment Courts to a Multilateral Investment Court: Options Regarding the Institutionalization of Investor-State Dispute Settlement* (Springer Nature 2020)

Cacciolatti L and others, 'Strategic Alliances and Firm Performance in Startups with a Social Mission' (2020) 106 Journal of Business Research 106

Casella B, 'Looking Through Conduit FDI in Search of Ultimate Investors—a Probabilistic Approach' (2019) 26 Transnational Corporations 109

Council of the European Union, 'Joint Interpretative Instrument on the Comprehensive Economic and Trade Agreement (CETA) Between Canada and the European Union and Its Member States' (2016) 13541/16 <https://data.consilium.europa.eu/doc/document/ST-13541-2016-INIT/en/pdf>

Desierto DA, 'ASEAN Investment Treaties, RCEP, and CPTPP: Regional Strategies, Norms, Institutions, and Politics' (2017) 27 Washington International Law Journal 349

Gakuto T, 'RCEP to Remove Tariffs on 86% of Japan's Exports to China' *Nikkei Asia* (15 November 2020) <https://asia.nikkei.com/Politics/International-relations/RCEP-to-remove-tariffs-on-86-of-Japan-s-exports-to-China> accessed 15 November 2020

Howse R, 'Designing a Multilateral Investment Court: Issues and Options' (2017) 36 Yearbook of European Law 209

Kingsbury B and others (eds), *Megaregulation Contested: Global Economic Ordering After TPP* (OUP 2019)

Krajewski M, 'A Nightmare or a Noble Dream? Establishing Investor Obligations Through Treaty-Making and Treaty-Application' (2020) 5 Business and Human Rights Journal 105

101 Markus Krajewski, 'A Nightmare or a Noble Dream? Establishing Investor Obligations Through Treaty-Making and Treaty-Application' (2020) 5 Business and Human Rights Journal 105, 116.

Moran TH, 'The United Nations and Transnational Corporations: A Review and a Perspective' (2009) 18 Transnational Corporations 91

Organisation for Economic Cooperation and Development (OECD), *The OECD Declaration and Decisions on International Investment and Multinational Enterprises: Basic Texts* (OECD 2012)

Sauvant KP, 'The Negotiations of the United Nations Code of Conduct on Transnational Corporations: Experience and Lessons Learned' (2015) 16 The Journal of World Investment & Trade 11

Schacherer S, 'The CETA Investment Chapter and Sustainable Development: Interpretative Issues' in Makane Moïse Mbengue and Stefanie Schacherer (eds), *Foreign Investment Under the Comprehensive Economic and Trade Agreement (CETA)* (Springer International Publishing 2019)

Titi C, 'The Right to Regulate' in Makane Moïse Mbengue and Stefanie Schacherer (eds), *Foreign Investment Under the Comprehensive Economic and Trade Agreement (CETA)* (Springer International Publishing 2019)

United Nations Centre on Transnational Corporations (UNCTC), 'World Investment Report 1991: The Triad in Foreign Direct Investment' (United Nations 1991) ST/CTC/118

United Nations Commission on Trade and Development (UNCTAD), 'World Investment Report 1993: Transnational Corporations and Integrated International Production' (United Nations 1993) ST/CTC/156

United Nations Commission on International Trade Law (UNCITRAL), 'World Investment Report 1994: Transnational Corporations, Employment and the Workplace' (United Nations 1994) UNCTAD/DTCI/10

United Nations Commission on International Trade Law (UNCITRAL), 'World Investment Report 1998: Trends and Determinants' (United Nations 1998)

United Nations Commission on International Trade Law (UNCITRAL), 'World Investment Report 1999: Foreign Direct Investment and the Challenge of Development' (United Nations 1999)

United Nations Commission on International Trade Law (UNCITRAL), 'World Investment Report 2000: Cross-Border Mergers and Acquisitions and Development' (United Nations 2000)

United Nations Commission on International Trade Law (UNCITRAL), 'World Investment Report 2008: Transnational Corporations and the Infrastructure Challenge' (United Nations 2008) UNCTAD/WIR/2008

United Nations Commission on International Trade Law (UNCITRAL), 'World Investment Report 2012: Towards a New Generation of Investment Policies' (United Nations 2012) UNCTAD/WIR/2012

United Nations Commission on International Trade Law (UNCITRAL), 'World Investment Report 2013: Global Value Chains: Investment and Trade for Development' (United Nations 2013) UNCTAD/WIR/2013

United Nations Commission on International Trade Law (UNCITRAL), 'World Investment Report 2014: Investing in the SDGs: An Action Plan' (United Nations 2014) UNCTAD/WIR/2014

United Nations Commission on International Trade Law (UNCITRAL), 'Investment Policy Framework for Sustainable Development' (2015) UNCTAD/DIAE/PCB/2015/5

United Nations Commission on International Trade Law (UNCITRAL), 'World Investment Report 2015: Reforming International Investment Governance' (United Nations 2015) UNCTAD/WIR/2015

United Nations Commission on International Trade Law (UNCITRAL), 'World Investment Report 2016: Investor Nationality: Policy Challenges' (United Nations 2016) UNCTAD/WIR/2016

United Nations Commission on International Trade Law (UNCITRAL), 'Possible Future Work in the Field of Dispute Settlement: Concurrent Proceedings in International Arbitration' (United Nations General Assembly 2017) A/CN.9/915

United Nations Commission on International Trade Law (UNCITRAL), 'Reform Package for the International Investment Regime' (United Nations 2018)

United Nations Commission on International Trade Law (UNCITRAL), 'World Investment Report 2018: Investment and New Industrial Policies' (United Nations 2018) UNCTAD/WIR/2018

United Nations Commission on International Trade Law (UNCITRAL), 'Possible Reform of Investor-State Dispute Settlement (ISDS)' (United Nations General Assembly 2019) A/CN.9/WG.III/WP.166

United Nations Commission on International Trade Law (UNCITRAL), 'Report of Working Group III (Investor-State Dispute Settlement Reform) on the Work of Its Thirty-Eighth Session' (United Nations General Assembly 2019) A/CN.9/1004

United Nations Commission on International Trade Law (UNCITRAL), 'World Investment Report 2019: Special Economic Zones' (United Nations 2019) UNCTAD/WIR/2019

United Nations Commission on International Trade Law (UNCITRAL), 'International Investment Agreements Reform Accelerator' (2020) UNCTAD/DIAE/PCB/INF/2020/8

United Nations Commission on International Trade Law (UNCITRAL), 'World Investment Report 2020: International Production Beyond the Pandemic' (United Nations 2020) UNCTAD/WIR/2020

United Nations Commission on International Trade Law (UNCITRAL), 'World Investment Report 2021: Investing in Sustainable Recovery' (United Nations 2021) UNCTAD/WIR/2021

United Nations Commission on International Trade Law (UNCITRAL), 'World Investment Report 2023: Investing in Sustainable Energy for All' (United Nations 2023)

United Nations Commission on International Trade Law (UNCITRAL), 'Possible Reform of Investor-State Dispute Settlement (ISDS): Draft Statute of a Standing Mechanism for the Resolution of International Investment Disputes' (United Nations General Assembly 2024) A/CN.9/WG.III/WP.239

United Nations Commission on International Trade Law (UNCITRAL), 'Possible Reform of Investor-State Dispute Settlement (ISDS): Annotations to the Draft Statute of a Standing Mechanism for the Resolution of International Investment Disputes' (United Nations General Assembly 2024) A/CN.9/WG.III/WP.240

United Nations Commission on International Trade Law (UNCITRAL), 'World Investment Report 2024: Investment Facilitation and Digital Government' (United Nations 2024) UNCTAD/WIR/2024

United Nations Department of Economic and Social Development, 'World Investment Report 1992: Transnational Corporations as Engines of Growth' (United Nations 1992) ST/CTC/130

United Nations Economic and Social Commission for Asia and the Pacific (UNESCAP), 'Foreign Direct Investment and Sustainable Development in International Investment Governance' 90 <https://unescap.org/publications/studies-trade-investment-and-innovation-no-90-foreign-direct-investment-and-sustainable>

United Nations Economic and Social Commission for Asia and the Pacific (UNESCAP), United Nations Environment Programme (UNEP), and United Nations Commission on Trade and Development (UNCTAD), *Accelerating Climate-Smart Trade and Investment for Sustainable Development* (United Nations 2021)

United Nations Inter-Agency Task Force on Financing for Development, 'Financing for Sustainable Development Report 2020' (United Nations 2020) Report of the Inter-agency Task Force on Financing for Development E/FFDF/2020

Walzenbach G, 'Procedure Over Substance? CETA and the Political Economy of Subsidiarity' (2019) 57 Commonwealth & Comparative Politics 153

Wang H, 'The Future of Deep Free Trade Agreements: The Convergence of TPP (and CPTPP) and CETA?' (2019) 53 Journal of World Trade

World Bank Group (WBG), 'Legal Framework for the Treatment of Foreign Investment, Volume II' (1992) Report to the Development Committee and Guidelines on the Treatment of Foreign Direct Investment

Wu C-H, 'ASEAN at the Crossroads: Trap and Track Between CPTPP and RCEP' (2020) 23 Journal of International Economic Law 97

4 Notion of sustainable investment

4.1 Background and scope

The first three chapters of this work identified the role of the right to regulate for the public interest within international investment law, revealed the presence of an incomplete assessment when involving the public interest of sustainable development, and established the importance of a multilateral approach founded through the UN system in responding to that incomplete assessment. As these chapters further demonstrated, the incomplete assessment of investor/investment contribution to sustainable development when measured against a host state government measure taken in the right to regulate for the public interest has been in part due to conceptual limitations of what constitutes a contribution to sustainable development. Furthermore, as explained in Chapters 2 and 3, the UN system provides a framework concerning the way in which international investment contributes to sustainable development. While the multilateral nature of UN system renders an optimal conceptual basis in completing the assessment of international investor/investment contribution to sustainable development, it provides limited guidance on assessing the investment's development contribution. This chapter thus identifies a "notion of Sustainable Investment" to aid in such an assessment.

The "notion of Sustainable Investment" (hereinafter "Notion"), as it is analysed within this work, complements the international investment–sustainable development framework ("Framework") introduced in the previous chapter. Together, they form the "Consolidated Method" constructed through this work. Like the Framework, the Notion is also based on multilateral negotiation and consensus, and is grounded in the working definition and broader concept of the role of investment in sustainable development identified in Chapters 1 and 2. The Notion adds to the approach offered in this work two broad platforms that are derived from Sustainable Investment. The first is that it provides a system of indicators and metrics that can be used to clarify the extent to which an investment has sustainable development impact. The second is the standards established for how such indicators and metrics are monitored, reviewed, and verified. By leveraging these platforms, the Notion adds to the overall approach offered by this book a means to analyse and verify the development impact of investment.

DOI: 10.4324/9781003495871-4

In line with the conceptual framework provided in Chapter 2, the Notion finds basis only in the UN system.[1] Recalling the institutional history offered in the same chapter, the first signs of the UN system's engagement with Sustainable Investment began in 1991 with Rio+20, expanding then into the Financing for Development Framework. The increasing interest in Sustainable Investment in part responded[2] to the growing centrality of the private sector in not only bridging the climate finance gap,[3] but also in contributing to the factors that cause climate change.[4] To this end, engagement by the UN system recognized the need to monitor, review, and verify the effects of investment on sustainable development, leading to the launch of key UN system engagements that are analysed throughout this chapter.

Before delving into the Notion, this chapter begins by providing an overview of the broader concepts and methodology of Sustainable Investment. Unlike conventional portfolio investment assessments that centre on financial performance, such as rates of return, Sustainable Investments assess portfolio investments based on environmental, social, and corporate governance–related performance. As was examined in greater length in Chapter 2, while Sustainable Investments enjoyed exponential growth across a wide range of asset classes, they have also been confronted with core challenges concerning definition, measurement, and equivalence between divergent methodologies of environmental, social, and governance (ESG) assessment.

As this chapter shows, while the development of ESG methodology has seen its most notable growth through the private sector, it presents many key similarities to the engagements by the UN system. This chapter also takes elements of these engagements and distils them into a framework—the Notion—that not only encapsulates the position advanced by the UN system on Sustainable Investment, but also identifies those engagements that would have the largest impact in informing the right to regulate for sustainable development in the setting of investment treaty arbitration. The Notion formulated in this chapter and the Framework produced in the previous chapter are brought together into a Consolidated Method in Chapter 5.

1 In line with the reasoning provided in Chapter 2, this excludes multilateral activities where the UN may be involved but in a more supporting role. For instance, the COP26 Finance Coalition Coordination Mechanism (United Nations Environment Programme (UNEP), 'How UNEP FI Is Supporting Finance Action Ahead of COP26' (*United Nations Environment—Finance Initiative*, 14 December 2020) <www.unepfi.org/news/how-unep-fi-is-supporting-finance-action-ahead-of-cop26/> accessed 17 December 2020). Another example would include pledges by multilateral banks and financial institutions (Maddy White, 'Development Banks Pledge to Align Trade Finance with SDGs but Skirt Around Fossil Fuels' (*Global Trade Review (GTR)*, 25 November 2020) <www.gtreview.com/news/sustainability/development-banks-pledge-to-align-trade-finance-with-sdgs-but-skirt-around-fossil-fuels/> accessed 17 December 2020).

2 This correlation is further explored in Richard Roberts and John Elkington, 'Innovation and Transformation: What It Will Take to Finance Net Zero' (EIT Climate-KIC and the UN Environment Finance Initiative 2021) Thought Leadership Series.

3 See J Timmons Roberts and others, 'Rebooting a Failed Promise of Climate Finance' (2021) Nature Climate Change 1.

4 See Thierry Philipponnat, *Breaking the Climate-Finance Doom Loop* (Finance Watch 2020).

4.2 Sustainable investment in the private sector

Evaluating the Sustainable Investment performance of portfolio investments is quickly becoming a mainstay of portfolio investment analysis.[5] Sustainable Investments, which can include a wide range of financial instruments such as bonds or funds, have not only overtaken traditional funds in Europe,[6] but have also outperformed traditional funds on more conventional measurements of financial performance. For example, this was the case on the S&P 500, which is an index of the 500 largest companies in the United States.[7] The popularity of Sustainable Investments is in part generated by an increasing demand by investors, particularly institutional investors, for extra-financial information on companies. This information helps determine the long-term market value of such investee companies, such as its practices, reputational risks, and long-term commitments.[8] As was explored in Chapter 2, firms are inclined to align their operations to ESG standards, such as through corporate social responsibility activities as a form of insurance against risk. The insurance here, however, is not financial capital to dispense as a buffer against losses derived from a risk event, such as a corporate scandal, but rather moral capital in the form of positive reputational gains in the eyes of investors and consumers. Should the company with a high ESG standard therefore experience a risk event, the built-up moral capital would theoretically buffer against reputational damage that would lead to material injury and/or performance losses.[9]

4.2.1 ESG disclosures and impacts on performance

In response to the growing market for the disclosure of extra-financial information, an array of disparate reporting standards was released starting from the Global Reporting Initiative (GRI) in 2000 to more recently the Task Force on Climate-Related Financial Disclosures (TCFD) in 2017 and the Sustainability

5 Specific issues included into these three broad categories vary depending on the level of analysis. For instance, equity and corporate bond investors may frequently examine ESG issues such as contributions to climate change, labour safety, and business integrity whereas sovereign debt investors would examine ESG issues such as the impacts of climate change, political freedoms, and rule of law (CFA Institute and Principles for Responsible Investment (PRI), 'Guidance and Case Studies for ESG Integration: Equities and Fixed Income' (2018) 18–20 <https://www.cfainstitute.org/-/media/documents/survey/guidance-case-studies-esg-integration.pdf>).

6 Alastair Marsh, 'Almost 60% of Mutual Fund Assets Will Be ESG by 2025, PwC Says' (*BNN Bloomberg*, 19 October 2020) <www.bnnbloomberg.ca/almost-60-of-mutual-fund-assets-will-be-esg-by-2025-pwc-says-1.1509837> accessed 4 February 2021.

7 FINSUM, 'ESG Investing Is Beating the S&P 500' (*Nasdaq*, 29 January 2021) <www.nasdaq.com/articles/esg-investing-is-beating-the-sp-500-2021-01-30> accessed 4 February 2021.

8 Upalat Korwatanasakul, 'Environmental, Social, and Governance Investment: Concepts, Prospects, and the Policy Landscape' in Naoko Nemoto and Peter J Morgan (eds), *Environmental, Social, and Governance Investment: Opportunities and Risks for Asia* (Asian Development Bank Institute 2020) 3.

9 Paul C Godfrey, Craig B Merrill and Jared M Hansen, 'The Relationship Between Corporate Social Responsibility and Shareholder Value: An Empirical Test of the Risk Management Hypothesis' (2009) 30 Strategic Management Journal 425, 428, 441.

Accounting Standards Board (SASB) in 2018. The formulation of metrics and standards has largely been engrossed in private sector activity, in response to the growing scrutiny and regulation of transnational corporations. The lack of harmonization and coordination between these activities, however, has resulted in a patchwork of competing approaches.[10] This has also resulted in the formation of "data holes", whereby for certain topics or themes, such as biodiversity, there is a dearth of reporting standards and datasets, making it difficult to meaningfully assess the extent to which investment positively contributes to these aspects of sustainable development.[11] Attempts at consolidation have been strategic and competitive, seeking widest adoption rather than harmonization. This resulted in overlapping metrics based on divergent data, concealed under a thick cloak of confidentiality. For users, this resulted in "reporting fatigue" as companies and investors attempt to report across different standards.[12] This can be seen as a bottom-up approach to consolidation led by the market and based on competitive standards. While such a bottom-up approach faces these challenges, research has shown that it also results in more effective convergence due to steady progression. This is in contrast to a top-down, rules-based approach,[13] where a regulatory authority provides definition and enforces compliance. Companies and investors may respond to such a top-down approach with resistance and noncompliance by seeking loopholes and cherry-picking interpretation.

4.2.1.1 ESG and corporate financial performance

Whether applied bottom up or top down, the actual correlation between ESG and corporate financial performance remains a matter of contention. Research in Sustainable Investment that seeks to link ESG indicators and corporate performance remains inconclusive, due to such variables as for instance the type of financial

10 Leslie P Norton, 'ESG Standards Convergence Could Happen in Next 12 to 24 Months, Accounting Body Chief Says' *Barrons* (14 December 2020) 24 <www.barrons.com/articles/esg-standards-convergence-could-happen-in-next-12-to-24-months-accounting-body-chief-says-51607968355> accessed 16 December 2020.

11 Sophie Robinson-Tillett, 'UN-Backed Body Identifies Main Obstacles for ESG Data, Plans to Engage with Regulators' (*Responsible Investor*, 14 December 2020). See also Bjorg Jonsdottir and others, 'Barriers to Using ESG Data for Investment Decisions' (2022) 14 Sustainability 5157.

12 Toshikazu Hayashi, 'Competition in Extra-Financial Information Disclosure Frameworks and Standards: Significance and Challenges for Effective Convergence' in Naoko Nemoto and Peter J Morgan (eds), *Environmental, Social, and Governance Investment: Opportunities and Risks for Asia* (Asian Development Bank Institute 2020) 33.

13 One such a top-down approach may occur through "specialised administrative, regulatory, financial, and knowledge structures" that define the environmental obligations and entitlements between the state and society (Andreas Duit, Peter H Feindt and James Meadowcroft, 'Greening Leviathan: The Rise of the Environmental State?' (2016) 25 Environmental Politics 1, 6–12). Du and others, for instance, determine that the influence of these institutions have a direct effect on green investment in China (Helen S Du and others, 'The Influencing Mechanism of Multi-Factors on Green Investments: A Hybrid Analysis' (2019) 239 Journal of Cleaner Production 117977).

institution involved, i.e. an institutional investor versus a bank;[14] the presence of corporate controversies with adverse impacts on financial performance;[15] or the size of the firm.[16] In connection to sovereign debt instruments, for example, country ESG ratings have an unclear influence on borrowing costs[17] compared to more established ratings that look exclusively at economic productivity. At the firm level, returning to a comparison with the S&P 500, for instance, the correlation between a higher placement on the S&P 500 and financeability was shown to be three times more positive than a coefficient between a high ESG rating and financeability.[18] However, empirical studies have pointed in both directions, with meta-studies showing a clearly positive relationship between ESG impact and both corporate financial performance and investment performance.[19]

The connection between greater ESG integration and performance with shareholder value creation also remains a matter of contention. During periods of crisis, for example like a global pandemic, Sustainable Investments were widely believed to have greater resilience to such exogenous impacts—a presumption that has been refuted as stylistic[20] and not supported by the actual performance of Sustain-

14 See, for instance, Oana Marina Bătae, Voicu Dan Dragomir and Liliana Feleagă, 'The Relationship between Environmental, Social, and Financial Performance in the Banking Sector: A European Study' (2021) 290 Journal of Cleaner Production 125791.

15 Niccolò Nirino and others, 'Corporate Controversies and Company's Financial Performance: Exploring the Moderating Role of ESG Practices' (2021) 162 Technological Forecasting and Social Change 120341, 5.

16 See, for instance, Juan Pablo Sánchez-Infante Hernández, Benito Yañez-Araque and Juan Moreno-García, 'Moderating Effect of Firm Size on the Influence of Corporate Social Responsibility in the Economic Performance of Micro-, Small- and Medium-Sized Enterprises' (2020) 151 Technological Forecasting and Social Change 119774.

17 Nemoto and Liu in their empirical testing of the literature found that the impact of ESG ratings and the use of credit default swaps (CDS), which is a form of insurance more widely used in higher risk settings, varies depending on numerous macroeconomic factors and performance of specific ESG themes, which in turn show regional and country variance. In general, however, a high ESG ranking has been associated to reduced CDS spread (Naoko Nemoto and Lian Liu, 'How Will Environmental, Social, and Governance Factors Affect the Sovereign Borrowing Cost?' in Naoko Nemoto and Peter J Morgan (eds), *Environmental, Social, and Governance Investment: Opportunities and Risks for Asia* [Asian Development Bank Institute 2020] 82).

18 Naoko Nemoto and Lian Liu, 'How Will Environmental, Social, and Governance Factors Affect the Sovereign Borrowing Cost?' in Naoko Nemoto and Peter J Morgan (eds), *Environmental, Social, and Governance Investment: Opportunities and Risks for Asia* (Asian Development Bank Institute 2020) 77.

19 See Tensie Whelan and others, 'ESG and Financial Performance: Uncovering the Relationship by Aggregating Evidence from 1,000 Plus Studies Published Between 2015–2020' (Rockefeller Asset Management and NYU Stern Center for Sustainable Business 2021); Gunnar Friede, Timo Busch and Alexander Bassen, 'ESG and Financial Performance: Aggregated Evidence from More Than 2000 Empirical Studies' (2015) 5 Journal of Sustainable Finance & Investment 210, 212.

20 Baruch Lev and others, 'ESG Didn't Immunize Stocks Against the Covid-19 Market Crash' (*The Harvard Law School Forum on Corporate Governance*, 8 September 2020) <https://corpgov.law.harvard.edu/2020/09/08/esg-didnt-immunize-stocks-against-the-covid-19-market-crash/> accessed 17 February 2021.

able Investment funds.[21] However, a blanket dismissal of this kind is difficult to argue. If a company is excluded from an investment because it does not meet the investment's ESG scope, but it is then compelled to undergo reformation to meet those requirements, then the firm's willingness to shoulder those reformation costs towards ESG compliance can be viewed as impactful.[22] This endogeneity of ESG disclosures on value creation also finds support in research pointing to the "moderating role" of ESG disclosures: negative valuation linked to ESG performance is alleviated through disclosures that affect investor sentiment.[23] Verifiable progress towards improving distressed ESG performance can signal to investors that the company is responsive not only to investor sentiment, but also to the rapidly changing milieu of international investment. For instance, if investors express concern about the plastic waste arising from a sporting goods company, and in response the company embarks on initiatives that have an actual impact on reducing plastic waste, this initial progress has shown to mitigate investor concerns and thus boost confidence and performance.[24]

As was described in Chapter 2, Sustainable Investment does not exclusively operate on pecuniary, shareholder-centric objectives. To assess a correlation between ESG indicators and strictly financial performance, therefore, remains inherently limited due to incongruent objectives. The shift to stakeholderism as an objective is perhaps best embodied by sovereign wealth funds, which are "managed according to the objectives of the sovereign", thereby making the "ultimate beneficiary . . . not a specific individual but rather the government itself, the State, the current or future generations". Therefore, as long-term institutional investors, sovereign wealth funds "have the responsibility to promote sustainable development and social justice through their investment, in order to give future generations the opportunity to reap the awards of the investment".[25] When viewed in this manner, sovereign wealth funds effectively extended the concept of fiduciary duty from the relatively immediate horizon of profitability to the long-term objective of intergenerationality.

21 Laura Mervelskemper, Daniel Kaltofen and Stefan Stein, 'Are Sustainable Investment Funds Worth the Effort?' (2014) 4 Journal of Sustainable Finance & Investment 127, 136. For the correlation between stringent ESG requirements and investment performance, see L Renneboog, J Ter Horst and C Zhang, 'Socially Responsible Investments: Institutional Aspects, Performance, and Investor Behavior' (2008) 32 Journal of Banking and Finance 1723.

22 A Barnea, R Heinkel and A Kraus, 'Green Investors and Corporate Investment' (2005) 16 Structural Change and Economic Dynamics 332, 342.

23 Ali Fatemi, Martin Glaum and Stefanie Kaiser, 'ESG Performance and Firm Value: The Moderating Role of Disclosure' (2018) 38 Global Finance Journal 45–46.

24 See, for instance, a study on performance metrics involving Adidas and Parley in Martin Vezér and Doug Morrow, *Blue Investing: Searching for Solutions to Ocean Plastics* (Analytics Firm Sustainalytics 2018) 5.

25 Xenia Karametaxas, 'Sovereign Wealth Funds as Socially Responsible Investors' in Giovanna Adinolfi and others (eds), *International Economic Law: Contemporary Issues* (Springer International Publishing 2017) 276.

Admittedly, while such a principle may not universally apply to the actual practice of sovereign wealth funds,[26] it does help to illustrate the form through which Sustainable Investments may take place, their underlying reasons, and in turn their significance to the Notion in this book.

4.2.2 ESG strategies and measurements

Turning now to the methodology of ESG investing, there are three broad strategies employed.[27] The first strategy involves screening companies prior to an investment based on a negative list, a positive list, and/or based on certain principles. A negative list approach screens out companies that exhibit certain activities or traits, or exclusionary criteria, from potential investments. For instance, companies that deal in firearms, tobacco, and fossil fuels may be excluded from receiving certain Sustainable Investments. Conversely, a positive list or best-in-class approach identifies favourable activities and/or traits of companies that would qualify them for investments. Rules-based or principles-based screening applies a set of widely recognized norms like human rights in determining whether companies would qualify for investment.[28]

The second strategy is known as ESG overlay or integration, which seeks to apply ESG principles to corporate practices as a means to work towards fulfilling Sustainable Investment conditionality. This is achieved either internally or externally, with the former involving self-regulatory decisions by the business enterprises in an effort to more closely align their operations to a set of ESG standards. External pressure by shareholders, particularly institutional investors and asset management firms with sizeable positions, leveraging equity can also be exerted on corporate leadership to pressure companies to integrate ESG standards into business practices.

Finally, the third strategy is broadly embodied by active investing, which seeks to arrange investments around a certain theme, such as sustainability, biodiversity, and so forth. This strategy also includes impact investing, which is made "with the intention to generate positive, measurable social and environmental impact alongside a financial return".[29]

26 For instance, proposed amendments to the Employee Retirement Income Security Act of 1974 (United States) to limit the duty of loyalty to beneficiaries of pension funds to pecuniary factors alone rather than any ESG factors.

27 Upalat Korwatanasakul, 'Environmental, Social, and Governance Investment: Concepts, Prospects, and the Policy Landscape' in Naoko Nemoto and Peter J Morgan (eds), *Environmental, Social, and Governance Investment: Opportunities and Risks for Asia* (Asian Development Bank Institute 2020) 6.

28 For example, the Guiding Principles on Business and Human Rights (2011) attributes the responsibility of due diligence to respect human rights not only to business enterprises, but also to the states in which they are domiciled and/or originated (Office of the High Commissioner on Human Rights (OHCHR), *Guiding Principles on Business and Human Rights* (United Nations 2011) 4).

29 Global Impact Investing Network (GIIN), 'What You Need to Know About Impact Investing' (*About Impact Investing*) <https://thegiin.org/impact-investing/need-to-know/> accessed 7 February 2021.

4.2.2.1 Measuring ESG performance

The diversity of ESG metrics arise from their equally assorted authorship. While there have been efforts at harmonization,[30] the variations of challenges facing these efforts are essentially limited only by the imagination given that financial products are passed through many hands during the securitization process and the rise of alternative financial systems.[31] For example, an exchange-traded fund (ETF) may demonstrate ESG behaviour overall as a basket of assets, but the individual assets that are structured into the ETF may not achieve that same level of performance, or may themselves be involved in a longer global value chain that is noncompliant.[32]

Rating agencies and institutions have generally been at the helm in navigating ESG measurements. For instance, the ESG measuring system developed by Morgan Stanley Capital International (MSCI) defines ESG performance as existing between ESG and financial performance. The MSCI thus measures ESG performance through three transmission channels between ESG and financial performance. The first transmission channel between ESG and financial performance assumes that business practices that are more aligned with ESG signal more stability in revenue streams for the company, which can in turn be identified by increasing yields from dividends. In reverse, for instance, a company with unstable earnings would be less likely to absorb the reformation costs to align its practices with ESG standards, just as it would also be unlikely to provide higher steady income coupon rates for its investors at the risk of reneging on such expectations.

30 See, for instance, Siobhan Riding, 'CFA Forges Ahead with ESG Standard Despite Criticism' *Financial Times* (23 November 2020) <www.ft.com/content/5430ff68-2a73-4e1b-bf40-8de6a76389a2> accessed 20 February 2021; Khalid Azizuddin, 'Russian Banks to Develop National ESG Principles and Support Green Taxonomy' (*Responsible Investor*, 27 October 2020); Michael Holder, 'Morgan Stanley Will Measure CO2 Impact of Loans and Investments' (*GreenBiz*, 27 July 2020) <www.greenbiz.com/article/morgan-stanley-will-measure-co2-impact-loans-and-investments> accessed 20 February 2021; Global Impact Investing Network (GIIN), 'What You Need to Know about Impact Investing' (*About Impact Investing*) <https://thegiin.org/impact-investing/need-to-know/> accessed 7 February 2021; 'DBS Rolls Out Sustainable and Transition Finance Framework, Taxonomy' *The Straits Times* (29 June 2020) <www.straitstimes.com/business/banking/dbs-rolls-out-sustainable-and-transition-finance-framework-taxonomy> accessed 20 February 2021.

31 For example, there is considerable business interest surrounding the idea of ESG-aligned cryptocurrencies. See, for instance, 'Wall Street ESG Gold Rush Sees a "Green" Bitcoin' *Bloomberg Professional Services* (3 June 2021) <www.bloomberg.com/professional/blog/wall-street-esg-gold-rush-sees-a-green-bitcoin/> accessed 18 June 2021.

32 See, for instance, Steve Johnson, 'BlackRock ETF Thrusts Climate Change into Political Sphere' *Financial Times* (6 October 2020) <www.ft.com/content/112e536a-91db-426a-aef6-3106f0717972> accessed 20 February 2021; 'BNP Paribas Asset Management Launches First Blue Economy ETF' (*Mondo Visione*, 13 October 2020) <https://mondovisione.com/media-and-resources/news/bnp-paribas-asset-management-launches-first-blue-economy-etf/> accessed 20 February 2021; 'JP Morgan's Launch of Carbon Transition ETF Signals Strong Investment Flows Into ESG' (*Banking Exchange*, 20 December 2020) <www.bankingexchange.com/sri-exchange/item/8513-jp-morgan-s-launch-of-carbon-transition-etf-signals-strong-investment-flows-into-esg> accessed 20 February 2021.

The second transmission channel is that higher ESG performance also acts as a buffer against idiosyncratic risk, which are risk events that are particular to specific industries or contexts, which in turn have a negative impact on financial performance known as financial drawdown events. An enlightening case study is that of Ørsted, the Danish oil giant that was left nearly bankrupt during its transition to eventually become the world's largest developer of offshore wind energy. As a result, Ørsted was not only able to largely avoid the risk increasingly faced by oil companies,[33] but also exceeded the market value of its former rivals Occidental Petroleum Corporation and Eni SpA.[34]

The final transmission channel between ESG performance and financial performance is in the increased efficiency of capital investment that arises from higher resilience against volatility originating in risk events or risk characteristics of the investment itself. This returns to the idea of moral capital serving as a buffer between a high-risk event or investment and its direct materiality on financial performance. Signalling this ESG performance, such as by joining highly public ESG initiatives, can enhance investor and/or business confidence, which can then materialize into heighted financial performance.[35] For example, the main beneficiaries of palm oil, such as global corporations like Nestlé, PepsiCo, and Procter & Gamble, participate in a private sector initiative to finance forest conservation and reforestation called the "Rimba Collective".[36] This participation follows the uncovering of mass deforestation by palm oil producers that are linked by supply chain to these and other global corporations.[37] In doing so, these corporations attempt to insulate themselves with moral capital against reputational damage.

Yet beyond the correlation between ESG and corporate financial performance, of greater interest to this study is the assessment of ESG performance as an approach

33 See, for instance, litigation brought against Royal Dutch Shell (Neil Munshi and Anjli Raval, 'Shell Loses Dutch Case over Nigeria Oil Spills' *Financial Times* (29 January 2021) <www.ft.com/content/663c6261-338e-4f6a-8ae4-11416607db71> accessed 18 February 2021; Daniel Boffey, 'Court Orders Royal Dutch Shell to Cut Carbon Emissions by 45% by 2030' *The Guardian* (26 May 2021) <www.theguardian.com/business/2021/may/26/court-orders-royal-dutch-shell-to-cut-carbon-emissions-by-45-by-2030> accessed 18 June 2021).

34 Sarah McFarlane, 'One Oil Company's Rocky Path to Renewable Energy' *Wall Street Journal* (8 June 2021) <www.wsj.com/articles/one-oil-companys-rocky-path-to-renewable-energy-orsted-11623170953> accessed 18 June 2021.

35 Guido Giese, Zoltan Nagy and Linda-Eling Lee, 'Deconstructing ESG Ratings Performance: Risk and Return for E, S and G by Time Horizon, Sector and Weighting' (MSCI ESG Research LLC 2020) 7 <www.msci.com/www/research-paper/deconstructing-esg-ratings/01921647796> accessed 13 July 2020.

36 Robin Hicks, 'Indonesian Palm Oil Firm to "Remedy Past Mistakes" with Forest Restoration Plan' *Eco-Business* (15 June 2021) <www.eco-business.com/news/indonesian-palm-oil-firm-to-remedy-past-mistakes-with-forest-restoration-plan/> accessed 20 June 2021.

37 'The Chain: Detected Deforestation Within Oil Palm Concessions Has Decreased so Far in 2020' (*Chain Reaction Research*, 20 August 2020) <https://chainreactionresearch.com/the-chain-detected-deforestation-within-oil-palm-concessions-has-decreased-so-far-in-2020/> accessed 5 July 2021.

to measuring the sustainable development impact of foreign investment. A few of the main measurements used in the financial sector are identified below.

Returning to the MSCI, research finds that varying methodologies in the sourcing of ESG data, e.g. company disclosures and media reports, as well as weighting of the different ESG dimensions, both impact the resultant ESG score. For instance, the combination of availability of data and weighting for lacking data is in practice accounting for data holes: the lack of ESG data for a certain industry is compensated by applying a weight to the ESG data that is available. Adjusting weights depends on the methodology selected. The MSCI ESG Ratings choose to curate key ESG issues within specific industries or sub-industries[38] based on their relevance to those sectors. This is determined by the strength of the transmission channel between ESG and financial performance for that particular industry,[39] which are then weighted against the remaining issues in calculating the aggregate score.

In application to, for instance, Coca-Cola, the MSCI ESG Ratings place particular weight on "Packaging Material & Waste" under the environmental pillar, which is then followed by "Health & Safety" under the social pillar as representing the two predominant ESG issues for the industry. The remaining issue in this case would be governance, which here is a broad overlay in governance, referring to factors that are common across all corporations such as anticorruption or demographic equality in executive positions and pay.[40] The ESG data rendered for the environmental and social pillars would be weighted to affect the company's aggregated score more significantly. Neutralizing differences in sectors and industries through a normalization process is important in rendering informative aggregate ESG scores. This can involve accounting for total volatility of an ESG factor applicable to certain industries in the total performance of individual firms in that industry, resulting in a return to volatility ratio. Returning to the Coca-Cola example, the impact on the health of consumers would be of heightened risk for the beverage industry in general, which means that the returns of positive performance in this risk area would need to be weighted higher to normalize differences in volatility specific to the industry and to the product that may not exist as prominently for other industries and/or products.

Refinitiv, a global provider of financial market data, categorizes 186 key performance indicators (KPIs) thematically in scoping its ESG performance measurement.[41] Under environment, categories include "resource use", "emissions", and "innovation", within which 68 indicators are categorized. More than 450 data points inform the indicators used in the Refinitiv assessment in the form of either Boolean data (yes, no, or null) or numeric values, which will either be positive or

38 Defined by the Global Industry Classification Standard (GICS) developed by MSCI and S&P.

39 Based on "active exposure" or the t-statistic correlation between the selected key issue and the three channels of economic transmission (profitability, valuation, and volatility) in a positive relationship between ESG factor and corporate financial performance.

40 Giese, Nagy and Lee (n 35) 8–9.

41 Extracted from 'Environmental, Social and Governance (ESG) Scores from Refinitiv' (Refinitiv 2020).

negative (water conserved is a positive, whereas the amount of emissions is a negative). Category scores are also weighted differently based on their ESG magnitude, or materiality. Weights are based on the impact of a certain sector or industry on a ESG dimension as well as the level of transparency on questions of high impact. For instance, Coca-Cola is weighted on themes of health and on whether it is transparent in disclosing its health-related data. A low health rating would thus have a much greater impact on the ESG rating of Coca-Cola, as would the decision not to disclose nutritional information on the product. After the ESG rating is calculated, Refinitiv then applies an "ESG controversy overlay" to provide a readjusted aggregate score based on the severity of the controversy as well as benchmarking whether such controversies are common and/or specific to the company's industry. An ESG controversy can be a "toxic waste spill (environmental), human rights violation (social), or corrupt CEOs (governance)".[42] The "controversy score" is derived from the number of controversies, based on a list of 23 controversy topics, published in the media about a company over a fiscal year. The "severity rate" of the controversy is weighted down for companies with larger market capitalization (0.33 for large companies, 0.67 for mid-sized companies, and 1 for small companies), which is their aggregate market value, since they are more likely to receive media attention. The number of controversies is multiplied by the severity rate resulting in the controversy score, which if lower than the ESG score, and the resulting "ESGC score" (the added "C" referring to *controversy*) is the average between the two values.[43]

The S&P 500 Dow Jones Indices (DJI) ESG Score bases its scoping on characteristics decided to be unique to specific industries across 61 industry types. This is at the core of its materiality assessment.[44] Indicators are weighted differently between industries based on their level of impact building on 600 to 1,000 data points. Weighting also compensates for data gaps, meaning that if a company does not disclose information concerning a certain indicator, it is penalized and another indicator is weighted more heavily as a result. Weights are then normalized so that they are comparable across industries without one industry becoming innately higher scoring than another due to the internal characteristics assigned to that industry grouping. S&P also applies an exclusionary criterion, which automatically eliminates certain companies from being rated if they produce or primarily profit from tobacco, are involved in controversial weapons, score in the bottom 5% of the UN Global Compact scoring, and/or derive more than 5% of their profit from thermal coal. These exclusionary criteria undergo continued adjustments based on

42 Refinitiv, 'Detecting ESG Controversies' <www.refinitiv.com/en/labs/projects/esg-controversy-prediction> accessed 28 April 2021.

43 Refinitiv, 'Environmental, Social and Governance (ESG) Scores from Refinitiv' (2021) 14–15. A similar approach is taken by Sustainalytics (see Sustainalytics, 'Identify Controversies Affecting Portfolio Companies' (*Controversies Research*) <www.sustainalytics.com/investor-solutions/esg-research/controversies-research> accessed 29 April 2021).

44 Extracted from Reid Steadman and others, 'The S&P 500 ESG Index: Defining the Sustainable Core' (S&P Dow Jones Indices 2021).

investor consultations. Scores are then rebalanced when confronted with ESG controversies. One unique practice by the S&P DJI ESG Score is assessing the potential of a firm of realizing its ESG potential to rebalance scoring for firms that are not inherently more aligned with the ESG indicators.

Deconstructing such ESG rating systems, such as those briefly introduced above, renders three core elements.[45] The scope provides the operative denotation of ESG, such as through the identification of key issues or KPIs within each ESG pillar. Indicators provide the numerical measurement of ESG performance within the defined scope based on different scales of materiality, which is weighting certain indicators during assessment. Finally, the aggregation rule is how indicators are neutralized into a single rating. A study of major ESG ratings providers demonstrated that while these three core elements may be a common feature in all ratings, there is considerable divergence in the resulting aggregated ESG rating, largely due to differences in the way that rating agencies assess the same firm's performance on the same indicator.[46]

There have been efforts to produce shared standards on disclosures and rating methods, such as by the GRI, the SASB, and the TFCD. The TFCD, for instance, was the first finance sector initiative to identify "scenario-based risk assessment in financial disclosure" in line with the Paris Agreement.[47] With it, investors can better assess the "climate-related risk and opportunity" in making investment decisions, based on factors such as the materiality of climate risk on investment as well as "stress tests" to measure the extent to which an investment can be compatible with an emission reduction target before exceeding a certain amount of risk exposure.[48] While the standards produced by these initiatives are disparate, resulting in some of the consequences identified earlier in this chapter such as overburdening companies with the reporting process,[49] standard-based disclosures nevertheless remain important to the notion of Sustainable Investment. For instance, research shows that the indicators employed by SASB are 70% aligned with the UN SDG country indicators, meaning that they bear considerable and direct relevance to the achievement of the Sustainable Development Goals (SDGs).[50]

Efforts at unifying these standards remain ongoing. For instance, the World Economic Forum (WEF) in 2020 collaborated with the four largest accounting firms,

45 Florian Berg, Julian F Kölbel and Roberto Rigobon, 'Aggregate Confusion: The Divergence of ESG Ratings' (MIT Sloan School of Management 2019) 5822-19 3.

46 Florian Berg, Julian F Kölbel and Roberto Rigobon, 'Aggregate Confusion: The Divergence of ESG Ratings' (MIT Sloan School of Management 2019) 5822-19 8.

47 United Nations Environment Programme Finance Initiative (UNEP FI), 'Changing Course: A Comprehensive Investor Guide to Scenario-Based Methods for Climate Risk Assessment, in Response to the TCFD' (United Nations 2019) 17 <www.unepfi.org/investment/tcfd/>.

48 United Nations Environment Programme Finance Initiative (UNEP FI), 'Changing Course: A Comprehensive Investor Guide to Scenario-Based Methods for Climate Risk Assessment, in Response to the TCFD' (United Nations 2019) 19 <www.unepfi.org/investment/tcfd/>.

49 Andreea Papuc, 'Patchwork of ESG Ratings Sow Investor Confusion as Flows Surge' *Bloomberg* (9 July 2021).

50 Gina Gambetta, 'BlackRock Finds Large Overlap between SASB and SDG Indicators' (*Responsible Investor*, 1 July 2021).

Deloitte, Ernst & Young, Klynveld Peat Marwick Goerdeler (KPMG), and PricewaterhouseCoopers (PwC), to produce a set of metrics aligned with the SDGs that sought to combine these different disclosure standards.[51] The result was four pillars of "principle ESG domains"—Principles of Governance, Planet, People, and Prosperity—consisting of core metrics that sought universality across industries and firms insofar as they were material to a given company's long-term value creation. The metrics are organized into themes and divided into core and expanded metrics, the latter serving as a means for companies to improve their long-term value by providing more in-depth disclosures. The WEF's proposed common metrics add a "prosperity" pillar, which seeks to capture the value creating impact of companies and investment. The prosperity pillar includes such metrics as job creation, amount spent as research and development, investment into communities, and tax reporting.[52]

The attempt by the WEF in proposing a common metric illustrated the primary limitations of Sustainable Investment: competing frameworks leading to limitations imposed on both the availability of data sources as well as transparency in methodologies. Incompatibility between these frameworks remains difficult to analyse due to the inaccessibility of data, weighting algorithms, and aggregation calculations, which are closely guarded secrets. They remain out of reach for fear of losing a growing competition to lead the exponential rise in demand for Sustainable Investment by both the private and public sectors.

Elsewhere, there has been scepticism concerning whether underdeveloped metrics like ESG, a fact embodied by the lack of coherence between competing ratings, can (or should) be reflected in market valuations. This has been in part due to the presence of anomalies that while having materiality on ESG performance cannot be explained through conventional approaches to modern portfolio theory, such as the capital asset pricing model, which attempts to capture reduced risk following asset diversification.[53]

Continuing from this overview of the main concepts and challenges of Sustainable Investment, the following section is now well postured to assemble the Notion of Sustainable Investment, which is the latter half of the Consolidated Method that this book advances.

4.3 Notion of sustainable investment

This final section distils common and defining features across the main multilateral initiatives of the UN system[54] and proposes a comprehensive notion of

51 Extracted from WEF, *Toward Common Metrics and Consistent Reporting of Sustainable Value Creation* (World Economic Forum (WEF) 2020).

52 WEF, *Toward Common Metrics and Consistent Reporting of Sustainable Value Creation* (World Economic Forum (WEF) 2020) 23.

53 Tadahiro Nakajima, 'ESG Investment' in Tadahiro Nakajima and others (eds), *ESG Investment in the Global Economy* (Springer 2021) 13.

54 The UN Environment Programme Finance Initiative (UNEP FI), UN-Backed Principles for Responsible Investment (PRI), UN-Convened Net-Zero Asset Owner Alliance (NZAOA), Global Investors for Sustainable Development (GISD), and the UN Sustainable Stock Exchange (SSE).

Sustainable Investment ("Notion").[55] The notion complements the international investment-sustainable development framework ("Framework") assembled in Chapter 3, both of which are based on the SDGs, but in application to the wide range of private sector investors in what the UN system identifies as the modern fiduciary duty.[56] The PRI defines this modern fiduciary duty as considering "all financially material factors regardless of their origin . . . positive duties on investors to incorporate [sustainability issues]".[57]

As identified earlier in Chapter 2, the UN system has historically taken and continues to take a facilitative role towards the substantive elements of modern fiduciary duty, supporting private and public sector initiatives to navigate monitoring, reporting, and verification of sustainability performance. As identified in the present chapter, the extent to which the UN system becomes involved in this regard has varied across agencies. With only a few exceptions, UN agencies have taken largely a supportive role, such as in knowledge sharing and technical guidance. The alternative has been UN agencies working more closely with the private sector, forming networks such as the Principles for Responsible Investment (PRI), Net-Zero Asset Owner Alliance (NZAOA), and more recently the Global Sustainable Finance Observatory operated by UN Trade and Development (UNCTAD). The Global Sustainable Finance Observatory does well to embody the partnership between the UN and public and private sector entities engaged in Sustainable Investment: the facilitative role of the UN system brings legitimacy to private and public sector initiatives, which in return provides the UN system with the opportunity to observe and analyse performance and trends.[58]

For the purposes of this chapter, however, the Notion examines main instances of the UN intervening more substantively in the operative level of Sustainable Investment. As seen in private sector approaches to Sustainable Investments, the Notion consists also of three components: scope, KPIs, and an aggregated metric. The scope and the indicators that constitute it define the characteristics of Sustainable Investment. As demonstrated in the previous section, both the scope and its KPIs differ by the ESG measurement applied. Broadly, however, "sustainability-themed funds" are those that use "ESG criteria as part of their security selection process

55 See Appendix 2 for a tabular summarization of the Notion.

56 Kris Douma, Louise Scott and Anna Bulzomi, *The SDG Investment Case* (Principles for Responsible Investment (PRI) 2017) 7.

57 The PRI identifies three principles: (1) financially material ESG factors should be incorporated in investment decision-making, (2) investors should consider ESG factors consistent with the time frame of the obligation, and (3) investors should understand and incorporate the sustainability preferences of their clients/beneficiaries/savers (Kris Douma, Louise Scott and Anna Bulzomi, *The SDG Investment Case* (Principles for Responsible Investment (PRI) 2017) 14).

58 See, for instance, the "UNCTAD Sustainability Integration Framework for Institutional Investors", which summarizes observations made by UNCTAD of major pension and sovereign wealth funds (United Nations Trade and Development (UNCTAD), 'Asset Owner Rankings' (*Global Sustainable Finance Observatory*) <https://gsfo.org/assets-owner-rankings> accessed 2 August 2024).

or seek a measurable positive impact alongside financial returns".[59] This includes KPIs categorized into themes or dimensions, such as ESG, which as a scope defines the normative content of sustainable development to be measured. The key features of the Notion are explored in greater length below.

4.3.1 Key feature 1: scope

Scope in the Notion can be reduced to two core elements: net positive impact and catalyst effect. These themes are present across the Sustainable Investment initiatives and programmes of the UN system examined in this book.

4.3.1.1 Element 1.1: net positive impact

Perhaps the most fundamental element to the scope of the Notion is net positive impact. This refers not only to the extra-financial value added that results from the investment, but also accounts for the negative impacts of the investment as well. An investment that results in a positive environmental impact at the cost of a larger social consequence, for instance, would not result in a net positive impact. However, an investment that contributes to an area that is a priority in achieving the SDGs, or a key SDG sector, may result in a large enough positive impact to outweigh potential negative costs in the process.

The World Investment Report 2014 identified ten key SDG sectors where approximately USD 3.3 to 4.5 trillion of investment per annum was required in order to meet the goal set out by the 2030 Agenda.[60] Investments in key SDG sectors include (1) power generation, transmission, and distribution; (2) roads, airports, ports, and rail; (3) telecommunications infrastructure; (4) water provision and sanitation for industry and households; (5) agriculture and/or rural development, research, and safety nets; (6) climate change mitigation–relevant infrastructure, such as in renewable energies and the research and development of climate-friendly technologies; (7) adaptation capacities against the impact of climate change in inter alia agriculture, infrastructure, water, and coastal management; (8) conservation and safeguarding of ecosystems; (9) health infrastructure; and (10) education infrastructure.[61]

However, while these key sectors represent financing gaps in achieving the SDGs, they do not necessarily represent the normative aspects of the Notion. In other words, any investment in a key SDG sector would not embody the Notion,

59 United Nations Trade and Development (UNCTAD), 'World Investment Report 2020: International Production Beyond the Pandemic' (United Nations 2020) UNCTAD/WIR/2020 187.

60 United Nations Trade and Development (UNCTAD), 'World Investment Report 2014: Investing in the SDGs: An Action Plan' (United Nations 2014) UNCTAD/WIR/2014 140.

61 United Nations Trade and Development (UNCTAD), 'World Investment Report 2014: Investing in the SDGs: An Action Plan' (United Nations 2014) UNCTAD/WIR/2014 142.

but it would add to the extent to which that investment results in net positive impact.[62]

The idea of a net positive impact is perhaps best captured by the Sustainable Development Investment (SDI) concept advanced by the Global Investors for Sustainable Development (GISD). SDI bases the measurement of an investment's positive contribution to sustainable development on the SDGs,[63] spelling out the fundamental balance between positive and negative impacts: positive (SDG-aligned) contribution weighed against negative (not SDG–aligned) consequence. For this reason, divestment and exclusionary screens alone do not qualify as SDI because while they help to reduce potential negative impacts of investment, divestment does not necessarily result in a positive contribution. In fact, divestment may exacerbate capacities to advance the SDGs by detracting from its capital base, such as in the form of unemployment.

Evaluating positive contribution to the negative impact in SDI occurs at either two levels: (1) private sector enterprise or (2) investment project.[64] This means that while a transnational corporation may exhibit many of the characteristics of the Sustainable Investment in its operations, this does not mean that its investments qualify as SDI under that pedigree alone. Conversely, an investment project may by its own merits be considered an SDI even if the company does not demonstrate as a corporate entity the characteristics of the Sustainable Investment in its operations.[65] In other words, both the investor and the investment are taken into consideration when assessing an investment as SDI. As per the former, characteristics of the corporate entity include:

1 Integrating the SDGs into core business models by aligning internal strategies, policies, and guidelines with the SDGs and introducing long-term performance metrics, accelerated company disclosures, and reporting on social and environmental issues;[66]
2 Demonstrating directional gestures, such as net zero, as well as costs for failing to fulfil those commitments;

62 Investments in key SDG sectors are examined from the perspective of the notion of Sustainable Investment.

63 In contrast to ESG, gauging investment against the SDGs means "looking primarily at maximizing opportunities by addressing risks to people and the environment throughout operations and value chains and, in addition, developing beneficial products, services or investments that help advance the SDGs" (United Nations Global Compact (UNGC), Principles for Responsible Investment (PRI), and Global Reporting Initiative (GRI), 'In Focus: Addressing Investor Needs in Business Reporting on the SDGs' (2018) 5).

64 'Definition of Sustainable Development Investing' (Global Investors for Sustainable Development Alliance (GISD) 2020) 2.

65 Based on the policy document, Global Investors for Sustainable Development Alliance (GISD), 'Renewed, Recharged and Reinforced: Urgent Actions to Harmonize and Scale Sustainable Finance' (2020).

66 Global Investors for Sustainable Development Alliance (GISD), 'Renewed, Recharged and Reinforced: Urgent Actions to Harmonize and Scale Sustainable Finance' (2020) 21.

3 Instituting "fit and proper" tests for board members and directors to ensure that they are appropriately informed and skilled to scrutinize sustainability issues, including members with relevant expertise when involving industries or companies with high ESG risk exposure;[67] and
4 Integrating the SDGs into stewardship codes[68] with the involvement of governments and international bodies negotiated at the international level (norms-based screening).[69]

As per the investment, the GISD identifies the following characteristics:

1 Reporting sustainability and contributions to SDGs aligned with standards that are globally comprehensive, science-based and empirical;[70]
2 Revealing portfolio alignment to climate scenarios with reference to temperature pathways, e.g., 1.5°C;[71] and
3 Reporting supply chain due diligence[72] based on internationally established principles and guidelines with multinationals subject to stricter requirements.[73]

Net positive impact is also at the centre of the SDG Impact Standards and SDG Finance Taxonomy by the United Nations Development Programme (UNDP), which bases scope of assessment ("impact thesis") on the extent to which the assessed activity promotes achieving the SDGs.[74] Standard 1 of the Impact Standards identifies three elements of an impact thesis, namely the specification of:

1 A clearly identified positive impact target based on a SDG "and/or other sustainable development outcome area";

67 Global Investors for Sustainable Development Alliance (GISD), 'Renewed, Recharged and Reinforced: Urgent Actions to Harmonize and Scale Sustainable Finance' (2020) 22–23.
68 A stewardship code is an instrument, whether regulatory or private, that defines management responsibilities between an agent and the beneficiary of that agent's management. Based on that understanding between the agent and the beneficiary, a stewardship code is a "market-based system for investors to hold companies to account for their corporate governance practices" (International Corporate Governance Network, *ICGN Global Stewardship Principles* (2016) 5–7).
69 For example, the Tripartite Declaration of Principles Concerning Multinational Enterprises and Social Policy or the UN Global Compact Principles (Dirk Willem te Velde, 'The Impact of Codes and Standards on Investment Flows to Developing Countries' [International Labour Organization (ILO) 2008] Employment Working Paper No 25 8).
70 'Definition of Sustainable Development Investing' (n 64) 20.
71 'Definition of Sustainable Development Investing' (n 64).
72 This refers to ensuring SDG alignment along the entire lifecycle of a value chain. For instance, starting from the sourcing raw materials in line with SDG 15 to logistics, distribution, consumption, and ending with the final disposal of the product aligned to SDG 12 (United Nations Global Compact (UNGC), Principles for Responsible Investment (PRI), and Global Reporting Initiative (GRI) (n 63) 12).
73 Global Investors for Sustainable Development Alliance (GISD) (n 64) 23.
74 United Nations Development Programme (UNDP), 'SDG Impact Standards: Private Equity Funds' 12.

2 The type of positive impact that the activity seeks to achieve based on a certain scope or other predetermined performance indicator; and
3 The contextual factors of the activity, such as the extent to which the activity should tolerate risk based on its specific industrial, geographical, and/or development setting as well as the extent to which a certain amount of risk burden is permissible based on the necessity of the activity in the context where it is to be implemented (or the impact risk appetite).[75]

The third of these adds an extra dimension to the concept of net positive impact. In addition to differentiating between industry-level and project-level impact assessments, UNDP adds a "leave no one behind" principle,[76] which considers the extent of impact to different stakeholders. In doing so, net positive impact becomes multidimensional, accounting for disparities in the amount of SDG-aligned benefits gained, at what cost, and to whom. This is designed into the impact thesis based on what the UNDP SDG Impact Standards identifies as the "Five Dimensions of Impact". These five dimensions "help fully understand an individual impact and compare or choose between different impacts" through the following set of questions:

1 *What*: What outcome level is occurring in the period? Is it positive or negative relative to an outcome threshold? How important is the outcome to the people (or planet) experiencing it?
2 *Who*: Who experiences the outcome? How underserved are the affected Stakeholders in relation to the outcome (when comparing the baseline to the outcome threshold)?
3 *How much*: What is the change in outcome? For how many people? And for how long does it last?
4 *Contribution*: Would the change likely have happened anyway?
5 *Risk*: What is the risk to people and planet that impact does not occur as expected?[77]

Where a clear impact thesis is central to UNDP assessments of Sustainable Investment, the PRI identifies how a similar stakeholder analysis can take place at the investment implementation and assessment phases. This analysis is based on two principles. The first is by establishing technical or performance criteria that can identify how different segments in society are impacted by the investment.[78]

75 United Nations Development Programme (UNDP), 'SDG Impact Standards: Private Equity Funds' 14.
76 Xu Qing and Christoph Nedopil Wang, 'Technical Report on SDG Finance Taxonomy (China)' (United Nations Development Programme (UNDP) 2020) 14–16.
77 United Nations Development Programme (UNDP), 'SDG Impact Standards Glossary' (United Nations 2021) 7.
78 The categories are as follows: (1) general public; (2) unemployed or under-employed; (3) under-served, e.g. people living in remote areas; (4) under-educated; (5) migrants and/or displaced

Following this analysis is to pursue investment models that pose the least harm overall with the most contribution.[79] The second principle is installing minimum safeguards, such as "do no significant harm",[80] which seeks to prevent an economic activity, such as an investment, from exacerbating progress on sustainable development—even if that economic activity may contribute to another sustainable development objective.[81]

Application of the do no harm principle resonates in two readings of the net positive impact element that attach performance to an anthropocentric effect on the environment. The first is in connection to climate change and the interpretation of net positive impact in "climate solution investments" as defined by the NZAOA. These are investments made in "economic activities considering to contribute substantially to climate change mitigation [and/or climate] change adaptation . . . ensur[ing that] they do not cause significant harm to all remaining environmental or social objectives".[82]

The second relates to human impacts on biodiversity. The Post-2020 Global Biodiversity Framework, a product of the 15th Conference of the Parties and a continuation of efforts to implement the Convention on Biological Diversity (CBD), carved out a clear role for private sector entities and finance. Of the 2030 Milestone set out therein, Goal B.2 identifies that "[n]ature is valued through green investments, ecosystem service valuation in national accounts, and public and private sector financial disclosures".[83] In recognition of the elevated role of private sector finance, particularly in relation to disclosures, the UNEP Finance Initiative

persons; (6) people with disabilities; (7) vulnerable groups, e.g. children, senior citizens, and pregnant women; (8) excluded/marginalized populations; and (9) those living below the poverty line.

79 Qing and Wang (n 76) 19.

80 The "Do No Significant Harm" principle is identified in Article 3b of the EU Taxonomy Regulation and is based on whether an investment has a deleterious effect on the six environmental objectives covered by the EU Taxonomy. So violations of the principle would include those investments that negatively affect (1) climate change mitigation by resulting in significant greenhouse gas emissions, (2) climate change adaptation by resulting in adverse impact to the current and expected future climate, (3) sustainable use and protection of water and marine resources by resulting in the detriment of the good status or good ecological potential of bodies of water and their ecosystems, (4) circular economy by resulting in significant inefficiencies in the use of materials and/or natural resources, (5) pollution prevention and control by resulting in significant increases of pollutants in all its forms, and (6) protection and restoration of biodiversity and ecosystems by resulting in detriment to the resilience and/or conservation of habitats and species (European Commission, 'Technical Guidance on the Application of "Do No Significant Harm" Under the Recovery and Resilience Facility Regulation' (2021) Commission Notice C(2021) 1054 final 2).

81 Margarita Pirovska and others, *Toolkit for Sustainable Investment Policy and Regulation* (Principles for Responsible Investment (PRI) and the World Bank Group (WBG) 2021) 23.

82 UN-Convened Net-Zero Asset Owner Alliance (NZAOA), 'Inaugural 2025 Target Setting Protocol: UN-Convened Net-Zero Asset Owner Alliance Monitoring Report and Verification Track' (United Nations Environment Programme Finance Initiative (UNEP FI) and Principles for Responsible Investment (PRI) 2021) 61.

83 Convention on Biological Diversity (CBD), 'Update of the Zero Draft of the Post-2020 Global Biodiversity Framework' (United Nations Environment Programme (UNEP) 2020) CBD/POST2020/PREP/2/1 4.

(UNEP FI), PRI, Secretariat of the CBD and private sector and civil society initiatives produced the Financial Sector Guide for the Convention on Biological Diversity, which elaborated on ways that private sector finance can result in net positive impact ("nature positive") and do no harm ("nature negative"). The Guide interprets net positive impact as "align[ing] financial flows to nature positive outcomes" that "increase opportunities for positive outcomes on the ground, including restoration".[84] The approach, the Post-2020 Global Biodiversity Framework proposes, is not only in requiring disclosures, but also understanding whether investments are "harming or building the resilience of biodiversity" as well as whether they are aligned with "global/regional biodiversity targets".[85]

The Human Rights Guidance Tool for the Financial Sector (2014) of the UNEP FI also demonstrated the net positive impact element.[86] The guidance tool identified human rights risks specific to certain sectors that would arise from economic activity, such as in infrastructure (i.e., forced resettlement of communities due to construction) and agricultural (i.e., impact on traditional livelihoods due to monoculture). The Guidance Tool provided a means to view the positive impacts of an investment, such as employment, against its consequences, such as those to the environment, on a sectoral basis. One important reason behind accounting for eccentric risk specific to each sector was to maximize participation. Companies were encouraged to join voluntary initiatives to assist and certify their efforts in addressing human rights risks, which would be adjusted to meet sector-specific standards.[87] For example, this may include anything from joining initiatives in the resource extraction sector to source materials responsibly through the Kimberley Process against conflict diamonds. In other instances, signing onto self-governing principles like those by the International Organization for Standardization or the International Labour Organization (ILO) may be important for labour-intensive production. Elsewhere, standards of reporting on supply chains such as through the GRI remain central in disclosure processes.

While net positive impact is a near-universal feature in the Notion, there remains limited guidance on confronting trade-off risks. At the same time, how does the positive impact of an investment essentially cancel out or equalize the consequences of that same investment? For instance, an investment in sustainable agricultural production may advance SDG 2 (Zero Hunger) by increasing agricultural

84 Secretariat of the Convention on Biological Diversity (SCBD) and others, *Financial Sector Guide for the Convention on Biological Diversity* (United Nations Environment Programme (UNEP) 2021) 11.

85 Secretariat of the Convention on Biological Diversity (SCBD) and others, *Financial Sector Guide for the Convention on Biological Diversity* (United Nations Environment Programme (UNEP) 2021) 14.

86 United Nations Environment Programme Finance Initiative (UNEP FI), 'Human Rights and Business: Basic Questions' (*Human Rights Guidance Tool for the Financial Sector*, December 2014) <www.unepfi.org/humanrightstoolkit/fundamentals.php> accessed 25 February 2021.

87 United Nations Environment Programme Finance Initiative (UNEP FI), 'Human Rights Issues by Sector' (*Human Rights Guidance Tool for the Financial Sector*, December 2014) <www.unepfi.org/humanrightstoolkit/agriculture.php> accessed 25 February 2021.

productivity while maintaining ecosystems but may necessarily require costs that take away from SDG 15 (Life on Land) through working against afforestation and reforestation (15.2) as a result of clearing land needed for agricultural production. In scholarship, these tensions between the SDGs were recognized in efforts to classify trade-offs and co-benefits between the goals to understand their "horizontal coherence across sectors".[88] While no clear technical response is offered within the Notion, these tensions are broadly addressed. In the 2021 Financing for Sustainable Development Report, the UN system's position on this tension is that the risks of trade-offs from SDG-aligned financing are far outweighed by its benefits based on two premises.[89]

The first is that there are different levels of resilience among segments in society. While the most vulnerable populations have heightened exposure to the risks of trade-offs, there are also actors who are more resilient, such as governments and private sector companies and investors. Either individually or shared, these resilient actors can strengthen the overall resilience of societies and economies by internalizing the trade-off risks that may arise from Sustainable Investment. This can be, for instance, offsetting the costs of retraining labour with the advent of new technologies, such as in renewable energies. In practice, however, the private sector actor may be less able and/or willing to absorb those trade-off risks, ultimately requiring the government to retain the responsibility as the risk bearer of last resort for Sustainable Investments based on its duty of care in its role as the "custodian of the sustainable development agenda".[90] The result is that private sector actors transfer risk to the government, such as through insurance or public financing.[91]

Second, the UN system identifies that the trade-off risk associated with Sustainable Investment arises from knowledge gaps concerning long-term and nonpecuniary risk. For that reason, investment flows can be limited by the "tragedy of the horizon", which seeks to limit risk within an acceptable horizon of time and materiality, e.g., pecuniary. In addressing these knowledge gaps, however, it becomes

88 International Council for Science, 'A Guide to SDG Interactions: From Science to Implementation' (2017) 9. The system proposed therein suggest quantifying positive interactions, or "co-benefits", between SDGs as being +1 (enabling), +2 (reinforcing), or +3 (indivisible). On the other hand, negative relationships or trade-offs are quantified as −1 (constraining), −2 (counteracting), or −3 (cancelling). For related studies, see also Håvard Hegre, Kristina Petrova and Nina von Uexkull, 'Synergies and Trade-Offs in Reaching the Sustainable Development Goals' (2020) 12 Sustainability 8729; Måns Nilsson and others, 'Mapping Interactions Between the Sustainable Development Goals: Lessons Learned and Ways Forward' (2018) 13 Sustainability Science 1489.

89 United Nations Inter-Agency Task Force on Financing for Development, 'Financing for Sustainable Development Report 2021' (United Nations 2021) Report of the Inter-Agency Task Force on Financing for Development E/FFDF/2020 16–17.

90 United Nations Inter-Agency Task Force on Financing for Development, 'Financing for Sustainable Development Report 2021' (United Nations 2021) Report of the Inter-Agency Task Force on Financing for Development E/FFDF/2020 25–26.

91 United Nations Inter-Agency Task Force on Financing for Development, 'Financing for Sustainable Development Report 2021' (United Nations 2021) Report of the Inter-Agency Task Force on Financing for Development E/FFDF/2020 64–65.

necessary to assess the sources of risks across societal, technological, economic, environmental, and (geo)political hazards, in relation to the extent of exposure, vulnerabilities, capabilities, and potential impacts.[92] An important aspect of filling these knowledge gaps through such assessments is via disclosures by large corporations. Here, as has been identified throughout this chapter, the UN system recognizes that such disclosures should be "further enhanced through norm-setting and standardization, mandatory reporting measures, going beyond financial material risks, consistently addressing all SDG impacts".[93]

In this regard, the UN system acknowledges that the methodological limitations facing disclosures also face assessments of net positive impact as a whole. In confronting these methodological limitations, the inter-agency authors of the Financing for Sustainable Development Report come to two reflections. The first is that the alternative to Sustainable Investment is the "cost of doing nothing". While there may be no (or at least fewer) trade-off risks to such traditional investments, these investments are also devoid of any positive SDG impacts. Moreover, the disproportionate risk faced by vulnerable populations remains unaddressed.[94] The second reflection is that when facing the consequences of a trade-off risk (or hazard) scenario, learning and adaptation equips future Sustainable Investment with the knowledge to help mitigate those risks in the future, resulting in a larger margin of net positive impact from the investment. This dynamic learning process, when engaged inclusively across many stakeholders, is necessary to "ensure that recovery interventions overcome rather than reinforce existing inequalities"[95] and Sustainable Investments may optimize their net positive impact.

4.3.1.2 Element 1.2: catalyst effect

The second element to the scope of the Notion is the extent to which the investment acts as a catalyst to sustainable development. Investors as shareholders can serve as catalysts through engagement by using their voting or stewardship rights from owning equity in companies to influence corporate behaviour and decision-making. Should investors use their voting rights to compel investee companies to become more accountable to ESG-related risks, it can catalyse those companies to adjust their operational and financial management to avoid or mitigate such risks. When

92 United Nations Inter-Agency Task Force on Financing for Development, 'Financing for Sustainable Development Report 2021' (United Nations 2021) Report of the Inter-Agency Task Force on Financing for Development E/FFDF/2020 20–23.

93 United Nations Inter-Agency Task Force on Financing for Development, 'Financing for Sustainable Development Report 2021' (United Nations 2021) Report of the Inter-Agency Task Force on Financing for Development E/FFDF/2020 27.

94 United Nations Inter-Agency Task Force on Financing for Development, 'Financing for Sustainable Development Report 2021' (United Nations 2021) Report of the Inter-Agency Task Force on Financing for Development E/FFDF/2020 19.

95 United Nations Inter-Agency Task Force on Financing for Development, 'Financing for Sustainable Development Report 2021' (United Nations 2021) Report of the Inter-Agency Task Force on Financing for Development E/FFDF/2020 23.

mainstream finance integrates ESG factors, the UNEP FI phrases the idea of catalysing change as a dual focus of not only "changing finance" but also "financing change"[96] by directing private sector finance into applicable technologies and/or services that in turn catalyses sustainable development.[97] Three thematic workstreams are identified as causing this catalyst effect: (1) climate change (including energy efficiency), (2) biodiversity and ecosystem services, and (3) social issues including human rights.[98] Investment that falls into these workstreams are seen as catalysing impact in a priority development area.

Private sector finance as a catalytic agent in advancing sustainable development finds further definition in the NZAOA "theory of change". According to the "theory of change", investments are made across a wide range of asset classes and sectors that are exposed to sectors associated with climate and other systemic vulnerabilities. As such, these investments, and the shareholder leverage that comes with equity, are well positioned to catalyse and boost decarbonization and climate-resilience.[99] In order to best take advantage of this position towards advancing sustainable development, NZAOA signatories commit to a common goal. This has traditionally been the target scenario identified in Article 2.1a of the Paris Climate Agreement,[100] which is keeping global warming below 1.5°C.[101] This specific focus serves as a rallying point around which asset holders and managers as investors are able to leverage their equity towards influencing firm behaviour, turning their shareholder rights into catalysts towards "making finance flows consistent with a pathway towards low greenhouse gas emissions and climate-resilient development" (Article 2.1c of the Paris Agreement).

One specific manifestation of the catalyst effect would be if NZAOA signatories work in tandem to employ capital allocation strategies, such as sector weighting, which reallocates capital between sectors or companies based on ESG performance. In doing so, firms with higher "carbon efficiency", which is minimizing the amount of carbon output for input of economic value creation, outcompete other firms for NZAOA investments.[102] An example of in tandem strategies like sector

96 United Nations Environment Programme Finance Initiative (UNEP FI), 'UNEP Finance Initiative: Unlocking Private Finance for the Implementation of the 2030 Agenda' <www.unepfi.org/fileadmin/documents/UNEPFIandSDG2015_01.pdf>.

97 United Nations Environment Programme Finance Initiative (UNEP FI), 'Background' <www.unepfi.org/about/background/> accessed 24 February 2021.

98 United Nations Environment Programme Finance Initiative (UNEP FI), 'UNEP Finance Initiative: Unlocking Private Finance for the Implementation of the 2030 Agenda' (n 96).

99 UN-Convened Net-Zero Asset Owner Alliance (NZAOA) (n 82) 18–19.

100 Based on evidence of the climate-related risks arising from "robust differences in regional climate characteristics between present-day and global warming of 1.5°C, and between 1.5°C and 2°C" (Intergovernmental Panel on Climate Change, *Global Warming of 1.5°C* (IPCC 2018) 7).

101 Article 2.1a reads, "Holding the increase in the global average temperature to well below 2°C above pre-industrial levels and pursuing efforts to limit the temperature increase to 1.5°C above pre-industrial levels, recognizing that this would significantly reduce the risks and impacts of climate change".

102 UN-Convened Net-Zero Asset Owner Alliance (NZAOA) (n 82) 20–21.

weighting can involve NZAOA investors taking joint action against certain types of companies in order to affect their behaviour, such as divesting from fossil fuel companies and reallocating that financing to renewable energy firms. In this manner, the NZAOA leverages the sheer magnitude of its collective assets (USD 5.7 trillion) to catalyse companies towards contributing to sustainable development.

Another form of the catalyst effect occurs through active ownership, which refers to an approach to asset management that bases decisions to trade positions based on a set principle, such as the extent to which investment position results in excess returns ("alpha") or alternatively, whether it is aligned with the SDGs. Active ownership within the context of Sustainable Investment would refer to an owner expressing to their agent, such as the institutional investor, to exclude certain types of assets from the managed portfolio based on, for example, their detrimental impact on the environment.

The PRI also encourages its members towards active ownership, targeting asset owners, from real estate owners to commodity traders, in leveraging their equity share to "directly influence companies, markets, and economies; and, in turn, society and the environment as a whole".[103] Members are encouraged to practice principle-based active ownership based on the six "Principles for Responsible Investment", followed up by institutionalized procedures to monitor, report, and verify the incorporation of SDG-related issues into both asset ownership and management.[104]

Another common means of investment as taking on a catalyst effect is through policy advocacy. Whether as individuals or through institutions, when considerable amounts of capital are mobilized under a uniform platform, such as advancing sustainable development, it sends policy signals to regulators to support SDG-aligned investment practices.[105] This form of the catalyst effect is central to the "Investor Agenda", an initiative bringing together organizations including the UNEP FI and PRI to advance Sustainable Investment in law and policy. The Investor Agenda identifies "four interlocking areas" in the role of investment as a catalyst to sustainable development, which in addition to the conduct of the corporation, investor, and investment also recognizes the influence of private sector finance as means of policy advocacy.[106] This influence takes three forms: (1) investor statements that call on governments to achieve emissions reduction targets, such as phasing out

103 Susheela Peres da Costa and Regnan Paul Chandler, *Active Ownership 2.0: The Evolution Stewardship Urgently Needs* (Principles for Responsible Investment (PRI) 2019) 4.

104 The six Principles are to (1) incorporate ESG issues into investment analysis and decision-making processes, (2) be active owners and incorporate ESG issues into our ownership policies and practices, (3) seek appropriate disclosure on ESG issues by the entities in which we invest, (4) promote acceptance and implementation of the Principles within the investment industry, (5) work together to enhance our effectiveness in implementing the Principles, and (6) report on our activities and progress towards implementing the Principles.

105 Principles for Responsible Investment (PRI), *A Blueprint for Responsible Investment: Genesis, Assumptions and Process* (PRI 2017) 12.

106 The Investor Agenda, 'About Us' <https://theinvestoragenda.org/about-the-agenda/> accessed 15 June 2021.

coal; (2) membership in trade associations that lobby for sustainable development while remaining vigilant in ensuring that those associations are working in line with global development goals like those of the Paris Agreement; and (3) actively engaging governments to advocate for policy measures that achieve net-zero emissions by 2050 and/or ensure 1.5°-aligned financial flows.[107]

Another powerful format of policy advocacy has been engaging stock exchanges. Sustainable Stock Exchanges (SSE) seeks to leverage its membership of exchanges around the world to influence the financial or securities regulations that govern portfolio investment. Stock exchanges can include the integration of material ESG factors in listing requirements for companies, pressuring companies towards more comprehensive disclosures. Companies listed on those exchanges will then be pressured to comply with these listing requirements, with insufficient performance met with delisting. SSE also avails incentives to encourage listed companies to disclose information related to Sustainable Investment, such as through tax incentives and promoting efforts in Sustainable Investment by investors and/or companies.[108]

4.3.2 Key feature 2: indicators

An early attempt by the UNEP FI to expand Sustainable Investment was in 2014 with the Portfolio Decarbonization Coalition, which aimed at encouraging institutional investors to take "systematic efforts to align their investment portfolios with the goals of a low carbon economy".[109] From its launch, the Portfolio Decarbonization Coalition was overwhelmed by challenges arising from the lack of a harmonized approach to decarbonization, permitting member institutions to define the scope of their involvement unilaterally. In its annual report, the Portfolio Decarbonization Coalition identified that it quickly encountered limitations in terms of reliability[110] and an understanding of the connection between investment performance and decarbonization.[111] The Portfolio Decarbonization Coalition demonstrated the difficulty in balancing a bottom-up approach led by private sector actors in designing the scope of Sustainable Investment and the top-down role of the UN

107 The Investor Agenda, 'Expectations Ladder' (2021) 5. The level policy advocacy undertaken by the investor corresponds with a higher tier of an "Expectations Ladder", with each increasing tier up to four representative of greater ambition. The specific measures within each of the tiers can be found in The Investor Agenda, 'Guidance on Using the Expectations Ladder' (2021) 27.

108 United Nations Sustainable Stock Exchanges (SSE) Initiative, 'Model Guidance on Reporting ESG Information to Investors' (2015) 21.

109 Rory Sullivan, Lisa Petrovic and Remco Fischer, *From Disclosure to Action: The First Annual Report of the Portfolio Carbonization Coalition* (United Nations Environment Programme (UNEP) 2015) 7.

110 Rory Sullivan, Lisa Petrovic and Remco Fischer, *From Disclosure to Action: The First Annual Report of the Portfolio Carbonization Coalition* (United Nations Environment Programme (UNEP) 2015) 14.

111 Rory Sullivan, Lisa Petrovic and Remco Fischer, *From Disclosure to Action: The First Annual Report of the Portfolio Carbonization Coalition* (United Nations Environment Programme (UNEP) 2015) 18.

system as a governing authority in ensuring that investments were actually contributing to sustainable development.

Following the Portfolio Decarbonization Coalition, the UN system continues to leave the conceptualization of KPIs to the private sector, rarely getting directly involved in the production of an already rapidly expanding universe of KPIs. The UN system also does not advocate the exclusive use of a single directory of KPIs, but rather embraces the diversity of metrics by seeking their correlation with the SDGs. This was apparent with the UN Global Compact and its partners providing an inventory of existing business indicators across more than 1,500 indicators through the SDG Compass based on SDG targets.[112] The UN system instead takes a more pronounced role in the principles that inform the generation of KPIs. As explained in this section, two broad principles are at the heart of that endeavour: (1) indicators should measure the extent to which the investment has real-world impact and (2) indicators should also assess whether performance results in more additionality, which is when more private sector entities are influenced to embrace Sustainable Investment practices.

4.3.2.1 Element 2.1: real-world impact

Verification of the actual sustainable development impact of Sustainable Investment is crucial to its appeal of long-term value creation. In verifying the real-world impact on sustainable development, the UN system generally leans towards science-based and/or quantitative measures. This was especially evident in the report of the United Nations' High-Level Expert Group on the Net Zero Emissions Commitments of Non-State Entities, which emphasized the need to align with science-based goals in net zero commitments in accordance with Intergovernmental Panel on Climate Change (IPCC)-modelled pathways every five years and "demonstrate alignment to funding and enabling real-world decarbonisation".[113] The emphasis on science-based climate action by the private sector has consistently been a unified approach across involved UN agencies, the culmination of which was perhaps the "Business Ambition for 1.5°C" organized by the UN Global Compact in 2019 and backed by key UN agencies and organs. The Business Ambition called for a "1.5°C-compliant business model" is based on the Paris Climate Agreement, which required "science-based climate action".[114]

The science-based approach identified by the Business Ambition finds definition through the Science Based Targets initiative (SBTi), which in application to greenhouse gas (GHG) reduction targets requires that emissions reduction targets are "in

112 United Nations Global Compact (UNGC), 'Inventory of Business Indicators' (*SDG Compass*) <https://sdgcompass.org/business-indicators/> accessed 22 March 2021.

113 High-Level Expert Group on the Net Zero Emissions Commitments of Non-State Entities, *Integrity Matters: Net Zero Commitments by Businesses, Financial Institutions, Cities and Regions* (United Nations 2022) 15, 20–22.

114 UN Global Compact (UNGC), 'Business Ambition for 1.5°C' <www.unglobalcompact.org/take-action/events/climate-action-summit-2019/business-ambition> accessed 2 June 2021.

line with what the latest climate science says is necessary to meet the goals of the Paris Agreement—to limit global warming to well-below 2°C above pre-industrial levels and pursue efforts to limit warming to 1.5°C".[115] Basing the design of KPIs against the broad qualification of "science" illustrates that one dimension of real-world impact is relevance on a threshold of current scientific understanding. Alternatively, the extent to which impact can be considered real world within the extent that it is science based also refers to the extent that the metric of that impact is dynamic and remains updated to the most recent scientific understanding. This is directly identified in the post-2020 Global Biodiversity Framework, which attaches performance to the "best available science [as] increas[ing] significant positive and reduc[ing] significant negative impacts on biodiversity".[116]

The NZAOA KPIs were shaped through this science-based approach, reflecting the recommendations of the IPCC founded on the current state of scientific understanding of the anthropocentric impacts on climate change. In application to the actual evaluation of KPIs, this translated into:

1 Differentiating between Scope 1 and 2 emissions for investment portfolios against a 2019 base year;
2 Formulating carbon reduction pathways on a sector-by-sector basis to optimize their configuration around characteristics that are specific to certain industries or sectors; or
3 Recognizing "climate solution investments", which are investments in the supply of low carbon assets, such as green energy, carbon capture solutions, and energy storage systems.[117]

Elsewhere in areas where no such clear scientific revelation exists, real-world impact emphasizes the importance of data-based results. The SDG Finance Taxonomy of the UNDP accentuates this empirical basis in approaching environmental and social impact assessments. It does this by first producing an ex ante management analysis, which should result in both the objective and baseline measurements in assessing determined goal. This is followed by analysing impact data following the investment in ex post assessment.[118] The SDG Impact Standards defines "realistic portfolio impact" as drawing on "available evidence and relevant SDG impact data and information from reputable government and scientific and civil society organizations".[119] They further include as a dimension of operations and management the introduction of "robust, reliable and practical processes to collect, manage and use its impact data", which involves "systematically capturing results from across its impact management activities"; integrating impact data into financial

115 Science Based Targets initiative (SBTi), 'SBTi Corporate Manual' (2021) TVT-INF-003 4.
116 Secretariat of the Convention on Biological Diversity (SCBD) and others (n 84) 15.
117 UN-Convened Net-Zero Asset Owner Alliance (NZAOA) (n 82) 25.
118 Qing and Wang (n 76) 21–22.
119 United Nations Development Programme (UNDP), 'SDG Impact Standards: Private Equity Funds' (n 74) 15.

data to "inform investment decision making"; "managing data ownership"; and determining risk on "impact data, impact assessments and evaluations".[120]

Simultaneously, however, the UNDP cautions against an overreliance on metrics. SDG Impact Standard 2.3.6 identifies that "selecting and using metrics that wherever possible include context and valuation and provide the required level of confidence that the impact is being achieved" while recognizing that there may be "unintended negative and perverse outcomes in the framing of its investment impact targets and the metrics it selects and how it uses them". These "unintended negative and perverse outcomes" refer to using metrics to emphasize the positive impact of an investment while masking the costs and negative consequences to achieve those impacts.[121] Based on these limitations, the SDG Impact Standards call for investors to make "relative and absolute" choices between options that account for those risks and contributions to sustainable development.[122]

The last dimension of real-world impact in addition to science based and quantifiability is the extent to which KPIs are forward-looking and/or demonstrate forward-looking ambition. These essentially mean that KPIs should not be static in their assessment, but rather incentivize a progressive upscaling of commitment to sustainable development. The extent to which its members show forward-looking ambition towards decarbonization is a central tenet to the NZAOA. Therein, a "quantified view of the impact of their investments on climate change" must also include "forward-looking data" that facilitate methodologies that are able to factor in "strategic orientation commitments" towards decarbonization made either at the corporate, sectorial, and/or regional levels. Increasingly ambitious GHG footprinting by covering Scope 3 emissions or accounting for temperature alignment requirements or plans based on the Paris Agreement, for instance, would constitute forward-looking data.[123]

Similar language exists in the SBTi, which requires participating companies to first identify a base year or base period that is representative of the company's GHG profile used to track emissions reduction performance.[124] For example, this

120 United Nations Development Programme (UNDP), 'SDG Impact Standards: Private Equity Funds' (n 74) 18.

121 Refer to earlier discussion on SDG tensions and trade-offs. See also Stephen Morton, David Pencheon and Neil Squires, 'Sustainable Development Goals (SDGs), and Their Implementation: A National Global Framework for Health, Development and Equity Needs a Systems Approach at Every Level' (2017) 124 British Medical Bulletin 81, 87.

122 United Nations Development Programme (UNDP), 'SDG Impact Standards: Private Equity Funds' (n 74) 21.

123 UN-Convened Net-Zero Asset Owner Alliance (NZAOA), 'Live Version 2.0 of Methodological Principles' 3–4 <www.unepfi.org/wordpress/wp-content/uploads/2020/11/AO-Alliance_Request-For-Comment-on-Methodological-Principles_Live-V2.pdf>.

124 Emissions reductions "cover all relevant emissions of the seven different GHGs or classes of GHGs covered by the UNFCCC/Kyoto Protocol. These are carbon dioxide (CO_2), methane (CH4), nitrous oxide (N2O), perfluorocarbons (PFCs), hydrofluorocarbons (HFCs), sulfur hexafluoride (SF6), and nitrogen trifluoride (NF3)" (Science Based Targets initiative (SBTi) (n 115) 12–13).

might be a 40% reduction of Scope 1 and 2 emissions by 2025 from the 2016–2018 base period. The base year or period is also used as a threshold to measure to extent to which the company's reduction targets demonstrate "forward-looking ambition", the opposite of which would be to pursue "low-hanging fruit" for the sake of reporting.[125] Ambition is provided with specific targets based on the scope of emissions. In application to Scopes 1 and 2 emissions, this would involve a linear rate of annual reductions between a range of 1.23% to 4.2% in order to achieve long-term goals of limiting temperature rise.[126] "Ambitious" in application to Scope 3 emissions is defined as "reduction targets that are consistent with the decarbonization required to keep global temperature increase to 2°C compared to preindustrial temperatures [or] at least "7% year-on-year reductions of emissions per unit value added".[127]

4.3.2.2 Element 2.2: additionality

Expanding the number of participants in Sustainable Investment, whether they are asset owners or managers, is one the primary objectives of the UN system. For that reason, additionality, which here should be understood as the resultant added engagement in Sustainable Investment, is a recurring KPI in the Notion.[128] For institutional investors, this means the extent to which they catalyse investee companies towards alignment with the SDGs. For example, a measure by the investor may cause investee companies to undertake climate mitigative action that would not have occurred in the absence of the measure taken by the investor.

Additionality as a material factor in the Notion is based on the fact that the wider adoption of sustainable investment in the private sector, or universality, remains an important objective for the UN system.[129] Yet in meeting that objective, additionality or universality and criteria for materiality may operate in opposition, where overly strict requirements can crowd out new signatories while an over-facilitative approach can reduce the impact of Sustainable Investment. To that end, the UN

125 Science Based Targets initiative (SBTi) (n 115) 11.

126 Science Based Targets initiative (SBTi), 'SBTi Criteria and Recommendations' TWG-INF-002 16.

127 Science Based Targets initiative (SBTi), 'SBTi Criteria and Recommendations' TWG-INF-002 10.

128 The idea of additionality, however, is commonly associated with carbon offsets, which refers to an action or measure, such as a corporate and public policy, that results in additional climate change mitigation. The World Bank defines additionality as being identifiable to a mitigation action that would not have occurred should the measure not have taken place, such as the incentive provided by a carbon crediting scheme (Pedro Martins Barata, 'Carbon Credits and Additionality Past, Present, and Future' (2016) 13 Partnership for Market Readiness 4–5). The importance of isolating the meaning of additionality in this context is to distinguish its mechanics from that of carbon offsetting, which remains contentious. See, for instance, Heather McKenzie, 'Carbon Pricing too Low to Meet Paris Agreement Goals' (*ESG Investor*, 7 June 2021) <www.esginvestor.net/carbon-pricing-too-low-to-meet-paris-agreement-goals/> accessed 10 June 2021.

129 United Nations Trade and Development (UNCTAD), 'Guidance on Core Indicators for Entity Reporting on Contribution Towards Implementation of the Sustainable Development Goals' (United Nations 2019) UNCTAD/DIAE/2019/1/Corr.1 12.

system has advanced an "incremental approach" to facilitating the transition into increasingly forward-looking Sustainable Investment engagements as a means to prevent "placing an excessive burden on companies [that] may be detrimental to engaging the private sector under the 2030 Agenda".[130]

The activities of SSE are demonstrative of the approach to additionality within the Notion. Member stock exchanges not only work on "outward-facing activities", but they also engage in "inward-facing activities". Outward-facing activities pertain to issues more broadly relevant to Sustainable Investment, such as developing specialized labels to ensure transparent reporting on ESG issues and a continuous review of materiality in light of emerging topics.[131] Inward-looking activities are those that seek to mobilize national stock exchanges to increase participation in Sustainable Investment among listed companies.[132]

In its "Model Guidance on Reporting ESG Information to Investors", SSE identifies both the inward activities that stock exchanges can execute to increase additionality, and what investor and/or corporate activities qualify as additionality. These include:

1 Forming dedicated Sustainable Investment-related responsibility and oversight to lend "credibility to a company's claims about its sustainability commitments and performance". This can include forming dedicated teams or departments as well as dedicating board activity to address forthright the reasoning behind the selection of certain ESG factors in relation to different stakeholders and implementation timelines[133];
2 Reporting ESG information and key themes in accordance with national and/or international standards that is material to company financial and extra-financial performance at different parts of the company's value chain in financial disclosures, mandatory investor communications, and regulatory filings[134];
3 Adopting KPIs that are widely accepted, featuring ESG information with quantitative data that can compare across time, within the same company, and against other companies with explanations of methodology[135]; and
4 Engaging stakeholders on ESG factors as a "preventative rather than reactionary activity" to help "identify, mitigate, and manage ESG risks and opportunities".[136]

130 United Nations Trade and Development (UNCTAD), 'Guidance on Core Indicators for Entity Reporting on Contribution Towards Implementation of the Sustainable Development Goals' (United Nations 2019) UNCTAD/DIAE/2019/1/Corr.1 13.

131 United Nations Sustainable Stock Exchanges (SSE) Initiative, 'How Exchanges Can Embed Sustainability Within Their Operations: A Blueprint to Advance Action' (2019).

132 United Nations Sustainable Stock Exchanges (SSE) Initiative, 'United Nations SSE Initiative: 10 Years of Impact and Progress' (2019) 31–33.

133 United Nations Sustainable Stock Exchanges (SSE) Initiative, 'Model Guidance on Reporting ESG Information to Investors' (n 108) 13.

134 United Nations Sustainable Stock Exchanges (SSE) Initiative, 'Model Guidance on Reporting ESG Information to Investors' (n 108) 14–15.

135 United Nations Sustainable Stock Exchanges (SSE) Initiative, 'Model Guidance on Reporting ESG Information to Investors' (n 108) 16.

136 United Nations Sustainable Stock Exchanges (SSE) Initiative, 'Model Guidance on Reporting ESG Information to Investors' (n 108) 18.

The PRI and NZAOA also clearly feature additionality as having clear materiality.[137] The NZAOA features "engagement targets" as measured through additionality resulting from the number of companies or asset managers engaged and/or positions papers published seeking to expand membership or contribution to the commonly held decarbonization targets held.

4.3.3 Key feature 3: metrics and data

In the absence of top-down, formalized operational guidance on the type and source of data, the UN system generally encourages an aggregative approach that brings together varied methodologies, known as metric sets, recognizing both their distinct limitations and unique contributions. A major reason behind this aggregative approach is that if metrics become too esoteric in the way that they are curated, then they lose relevance in specific sustainable development applications and/or contexts.

Conversely, metrics that are too universal enable opportunities for "cherry-picking" that can give a distorted composite score for certain types of firms or sectors that enjoy advantages in ESG performance.[138] Furthermore, data-centric approaches, including those pushed by the UN system,[139] face persistent challenges concerning data availability and reliability, such as those concerning Scope 3 emissions.

Despite their limitations, tailoring metrics is crucial to identifying the most pertinent data points out of a plethora of disclosures provided by companies (primary data) and providers that analyse primary and public data for the sake of scoring, harmonization, and/or analysis (secondary data).[140] In this respect, the UN system emphasizes the importance of normalizing in approaching metrics to account for idiosyncratic variables in the measurement process, such as methodological limitations and other contextual factors. In addition to appropriately scoping

137 Principles for Responsible Investment (PRI) (n 105) 26.

138 There is considerable research linking size or certain industries, namely, technology sectors, with impact of ESG activities. Nazir and others (2021), for instance, finds that while at a greater cost, the social capital derivative of ESG activities has more significant positive impact for large, multinational tech companies (Marina Nazir and others, 'The Nexus Between Corporate Environment, Social, and Governance Performance and Cost of Capital: Evidence from Top Global Tech Leaders' (2022) 29 Environmental Science and Pollution Research 22623). Drempetic and others (2020) further identified that larger companies report their ESG performance more often and that "more disclosure, independent from the quality and content of the information, implicates a better CSR reputation" (Samuel Drempetic, Christian Klein and Bernhard Zwergel, 'The Influence of Firm Size on the ESG Score: Corporate Sustainability Ratings Under Review: Journal of Business Ethics' (2020) 167 Journal of Business Ethics 333, 354).

139 For instance, the Science Based Target initiative (SBTi) with the UN Global Compact provides guidance on how to be forward-looking with Scope 3 emissions, but ultimately advises to "select data that are the most complete, most reliable, and most representative in terms of technology, time, and geography" (Science Based Targets initiative (SBTi) [n 115] 23).

140 Stan Dupré and others, 'Climate Strategies and Metrics: Exploring Options for Institutional Investors' (World Resources Institute, United Nations Environment Programme Finance Initiative (UNEP FI), and 2° Investing Initiative) 39–40.

metrics and data, normalization can help express materiality of indicators so that they are relevant not only to the context in which they are being applied, but also in cross-contextual applications of sustainable development.

The UN system provides normalization guidance in order to ensure that the data used to measure indicators are averaged out or levelized and that firms in inherently more polluting sectors are encouraged to participate. Without normalization, such firms may be apprehensive in embracing the Notion because of significant barriers to entry. For instance, one central process in normalizing includes ensuring an alignment between micro- and macro-level indicators. This refers to ensuring that indicators are sufficiently scaled to represent sufficiently the micro- or macro-level scale of what the indicator is attempting to measure.[141]

One illustration of this is the UN Environment Programme Finance Initiative's accounting for climate mitigative (green) and adverse (brown) exposure adjusted for each industry in order to factor in these activities into resultant sustainable investment metrics. For instance, in the power sector, a green metric may include the share of renewable energy-related research and development and capital expenditures while a brown metric may include the share of high-carbon electricity generation in the total energy mix.[142] Assets involving equity, such as investment, are more holistically measured through data-based metrics involving the amount of exposure to GHG emissions (GHG footprinting) when accounting for these green/brown metrics as a complement to ESG scores.

Another benefit of normalization is that they render a highly aggregated, single-figure metric, which is more geared towards promoting public awareness and a general understanding of Sustainable Investment. However, as the UN Environment Programme Finance Initiative warns, these aggregated figures "cannot be both comprehensive (cover different sectors, assets, and strategies available to an investor) and meaningful vis-à-vis economic trends".[143]

A pertinent illustration of this trade-off was with GHG footprinting, or carbon footprinting, which is a form of emissions allocations that apportions GHG emissions to a company, its activities, or asset holders based on the allocation method.[144] Using this method, the sustainable development-related impacts of a company were aggregated into a GHG emissions value, i.e., tonnes of carbon dioxide-equivalents (CO_2e). The annual GHG emissions of a company were then normalized for comparison across different sectors and portfolios against such values as revenue or sales, i.e. tonnes of CO_2e by items sold categorized by industry. This absolute value is a sum of three scopes of emissions: direct emissions by activity of the company being measured (Scope 1); upstream emissions such as purchasing energy for production (Scope 2); and supply chain emissions that include emissions resulting

141 See, for instance, United Nations Trade and Development (UNCTAD), 'Guidance on Core Indicators for Entity Reporting on Contribution towards Implementation of the Sustainable Development Goals' (n 129) 8–10.

142 Dupré and others (n 140) 49.

143 Dupré and others (n 140) 60.

144 Dupré and others (n 140) 74–77.

from the use of goods and services produced as well as investments made by the company (Scope 3).[145]

While GHG footprinting is the most comparable metric, its uses in evaluating the climate impact of investments are limited by the use of historic data on emissions, meaning that they do not include the potential (locked-in) emissions that would arise from, for example, latent sources (as per the lifetime of the asset), such as fossil fuel reserves. Furthermore, GHG footprinting is unable to account for different classes or horizons of assets. The climate impact of a long-term bond, for example, may be difficult to assess because of the lack of data in how the bond issuer employs the resulting financing over a horizon of decades. Similarly, GHG footprinting may not account for investment in sustainable development-aligned technology development, which has a much longer horizon of impact that may not be realized until the technology is in general use.[146]

Other forms of normalization permit adjustments between companies and sectors based on existing liabilities, geographical attributes, access to finance, size of company, rate of growth, and sectoral differences such as those where decarbonization is inherently more difficult.[147] By normalizing for companies of different sizes and scopes of operation, such as a company that works locally versus one that exports globally, these adjustments add to the granularity of metrics. For financial intermediaries and investors, addressing different value chain lengths and carbon leakage that may occur at each stage of that value chain show that there are different levels of "carbon asset risk", which are "non-physical climate change-related factors . . . encompass[ing] policy and legal, technology, market and economic factors as well as reputational risks".[148] By identifying carbon asset risk at each stage of securitization that lead into the investment, from the underwriter to the investor, financial intermediaries and investors would be better able to mitigate or avoid such risks,[149] which is reflected into the Notion.

Adjustments made for the amount of control over emissions also exist within the methodology of the SBTi, which provides three categories of "organizational boundaries" in defining corporate GHG inventories.[150] The first is operational control, which are the emissions accountable to the operations under the authority of the company. The second is financial control, which refers to the emissions accountable to the financial activities directed by the company. The third is equity share, which refers to the emissions produced by the share of equity held by a company in an operation. Another means to normalize organizational boundaries within the SBTi methodology includes choosing between two allocation approaches: absolute

145 Dupré and others (n 140) 41.

146 Dupré and others (n 140) 44.

147 UN-Convened Net-Zero Asset Owner Alliance (NZAOA) (n 82) 27.

148 Mark Fulton and Christopher Weber, *Carbon Asset Risk: Discussion Framework* (World Resources Institute and United Nations Environment Programme Finance Initiative (UNEP FI)) 14.

149 Mark Fulton and Christopher Weber, *Carbon Asset Risk: Discussion Framework* (World Resources Institute and United Nations Environment Programme Finance Initiative (UNEP FI)) 17–20.

150 The following definition are found in Science Based Targets initiative (SBTi) (n 126) 12.

contraction or sectoral decarbonization. The absolute contraction approach involves a company reducing its emissions at the "same rate, irrespective of initial emissions performance" based on a global emissions reduction pathway, such as the well below 2°C scenarios identified in the Paris Agreement.[151] Sectoral decarbonization, on the other hand, defines emissions reductions relative to another aggregation metric, such as tonnes CO_2 equivalent per of tonne product produced. This permits for adjustments for sectors with natively higher emissions, such as power generation, manufacturing, and transportation.[152]

Another form of normalization includes appreciating the value added of Sustainable Investment when addressing areas of high need. This methodology was employed in the SDG Investor Platform, which was launched as part of the SDG Impact initiative of the UNDP in collaboration with the UN Environment Programme Finance Initiative, UN Global Compact, and the UN Department of Economic and Social Affairs, which houses the GISD. The SDG Investor Platform begins by identifying investment SDG priority areas at sectoral, subsectoral, and subregional levels in order to construct a database of "investment opportunity areas" for consideration by potential investors.[153] The 200+ investment opportunity areas identified on the SDG Investor Platform are classified by sector and country and each provides an impact thesis—key beneficiaries, SDGs addressed, and so forth. The normalization that takes place in these assessments is by weighting the extent to which the given SDG priority area is addressed by the investment. These investment areas are considered sustainable based on an assessment that they produce enough value to outweigh any "outcome risks", which are consequences resulting from the investment.

One example of "outcome risks" includes an investment opportunity area for affordable housing in Nigeria. The SDG Investor Platform contextualizes the investment in terms of the gravity of need, which in this case is a housing shortage despite a growing population, which is set to have a more accentuated impact for low- to medium-income earners. An investment in affordable housing through new constructions, property acquisitions, or equity investments in companies that operate in the Nigerian housing industry would result in two main development outcomes. The first is in SDG 10 by decreasing infrastructural and housing gaps between different income levels. The second is through SDG 11, which would increase the number of women and rural communities living in safe and clean environments. These development outcomes in turn outweigh the risk factors of potential investment, which include driving environmental pollution and overpopulation as well as potentially causing further exclusion of certain regions and/or communities where the affordable housing projects are to be located.[154] While

151 Science Based Targets initiative (SBTi) (n 126) 17.

152 Science Based Targets initiative (SBTi) (n 126) 18.

153 United Nations Development Programme (UNDP), 'Methodology' (*SDG Investor Platform*) <https://sdginvestorplatform.undp.org/methodology> accessed 21 May 2021.

154 'Affordable Mass Housing' (*SDG Investor Platform*, 13 May 2021) <https://sdginvestorplatform.undp.org/market-intelligence/affordable-mass-housing> accessed 1 June 2021.

the SDG Investor Platform does not provide how and to what extent this weighting takes place, such as the gravity of the need for housing in Nigeria against the potential consequences of advanced pollution resulting from construction, it does demonstrate that the UN system engages in such normalization methodologies and is thus pertinent to the Notion.

4.4 Concluding remarks

The Framework and Notion presented in Chapters 3 and 4, respectively, are two approaches to assessing how foreign investment and the government measures that affect foreign investment contribute to sustainable development. Both the Framework and Notion, as a Consolidated Method, are based on a comprehensive investigation across the diverse bodies that constitute the UN system and its extensive corpus of substantive materials. In doing so, the Consolidated Method, which is explored further in Chapter 5, finds basis in normative and policy positions derived from multilateral negotiation and agreement. As was argued in Chapter 1, this is necessary for application in international investment law, where while the interaction between international investment and sustainable development is not specified, interpretations of that nexus have looked beyond the conventional boundaries of the international investment law regime. Indeed, the need for both regulation and the harmonization of regulation was the overarching conclusion of the report by the United Nations' High-Level Expert Group on the Net Zero Emissions Commitments of Non-State Entities.[155]

The Notion presented in this chapter, while complementing the Framework as the latter half of the approach that constitutes the Consolidated Method, also presents key differences. The most obvious, perhaps, is the fact that the Notion applies to foreign portfolio investment whereas the Framework is largely applicable to foreign direct investment (FDI). Despite significant differences between FDI and portfolio investment, a few of which were explained in Chapter 2, they are both regulated on the basis of an agreement that is shaped between the interests of the host state where the investment is located and the interests of the foreign investor. This agreement is either in the form of provisions of an international investment agreement or stipulated by contract as part of the obligations of becoming an asset owner. It is this aspect of foreign investment, whether direct or portfolio, as well as the policies that influence it that the Consolidated Method finds application.

For FDI, this relationship is defined by the prevailing international investment agreement. That agreement will dictate the interaction between the treatment provided to the foreign investment as a covered investment and manoeuvrability of the host state in implemented government measures. On the other hand, treatment surrounding foreign portfolio investment are dictated by the combination of prudential regulation and company law, which traditionally does not require foreign

155 High-Level Expert Group on the Net Zero Emissions Commitments of Non-State Entities (n 113) 15.

investors to consider their impact on the public interest of the host state. However, as both Chapter 2 and the present chapter demonstrated, there has been a departure from this shareholder primacy model for a multistakeholder view of private sector portfolio investment, which holds companies and investors responsible for their sustainable development impact.[156] Finally, irrespective of the legal requirements of the host state, there remains a legal obligation by means of fiduciary duty to stakeholders to consider the sustainable development impacts of foreign investments.[157] When the analysis of potential investments exhausts financial criteria resulting in equal alternatives in terms of profitability, choosing an investment with lower ESG performance would constitute a breach of fiduciary duties.[158]

This chapter extracted key engagements by the UN system in Sustainable Investment to synthesize into the Notion, which could then be applied to this book's dual approach, the Consolidated Method, towards addressing the incomplete assessment in the right to regulate defined in Chapter 1. As demonstrated throughout this chapter, Sustainable Investment in the Notion is structurally equivalent to that of the private sector: a normative scope defined by a series of KPIs that is in turn composed of a galaxy of data and metrics. At the same time, while the UN system does not participate in developing specific methodologies in defining metrics or data collection, it does engage in enshrining principles that are applicable at different stages of the Sustainable Investment. The Notion is an encapsulation of those principles, making it a valuable component to the Consolidated Method. Namely, the Notion furnishes the tools and concepts to analyse the development impact of foreign investment.

156 For instance, in addition to the EU taxonomy, which establishes a list of environmentally sustainable economic activities, there is a growing number of states that are mandating stricter regulation on the impact of finance on sustainability. Most commonly, this has been in the form of financial regulators and/or central banks requiring ESG disclosure. See, for instance, Katya Golubkova, 'Russia's Central Bank Advises Companies to Disclose ESG Agenda' *Reuters* (19 July 2021); Shih-ching Kao, 'FSC Mandates ESG-Related Data Disclosure from 2022' *Taipei Times* (17 June 2021) 12; 'Disclosure Request for "Showed ESG" to Stop the Application and Financial Agency, Operation and Evaluation (「見せかけESG」に歯止め 金融庁、運用・評価に開示要求)' *Nihon Keizei Shimbun (日本経済新聞)* (28 May 2021); Bob Pisani, 'SEC Chair Gensler Says Agency Will Enforce Rules "Aggressively" Against Bad Actors' *CNBC* (20 May 2021).

157 Freshfields Bruckhaus Deringer LLP, *A Legal Framework for the Integration of Environmental, Social and Governance Issues into Institutional Investment* (United Nations Environment Programme Finance Initiative (UNEP FI) 2005) 12–13.

158 The UN Environment Programme Finance Initiative and the Principles for Responsible Investment in a 2021 report observed that this expansive interpretation of fiduciary duty is much needed. They write that "[n]egative sustainability outcomes can clearly be a threat to the long-term prosperity of any business. . . . This is the main reason for a potential obligation to consider engaging in instrumental [investing for sustainability impact]. . . . [I]f one or more sustainability factors posed a material risk to meeting [their] investment objective[s] . . . [asset owners and investment managers are] legally obliged to consider what steps [they] can take to mitigate the risk" (Freshfields Bruckhaus Deringer LLP, *A Legal Framework for Impact: Sustainability Impact in Investor Decision-Making* (United Nations Environment Programme Finance Initiative (UNEP FI) and Principles for Responsible Investment (PRI) 2021) 89).

In addition, the Notion is constructed from the results of a multilaterally participatory process. The diverse modalities drawn out in this and the previous chapter string together the many different activities and substantive positions within the UN system. Namely, that international investment should not only catalyse sustainable development, but also facilitate both the host state and its key stakeholders becoming the primary beneficiaries of that development progress. This position is largely identical to the UN system's approach to FDI and its role in sustainable development. That is, recognizing that attracting international investment is not the primary objective, but rather it is to enable international investment to become a means towards achieving sustainable development. Instilling this theme into the agreement(s) that govern international investment in the ways identified in this and the previous chapter thus remains the final task of this book, which is taken up in Chapters 5 and 6.

5 Consolidated method and its application

5.1 Background and scope

International investment, its governance, and their combined impact on the process of sustainable development elicited increased attention and scrutiny as they became inseparable features of progressively integrated economies. Seen as a remedy to trailing economic growth, international investment would quench the need for financing in areas and sectors where little to none was available.[1] Chapters 2 and 3 broadly curated the historical and conceptual milieu of international investment and sustainable development, which chronicled both the exponential growth of transnational corporations (TNCs) and investment evoked as well as the rethinking of the balance between the risks and benefits of admitting foreign investment. Meanwhile, the international investment law regime provisioned an ex ante (international investment agreements) and ex post (investment treaty arbitration) governance system. Yet as examined in Chapter 3, that governance system remained limited in facilitating government measures and private sector investment that sought to advance sustainable development within the confines of international investment law.

In confronting those limitations, Chapter 3 distilled the international investment–sustainable development framework ("Framework") to delineate the ways in which international investment was viewed as being able to advance sustainable development based on conceptualizations and documents materialized through multilateral negotiations. The Framework remains indispensable to the objective of this work in its entirety, which was to investigate international investment and its governance as means to advance sustainable development. A main limitation, which was also raised in Chapter 1, was that the international investment law regime, particularly investment treaty arbitration tribunals, were unable and/or unwilling to assess the relationship between an international investment and sustainable development. This was captured through the three forms of incomplete assessment introduced in Chapter 2, which together showed how investment treaty arbitration either misinterpreted or did not consider the substantive merits of

1 As outlined by the first pillar provided in Chapter 2.

DOI: 10.4324/9781003495871-5

sustainable development within the context of the dispute, even after the issue was raised by either of the disputing parties.

Chapter 4 turned to Sustainable Investment, providing an overview of its evolution across private sector engagement, financial regulation, and involvement by multilateral institutions. The resultant notion of Sustainable Investment ("Notion") extracted the types and characteristics of investments that could be identified as "sustainable" as well as the methodologies employed, and considerations taken to reach such a conclusion based on the results of a multilateral process, which was a defining parameter in both the Framework and the Notion. Where the Framework is primarily applicable to government measures, the Notion serves as a complement by focusing on the extent to which investments themselves impact sustainable development.

The present chapter synthesizes the Framework and Notion into a Consolidated Method ("Method") in advancing the thesis at the centre of this book: when determining the legitimacy of a government measure implemented in the right to regulate for the public interest of sustainable development, the conduct of the investor (and/or the performance of the investment) must be taken into consideration in order to avoid an incomplete assessment of their respective impact on sustainable development.

The importance of the Method advanced by this work becomes clearer in the context of investment treaty arbitration when the claimant party (the international investor) and the respondent (the host state) present opposing claims concerning impact on sustainable development. Such circumstances arise when the host state implements a government measure that directly or indirectly harms the international investment but recuses itself of violating an applicable international investment agreement on the basis of evoking its right to regulate for the public interest.[2]

The Method addresses this specific set of circumstances in international investment law, seeking to better align the international investment law regime with multilaterally conceived sustainable development ambitions. As identified at the end of Chapter 4, the Method does this by bringing together the Framework and Notion in application to the international agreements that affect foreign investment. The form of application envisioned by this project, to which this chapter is committed, is in the drafting an interpretation of international agreements in the form of model provisions that are aligned with international investment and sustainable development nexus advanced by this work.[3]

5.2 Interdisciplinarity in the investment law scholarship

Interdisciplinary approaches to international investment law populate large swathes of the scholarship, expanding the frontiers on how both scholars and practitioners

2 Chapter 1 details these circumstances in greater length.
3 As substantiated in Pillar One.

view the subject.[4] In continuing from Chapter 2, which constructs the three-pillar conceptual framework that forms the interdisciplinary approach of this work, this section provides a more accurate location of this Method's approach within the evolutionary position. This evolutionary view of international investment law, as was described in Chapter 1, is a conceptually loose grouping of research that identifies institutional pathways for international investment law to confront its limitations.[5] The Method combines two approaches within the evolutionary view. The first seeks to understand the international investment law regime by employing concepts from an external discipline (identified as "centripetal approaches"). The second applies the international investment law regime to concepts of an external discipline (identified as "centrifugal approaches"). This bifurcation, while coarse, is helpful in better locating the Method within the expansive body of international investment law research and scholarship.

5.2.1 Centripetal approach

Centripetal approaches can be defined as those that seek to shed light on the obfuscated inter-workings of the international investment law regime, particularly investment treaty arbitration, by drawing connections and insights from disciplines that can be considered external to international investment law. The value of this approach becomes apparent when viewed in connection to the institutional eccentricities of international investment law,[6] specifically the considerable discretion endowed to investment treaty arbitration tribunals. In specific disputes, an arbitral tribunal may be tasked with assessing the legitimacy of a state's policymaking when it falls within its jurisdiction. Indeed, Kethireddy described investment treaties as being "replete with open-textured provisions that can sustain a wide range of understandings", requiring tribunals to "reinvent the wheel all the time" because "investment treaties are instruments of public international law that turn investors into rights-holders".[7] This is invariably worrisome in application to such multimodal concepts as sustainable development, as this book attempted to depict through the presence of an incomplete assessment.[8]

4 See, for example, Emma Aisbett and others, *Rethinking International Investment Governance: Principles for the 21st Century* (Columbia Center on Sustainable Investment 2018). See Chapter 1.

5 A prototypical approach in the evolutionary position may be found in Stephan W Schill and Vladislav Djanic, 'Wherefore Art Thou? Towards a Public Interest-Based Justification of International Investment Law' (2018) 33 ICSID Review 29.

6 These are addressed in Chapter 1.

7 Srinath Reddy Kethireddy, 'Still the Law of Nations: Legitimate Expectations and the Sovereigntist Turn in International Investment Law' (2019) 44 Yale Journal of International Law 315, 318–21.

8 Batifort and Larkin, for instance, identified that arbitral tribunals subjecting such "treaty silence" to "creative" interpretation has "played a significant role in driving many key controversies currently facing international investment law" (Simon Batifort and Andrew Larkin, 'The Meaning of Silence in Investment Treaties' [2022] ICSID Review 1, 23). such as those identified in Chapter 1.

Much of the research that typifies this centripetal approach takes to analysing procedural reform[9] in the international investment law regime as well as ongoing efforts at the multilateral level in addressing procedural concerns.[10] While the Method opts for an interdisciplinary approach, much of the research in reforming investment law adopt methods from within international economic law or more broadly in legal studies.[11]

In terms of interdisciplinary centripetal approaches, the most predominant of these have been in empirical analysis, leveraging the explanatory power of "quantitative, qualitative and computational [methods] to analyze the international investment regime, probing its origins, functioning and effects, and to address doctrinal questions".[12] The variation in how this research is scoped is broad. Some work seeks to draw observations regarding the mechanical features of international investment law practice through empirical study.[13] For example, Franck investigated the psychology of arbitrators in an empirical investigation of the quality of decisions, finding that arbitrators "often made intuitive and impressionistic decisions rather than the fully rational and deliberative decisions that might be normatively desirable".[14]

9 Meg Kinnear, Secretary General of the International Centre for Settlement of Investment Disputes (ICSID), provides a short overview of reform issues and current progress in Meg Kinnear, 'The Launch of a New Generation of the ICSID Rules' (2022) 326 Columbia FDI Perspectives. In March 2022, Member States approved and thereby concluded a five-year process of revising the ICSID Regulations and Rules, which come into effect in July 2022 (International Centre for Settlement of Investment Disputes (ICSID), 'ICSID Administrative Council Approves Amendment of ICSID Rules' [*News Releases*, 21 March 2022] <https://icsid-worldbank-org/news-and-events/communiques/icsid-administrative-council-approves-amendment-icsid-rules> accessed 14 April 2022). Investment Arbitration Reporter offers an overview of this process in Lisa Bohmer, 'New ICSID Rules and Regulations Will Come into Effect on 1 July 2022, as Member States Approve Proposed Amendments' (*Investment Arbitration Reporter*, 22 March 2022) <https://www-iareporter-com/articles/breaking-new-icsid-rules-and-regulations-will-come-into-effect-on-july-1-2022-as-member-states-approve-proposed-amendments/> accessed 14 April 2022.

10 See Chapter 3 for an overview of these efforts.

11 The 2020 special issue of *The Journal of World Investment & Trade* on "UNCITRAL and Investment Arbitration Reform", for example, features numerous disciplinary (within international economic law) approaches to the research on reform. For example, Arato, Brown and Ortino's article present an analysis based on arbitral decisions and principles of international economic law (Julian Arato, Chester Brown and Federico Ortino, 'Parsing and Managing Inconsistency in Investor-State Dispute Settlement' (2020) 21 The Journal of World Investment & Trade 336). An analysis of criticism and reform concerning investment treaty arbitration that borrows from sources of law that are found outside the conventional investment law regime but within general legal scholarship is also included in this disciplinary format. For example, in the same issue, Giorgetti and others seek to apply different guidelines of impartiality on the topic of arbitrator bias in investment arbitration (Chiara Giorgetti and others, 'Independence and Impartiality of Adjudicators in Investment Dispute Settlement: Assessing Challenges and Reform Options' [2020] 21 The Journal of World Investment & Trade 441).

12 Daniel Behn, Malcolm Langford and Laura Létourneau-Tremblay, 'Empirical Perspectives on Investment Arbitration: What Do We Know? Does It Matter?' (2020) 21 The Journal of World Investment & Trade 188–89.

13 See, for example, Zoe Williams, *The Political Economy of Investment Arbitration* (OUP 2022).

14 Susan D Franck and others, 'Inside the Arbitrator's Mind' (2016) 66 Emory Law Journal 1115–66.

Franck also uncovered similarly stirring results in her investigation on the correlation between the costs of investment treaty arbitration and the outcomes of arbitration, identifying that "the cost of counsel (PLC) for investors was reliably more expensive when investors won, and where states won, investor PLC cost reliably less".[15]

Other works mount more farsighted examinations, identifying potential exogenous influences on international investment law. For example, Franck empirically contested the correlation between the outcome of an investment treaty arbitration and the development status of the respondent or arbitrator[16] while levels of "internal democracy" and governance infrastructure "could exert more influence on [investment treaty arbitration] outcomes".[17] Bjorklund and others identified through this empirical method that the arbitrator diversity remains low due to systemic reasons involving a preference for more experienced arbitrators and a lack of coordinated effort to "broaden the adjudicator pool" in a system where arbitrators are appointed on a case-by-case basis as opposed to being a more permanent presence at an institution.[18] Chriki identified in an empirical study that when host states implement government measures that are "inconsistent with the Washington Consensus", they have a "larger and significantly higher chance [44%] of being in violation of [fair and equitable treatment] than other cases".[19] Of these measures, restructuring treasury bills, enforcing mandatory standards and bans, imposing a temporary administrator, increasing taxes, and regulating price had a 90% to 100% chance of resulting in a claim of violating fair and equitable treatment.[20]

As these centripetal interdisciplinary approaches have done, empirical investigations of international investment law are able to formulate the basis for self-reflexive observations. While capitulating empirical evidence does not necessarily provide the means to draw broader, normative conclusions, the research ascribable to this approach affords the capacity to pronounce with greater precision the challenges facing international investment law.

While the Method does not take to empirical analysis, but rather the financial analysis of sustainable investment, it also seeks to employ the lens of external

15 Susan D Franck, 'The Potential Drivers—Predicting ITA Costs' in *Arbitration Costs* (OUP 2019) 257.

16 Susan D Franck, 'Development and Outcomes of Investment Treaty Arbitration' (2009) 50 Harvard International Law Journal 435.

17 Susan D Franck, 'Conflating Politics and Development: Examining Investment Treaty Arbitration Outcomes' (2014) 55 Virginia Journal of International Law 13, 60. The robustness of these relationships is further explored in explored in Daniel Behn, Tarald Laudal Berge and Malcolm Langford, 'Poor States or Poor Governance: Explaining Outcomes in Investment Treaty Arbitration' (2017) 38 Northwestern Journal of International Law & Business 333.

18 Andrea K Bjorklund and others, 'The Diversity Deficit in International Investment Arbitration' (2020) 21 The Journal of World Investment & Trade 410, 426–27.

19 David Chriki, 'Is the Washington Consensus Really Dead: An Empirical Analysis of FET Claims in Investment Arbitration' (2018) 41 Suffolk Transnational Law Review 291, 324.

20 David Chriki, 'Is the Washington Consensus Really Dead: An Empirical Analysis of FET Claims in Investment Arbitration' (2018) 41 Suffolk Transnational Law Review 323.

disciplines in committing to that same task. Within the Method, the Framework offers a means to analyse investment and development as they exist as concepts in development economics. In doing so, as Chapter 3 attempted to demonstrate, the Framework exists to enhance how the effect of investment on development is understood within the study of international investment law. Likewise, the Notion brings from its progeny in financial analysis the means to understand sustainability as it applies to investment. As Chapter 4 demonstrated, the result was a more comprehensive assessment of the way in which a private sector investment may impact sustainable development progress.

5.2.2 Centrifugal approach

Research that seeks to expand international investment law by extending its concepts beyond its conventional boundaries is broadly classified here as a centrifugal approach. Centrifugal approaches undoubtedly represent the bulk of the interdisciplinary research in international investment law. Such work seeks to expand the scope of international investment law through "cross-fertilization"[21] between the language of international law and that of inter alia sustainable development. Thus, a centrifugal study would, for instance, isolate a dimension of international investment law, such as public interest safeguards,[22] and cross-fertilize it with the idea of leave no one behind in sustainable development[23] in an effort to expand its interpretation.

Gordon, Pohl, and Bouchard, for example, examined how responsible business conduct is integrated into the language of international investment agreements through cross-fertilization. They describe these centrifugal approaches as warranted by "adjudicative bodies in international law increasingly seek[ing] to apply international law (including investment treaty law) in its general context—that is, interpreting treaties while also integrating, where relevant and applicable, other components of international law (both customary and international) and of domestic law".[24] This implies, they conclude, that investment treaty arbitration tribunals have been and should continue to consider "principles of other fields of international law, including bodies of law related to [responsible business conduct]".[25]

21 Philippe Sands, 'Treaty, Custom and the Cross-Fertilization of International Law' (1998) 1 Yale Human Rights & Development Law Journal 85.

22 See Chapter 2.

23 See 'Universal Values Principle Two: Leave No One Behind' (*UN Sustainable Development Group*) <https://unsdg.un.org/2030-agenda/universal-values/leave-no-one-behind> accessed 20 April 2022.

24 Kathryn Gordon, Joachim Pohl and Marie Bouchard, *Investment Treaty Law, Sustainable Development and Responsible Business Conduct: A Fact Finding Survey* (Organisation for Economic Cooperation and Development (OECD) 2014) 22.

25 Kathryn Gordon, Joachim Pohl and Marie Bouchard, *Investment Treaty Law, Sustainable Development and Responsible Business Conduct: A Fact Finding Survey* (Organisation for Economic Cooperation and Development (OECD) 2014).

Generally, centrifugal approaches to interdisciplinary international investment law research attempt to cross-fertilize matters related to "transnational public policy", which refer to "fundamental values and interests of the international society as a whole".[26] In this manner, transnational public policy concerns provide a contrast to the "conception of international law that strictly relies on the will of sovereign States"[27] by examining matters of importance multilaterally, such as sustainable development. As was examined in greater length in the conceptual framework provided in Chapter 2, the integration of these matters of transnational public policy, e.g., sustainable development, into the international investment law regime is based on the commonly held view that the object and purpose of trade and investment agreements include sustainable development as an objective.[28]

The Organisation for Economic Cooperation and Development also engages these issues of transnational public policy in application to the international investment law regime regularly. In 2020, for example, Gaukrodger traced the process of "business and investor responsibilities" becoming regular features in international investment agreements.[29] In this new generation of investment treaties, governments have "acted to protect policy space. They have also affirmed more strongly government duties to regulate in key policy areas in extensions of earlier trade agreement policies" though none has referred to international agreements on responsible business conduct like the UN Guiding Principles on Business and Human Rights.[30] The distinct absence of human rights considerations in international investment law is a focal point within the scholarship that can be classified into the centrifugal approach, many of which seek to address how the international investment law regime has and should engage human rights as a transnational public policy interest.[31]

Another source of centrifugal approaches to international investment law has been in reaction to the increasing prominence of new trends or phenomena that remain insufficiently addressed. For example, Chaisse identifies how the rise of

26 Jean-Michel Marcoux, 'Transnational Public Policy as a Vehicle to Impose Human Rights Obligations in International Investment Arbitration' (2020) 21 The Journal of World Investment & Trade 809, 816.

27 Jean-Michel Marcoux, 'Transnational Public Policy as a Vehicle to Impose Human Rights Obligations in International Investment Arbitration' (2020) 21 The Journal of World Investment & Trade 811–12.

28 A recent example includes Marie-Claire Cordonier Segger, 'International Trade and Investment Agreements in Light of the Integration Principle' in *Crafting Trade and Investment Accords for Sustainable Development: Athena's Treaties* (OUP 2021).

29 David Gaukrodger, 'Business Responsibilities and Investment Treaties' (Organisation for Economic Cooperation and Development (OECD) 2020) Consultation paper by the OECD Secretariat 22.

30 David Gaukrodger, 'Business Responsibilities and Investment Treaties' (Organisation for Economic Cooperation and Development (OECD) 2020) Consultation paper by the OECD Secretariat 89.

31 Markus Krajewski, 'Framing the Broader Context of Business and Human Rights: The Impact of Trade Agreements on Human Rights' in Surya Deva and David Birchall (eds), *Research Handbook on Human Rights and Business* (Edward Elgar Publishing Limited 2020) 288.

"state capitalism" with state-controlled entities and sovereign wealth funds evoked controversy concerning the "role of government in a capitalist economy", especially involving "potential for abuse or corruption where elements of state capitalism interfere in a tradition of market capitalism".[32] Mounting a response to such challenges requires countermeasures that are not easily located in international investment law,[33] which was demonstrated by the need of Tribunals deliberating questions of weaponizable dual-use technologies, exposure to cybersecurity threats, and critical infrastructure prone to incursion as matters of geopolitical intrigue.[34] In line with this risk-benefit calculus in engaging with the international investment law regime, another subject of centrifugal interdisciplinary research has been the political economics of economic integration. Bonnitcha, Poulsen, and Waibel in their exploration of this issue identified that a primary motivation behind entering into an international investment agreement is the result of the strategic behaviour to "lock in" and/or push forward domestic reforms, preventing successors from easily rolling back policy changes.[35]

Linarelli, Salomon, and Sornarajah take this interdisciplinary investigation deeper, observing that if the "policy prescriptions of the law are based on untruths or unprovable hypothesis, then, the law itself will lack legitimacy based on epistemological grounds alone, quite apart from any normative grounds that threaten its legitimacy".[36] From this orientation, any view of international investment law must depart from the understanding that the "creation of inflexible systems of investment protection through a network of treaties and the expansionary interpretation of the standards of protections in the treaties by arbitral tribunals" is the product of the monopolization of power by the "institutions and individuals who have promoted a neoliberal vision".[37] These views can be attributed to the series of commentary and research that investigate democratization and governance issues in international investment law. Koivusalo scopes such works in a classification of "rights, regulation, and redistribution" based on how investment protections "restricts and directly or indirectly influences what governance can do and how governments

32 Julien Chaisse, 'State Capitalism on the Ascent: Stress, Shock, and Adaptation of the International Law on Foreign Investment' (2018) 27 Minnesota Journal of International Law 339, 19.

33 Julien Chaisse, 'State Capitalism on the Ascent: Stress, Shock, and Adaptation of the International Law on Foreign Investment' (2018) 27 Minnesota Journal of International Law 21.

34 Julien Chaisse, 'State Capitalism on the Ascent: Stress, Shock, and Adaptation of the International Law on Foreign Investment' (2018) 27 Minnesota Journal of International Law 33–35.

35 Jonathan Bonnitcha, Lauge N Skovgaard Poulsen and Michael Waibel, 'Politics of Investment Treaties in Developing Countries' in *The Political Economy of the Investment Treaty Regime* (OUP 2017) 216–20.

36 John Linarelli, Margot E Salomon and Muthucumaraswamy Sornarajah, 'The End of Empire and the Search for Justice' in *The End of Empire and the Search for Justice: NIEO and Beyond* (OUP 2018) 149–50.

37 John Linarelli, Margot E Salomon and Muthucumaraswamy Sornarajah, 'The End of Empire and the Search for Justice' in *The End of Empire and the Search for Justice: NIEO and Beyond* (OUP 2018) 151.

can—or often more precisely at what price they can—intervene or restrict markets or investor interests".[38]

Moving closer to the topic of this work, another illustration of the centrifugal approach stands at the intersection between international investment law and climate change. The absence of climate change concerns in international investment law has been a flashpoint both in the scholarship and initiatives to reform the international investment law regime. The Energy Charter Treaty, for instance, is representative of this absence, primarily in its technology-neutrality: strong investment protections are provided to unsustainable energy projects[39] while government policies that are "disruptive but necessary measures to address climate change" are targeted for penalization.[40] This misalignment between the measures necessary to mitigate the impacts of climate change and those that are compliant with international investment law shows the necessity of channelling centrifugal approaches. Van Harten, for instance, suggested that investment treaty arbitration carve-outs were a viable means towards reconciliation. He suggests that the "objective of stabilizing greenhouse gas concentrations in the atmosphere at a level that would prevent dangerous anthropogenic interference with the climate system" should override other considerations when climate change-related issues measures are in dispute.[41] In order to "safeguard against the risk of [investor-State dispute settlement] claims that frustrate or deter climate change action", the scope and application of relevant measures would fall within the "sole and exclusive jurisdiction" of the body or process pursuant to the relevant multilateral climate change agreement.[42]

Whether climate changes or social protections, through any of its multiple dimensions, sustainable development inhabits a central space in the interdisciplinary research on international investment law. Such research investigates how sustainable development interacts at different levels of the international investment law regime. A common entry point, as this work utilized in Chapter 4, has been at the stage of defining a covered investment in the context of investment treaty arbitration. More specifically, the criteria that need to be satisfied for an investment to be covered by the relevant international investment agreement. Tamada undertook

38 M Koivusalo, 'Rights, Regulation and Redistribution: The Global Politics of Investment Protection' (2019) 19 Global Social Policy 105–6.

39 Markus Burgstaller, 'Investment Protection and Sustainable Energy Projects in the Age of Climate Change' in Stephan Hobe and others (eds), *Evolution, Evaluation and Future Developments in International Investment Law: Proceedings of the 10 Year Anniversary Conference of the International Investment Law Centre Cologne* (Bloomsbury 2021) 114.

40 Markus Burgstaller, 'Investment Protection and Sustainable Energy Projects in the Age of Climate Change' in Stephan Hobe and others (eds), *Evolution, Evaluation and Future Developments in International Investment Law: Proceedings of the 10 Year Anniversary Conference of the International Investment Law Centre Cologne* (Bloomsbury 2021) 116.

41 Gus Van Harten, 'An ISDS Carve-Out to Support Action on Climate Change' (2015) 38/2015 Osgoode Legal Studies Research Paper Series 1.

42 Gus Van Harten, 'An ISDS Carve-Out to Support Action on Climate Change' (2015) 38/2015 Osgoode Legal Studies Research Paper Series 2–4.

this task by examining the way that investment treaty arbitration tribunals had responded to the Salini criterion of investment, which suggested that one characteristic of a covered investment is that it significantly contributes to the development of the host state's economy. He identified that while the issue is deliberated in investment treaty arbitration, it would remain technical rather than substantive, not touching upon the "essential problem of how one is to conceive development".[43]

Chi also takes to this challenge, identifying an "incompatibility" between international investment agreements and sustainable development because relevant provisions in international investment agreements "only represent some elements of sustainable development" and that they "in general fail to generate concrete and enforceable sustainable development obligations on states and foreign investors".[44] Chi advances that not only do more balancing provisions need to be introduced, which are provisions in international investment agreements that seek to balance rights of the investor and the right to regulate of the host state, but also that these balancing provisions must be based on a concrete normativity concerning sustainable development.[45] He offers pathways towards that objective, such as imposing more stringent requirements on international investors through national law that require the observation of norms related to corporate social responsibility and sustainable development.[46] Aust adds here that one aspect of international investment agreements that demonstrates this incompatibility is remedies for material injuries to the foreign investor caused by policy measures taken in the right to regulate. Compensation as the sole form of remedy, as well as its exclusively penal interpretation, necessarily establishes questions of remedy as resulting from violative state behaviour. To this, Aust asks:

> Why should, as a matter of policy, a violation of the standard of fair and equitable treatment only result in compensation? Is it not conceivable that such a violation may very well be undone and that thus a "return to legality" could be a viable option—and thus restitution?[47]

In addition to identifying the means from within the international investment law regime in order to expand the overall practice to integrate sustainable development

43 Dai Tamada, 'Must Investments Contribute to the Development of the Host State? The Salini Test Scrutinised' in Piotr Szwedo, Richard Peltz-Steele and Dai Tamada (eds), *Law and Development: Balancing Principles and Values* (Springer 2019) 110.

44 Manjiao Chi, 'Filling the Compatibility Gap Between IIAs and Sustainable Development' in *Integrating Sustainable Development in International Investment Law* (Routledge 2017) 163.

45 Manjiao Chi, 'Filling the Compatibility Gap Between IIAs and Sustainable Development' in *Integrating Sustainable Development in International Investment Law* (Routledge 2017) 164.

46 Manjiao Chi, 'Filling the Compatibility Gap Between IIAs and Sustainable Development' in *Integrating Sustainable Development in International Investment Law* (Routledge 2017) 165.

47 Helmut Philipp Aust, 'Investment Protection and Sustainable Development What Role for the Law of State Responsibility?' in Steffen Hindelang and Markus Krajewski (eds), *Shifting Paradigms in International Investment Law: More Balanced, Less Isolated, Increasingly Diversified* (OUP 2016) 217.

issues into the international investment law regime, research has also looked beyond the practice to multilateral agreements concerning sustainable development that together formulate a "legitimate expectation" to "prevent, or at least mitigate, the environmental and social development impacts of trade and investment agreements".[48] The methodology shaped in this work takes a similar view, seeking to extend the commitment made by governments to UN resolutions, standards, and initiatives into international investment law.

5.2.3 Approach of the present study

As the studies briefly overviewed in the preview section identified, and more extensively in Chapter 1, interdisciplinary approaches to international investment law research draw attention to issues in the subject that are comparatively less understood.[49] This book takes to the same endeavour in considering the interdisciplinary approach, specifically in seeking to understand the impact of incomplete assessments involving the public interest of sustainable development in international investment law.

As this chapter will attempt to demonstrate, the Framework and Notion take up both centripetal and centrifugal approaches to interdisciplinary international investment law research. The Framework and Notion both introduce extra-disciplinary methods to the analysis of international investment law, as well as broaden the scope of issues that are considered within the field. For instance, the three key features of the Notion together form a methodology in assessing the contribution of international investment to sustainable development. Meanwhile, the Framework stretches the margins of international investment law research to include issues and topics that would otherwise be considered extraneous to its conventional framing.

5.3 Consolidated method

Throughout this work, the Framework and Notion were grouped into a single "Consolidated Method" ("Method"). The primary objective of this chapter is now to apply the Method to the nexus between international investment law regime and

48 Marie-Claire Cordonier Segger, 'Policy and "Soft Law" Rationales for Addressing Social and Environmental Concerns in Trade and Investment Treaties' in *Crafting Trade and Investment Accords for Sustainable Development: Athena's Treaties* (OUP 2021) 106–7.

49 In reference to what scholars have used to describe the veiled and siloed thinking that at times commandeer the practice of international investment law. See, for example, Jeffrey L Dunoff and Mark A Pollack, 'International Judicial Practices: Opening the Black Box of International Courts' (2018) 40 Michigan Journal of International Law 47; Bernhard Berger and Michael E Schneider (eds), *Inside the Black Box: How Arbitral Tribunals Operate and Reach Their Decisions* (Juris 2014); Axel Berger and others, 'Do Trade and Investment Agreements Lead to More FDI? Accounting for Key Provisions Inside the Black Box' (2013) 10 International Economics and Economic Policy 247; Todd Tucker, 'Inside the Black Box: Collegial Patterns on Investment Tribunals' (2016) 7 Journal of International Dispute Settlement 183.

sustainable development, both as defined in Pillar Two of the Conceptual Framework provided in Chapter 2.

The Framework assembled in Chapter 3[50] extracted key policy strategies from the UN system as a means to, at the multilateral level, more closely integrating international investment and sustainable development. The Framework provided a more detailed depiction of government measures employable by a host state in working towards the advancement of sustainable development as a transnational public policy interest. Each government measure was then categorized into thematic strategies, which in turn were classified under broad development policy objectives. The five objectives, explained at greater length throughout Chapter 3, were formed into questions and provided an accessible means to determine whether a government measure or broad development policy strategy is consistent with multilateral consensus on the use of such measures.[51]

The Notion introduced in Chapter 4[52] assembled key features from the substantive works across the UN system on sustainable investment. While the Notion does not have at its disposal the repository of multinational research and policy guidance that UNCTAD was able to provide for international investment, there have been considerable albeit disconnected efforts within the system. One reason behind this disconnect, as Chapter 4 showed, is the prominent role given to the private sector in defining the specific parameters of sustainable investment governance, which can be traced to the UN's work on TNCs and corporate social responsibility.

One of the most important of these parameters commissioned to the private sector is the collection of data as well as the design and use of calculations to render sustainable investment, or more broadly environmental, social, and governance (ESG) performance, as a numerical score. The Notion thus finds substance in the substantive materials that are available through the UN system, particularly those areas of sustainable investment in which the UN system has engaged. The Notion is composed of the three key features that would be found in any approach to defining and/more measuring sustainable investment: scope, indicators, and metrics. Based on a comprehensive investigation of the substantive materials by the UN

50 Summarized into tabular form in Appendix 1.

51 They are:

(1) Does the international investment or government measure contribute to advancing the host state's national sustainable development ambitions and/or needs?
(2) Does the international investment or government measure promote a relationship between the investor and host state that is conducive to advancing sustainable development?
(3) Does the international investment or government measure promote productive economic interaction conducive to advancing sustainable development between states and/or economic actors, both domestic and international?
(4) Is then international investment or government measure harmonized with multilateral standards related to sustainable development?
(5) Does the international investment or government measure sufficiently prevent abusive practices that hamper sustainable development?

52 Summarized into tabular form in Appendix 2.

system on sustainable investment, elements that are broadly shared across these materials were extracted for each key feature. The result is a guideline for determining whether an investment (while designed for portfolio investment but can be readily applied to foreign direct investment [FDI]) is aligned with the UN system's conceptualization of Sustainable Investment.

The Framework and Notion are sourced from two entirely different forms of investment: foreign direct and foreign portfolio investment, respectively. Despite this difference, the Framework and Notion share a central set of two unifying tenets that guide the Method's application. Furthermore, the Framework and Notion are bound together in Method's overall objective of mobilizing investment towards Financing for Sustainable Development.[53] At the same time, however, satisfying one tenet of the Method does not necessarily equate to a contribution to sustainable development; an investment or government measure ("Action") that satisfies one tenet at the undue cost of another would be both counterintuitive and potentially detrimental to sustainable development.

After defining each tenet of the Method, this section applies them in the form of model law provisions in the latter half of this chapter. As discussed later, model laws are regularly employed tools in better aligning legal systems towards the objectives of the UN system, such as sustainable development. As such, they make apt platforms for applying the findings and analysis of this work. While model laws certainly lack the permanence of a total reformation of the international investment law regime, the calls for which were reviewed in Chapter 1, they seek to provide intermediary measures in the longer journey of actualizing permanent, institutional change. Simultaneously, the humility of this effort is also in recognition of (or perhaps subscription to) the evolutionary conviction on the important role that the international investment law regime retains in directing international investment to areas of development need and thus the need to enhance rather than eradicate the regime entirely.

5.3.1 First tenet: coherence with sustainable development[54]

The first tenet in the Method is whether the Action[55] is coherent with sustainable development as a matter of national or international public policy.[56] Evaluating whether an Action is coherent with sustainable development was identified in

53 As defined through its institutional history in the UN system in Section 2.2.1.

54 Appendices 1 and 2 categorize each Framework Measure and Notion Element into the First and Second Tenets.

55 Defined earlier as referring to either a (1) government measure by the host state, such as the implementation or termination of a certain policy, or (2) foreign direct investment.

56 International public policy and its inclusion of sustainable development were well established in Chapter 2. International public policy can be understood here as defined by the *Resolution of the International Law Association on Public Policy as a Bar to Enforcement of International Arbitral Awards*, which includes:

(1) fundamental principles, pertaining to justice or morality, that the State wishes to protect even when it is not directly concerned

Chapter 2 as one of the primary causes of the three forms of limited assessment demonstrated in investment treaty arbitration. Specifically, when sustainable development lacks normative substance in the international investment agreement, it is left to the discretion of investment treaty arbitration tribunals to fill those gaps in the instance of a dispute.

Two questions help to contour the type of considerations that may fall under this tenet:

1 Is the Action aligned with existing national policies meant to advance sustainable development?
2 Is the Action aligned with multilaterally accepted standards or agreements concerning sustainable development?

In answering the first question, assessing whether an Action is coherent with sustainable development is to examine the extent to which that Action corresponds with the sustainable development–related laws and policies of the host state. This has different meaning in application to an investment or a government measure. For international investment, this would refer to whether the investor and/or investment is not only in compliance with the host state's laws and regulations, but also aligned with its policy objectives and strategies in its nationally defined sustainable development ambition. In connection to government measures, this test would be in application to whether the measure is coherent with other laws and/or policies that are related to the state's sustainable development planning. For instance, whether the host state's laws and/or policies related to international investment, such as investment incentives, do not contradict its laws and/or policies that serve its sustainable development ambitions. This specification addresses instances when the host state (or a specific organ of the state) attempts to implement a government measure under false pretences of advancing its sustainable development and is inconsistent with the government's larger framework of sustainable development-related laws and/or policies.

The second question refers to the coherence of Actions with sustainable development beyond the laws and/or policies of any one host state. More specifically, this involves coherence with multilateral standards and obligations concerning sustainable development. The necessity to look beyond the domestic sphere can be ascertained when viewing sustainable development as a matter of transnational public policy with normativity beyond that which is provided by the host state alone.[57] In doing so, this second question of the first tenet emphasizes the existence

(2) rules designed to serve the essential political, social or economic interests of the State, these being known as "lois de police" or "public policy rules" and
(3) the duty of the State to respect its obligations towards other States or international organisations. ('Resolution of the ILA on Public Policy as a Bar to Enforcement of International Arbitral Awards' [2003] 19 Arbitration International 213 Art 1[d]).

57 As was established in Section 5.2.2.

of norms and standards that have been established at the multilateral level, such as the UN Sustainable Development Goals (SDGs),[58] and the obligation of states to ensure that they are observed. This applies to both a host state's government measures as well as in regulating covered investments in their territory. Coherence with established norms and standards at the multilateral level in applying the Method to international investment law is crucial in assessing claims concerning contributions to sustainable development beyond the strictures of national domain, which can be modified to be self-serving. Thus, in addition to retaining deference to national structures, the first tenet of the Method also acts as a bulwark against changes of political regime or direction that may seek to backpedal on obligations to servicing the forward-looking needs of sustainable development.

5.3.2 Second tenet: contribution to sustainable development

The advent of progressive international investment agreements sought to fill some of the normative gaps in relation to sustainable development.[59] The second tenet of the Method addresses the means to monitor, report, and verify (MRV) the extent to which Actions contribute to sustainable development. Harmonizing standards of MRV was identified as a core component of the nexus between international investment and sustainable development, both in the conceptual framework provided in Chapter 2 as well as throughout the Method itself, namely Framework Objective Four (harmonization with multilateral standards) and the second key feature of the Notion (indicators).[60]

The importance of the second tenet can be readily identified in the tendency of treaty arbitration tribunals to demonstrate a reluctance to stray from a purely "legal" analysis in deliberating disputes, dismissing a wide gamut of analytical claims such as those involving inter alia environmental impact. This second tenet in the Method thus concerns the ability to MRV the extent to which an Action contributes to sustainable development. The following questions contour the considerations that fall under this second tenet:

1 Is the extent of contribution to sustainable development by the Action falsifiable based on a threshold (such as being in line with the "best available science")[61] of empirical and/or science-based evidence?
2 Does the Action result in additionality, which is to expand investors and/or investments that are aligned with sustainable development?

58 As well as other binding multilateral agreements identified in the first pillar of the conceptual framework in Section 2.2.
59 Examples of such were provided in Section 3.2.
60 See Sections 3.3.4 and 4.2.2, respectively.
61 Oftentimes in reference to the findings of the Intergovernmental Panel on Climate Change (IPCC). See Section 4.2.2 regarding a science-based approach.

The first question represents a growing inclination towards empirical, data-backed, and quantitative evidence of whether Actions result in "real world impact". This movement mirrors a predilection towards "science-based" indications of policy commitments that are commonly linked with multilateral agreements as the Paris Agreement and its identification of a specific numerical targets in limiting the expansion of greenhouse gas-emitting activities to 1.5°C. This provided the basis for the idea of a "1.5°C-compliant business model" by the Business Ambition for 1.5°C organized by the UN Global Compact.

In addition to assessing Actions on their real-world impact on sustainable development, the second question also seeks to factor in the concepts of additionality and universality. As explained in Chapter 4, if an Action results in increasing the total amount of contribution to sustainable development (additionality) and/or advances harmonization concerning sustainable development (universality), then it can be seen as satisfying this tenet.

5.3.3 Examples of application

Actions, whether government measures or international investments, come with rich array of circumstantial factors and stakeholders. To then align these actions with the multiple dimensions of sustainable development to produce accurate portrayals of how the Action contributes to sustainable development is thus a complex task. Piecing together different dimensions of the Method confers numerous benefits while aiding in the navigation of that task. These benefits include a more comprehensive approach afforded through interdisciplinarity, which Chapter 2 laid out in detail. Furthermore, as Chapters 3 and 4 provided, each constituent part of the Method finds basis in multilateral deliberation and consensus through the United Nations system.

The chapters and section to this point have been dedicated to presenting the conceptual dimensions of the Method. Having done this to a sufficient level, the remainder of this work envisions how this Method can be applied so that it may achieve its intended effect. Preceding that endeavour, this section provides examples of recent Actions and how the Method can be employed as a means to analyse them.

5.3.3.1 National development and reform commission and the national high-standard farmland construction plan (China)

China's regular utilization of industrial policy and its increased prioritization of advancing its sustainable development in the face of large capital inflows from FDI do well to illustrate the first objective of the Framework.[62] In April 2022, the National Development and Reform Commission of China announced that it would it reorient its foreign investment targets to pair infrastructure development and

62 Does the Action facilitate greater development impact? (See Section 3.3.1.)

capital investment with clear implications for water and energy conservation and socioeconomic development.[63]

One example of this approach of integrating industrial, investment, and sustainable development policy was in targeting investment in artificial intelligence of things (AIoT) and drone technology to provide information on crop, soil, and weather conditions to farmers in Hainan. The aim of the measure was to provide both an increase in yield with spillover effects of providing technical training to farmers, irrespective of gender, in the use of technology.[64] Such investments would also nurture a better understanding of the prevailing ecological conditions, thereby enabling society's capacities to both protect and benefit from the ecosystem and its services. Furthermore, the measure is in line with a broader national policy objective (*National High-Standard Farmland Construction Plan 2021–2030*)[65] of expanding "high-standard farmland" that would employ technology to improve agricultural production to address food security while reducing the amount of water, fertilizer, and electricity used in that process.

When imagining this government measure into a hypothetical dispute, competing firms may contend that as a result, some amount of their value (or that of their investments) had been destroyed resulting from excluding producers that had less capacity to reduce their usage of fertilizer and/or electricity. Reduced agricultural yield from certain producers with limited access to technology due to more stringent requirements on resource use can be examples of exclusion if the government measure is not supplemented with broader safety nets. Alternatively, the affected investors may claim that their investment was contributing to the sustainable development of the host state, which may have been in producers that employ traditional knowledge to facilitate sustainable agricultural production. In its defence, the government may seek to dismiss the grounds for the investor's claim by appealing to its having served the public interest of sustainable development. In one such a predicament, the Method offers a diverse menu of tests to assess the appeals of both the investor and the host state.

For instance, the government measure would find justification in Framework Measure 1.3.1 (productive investment) in that it provides capacities creation to Hainanese farmers, better equipping them with the technical skills necessary to adapt to technological progress. The measure would certainly embody Framework Measure 1.3.2 (sustainable development sectors) in addressing food security,

63 Jiaping Shen and Gao Lei, 'National Development and Reform Commission: Focus on Expanding Effective Investment from Four Aspects (国家发改委：重点从四个方面做好扩大有效投资工作)' *People's Daily Online (人民网)* (15 April 2022) <http://finance.people.com.cn/n1/2022/0415/c1004-32400036.html> accessed 16 April 2022.

64 United Nations Development Programme (UNDP), 'AIoT Farming Solutions' (*SDG Investor Platform*, 26 October 2021) <http://sdginvestorplatform.undp.org/market-intelligence/aiot-farming-solutions> accessed 22 March 2022.

65 State Council, People's Republic of China, 'High-Standard Farmland Gets Push Over Next Decade' (*Latest Releases (Policies)*, 16 September 2021) <http://english.www.gov.cn/policies/latestreleases/202109/16/content_WS6142db85c6d0df57f98e0431.html> accessed 23 March 2022.

which may be a priority sustainable development sector for the region. Finally, the measure demonstrated that it was well aligned with the host state's overarching development strategy of reducing resource use and improving productivity, satisfying Framework Measure 1.2.3 (parallel instruments).

Meanwhile, the claimant would have at their disposal means to appeal the government measure on the second tenet of the Method, contribution to sustainable development. In offering a counterclaim on contribution to sustainable development, the investor directs the deliberation necessary in adjudicating this dispute to matters of real-world contribution (Notion Element 2.1). Furthermore, should the investor's claim that the measure excluded certain producers from benefitting from the policy prove true, then another dimension of the analysis would be to determine whether the measure was pursuant to net positivity (Notion Element 1.1), especially the extent to which it was built on multistakeholderism (Framework Strategy 2.1).

5.3.3.2 The 2021 Law on Investment (Cambodia)

The Law on Investment of the Kingdom of Cambodia was introduced in 2021 to inter alia attract high-quality foreign investment through a tiered investment incentive scheme. The first tier provided tax incentives for investments that are admitted by the state ("basic incentives").[66] The second tier provided additional tax exemptions for activities that improve the socioeconomic conditions of Cambodia, namely in such areas as human resource development through training or the provision of welfare.[67] Last, additional benefits were provided for investments in sectors that Cambodia recognized as critical, such as innovation, tourism, biodiversity conservation, circular economy, green energy, and climate change adaptation and mitigation.[68] In addition to these incentives, the Law on Investment also carved out safeguards that permitted the termination of an investment should it adversely affect the environment.[69]

Changes to the administrative requirements for investments to qualify for incentives in part resulted in investment treaty arbitration after the claimants were no longer included as beneficiaries.[70] While the proceedings remain confidential, one may assume that the investors identified that the circumstances in which they made

66 Law on Investment of the Kingdom of Cambodia 2021 Art 26.

67 Law on Investment of the Kingdom of Cambodia 2021 Art 27.

68 Law on Investment of the Kingdom of Cambodia 2021 Art 24.

69 Law on Investment of the Kingdom of Cambodia 2021 Art 31.

70 In *Qiong Ye and Jianping Yang v Cambodia* (ICSID/ARB/21/42), claimants filed for arbitration after having their license revoked as an internet service provider after being excluded from a list of approved providers in 2021 March (Lisa Bohmer, 'Cambodia Is Facing Its First Known Treaty-Based Arbitration, as Chinese Telecom Investors Lodge ICSID Claim' (*Investment Arbitration Reporter*, 3 September 2021) <www.iareporter.com/articles/cambodia-is-facing-its-first-known-treaty-based-arbitration-as-chinese-telecom-investors-lodge-icsid-claim/> accessed 23 March 2022). This follows a change in the administrative procedures for companies providing telecommunication services, requiring an additional approval by the Council for the Development of Cambodia to qualify

their investment had been changed so completely that they would have not been compelled to invest should the current conditions have existed at that time. To the claimant, this may represent an indirect expropriation if the new regulatory conditions were such that the investment would no longer be able to operate at a profit. In response to that challenge, Cambodia may appeal to its right to regulate for the public interest of sustainable development.

Similar to the previous example, a change in the laws on foreign investment, which include changes to investment incentives, may result in the exclusion of certain parties that may in turn have adverse impacts on their financial performance. If the government measure was intended to target socioeconomic conditions through improving its human capital, then changing its foreign investment laws alone without other domestic policy efforts to enhance absorptive capacities would constraint even the most high-quality, productive, and positive investment from contributing to the host state's sustainable development. In such a case, the investment treaty arbitration tribunal may look to the Method in assessing the government measure. First, whether the lack of other domestic policy measures to boost socioeconomic gain from foreign investment is implemented in parallel with the changes Cambodia's foreign investment incentive regime (Framework Strategy 1.2 on policy coherence), such as providing the means for human capital to absorb the benefits of investment (Framework Strategy 1.1 on selectively liberalizing international investment regulation).

Furthermore, whether the Council for the Development of Cambodia, which approves the eligibility of foreign investors to receive incentive benefits, pursues multistakeholder consensus (Framework Measure 2.1.2) and stakeholder analysis (Notion Element 1.1) to determine whether said government measures is supported by the most affected stakeholders in society. Finally, in the effort to bolster the socioeconomic gains from foreign investment, the arbitration tribunal may also look to examine the way in which the investments being targeted by the host state (alternatively the investment licenses revoked or denied) interact with other dimensions of sustainable development to ensure that there is no backpedalling in other areas such as in poverty reduction in priority areas and creating meaningful jobs through strong local linkages beyond manufacturing lines.

5.3.3.3 Business responsibility and sustainability reporting (India)

The Securities and Exchange Board of India (SEBI) implemented a government measure in 2021 that required the top 1,000 publicly listed entities to adopt a standardized form of reporting their sustainability-related disclosures.[71] The measure, a circular titled "Business Responsibility and Sustainability Reporting by Listed

as an "expanded qualified investment project" (Law on Investment of the Kingdom of Cambodia Art 10).

71 Securities and Exchange Board of India (SEBI), 'SEBI Issues Circular on "Business Responsibility and Sustainability Reporting by Listed Entities" (PR No 18/2021)'.

Entities", amended a previous circular from 2015 that prescribed a format for companies to disclose their sustainability-related performance and risks. In addition to expanding the mandatory basis of sustainability-related disclosures, the 2021 circular also attempted to standardize disclosures in a way that is informed by international accepted reporting frameworks.[72]

Following the release of the circular, there was concern about requiring an international standard of disclosures. This was not only due to the fact that it would make it difficult for firms to attract capital, but also because there was both potential overlap with existing corporate governance regulation in India, such as the Section 135 (Corporate Social Responsibility) of the Companies Act (2013),[73] as well as additional administrative burden places on companies. Imagining this government measure into the setting of a dispute may evoke recollections[74] of the revised Markets in Financial Instruments Directive (MiFID II, 2018).[75] The sudden imposition of disclosure requirements on corporate performance without the ability to opt-out could result in large administrative burdens for firms that may be a diminutive for Indian conglomerates but impose debilitating costs for smaller firms and foreign investors that may need to shoulder addition burden as non-national entities.

In assessing such a claim in the context of a right to regulate for the public interest defence by the host state, the Tribunal may find that the enforcement of an international standard in application to sustainability-related disclosures embodies many aspects of the Method. These include, for instance, formulating clear expectations between potential and existing foreign investors and SEBI (Framework Measure 2.1.1), increasing the transparency and consistency of the state's interpretation of disclosed sustainability-related performance (Framework Measure 2.2.1), espousal of a shared and communal understanding of good corporate citizenship (Framework Measure 2.2.2), and encouraging the adoption of harmonized reporting of sustainable development-related factors in an effort to better understand the impact of investment on a state's achievement of sustainable development (Framework Strategy 4.2) such as through the imposition of public listing requirements (Notion Element 1.2). The extent to which Indian companies comply with and actively adapt their disclosure practice to this and any future regulation remains to be seen. However, if the government measure closely mirrors existing international standards of reporting, then testing the extent to which investments contribute to sustainable development becomes a more straightforward task, especially when applying the elements identified in the Notion.

72 Securities and Exchange Board of India (SEBI), Business Responsibility and Sustainability Reporting by Listed Entities 2021 [SEBI/HO/CFD/CMD-2/P/CIR/2021/562].

73 The Companies Act 2013 [ACT No 18 of 2013].

74 Markus Fellner and Martin Wallner, 'Mifid II in Austria: An Example of Unintended Consequences' (*International Financial Law Review*, 15 December 2020) <www.iflr.com/article/b1pmnbkccpql9n/mifid-ii-in-austria-an-example-of-unintended-consequences> accessed 26 April 2022.

75 'MiFID II' (*European Securities and Markets Authority*) <www.esma.europa.eu/policy-rules/mifid-ii-and-mifir> accessed 26 April 2022.

5.4 Model laws as means of application

Equipped now with a clearer understanding of the Method, such as through its organizing tenets and its application in analysing government measures, the remaining half of this chapter explores its proposed application: model provisions. Model laws are an ideal medium for applying the Method because they facilitate the absorption of its normative substance at the legislative and/or treaty drafting stage, targeting harmonization in wording and interpretation. Furthermore, the model provisions proposed below aim to amend provisions in international investment agreements that have become largely similar in their substantive elements.

Model laws are especially useful in connection to efforts in modernizing existing stock of international investment agreements because they help renegotiate treaty terms to both reflect present realities as well as enhance compatibility in the spirit of nurturing greater harmonization in international economic relations.[76] Model laws as templates have shaped "salient features in negotiated [international investment agreements]", such as the International Institute for Sustainable Development's "Model International Agreement on Investment for Sustainable Development"[77] that was found to have "inspired the most comprehensive copying of entire clauses".[78]

The approach towards model law by the UN Commission on International Trade Law (UNCITRAL) is a high suitable platform for applications of the Method envisioned in this work. The texts of model laws are finalized and adopted at the UNCITRAL in its annual sessions, each requiring multilateral consensus.[79] Based on these agreed texts, states are then able to "accommodate local requirements that vary from system to system, or where strict uniformity is not necessary or desirable".[80] UNCITRAL model laws cover a broad range of international commercial topics, from public-private partnership and electronic commerce to international commercial arbitration and mediation.[81] Equally diverse are the issues that are considered when the Commission convenes through its Working Groups, which remain a primary method through which UNCITRAL Member States negotiate

76 United Nations Trade and Development (UNCTAD), *Reform Package for the International Investment Regime* (United Nations 2018) 25.

77 See Howard Mann and others, *IISD Model International Agreement on Investment for Sustainable Development* (International Institute for Sustainable Development (IISD) 2005).

78 Wolfgang Alschner, Manfred Elsig and Simon Wüthrich, 'Main Act or Side Show? Model Agreements by International Institutions and Their Reuse in Investment Treaty Texts' (2022) 2022 Journal of International Economic Law 19, 13, 17.

79 Howard M Holtzmann and Joseph E Neuhaus, *A Guide to the UNCITRAL Model Law on International Commercial Arbitration: Legislative History and Commentary* (Kluwer Law International 2015) 5.

80 See, for example, United Nations Commission on International Trade Law (UNCITRAL), 'A Guide to UNCITRAL: Basic Facts About the United Nations Commission on International Trade Law' paras 38–39. Other initiatives from the United Nations system are outlined in Section 3.2.

81 United Nations Commission on International Trade Law (UNCITRAL), 'Texts and Status' <https://uncitral.un.org/en/texts> accessed 28 March 2022.

draft conventions and model laws.[82] The final report leading up to the adoption of the Draft Model Law on International Commercial Arbitration (1985), for instance, illustrates the breadth of procedural issues discussed and conceded by the Member States of the Commission. While UNCITRAL model laws generally take a functional approach rather than confronting normative issues like contribution to sustainable development, the broader objective of modernizing and/or harmonizing treaties or legislation makes it difficult to disentangle the public interest considerations and impacts of model laws.[83]

Furthermore, public policy or public interest safeguards are in fact common features in the model laws. In the aforementioned final report on the Draft Model Law on Commercial Arbitration, for example, the staying power of public policy (interest) safeguards is evident despite concerns raised that they "might be interpreted as not covering notions of procedural justice".[84] Other safeguards can be found in the Model Law on Public Procurement that permits the suspension of a procurement proceeding for "urgent public interest considerations"[85] or the public policy exception built into the Model Law on Enterprise Group Insolvency "if the action would be manifestly contrary to the public policy of this State".[86] The UNCITRAL Model Law on Electronic Transferable Records goes further by identifying that while "party autonomy is a fundamental principle underpinning commercial law", the "UNCITRAL texts on electronic commerce contain some limits to party autonomy in order to avoid conflicts with rules of mandatory application, such as those on public policy".[87]

82 At the time of writing, the six Working Groups were deliberating micro, small and medium-sized enterprises (Working Group I from 2014); dispute settlement (Working Group II from 2000); investor-State dispute settlement reform (Working Group III from 2017); electronic commerce (Working Group IV from 1997); insolvency law (Working Group V from 1995); and judicial sale of ships (Working Group VI from 2019). See United Nations Commission on International Trade Law (UNCITRAL), 'Working Groups' (*Working Documents*) <https://uncitral.un.org/en/working_groups> accessed 26 April 2022.

83 For example, Akseli (2021) identifies how the "functional approach" of the model laws, in this case the Model Law on Secured Transactions (2019), helps to "eliminate the inherent problem of fragmentation in national laws" through modernization and harmonization. This in turn, "provide more certainty to financiers, leading to more favorable lending terms and greater access to credit" (Orkun Akseli, 'Financial Inclusion, Access to Credit, and Sustainable Finance: What Role for the UNCITRAL Model Law on Secured Transactions?' (2021) 84 Law and Contemporary Problems 181, 188–89).

84 'Report of the United Nations Commission on International Trade Law on the Work of Its Eighteenth Session' (United Nations General Assembly 1985) A/40/17 para 323.

85 United Nations Commission on International Trade Law (UNCITRAL), 'UNCITRAL Model Law on Public Procurement' Art 67(4)(b).

86 United Nations Commission on International Trade Law (UNCITRAL), 'UNCITRAL Model Law on Enterprise Group Insolvency' Art 6. This wording is also used in the UNCITRAL Model Law on Cross-Border Insolvency Law (para 22(e)).

87 United Nations Commission on International Trade Law (UNCITRAL), 'UNCITRAL Model Law on Electronic Transferable Records' para 47.

For the most part, other than establishing public policy or interest considerations as an overriding condition, UNCITRAL model laws do not substantiate what those considerations may entail. However, the UNCITRAL does recognize that public policy "has been found to include both substantive and procedural aspects".[88] However, as the Guide to Enactment of the Model Law on Electronic Transferable Records provides, since the "notion of public policy . . . may differ from State to State" there is no attempt to provide for a "uniform definition of that notion".[89] Perhaps one of the only notable exceptions to this is in the UNCITRAL Model Law on International Commercial Conciliation. In reference to exceptions to confidentiality of conciliation proceedings, the Model Law identifies "laws requiring disclosure if it is in the public interest, for example, to alert the public about a health or environmental or safety risk".[90]

As this brief overview of model law established, public policy or interest exceptions are common features in UNCITRAL model laws, which as a tool has shown to be effective in progressing multilateral consensus on legislative and treaty modernization and harmonization. This work proposes to further these substantiations in model law, advancing that sustainable development, as a matter of both national and transnational public interest, can be included into as provisions in model law related to international investment regulation.[91] While not identified as model laws, international investment agreements negotiated between the European Union and non–European Union states also provide useful illustrations of building such multilateral consensus.

One promising accomplishment has been the *EU–Angola: Sustainable Investment Facilitation Agreement*. While the extent to which the text of this agreement will retain its original ambition after continued negotiations and eventual ratification by the parties remains mercurial,[92] instruments of this kind provide the habitats in which international investment law may evolve. Within the Agreement, there are provisions that embody the Consolidated Method and are thus worth exploring.

Article 2.6 ("Linkages with the host economy") of the Agreement encourages international investment to "[strengthen] linkages with the local economy" as a means of "enhancing the contribution of investment to sustainable development". As Framework Measures 1.1.1 (Linkage Promotion Programmes) and 1.3.1

88 UNCITRAL, *2012 Digest of Case Law on the Model Law on International Commercial Arbitration* (United Nations 2012) 160.

89 United Nations Commission on International Trade Law (UNCITRAL), 'UNCITRAL Model Law on Enterprise Group Insolvency' (n 86) para 63.

90 United Nations Commission on International Trade Law (UNCITRAL), 'UNCITRAL Model Law on International Commercial Conciliation with Guide to Enactment and Use' para 63.

91 While UNCITRAL does engage in the topic of reforming investor-State dispute settlement (ISDS), as examined in Section 3.2, this proposal to employ model law as a means of application does not necessarily relate to the content of that work.

92 An overview of the progress on these negotiations can be found in 'EU and Angola Conclude First-Ever Sustainable Investment Facilitation Agreement' (*European Commission*, 18 November 2022) <https://ec.europa.eu/commission/presscorner/detail/en/IP_22_6136> accessed 21 November 2022.

(Productive Investment) embodied, encouraging such linkages can help that international investment is productive and impactful for the economy of the recipient state. Article 5.2 (Right to regulate and levels of protection) carves sustainable development-related safeguards as identified in Framework Measure 5.1.2 with a backstop described in Article 5.2.3 in the fashion suggested by Framework Measure 5.1.1. Articles 5.5 (Investment and climate change) and 5.6 (Investment contributing to sustainable development) seek to promote, facilitate, and encourage investment that has real-world sustainable development impact, which was an attribute of Notion Element 2.1 (Real-World Impact). This is particular the case in the instance of disputes as per Article 6.1 (Consultations) of the Agreement, which correlates with Framework Measure 5.1.3 (Clarified Conflict Rules between Parallel Instruments). A final notable aspect of the Agreement is in establishing a "Committee on Investment Facilitation", which has the capacity to update the substantive elements of the Agreement for the purposes of achieving the objectives of the Agreement, which refers then to a list of "legitimate policy objectives"[93] that in part recalls the General Exceptions provided in the chapeau of the General Agreement on Tariffs and Trade 1994.

The remaining segment of the present chapter constructs model provisions based on the Method that revise commonly worded articles in international investment agreements. Each model article is then connected to pertinent aspects of the Method to guide their enactment and/or interpretation.[94] In this approach, this chapter proposes three model provisions that both respond to the research question posed in Chapter 1[95] and affirm the thesis that guided this work.[96] In doing so, the three proposed model provisions confront contentious aspects of the overlay between international investment law and sustainable development that were identified throughout this work.[97]

5.4.1 Terms of a covered investment

Defining an investment to be covered by an international investment agreement can help to clarify questions concerning minimum standards of treatment, such as fair and equitable treatment, provided by the host state to the foreign investor. At the same time, the conditions for becoming a covered investor can help to define

93 European Union–Angola: Sustainable Investment Facilitation Agreement Art 1.2(2).

94 This approach roughly mirrors that of the UNCITRAL in the presentation of its model laws.

95 Which was in assessing a government measure with the purpose of advancing sustainable development within the host state's right to regulate, could and should investment treaty arbitration tribunals consider whether the conduct of the investor and/or their investment aimed to advance sustainable development? If so, how can the notion of 'sustainable investment' can help guide that determination?

96 As provided in Section 1.1.2, that a comprehensive assessment of contribution to sustainable development requires an analysis of both the government measure as well as the conduct of the investor and/or performance of the investment.

97 As was scoped in Section 1.3.

the expectations of the host state concerning the investor and/or their investment.[98] Failure to satisfy these expectations may result in a denial of benefits, limiting the protections of the international investment agreement from applying to the investment. For example, a common trend has been to deny benefits to investors that do not have substantial economic activities in the seat of incorporation (shell companies).[99] A commonly found wording of investment may be:

> The term "investment" means ["every kind of", "any kind of" or a set of defined] asset[s], invested by the investor of one Contracting Party in the territory of the other Contracting Party in conformity with its laws and regulations. Characteristics of an investment include the commitment of capital or other resources, the expectation of gain or profit, the assumption of risk [and a certain duration].[100]

Applying the Method to refine the above definition of a covered investment seeks to enhance a host state's capacities to target high-quality, productive, and positive investments that are aligned with sustainable development. Clarifying these qualifications before the admission of an investment can help to strengthen predictability concerning the policy directions of the host state. Meanwhile, clarifications can expand the manoeuvrability of the host state in pursuing measures in the public interest and mitigate potential disputes before they are formalized into investment treaty arbitration submissions. There are two main junctures where the Method can find application as reflected through the suggested model provision below.

> The term "investment" means ["every kind of", "any kind of" or a set of defined] asset[s], invested by the investor of one Contracting Party in the territory of the other Contracting Party in conformity with its laws and regulations *and coherent with their sustainable development policy objectives.*

98 For a survey on such provisions, see Catherine Yannaca-Small, *International Investment Law: Understanding Concepts and Tracking Innovations* (Organisation for Economic Cooperation and Development (OECD) 2008).

99 Article 8.1 of the EU-Canada Comprehensive Economic and Trade Agreement (CETA), for example, defines an enterprise as having "substantial business activities in the territory of the party" ('CETA Chapter by Chapter: Chapter Eight—Investment' (*Trade—European Commission*, 24 August 2018) <https://ec.europa.eu/trade/policy/in-focus/ceta/ceta-chapter-by-chapter/index_en.htm> accessed 20 August 2020). In *Pac Rim v El Salvador* (2009), El Salvador invoked a denial of benefits clause in the Central America Free Trade Agreement (CAFTA) to deny all benefits in the investment chapter of CAFTA to Pac Rim, which was established in the Cayman Islands (*Pac Rim Cayman LLC v Republic of El Salvador*, ICSID Case No ARB/09/12, The Republic of El Salvador's Memorial Objections to Jurisdiction (15 October 2010) para 115).

100 As found in, for example, the Georgia–Turkey BIT (2016), Japan–United Arab Emirates BIT (2018), Australia–Indonesia CEPA (2019), United States–Mexico–Canada Agreement (2018), Australia–Peru FTA (2018), Armenia–Korea, Republic of BIT (2018), Greece–Kuwait BIT (2014), Belarus–Georgia BIT (2017), Austria–Kyrgyzstan BIT (2016), and Singapore–Turkey FTA (2015).

> Characteristics of an investment include the commitment of capital or other resources, the expectation of gain or profit, the assumption of risk [and a certain duration], *and real-world significance for the host state's sustainable development.*[101]

The above model provision seeks to not only empower the host state to more effectively target investments, but also provides international investors with the capacity to seek verification of either their contributions to the host state's development or that of the challenged government measure.

The first addition of the model provision ("*and coherent with their sustainable development policy objectives*") seeks to add on to requirements of conformity with the host state's laws and regulations by ensuring that an investment is aligned with the current policy objectives and strategies of the host state. Falling under the first tenet of the Method, this addition seeks to ensure that investments, and government measures that affect them, when assessed for their coherence with sustainable development are based on their alignment with host state development policy objectives. The Method makes clear that a crucial aspect of the role of international investment in sustainable development is that relevant Actions (investments and related international investment laws and/or policies) are aligned with and parallel to the broader development policy objectives of the host state. Therefore, should the government measure not be compatible with the host state's sustainable development policy objectives but nevertheless seek justification by invoking the right to regulate for the public interest, the proposed model provision can help in emphasizing such discrepancies. Alternatively, international investors claiming to contribute to the host state's development based on a very broad definition of sustainable development will face the need to clarify how their investment(s) fit in the sustainable development needs of the host state.

In spite of policy objectives of the host state shifting to confront diverse sets of challenges, there have been attempts to maintain the same regulatory conditions at the time of admission through stabilization clauses, which has been flagged as a central item for reform by the UN system.[102] Functionally, therefore, these first additions attempt to better align international investment agreements with sustainable development planning (Framework Strategy 3.2) and carve out pre-admissions options and consensus in order to protect legitimate interests during the performance of the investment (Framework Strategy 5.1).

The Framework offers multiple pathways for how an Action can be coherent with the host state's development policy objectives. For example, when host states are designing measures that may affect existing obligations to covered investors,

101 As found in, for example, the Georgia–Turkey BIT (2016), Japan–United Arab Emirates BIT (2018), Australia–Indonesia CEPA (2019), United States–Mexico–Canada Agreement (2018), Australia–Peru FTA (2018), Armenia–Korea, Republic of BIT (2018), Greece–Kuwait BIT (2014), Belarus–Georgia BIT (2017), Austria–Kyrgyzstan BIT (2016), and Singapore–Turkey FTA (2015).

102 This was further examined in Section 3.2.

legislators and policymakers can identify how those measures, if implemented, align with existing industrial policies, sustainable development strategies, and development challenges the host state is facing (Framework Strategies 1.1 and 1.2) to demonstrate the government measure aligns with policy objectives that existed at the time of the investment. For international investments, ensuring coherence with the host state's development strategies can involve clarifying how their investments address the development priority areas of the host state or alternatively the host requiring such matchmaking as a prerequisite to entitlement (Framework Strategy 1.3). Another pathway towards observing coherence is for the foreign investor and the host state to secure pre-admission guarantees concerning development impact (Framework Strategy 2.1), such as agreeing on the conclusive interpretation of governance and performance standards regarding the investment (Framework Strategies 2.2 and 2.3) so that the expectations facing the investor to be covered by the applicable international investment agreement are definitive.

The latter set of additions in the model provision ("*real-world significance for the host state's sustainable development*") takes up the second tenet of the Method: contribution to sustainable development. While the contribution requirement has yet to have become a commonly found feature in international investment agreements, the inclusion of "significance for the host state's development" in the criteria of a covered investment has become widely accepted.[103] This set of additions to the model provision not only seeks to include this fourth criterion of investment to the instrument, but also to amplify it by replacing "significance" with "real-world". The purpose behind this modification is to deter some of the limited assessments of "significance" that were identified in Section 2.5.1 that would view an investment as significant to the host state's development in and of itself. Alternatively, such limited assessments would view the satisfaction of any of the characteristics of investment, such as extended duration or shared risk, as holding significance to the host state's development.

Real-world significance, or alternatively, real-world contribution to sustainable development, was identified as a core requirement in both the Framework and Notion in their respective efforts to materialize a link between international investment and sustainable development. Framework Measure 1.2.1 (Measurable Policy Effects) identifies the need for "clear resultant effects" of "direct and measurable" policies and government measures. Section 4.3.2.1 elaborates on Notion Element 2.1 (Real-World Impact), which identified that the verification of sustainable development impact remains inseparable to the process of identifying an investment as Sustainable Investment. While not explicitly correlated in the Method, for the sake of sparsity "real-world" includes not only Element 2.1 (Real-World Impact) of the second key feature identified in the Notion, but also Element 2.2 (Additionality). As defined in greater length in Section 4.3.2.2, additionality would include Actions that expand the participants engaged in Sustainable Investment as a key performance indicator.

103 As was explored in greater length in Sections 1.2.2 and 2.4.3.

Limitations of assessing the extent to which international investment contributes to sustainable development has been a common constituent in criticisms of the relevance of international investment law. As reviewed in Section 1.3.1, for instance, the revolutionary view in international investment law scholarship argues that the challenges facing the practice are so many and deeply systemic that the very regime remains incontrovertible. Some of these devaluations were further materialized in Section 2.5, which exhibited three forms of limited assessment facing investment treaty arbitration in connection to sustainable development, two of which were motivated in part by the lack of considering real-world impact of putative sustainable development contributions.

The model provision empowers the fourth criterion of investment with the formidable consensus[104] building around the push for verifying the impacts of international investment on sustainable development, as well as ongoing evolution of the employable methodologies of verification, both science based and forward-looking (Notion Element 2.1). In doing so, the model provision helps to partially dispel the normative reservations concerning what constitutes sustainable development. Given the availability of these methodologies and their widespread use by both private and public institutions,[105] as well as the multilateral consensus that has gathered around the key features of that methodology[106] (as demonstrated by the Notion), the continued exclusion of considering real-world impact from the practice of investment treaty arbitration would only further vindicate criticisms of the practice's antiquation.

One modification to the fourth criterion in this second set of additions of the model provision is the addition of "sustainable" as a qualification of development. The lack of concrete normativity of sustainable development motivated a reluctance towards including considerations of sustainable development in international investment agreements. This reluctance builds on pre-existing resistance against investment treaty arbitration admitting and deliberating on matters of sustainable development, which would expand the role of arbitrators to that of policymakers.[107] Yet this did not stop new generation international investment agreements from openly including sustainable development and its three dimensions (economic, social, and environmental).[108]

By adding to the model provision the "host state's sustainable development" following "real-world contribution", this set of additions seeks to not only appeal to the ongoing expansion of ways in which contributions are verified, but also the fact that parsing the meaning of sustainable development data has become a fundamental aspect of that verification process. As identified in the third key feature of the Notion (Metrics and Data), this could involve tailoring and adjusting the metrics

104 See Section 4.2 for a scoping of this trend.
105 As contoured in Section 4.2.2.
106 Pillar two of the conceptual framework (Section 2.3) outlines this procession.
107 This debate finds further discussion in Section 2.4, the third pillar of the conceptual framework.
108 For examples and analysis, refer to Section 3.2.

that constitute the means of assessing a contribution to sustainable development. This permits for a normalized assessment of how an investment may contribute to sustainable development more within the context of the host state (Framework Measure 1.3.2). One benefit of this approach is that it would permit for an Action in a high development priority area of the host state, to be weighted in league with the extent of its urgency in the host state's development agenda. These can factor in geological or climactic idiosyncrasies of the country, such as rising seas, receding coastlines, and submergence for small island developing states.[109]

Examining an investment treaty arbitration case within the scenario that the proposed model provision was adopted and ratified takes this analysis a step further. *Helnan v Egypt*, which was identified in Section 2.5.1 as embodying the first form of limited assessment (amalgamating contributions to host state's development), provides a suitable canvas for this exercise. In this dispute, Egypt challenged whether Helnan's constituted a covered investment as one part of dismissing the jurisdiction of the tribunal, seeking to deny Helnan with the benefit of submitting claims to the International Centre for Settlement of Investment Disputes. The arbitration tribunal decided Helnan had made an "obvious" contribution to the host state's economy premised on the importance of tourism for its economy.[110] The contested government measure was in reducing the property's star rating following an inspection by state authorities due to a lack of renovations necessary to improve the facility.[111] Claims concerning contributions to development raised by the host state received only limited assessment by the arbitration tribunal despite the relative centrality of its role in contesting the tribunal's jurisdiction.

The arbitration tribunal would have been harder pressed to have concluded on an "obvious" contribution due to the greater stringency of the test of contribution based on real-world significance. For instance, in assessing whether the investment contributed to development of Egypt, the arbitral tribunal might have assessed whether the hotel's management resulted in net positive impact (Notion Element 1.1) by weighing its environmental, social, and economic impacts against one another in order to account for possible drawdown effects. This can include, for example, domestic job or skills creation as opposed to reserving the highest skilled and salaried jobs for foreign nationals. Alternatively, whether Helnan's management encouraged firms in its supply chain or competing hotels in the region to adopt better environmental or social impact performance (Notion Element 2.2), or

109 See, for instance, Office of the High Representative for the Least Developed Countries, Landlocked Developing Countries and Small Island Developing States (OHRLLS), 'About Small Island Developing States' <www.un.org/ohrlls/content/about-small-island-developing-states> accessed 26 April 2022.

110 *Helnan International Hotels A/S v Arab Republic of Egypt*, ICSID Case No ARB/05/19, Decision of the Tribunal on Objection to Jurisdiction (17 October 2006) para 77.

111 Luke Eric Peterson, 'IN-DEPTH: ICSID Tribunal Finds No Breaches by Egypt in Treatment of Helnan International' (*Investment Arbitration Reporter*, 16 July 2008) <www.iareporter.com/articles/in-depth-icsid-tribunal-finds-no-breaches-by-egypt-in-treatment-of-helnan-international/> accessed 8 April 2022.

if Helnan maintained the same level of corporate social responsibility as it did in its home country (Framework Measure 2.2.2). The arbitration tribunal may also have considered whether the Helnan investment posed multistakeholder contributions taking into consideration the hotel's impact on the local community (Framework Measure 2.1.2).

Furthermore, the model provision would also help to address attempts to amalgamate contributions, under which an extremely permissive interpretation of contribution may render any economic activity in tourism as significant to the host state's economy. For instance, one assessment can involve comparing the economic value of the hotel, such as increased spending in the tourism sector, with the value of limiting the host state's capacities to apply relevant government measures. This may include forming clear expectations with foreign investors concerning building performance (Framework Measure 2.1.1) or maintaining dynamic policymaking capacities in order to respond to changing circumstances, such as more stringent building safety inspections as a response to climate change (Framework Measure 1.2.2).

5.4.2 Right to regulate for the public interest

The second model provision proposed by this work relates to the right to regulate, regulatory space, or regulatory power of the host state, which refers to its sovereign authority to implement government measures in order to achieve its public interests, particularly in response to changing circumstances facing the country.[112] By carving out these regulatory spaces in international investment agreements, the host state reserves this right to regulate, even should the resultant government measures be inconsistent with certain terms of the agreement, such as those related to fair and equitable treatment. A survey of international investment agreements that entered into force between 2019 and 2022[113] renders the following common wording:

> The provisions of this Agreement shall not affect the right of a Contracting Party to regulate through [non-discriminatory] measures necessary[, designed and applied] to achieve legitimate policy [and public welfare] objectives [such as . . .].

While the magnitude of the right to regulate carved out differs and there remain deviations in the of objectives listed thereafter, these provisions are generally in

112 Section 2.4 offers a more comprehensive examination of the concept.

113 As found in the Belarus–Hungary BIT (2019), EU–Japan EPA (2018), Ecuador–EFTA FTA (2018), Cabo Verde–Hungary BIT (2019), Montenegro–Turkey BIT (2012), Australia–Hong Kong Investment Agreement (2019), Cambodia–China FTA (2020), Regional Comprehensive Economic Partnership Agreement (2020), and Pacific Agreement on Closer Economic Relations Plus (2017).

consensus with the scope provided in the third pillar of the conceptual framework (Section 2.4).

Applying the Method in the formulation of a model provision would seek to modify the right to regulate as a safeguard of sustainable development. This endeavour is reflected by the model provision proposed below:

> The provisions of this Agreement shall not affect the right of a Contracting Party to regulate through [non-discriminatory] measures necessary[, designed and applied], *while doing no significant harm,* to achieve *not only* legitimate policy [and public welfare] objectives [such as . . .] *but also applicable objectives within the international public policy of sustainable development.*

The first set of additions of this model provision ("*while doing no significant harm*"), despite being only briefly mentioned as part of Notion Element 1.1 (Net Positive Impact)[114] represents a central theme in this Method. In application to government measures, do no significant harm would apply to policies that while attempting to achieve one public policy objective backpedals on another. For example, a state may seek to address balance of payments challenges with fiscal austerity measures, such as through the termination of certain investment incentives paired with public spending. However, implementing such austerity measures may insufficiently consider their socioeconomic consequences on individuals who may have their ability to enjoy their human rights challenged as a result.[115] In relation to investment, "do no significant harm" is a commonly featured principle in existing sustainable finance regulation, such as in the European Union and the Association of Southeast Asian Nations (ASEAN). As a central theme in the Method, do no significant harm more broadly represents those investments that are high-quality, productive, and positive.

High quality, as was further explained in Section 1.2.2, refers to international investments that seek to build on linkages with domestic capital factors (e.g. human capital allocation, environmental assets) that results in mutual benefit between the investor and the host state such as through technology transfers and other forms of public-private partnership. Productive investments refer to those investments that result in an additional value added beside the economic value of the investment itself, usually those that are not necessarily pecuniary. This can include, for example, an international investment part of a broader initiative towards clean energy transition that may also include retraining programmes to improve capital mobility while insulating workers who are more vulnerable to structural adjustment.

The second aspect refers to positive investments, which, as was described earlier, are investments that have a net positive impact on the host state after accounting

114 See Section 4.2.1.1.

115 Markus Krajewski, 'Human Rights and Austerity Programmes' in Christian Tietje, Rosa M Lastra and Thomas Cottier (eds), *The Rule of Law in Monetary Affairs: World Trade Forum* (CUP 2014) 508.

for not only financial gain, but also opportunity costs such as ecosystem service usage and societal costs. The idea of net positivity thus refers to after accounting for both financial and extra-financial costs of the investment, the total value of the investment is not in deficit. The concept of a positive investment was shown in Section 3.3 to be a recurring theme in the institutional history of Financing for Development and continues to be essential in the current Financing for Sustainable Development framework. Net positivity of investment also remains a core attribute of sustainable finance, embodying the stakeholder-centric view of investment and a view of investment performance that transcends solely financial profitability.[116]

In addition to the normative content of the do no significant harm emphasized in this section, the use of "do no significant harm" for the proposed model provision holds additional meaning. Do no significant harm as a principle is consequential insofar as it represents a comparatively high level of harmonization in financial regulation across different jurisdictions. Most notably, do no significant harm finds multilateral stature through the European Union, where it is a fundamental principle in the Taxonomy Regulation (EU 2020/852).[117]

The outcome of the EU Taxonomy Regulation, especially with issuance of a draft Social Taxonomy[118] and the Complementary Climate Delegated Act,[119] remains uncertain. However, in pioneering the push for multilateral regulatory harmonization concerning sustainable finance, the Taxonomy Regulation fashioned do no significant harm into a foundational concept in similar initiatives. One of the most notable of these initiatives is the ASEAN Taxonomy for Sustainable Finance, wherein do no significant harm is identified as an "essential criterion" in determining the compliance of economic activities in the region.[120] The interoperability of the do no significant harm concept across different jurisdictions and the recognition it has received as means of enhancing multilateral coordination and harmonization are demonstrative of its merits as a dimension of the proposed model provision.

These two aspects of the first set of additions in this model provision intersect with the Method at numerous junctures. Framework Strategy 1.1 identifies the value of shaping international investment law and policy in correspondence with the domestic capacities in order to form linkages with existing capital factors and industrial policy, particularly in the context of developing economies. Framework Strategy 1.3 calls for investment targeting based on economic and/or development

116 This is explored further in the second pillar of the conceptual framework (Section 2.3) and in the background to the notion of Sustainable Investment (Section 4.1).

117 Section 4.2.1 provides an overview of do no significant harm as it is featured in the EU Taxonomy Regulation.

118 See, for example, Gina Gambetta, 'EU Advisors Shake up Social Taxonomy Proposal to Better Align with Green Counterpart' (*Responsible Investor*, 21 February 2022).

119 See, for example, Elza Holmstedt Pell, 'European Commission Moves Ahead with Plans to Classify Gas and Nuclear as Sustainable in EU Taxonomy' (*Responsible Investor*, 2 February 2022).

120 ASEAN Taxonomy Board, *ASEAN Taxonomy for Sustainable Finance* (Association of Southeast Asian Nations (ASEAN) 2021) 44. See also Soo-hyun Lee, '"Do No Significant Harm" as a Core Principle in Sustainable Finance Regulation in the ASEAN Draft and Singapore Taxonomies' (2022) 29 Journal of International and Area Studies 21.

priority areas. Productive investments, as opposed to conventional ones, come with development value-added benefits that are best fit to advance attempts to fulfil development needs. The second key feature of the Notion on key performance indicators provides the means to evaluate the net impact of investments, such as through real-world and science-based assessments.

The second set of additions of this model provision ("*not only . . . but also applicable objectives within the international public policy of sustainable development*") seeks to modify the scope of a public policy safeguard to reflect the multilateral objectives and standards of sustainable development as a matter of transnational public policy. This is consistent with the first tenet of the Method[121] on cohering with sustainable development standards that are the result of multilateral consensus, such as, inter alia, the SDGs. The extent to which sustainable development is recognized as transnational public policy was addressed in the first pillar of the conceptual framework constructed in Chapter 2, which also traces the institutional history of sustainable development and its evolving multilateral stature.

As emphasized by the first tenet of the Method, assessing whether an Action (and later as expressed in the second tenet, the extent to which an Action) is consistent with multilaterally accepted standards concerning sustainable development aids in the defence against the misuse of safeguards. For instance, harmonized reporting on impacts of Actions (Framework Measure 4.1.2) has been key to remaining vigilant against green- (or SDG-)washing. These safeguards are crucial in preventing abusive practices by investors or host states that can obstruct progress towards sustainable development. The design and implementation of such safeguards as an overall objective of the Method was addressed in the fifth Framework Objective.

Applying this model provision in *Bernhard von Pezold and others v Zimbabwe*[122] shows that it could have aided the Tribunal's analysis of the right to regulate and its confrontation with the Salini requirement of contribution to the host state's development. Identified as demonstrating the second form of limited assessment of sustainable development within international investment law, specifically investment treaty arbitration,[123] the Tribunal in this dispute overlooked claims by both parties concerning the extent of development contribution and turned its attention instead to a more formalistic analysis, which concluded that Zimbabwe's measures were illegitimate. This followed Zimbabwe having appealed to its right to regulate for the public interest of the country and the investor advancing a counterclaim concerning its contributions to the host state's development based on testimonials by host state officials as well as citing a broad study on the role of "properly administered" exotic timber plantations in the Zimbabwean economy.[124]

121 See Section 5.3.1 for more on the first tenet.

122 *Bernhard von Pezold and Others v Republic of Zimbabwe*, ICSID Case No ARB/10/15, Award (28 July 2015).

123 See Section 2.5.2.

124 As well as engaging social dimensions of sustainable development (see Section 2.5.3).

Assessments of competing claims concerning contributions to sustainable development, such as in the application of the right to regulate for the public interest of sustainable development, take on greater methodological form when applying the earlier described aspects of do no significant harm. The extent to which the investment by Bernhard von Pezold and others qualified as a high-quality, productive, and positive impact would determine whether it was coherent with multilaterally accepted standards of Sustainable Development Investment. This would, in turn, lend to the Tribunal's analysis of whether Zimbabwe's implementation of government measures in its right to regulate was legitimate insofar that it served the transnational public policy of sustainable development. Should the investment been high-quality, productive, and positive while also aligning with the sustainable development planning of Zimbabwe, then the legitimacy in the host state's use of the right to regulate would have been dismissed on normatively substantive grounds rather than the limited assessment demonstrated in the Tribunal's deliberations.

5.4.3 Fair and equitable treatment

As was introduced in Chapter 2 in the third pillar of the conceptual framework to this work, fair and equitable treatment remains a regular feature in international investment agreements (or alternatively treaties with investment provisions), defining the minimum standard of treatment, such as rights and protections, that the international investor may expect. Austere readings of fair and equitable treatment tend to be preferential towards the investor because they maintain a restrictive approach to circumstances that would qualify a host state to implement government measures that would contradict the fair and equitable treatment provided to the foreign investor. In *Tecmed v Mexico*, for example, the Tribunal constrained the host state's sovereignty to ensure that its treatment towards the foreign investor did not affect the basic expectations of the investors at the time of the investment.[125]

The scope of interpreting fair and equitable treatment has been subject to contention, particularly regarding the extent to which it is able to constrain the host state's right to regulate. Such debates[126] revolve around whether fair and equitable treatment is viewed as an autonomous standard or, conversely, whether its interpretation fall within that of customary international law. While there is variation in the way that fair and equitable treatment is defined, common wording of the fair and equitable treatment provision is as follows:[127]

> Each Party shall accord to covered investments fair and equitable treatment and full protection and security, in accordance with the customary

125 *Técnicas Medioambientales Tecmed SA v The United Mexican States*, ICSID Case No ARB (AF)/00/2, Award (29 May 2003) para 153.

126 These are covered in greater length in Section 2.4.2.

127 As found in Regional Comprehensive Economic Partnership Agreement (2020); Hong Kong, China SAR–Mexico BIT (2020); Georgia–Turkey BIT (2016); Central America–Republic of Korea FTA (2018); Pacific Agreement on Closer Economic Relations Plus (2017); Australia–United

> international law minimum standard of treatment of aliens. The concepts of "fair and equitable treatment" and "full protection and security" do not require treatment in addition to or beyond that which is required by that standard, and do not create additional substantive rights.

Interpretation of the scope of fair and equitable treatment remains at the discretion of the arbitrator (and then ultimately one of ideological standing). This is in the absence of mechanisms like joint interpretation agreements, which more clearly contours what fair and equitable treatment entails.[128] While taking a stance on this specific issue[129] is beyond the endeavour taken up in the present chapter, the final proposed model provision instead attempts to facilitate bilateral or multilateral cooperation between treaty parties. Doing so seeks to provide greater clarity, based on consensus, as to the scope of fair and equitable treatment by reaching an explicit mutual understanding concerning the expectations that each party holds towards one another. The model provision is as follows:

> Each Party shall accord to covered investments fair and equitable treatment and full protection and security in accordance with the customary international law minimum standard of treatment of aliens *and commensurate to applicable commitments to sustainable development*. The concepts of "fair and equitable treatment" and "full protection and security" do not require treatment in addition to or beyond that which is required by *these* standard*s*, and do not create additional substantive rights.

The additions proposed above seek to extend considerations surrounding fair and equitable treatment beyond that of the minimum standard of treatment involving foreign nationals by including the state's commitments to sustainable development, whether at the national policy level or the bilateral or multilateral level. In that sense, "commensurate" seeks to refine the scope of fair and equitable treatment by encompassing the laws, policies, and treaty obligations of the host state as they relate to sustainable development. Regardless of whether fair and equitable treatment is treated as an autonomous standard or in accordance with customary international law, this model provision emphasizes that if an international investor seeks

Kingdom FTA (2021); and the Agreement Between the United States of America, the United Mexican States, and Canada (2018).

128 This is a trend in new generation investment agreements, which provide additional clarification on the limits of fair and equitable treatment, grandfather clauses, and the application of most favoured nation. For example, see the Agreement on Trade Continuity between the United Kingdom of Great Britain and Northern Ireland and Canada 2020 [CP 351] Joint Interpretive Instrument, Art 6(d). Elsewhere, in the EU-Japan EPA, the chapter on investment features a comprehensive treatment of general exceptions referring to Article XX of the GATT 1994 with fair and equitable treatment is not mentioned in the text (Agreement between the EU and Japan for an Economic Partnership 2018 Art 8.3).

129 This issue and the debate surrounding fair and equitable treatment is described in explained in greater detail through the third pillar of the conceptual framework offered in Section 2.4.

to benefit from the minimum standards of treatment provided by the host state, but then attempts to thwart the government's sustainable development objectives, then the investor loses claim to fair and equitable treatment.

Simultaneously, the proposed additions also seek to address instances when host states offer investment incentives or engage in investment liberalization that are inconsistent with their treaty obligations to sustainable development. This is in reference to the second aspect of the first tenet of the Method on coherence with sustainable development. Ensuring policy coherence (Framework Strategy 1.2) between policies intended to regulate investment and those that seek to achieve the state's sustainable development goals is a crucial step in shaping an equilibrium between creating an attractive investment climate and protecting sustainable development interests. The purpose of the above addition, therefore, is to establish a balance between providing an attractive investment climate for investors while supporting the host state's capacities to advance and keep true to its sustainable development ambition.

Ideal circumstances for enacting this model provision are in cohort with additional measures that clarify the expectations between both the international investor and the host state, as well as officials and ministries within the host state government, prior to the investment. Clear expectations concerning the policy objectives of the host state, whether with the international investor or within different authorities in the host state government, can help reduce the likeliness for upturned expectations to escalate into investor-State disputes while providing the regulatory space for the host state to service its treaty and policy commitments to sustainable development. As identified in Chapter 2, hostile investor-State disputes not only strain valuable public-private partnerships, but also impose high legal and opportunity costs that could arise from unfinished infrastructure projects. These consequences are magnified in application to host states that may already be facing strains on public finance.

The host state and investor may form clear expectations by shaping a relationship in the spirit of a public-private partnership rather than that of a host state and a foreign investor (Framework Strategy 2.1). One approach can be to form consensus on standards that apply to the investor and/or investment, such as corporate social responsibility (Framework Strategy 2.2) and approaches in monitoring, reporting, and verifying the investor/investment's performance in sustainable development-related areas (Framework Strategy 4.2). This can help create transparent and predictable interactions between the corporate entity and the governance structures of the host state. Furthermore, holding these clear expectations can help ensure that the international investor is aware of and aligned with the broader policy objectives of the host state, such as its identification of priority development areas (Framework Measure 1.3.2). The host state's use of safety valves (Framework Measure 5.2.2) in these predetermined priority development areas in effect need not necessarily embody risk factors for the investor and/or investment.

In carving out such policy flexibilities, however, it is important to clarify whether self-regulated public policy exceptions, such as those made to advance sustainable development, are actually given effect. As identified in Chapter 2, broad judicial discretion on whether public policy exceptions to minimum standards of treatment can result in incomplete (or non-existent) assessments of whether an Action contributed to the sustainable development objective. The proposed model provision, while maintaining a traditional approach to the observation of minimum standards of treatment, also seeks to appeal to the effect of committing to the application, and interpretation therein, of obligations to sustainable development-related agreements.

As mentioned earlier in reference to the second aspect of the first tenet of the Method, the latter half of the first addition ("*and commensurate to applicable commitments to sustainable development*") is a reference to existing multilateral sustainable development commitments, such as the Paris Agreement, as well as commitments that may exist between the home and host state as part of a bilateral international investment agreement. By viewing fair and equitable treatment as commensurate to such national and international commitments, this model provision seeks to ensure that host states remain able and willing to reach its sustainable development ambitions.

Furthermore, adding commensurability rallies behind the belief that fair and equitable treatment has no basis for taking precedence above the host state's commitments to bilateral or multilateral agreements on sustainable development. Conversely, the host state's capacity to provide for the investor's fair and equitable treatment should be commensurate on those commitments to both national and transnational public interest objectives. In addition to multilateral agreements, such as those identified in Pillar One of the conceptual framework,[130] a host state may seek consensus on such matters through bilateral instruments such as those identified in Framework Strategy 4.1 on formulating common interpretations of provisions in investment-related agreements and Framework Strategy 3.1 on harmonized international investment incentives. Of these, agreeing on joint interpretative statements (Framework Measure 4.1.1) as well as discouraged and encouraged investment incentive policies (Framework Measures 3.1.2 and 3.1.3) are especially relevant.

In this manner, the model provision can also serve the measures identified in the fifth Framework Objective, which safeguards a state's progress towards sustainable development at the level of international agreements. By adding the condition of commensurability to fair and equitable treatment, the model provision can serve to establish a backstop against abusive practices of international investment that are inconsistent with the host state's sustainable development progress (Framework Measure 5.1.1). The model provision also helps to carve out policy spaces targeted by the host state's sustainable development objectives (Framework Measure 5.1.2) by rebalancing the priority that the host state has towards the foreign investor and that it has towards ensuring intergenerational development.

130 This was provided in Section 2.2.

In addition to backstops and carve-outs, the applicability of commensurability would not be limited to pre-admissions, such as at the level of treaty negotiations. Should the conduct of the investor or the investment fail to meet the conditions agreed upon at the point of admission, then this model provision would suggest that the host state would have at its disposal reservations and safety valves in line with Framework Strategy 5.2. For instance, the extent to which a covered investor is able to claim fair and equitable treatment may factor in corporate behaviour that is recognized as abusive either at the national or international level. This can include asset-striping, leveraging anticompetitive market power, or reversing environmental or social standards imposed by the host state. Alternatively, if the international investor has committed to certain environmental, social, and/or governance standards in their home state, or as part of a self-regulatory initiative such as those identified in Section 4.2, its access to minimum standards of treatment may also be contingent on meeting those standards in the host state in accordance with Framework Strategy 2.3. This would help to hold the performance of an investment account to the commitments made by its transnational corporate owner.

Overall, the proposed model provision seeks to institute the view that fair and equitable treatment is a privilege attributed in accordance with the minimum standards of treatment as customary international law, but also existing commitments that the host state or international investor may hold towards sustainable development. In doing so, this model provision seeks to enable an interpretation of fair and equitable treatment that is balanced with the regulatory needs of the host state to achieve its public interest objectives in progressing towards sustainable development as a matter of both national and transnational public policy. Furthermore, the proposed model provision aids in confronting the limited assessment identifiable in investment treaty arbitration as was provided in Section 2.5 on the three forms of limited assessment in investment treaty arbitration. As identified therein, fair and equitable treatment and the right to regulate for the public interest conflict when the international investor and the host state hold different views towards mutual expectations and obligations.

5.5 Concluding remarks

The model provisions proposed in this chapter confront many of the major limitations facing the international investment law regime in its capacity to facilitate progress towards sustainable development. However, they are by no means systemic solutions to the challenges facing international investment law. One reason is that the process of ratifying and enacting these model laws into national legal systems is ripe with political travails in deciding omissions, which is only then punctuated with the vicissitudes of judicial interpretation. As such, the application of the Method envisioned here remains an intermediate step in the process of reforming the international investment law regime in a holistic enough manner so that it too advances, rather than merely complements or facilitates, the transnational public interest of sustainable development. The task therein does not end with the harmonization of the international investment law regime. Rather that remains but one part of a far more significant albeit difficult transformation: accepting sustainable development as a fundamental object and purpose of international investment and its governance.

Though sluggish, transformation is afoot. Sustainable Investment, while certainly not without its flaws, has helped turned the financial world away from highly destructive forms of consumption and production as the boundaries of stranded assets continue to expand. In the planning and execution of an investment, sustainable development impact is being elevated from a peripheral to a core concern. New generation investment and comprehensive economic agreements are leaving little room for investments in sectors that are clearly inconsistent with sustainable development progress. So long as persistent objectors continue their practices of abusive and unsustainable means of operations, the evolution of systems, such as that of international investment governance, will continue to be looked upon with expectations to evolve. Meanwhile, it remains in the vigilant powers of the host state policymaker and legislator, transnational investor, and the investment law practitioner and researcher to employ the tools available to them in advancing the nexus between sustainable development and international investment law.

The Method constructed in this work was designed as one such tool. The model provisions provide in this chapter illustrated how the Method may be used in order to gain a more definitive understanding of the sustainable development impact of international investments and their governance. In doing so, this work sought to locate points of convergence between international investment law and sustainable development as a means to exhibit their close compatibility. Whether through the Framework or the Notion, the Consolidated Method is the product of a closer synthesis of the nexus between international investment and sustainable development at the multilateral level.

Each individual segment of the Method represents the product of multilateral negotiation and consensus on a specific issue concerning that nexus. As such, they provide optimal points of departure in turning the international investment law regime, a system also built upon multilateral consensus, into a means towards advancing sustainability, rather than one disjoined from it.

References

'MiFID II' (*European Securities and Markets Authority*) <www.esma.europa.eu/policy-rules/mifid-ii-and-mifir> accessed 26 April 2022

'Report of the United Nations Commission on International Trade Law on the Work of Its Eighteenth Session' (United Nations General Assembly 1985) A/40/17

'Resolution of the ILA on Public Policy as a Bar to Enforcement of International Arbitral Awards' (2003) 19 Arbitration International 213 <https://academic.oup.com/arbitration/article/19/2/213/210498>

'Universal Values Principle Two: Leave No One Behind' (*UN Sustainable Development Group*) <https://unsdg.un.org/2030-agenda/universal-values/leave-no-one-behind> accessed 20 April 2022

Agreement Between the EU and Japan for an Economic Partnership 2018

Agreement on Trade Continuity Between the United Kingdom of Great Britain and Northern Ireland and Canada 2020 [CP 351]

Aisbett E and others, *Rethinking International Investment Governance: Principles for the 21st Century* (Columbia Center on Sustainable Investment 2018)

Akseli O, 'Financial Inclusion, Access to Credit, and Sustainable Finance: What Role for the UNCITRAL Model Law on Secured Transactions?' (2021) 84 Law and Contemporary Problems 181

Alschner W, Elsig M and Wüthrich S, 'Main Act or Side Show? Model Agreements by International Institutions and Their Reuse in Investment Treaty Texts' (2022) 2022 Journal of International Economic Law 19

Arato J, Brown C and Ortino F, 'Parsing and Managing Inconsistency in Investor-State Dispute Settlement' (2020) 21 The Journal of World Investment & Trade 336

ASEAN Taxonomy Board, *ASEAN Taxonomy for Sustainable Finance* (Association of Southeast Asian Nations (ASEAN) 2021)

Aust HP, 'Investment Protection and Sustainable Development What Role for the Law of State Responsibility?' in Steffen Hindelang and Markus Krajewski (eds), *Shifting Paradigms in International Investment Law: More Balanced, Less Isolated, Increasingly Diversified* (OUP 2016)

Batifort S and Larkin A, 'The Meaning of Silence in Investment Treaties' [2022] ICSID Review 1

Behn D, Berge TL and Langford M, 'Poor States or Poor Governance: Explaining Outcomes in Investment Treaty Arbitration' (2017) 38 Northwestern Journal of International Law & Business 333

Behn D, Langford M and Létourneau-Tremblay L, 'Empirical Perspectives on Investment Arbitration: What Do We Know? Does It Matter?' (2020) 21 The Journal of World Investment & Trade 188

Berger A and others, 'Do Trade and Investment Agreements Lead to More FDI? Accounting for Key Provisions Inside the Black Box' (2013) 10 International Economics and Economic Policy 247

Berger B and Schneider ME (eds), *Inside the Black Box: How Arbitral Tribunals Operate and Reach Their Decisions* (Juris 2014)

Bernhard von Pezold and Others v Republic of Zimbabwe, ICSID Case No ARB/10/15, Award (28 July 2015)

Bjorklund AK and others, 'The Diversity Deficit in International Investment Arbitration' (2020) 21 The Journal of World Investment & Trade 410

Bohmer L, 'Cambodia Is Facing Its First Known Treaty-Based Arbitration, as Chinese Telecom Investors Lodge ICSID Claim' (*Investment Arbitration Reporter*, 3 September2021)<www.iareporter.com/articles/cambodia-is-facing-its-first-known-treaty-based-arbitration-as-chinese-telecom-investors-lodge-icsid-claim/> accessed 23 March 2022

Bohmer L, 'New ICSID Rules and Regulations Will Come into Effect on July 1, 2022, as Member States Approve Proposed Amendments' (*Investment Arbitration Reporter*, 22 March 2022) <https://www-iareporter-com/articles/breaking-new-icsid-rules-and-regulations-will-come-into-effect-on-july-1-2022-as-member-states-approve-proposed-amendments/> accessed 14 April 2022

Bonnitcha J, Poulsen LNS and Waibel M, 'Politics of Investment Treaties in Developing Countries' in *The Political Economy of the Investment Treaty Regime* (OUP 2017)

Burgstaller M, 'Investment Protection and Sustainable Energy Projects in the Age of Climate Change' in Stephan Hobe and others (eds), *Evolution, Evaluation and Future Developments in International Investment Law: Proceedings of the 10 Year Anniversary Conference of the International Investment Law Centre Cologne* (Bloomsbury 2021)

Chaisse J, 'State Capitalism on the Ascent: Stress, Shock, and Adaptation of the International Law on Foreign Investment' (2018) 27 Minnesota Journal of International Law 339

Chi M, 'Filling the Compatibility Gap between IIAs and Sustainable Development' in *Integrating Sustainable Development in International Investment Law* (Routledge 2017)

Chriki D, 'Is the Washington Consensus Really Dead: An Empirical Analysis of FET Claims in Investment Arbitration' (2018) 41 Suffolk Transnational Law Review 291

The Companies Act 2013 [ACT No 18 of 2013]

Cordonier Segger M-C, 'International Trade and Investment Agreements in Light of the Integration Principle' in *Crafting Trade and Investment Accords for Sustainable Development: Athena's Treaties* (OUP 2021)

Cordonier Segger M-C, 'Policy and "Soft Law" Rationales for Addressing Social and Environmental Concerns in Trade and Investment Treaties' in *Crafting Trade and Investment Accords for Sustainable Development: Athena's Treaties* (OUP 2021)

Dunoff JL and Pollack MA, 'International Judicial Practices: Opening the Black Box of International Courts' (2018) 40 Michigan Journal of International Law 47

'EU and Angola Conclude First-Ever Sustainable Investment Facilitation Agreement' (*European Commission*, 18 November 2022) <https://ec.europa.eu/commission/presscorner/detail/en/IP_22_6136> accessed 21 November 2022

European Union—Angola: Sustainable Investment Facilitation Agreement

Fellner M and Wallner M, 'Mifid II in Austria: An Example of Unintended Consequences' (*International Financial Law Review*, 15 December 2020) <www.iflr.com/article/b1pmnbkccpql9n/mifid-ii-in-austria-an-example-of-unintended-consequences> accessed 26 April 2022

Franck SD, 'Development and Outcomes of Investment Treaty Arbitration' (2009) 50 Harvard International Law Journal 435

Franck SD, 'Conflating Politics and Development: Examining Investment Treaty Arbitration Outcomes' (2014) 55 Virginia Journal of International Law 13

Franck SD, 'Inside the Arbitrator's Mind' (2016) 66 Emory Law Journal 1115

Franck SD, 'The Potential Drivers—Predicting ITA Costs' in *Arbitration Costs* (OUP 2019)

Gambetta G, 'EU Advisors Shake up Social Taxonomy Proposal to Better Align with Green Counterpart' (*Responsible Investor*, 21 February 2022)

Gaukrodger D, 'Business Responsibilities and Investment Treaties' (Organisation for Economic Cooperation and Development (OECD) 2020) Consultation paper by the OECD Secretariat

Giorgetti C and others, 'Independence and Impartiality of Adjudicators in Investment Dispute Settlement: Assessing Challenges and Reform Options' (2020) 21 The Journal of World Investment & Trade 441

Gordon K, Pohl J and Bouchard M, *Investment Treaty Law, Sustainable Development and Responsible Business Conduct: A Fact Finding Survey* (Organisation for Economic Cooperation and Development (OECD) 2014)

Helnan International Hotels A/S v Arab Republic of Egypt, ICSID Case No ARB/05/19, Decision of the Tribunal on Objection to Jurisdiction (17 October 2006)

Holtzmann HM and Neuhaus JE, *A Guide to the UNCITRAL Model Law on International Commercial Arbitration: Legislative History and Commentary* (Kluwer Law International 2015)

International Centre for Settlement of Investment Disputes (ICSID), 'ICSID Administrative Council Approves Amendment of ICSID Rules' (*News Releases*, 21 March 2022) <https://icsid-worldbank-org/news-and-events/communiques/icsid-administrative-council-approves-amendment-icsid-rules> accessed 14 April 2022

Kethireddy SR, 'Still the Law of Nations: Legitimate Expectations and the Sovereigntist Turn in International Investment Law' (2019) 44 Yale Journal of International Law 315

Kinnear M, 'The Launch of a New Generation of the ICSID Rules' (2022) 326 Columbia FDI Perspectives

Koivusalo M, 'Rights, Regulation and Redistribution: The Global Politics of Investment Protection' (2019) 19 Global Social Policy 105

Krajewski M, 'Human Rights and Austerity Programmes' in Christian Tietje, Rosa M Lastra and Thomas Cottier (eds), *The Rule of Law in Monetary Affairs: World Trade Forum* (CUP 2014)

Krajewski M, 'Framing the Broader Context of Business and Human Rights: The Impact of Trade Agreements on Human Rights' in Surya Deva and David Birchall (eds), *Research Handbook on Human Rights and Business* (Edward Elgar Publishing 2020)

Law on Investment of the Kingdom of Cambodia 2021

Lee S, '"Do No Significant Harm" as a Core Principle in Sustainable Finance Regulation in the ASEAN Draft and Singapore Taxonomies' (2022) 29 Journal of International and Area Studies 21

Linarelli J, Salomon ME and Sornarajah M, 'The End of Empire and the Search for Justice' in *The End of Empire and the Search for Justice: NIEO and Beyond* (OUP 2018)

Mann H and others, *IISD Model International Agreement on Investment for Sustainable Development* (International Institute for Sustainable Development (IISD) 2005)

Marcoux J-M, 'Transnational Public Policy as a Vehicle to Impose Human Rights Obligations in International Investment Arbitration' (2020) 21 The Journal of World Investment & Trade 809

Office of the High Representative for the Least Developed Countries, Landlocked Developing Countries and Small Island Developing States (OHRLLS), 'About Small Island Developing States' <www.un.org/ohrlls/content/about-small-island-developing-states> accessed 26 April 2022

Pac Rim Cayman LLC v Republic of El Salvador, ICSID Case No ARB/09/12, The Republic of El Salvador's Memorial Objections to Jurisdiction (15 October 2010)

Pell EH, 'European Commission Moves Ahead with Plans to Classify Gas and Nuclear as Sustainable in EU Taxonomy' (*Responsible Investor*, 2 February 2022)

Peterson LE, 'IN-DEPTH: ICSID Tribunal Finds No Breaches by Egypt in Treatment of Helnan International' (*Investment Arbitration Reporter*, 16 July 2008) <www.iareporter.com/articles/in-depth-icsid-tribunal-finds-no-breaches-by-egypt-in-treatment-of-helnan-international/> accessed 8 April 2022

Sands P, 'Treaty, Custom and the Cross-Fertilization of International Law' (1998) 1 Yale Human Rights & Development Law Journal 85

Schill SW and Djanic V, 'Wherefore Art Thou? Towards a Public Interest-Based Justification of International Investment Law' (2018) 33 ICSID Review 29

Securities and Exchange Board of India (SEBI), 'SEBI Issues Circular on "Business Responsibility and Sustainability Reporting by Listed Entities" (PR No 18/2021)'

Securities and Exchange Board of India (SEBI), Business Responsibility and Sustainability Reporting by Listed Entities 2021 [SEBI/HO/CFD/CMD-2/P/CIR/2021/562]

Shen J and Lei G, 'National Development and Reform Commission: Focus on Expanding Effective Investment from Four Aspects (国家发改委：重点从四个方面做好扩大有效投资工作)' *People's Daily Online (人民网)* (15 April 2022) <http://finance.people.com.cn/n1/2022/0415/c1004-32400036.html> accessed 16 April 2022

State Council, People's Republic of China, 'High-Standard Farmland Gets Push Over Next Decade' (*Latest Releases (Policies)*, 16 September 2021) <http://english.www.gov.cn/policies/latestreleases/202109/16/content_WS6142db85c6d0df57f98e0431.html> accessed 23 March 2022

Tamada D, 'Must Investments Contribute to the Development of the Host State? The Salini Test Scrutinised' in Piotr Szwedo, Richard Peltz-Steele and Dai Tamada (eds), *Law and Development: Balancing Principles and Values* (Springer 2019)

Técnicas Medioambientales Tecmed SA v The United Mexican States, ICSID Case No ARB (AF)/00/2, Award (29 May 2003)

Tucker T, 'Inside the Black Box: Collegial Patterns on Investment Tribunals' (2016) 7 Journal of International Dispute Settlement 183

United Nations, *UNCITRAL 2012 Digest of Case Law on the Model Law on International Commercial Arbitration* (United Nations 2012)

United Nations Commission on International Trade Law (UNCITRAL), 'UNCITRAL Model Law on International Commercial Conciliation with Guide to Enactment and Use' <https://uncitral.un.org/en/texts/mediation/modellaw/commercial_conciliation>

United Nations Commission on International Trade Law (UNCITRAL), 'A Guide to UNCITRAL: Basic Facts About the United Nations Commission on International Trade Law' <https://uncitral.un.org/sites/uncitral.un.org/files/media-documents/uncitral/en/12-57491-guide-to-uncitral-e.pdf>

United Nations Commission on International Trade Law (UNCITRAL), 'UNCITRAL Model Law on Public Procurement' <https://uncitral.un.org/en/texts/procurement/modellaw/public_procurement>

United Nations Commission on International Trade Law (UNCITRAL), 'UNCITRAL Model Law on Electronic Transferable Records' <https://uncitral.un.org/en/texts/ecommerce/modellaw/electronic_transferable_records>

United Nations Commission on International Trade Law (UNCITRAL), 'UNCITRAL Model Law on Enterprise Group Insolvency' <https://uncitral.un.org/en/MLEGI>

United Nations Commission on International Trade Law (UNCITRAL), 'Texts and Status' <https://uncitral.un.org/en/texts> accessed 28 March 2022

United Nations Commission on International Trade Law (UNCITRAL), 'Working Groups' (*Working Documents*) <https://uncitral.un.org/en/working_groups> accessed 26 April 2022

United Nations Development Programme (UNDP), 'AIoT Farming Solutions' (*SDG Investor Platform*, 26 October 2021) <http://sdginvestorplatform.undp.org/market-intelligence/aiot-farming-solutions> accessed 22 March 2022

United Nations Trade and Development (UNCTAD), *Reform Package for the International Investment Regime* (United Nations 2018)

Van Harten G, 'An ISDS Carve-Out to Support Action on Climate Change' (2015) 38/2015 Osgoode Legal Studies Research Paper Series

Williams Z, *The Political Economy of Investment Arbitration* (OUP 2022)

Yannaca-Small C, *International Investment Law: Understanding Concepts and Tracking Innovations* (Organisation for Economic Cooperation and Development (OECD) 2008)

6 Discussion and future outlook

This chapter reflects on the implications of the Consolidated Method for three key stakeholders, namely the development policymaker, international investor, and the international investment law practitioner. From acknowledging the incomplete assessment of the right to regulate for the public interest of sustainable development, to engaging solutions to complementing that assessment, such as the ones offered in this text, these stakeholders are essential to each process. For the motivated stakeholder, the Consolidated Method, such as through the model provisions, offers a means to base their interpretation of and approach to the nexus of international investment law and sustainable development on tools and concepts that arise from a multilateral process through the UN system.

The ideas embodied in this text can best be described as a reserved optimism towards the nexus between international investment law and sustainable development.[1] This entails a reservation towards any assumed correlation between international investment and advancing sustainable development, yet an optimism in the sustainable development potential of international investment when mobilized effectively.[2] This work also subscribes to an optimism towards the role of institutions, such as international investment law and the UN system, in being able to administer international investment law in a capacity that reflects the needs of sustainable development. Simultaneously, that optimism is tempered by a reservation concerning the trajectory of the international investment law regime in confronting the realities imposed by sustainable development.[3] An aspect of that trajectory to which this work turned its focus was the incomplete assessment of sustainable development impact, the ongoing evidence of which[4] in international investment law, particularly investment treaty arbitration, does more to inspire reservation than optimism.

1 Defined in the first pillar of the conceptual framework (Chapter 2).

2 This view is constructed through Chapters 3 and 4 and finds more specific wording in Chapter 5. Sustainable developed as it is understood in this work was defined in Chapter 2, the first pillar of the conceptual framework.

3 A more precisely scoped stance within the existing body of research was provided at in Chapter 5, which builds off a more general position in the evolutionary view as defined in Chapter 1.

4 Defined in the fourth pillar of the conceptual framework (Chapter 2).

DOI: 10.4324/9781003495871-6

One need only to look to recent history for such evidence. In June 2022, the International Centre for the Settlement of Investment Disputes (ICSID) released its decision on an investment treaty arbitration between a foreign investor and Costa Rica[5] on the grounds that the latter had breached the fair and equitable treatment of the investor.[6] Evoked in the right to regulate for the public interest, Costa Rica ordered the closure of a poultry processing company acquired by the foreign investor after discovering that it had greatly expanded production capacity that exacted an unaccounted environmental cost. Despite having expanded production, the investor did not seek to update the company's existing environmental certifications that were only applicable to the circumstances prior to the expanded production capacity. The arbitration tribunal found that while the implementation of the government measure was well within the host state's right to regulate for the public interest, thus excusing any claims in that regard,[7] the means implemented to do so were a violation of the foreign investor's fair and equitable treatment.[8] The Tribunal determined that there would be no award, but ordered each party to pay their own legal fees and split the cost of arbitration, which meant a USD 1.956 million billing out of Costa Rica's public coffers.

This case does not stand out amongst its peers as many of the same themes are present in the decision made by the arbitral tribunal. These include a conviction in an autonomous standard of fair and equitable treatment that stands apart from the purview of international law (or in this case, even the applicable bilateral investment treaty). Adding to that is again an incomplete assessment of claims concerning the public interest value of the government measure, which the Tribunal's majority decided to overlook for narrower issues of procedure. In this case, that incomplete assessment spilled over into the award, which had it been in Costa Rica's favour would have imposed the arbitration and legal costs onto the claimant considering that the government measures were not seen to have had an injurious effect on the operations of the foreign investor (in fact the only detrimental decision was taken by the investor himself).

The continuation of these incomplete assessments will only serve to further disjoin international investment law from the intensifying needs of sustainable

5 *Alejandro Diego Díaz Gaspar v Republic of Costa Rica* (ICSID Case No ARB/19/13), Award (29 June 2022).

6 Based on a translation and analysis of the Award featured in Investment Arbitration Reporter, see Lisa Bohmer, 'Analysis: Unpacking the Reasons Why the *Diaz v Costa Rica* Tribunal Split on the Merits, but Unanimously Declined to Award Damages to the Claimant' (*Investment Arbitration Reporter*, 8 July 2022) <www.iareporter.com/articles/analysis-unpacking-the-reasons-why-the-diaz-v-costa-rica-tribunal-split-on-the-merits-but-unanimously-declined-to-award-damages-to-the-claimant/> accessed 29 July 2022.

7 One of the three arbitrators in their dissenting opinion claimed that prior to determining a breach of fair and equitable treatment was first whether the case was admissible to the investment treaty arbitration since Costa Rica was acting within its right to regulate and that the foreign investor had been operating at a production volume that was inappropriate to its existing environmental licenses.

8 The remedial or cure period of one day sanctioned by the government measure as well as premature public declarations by relevant ministries concerning the closure of the company were viewed as having violated fair and equitable treatment of the foreign investor.

development. As identified in both the scholarship[9] and in the work of intergovernmental organizations,[10] permitting international investment law to operate at business as usual would be diminutive not only to international investment governance, but also to channelling international investment towards advancing sustainable development. The Consolidated Method[11] was thus crafted to address the incomplete assessment of the impact of Actions.[12]

The two products of this book, the Consolidated Method and the model provisions, sought to find applicability to diverse stakeholders understanding that nothing less than a unified effort is required to exact much-needed change to the international investment law regime. In creating these products, this book sought to have practical significance, not only in connection to international investment and its governance, but also the process of sustainable development. Creating a work that traverses disciplinary boundaries and appeals to practical application, however, is faced with limitations in its theoretical contributions to the scholarship of international investment law, international development, or Sustainable Investment. Continuing from the key contentions raised throughout this text, this work adds to ongoing discussions on theory and acknowledges them as one step towards examining the specific issue at the centre of this work: supplementary means of assessing the right to regulate for the public interest of sustainable development.

6.1 The stakeholders

This chapter reflects on the implications of the Consolidated Method for three key stakeholders, namely the development policymaker, international investor, and the international investment law practitioner. From acknowledging the incomplete assessment of the right to regulate for the public interest of sustainable development, to engaging solutions to complementing that assessment, such as the ones offered in this text, these stakeholders are essential to each process. For the motivated stakeholder, the Consolidated Method, such as through the model provisions, offers a means to base their interpretation of and approach to the nexus of international investment law and sustainable development on tools and concepts that arise from a multilateral process through the UN system.

6.1.1 Development policymaker

Whether of the host or home state, policymakers are fundamental to ensuring that the foreign investment policies of their respective governments corroborate national sustainable development strategies. Positioning the state's policy stance

9 These can be found in the evolutionary views scoped in Chapter 1.

10 A review of such initiatives was identified in Chapter 3.

11 Defined in Chapter 1 as referring to the combination of the international investment-sustainable development framework defined in Chapter 3 and the notion of Sustainable Investment defined in Chapter 4. The Consolidated Method was detailed in Chapter 5.

12 Defined in Chapter 1 as referring to both foreign investments as well as government measures that affect foreign investments.

towards the international investment law regime so that it remains aligned with its sustainable development targets is essential to ensuring coherence between those divergent policy spheres. Policy coherence was introduced through the Framework in Chapter 3 and is a central tenet in this work, as identified later in Chapter 5. By applying these considerations to that policymaking process, as well as adopting the means of assessing investments through the approaches introduced in the Notion in Chapter 4, governments can maintain a forward-looking and policy coherent engagement with the international investment regime whilst protecting their sustainable development ambitions. This is especially timely as international investors have been increasingly seeking legal recourse against sustainable development policy in host states.[13]

Elsewhere, an increasing number of governments have been withdrawing their states from the international investment law regime[14] in a questioning of its legitimacy.[15] Yet this work is in support of the view that policymakers who advocate to withdraw the state from fundamental aspects of the international investment law regime in effect diminish the possibility of fostering a positive nexus between international investment and sustainable development. As the Framework attempted to illustrate, there is value in a comprehensive, progressive, and precautionary approach to engaging the international investment law regime. This is contrast to the view that prioritizes liberalization policies commonly associated with the Washington Consensus, which has shown to leave the state in a highly vulnerable position.[16] Lastly, the Framework provides a contouring of the type of government measures that have been employed and recognized by the UN system as effective means of balancing the rights offered to the foreign investor and the host state's own right to regulate for the public interest.

As was explored in Pillar One in Chapter 2, foreign investment is key to financing sustainable development, both at the national and transnational levels.

13 This trend has been particularly salient in connection to the Energy Charter Treaty, as was examined in Chapter 2. See also Blake Alexander Simmons, Kyla Tienhaara and Rachel Thrasher, 'How Treaties Protecting Fossil Fuel Investors Could Jeopardize Global Efforts to Save the Climate—and Cost Countries Billions' (*The Conversation*) <http://theconversation.com/how-treaties-protecting-fossil-fuel-investors-could-jeopardize-global-efforts-to-save-the-climate-and-cost-countries-billions-182135> accessed 4 August 2022.

14 Ecuador, for example, withdrew from 12 bilateral investment treaties in 2017 citing a threat to its "capacity to regulate corporate activities in order to protect its citizens" (See Kate Caervantes-Knox and Elinor Thomas, 'Ecuador Terminates 12 BITs—a Growing Trend of Reconsideration of Traditional Investment Treaties?' (*DLA Piper* 2017) <www.dlapiper.com/en/mexico/insights/publications/2017/05/ecuador-terminates-12-bits-a-growing-trend/> accessed 12 August 2022).

15 The legitimacy challenge facing the international investment law regime continues to be an evocative critique, which was examined in the overview of the revolutionary view in Chapter 1. See also Daniel Behn, Ole Kristian Fauchald and Malcolm Langford, 'The International Investment Regime and Its Discontents' in Daniel Behn, Malcolm Langford and Ole Kristian Fauchald (eds), *The Legitimacy of Investment Arbitration: Empirical Perspectives* (CUP 2022); Kathryn Gordon and Joachim Pohl, 'Investment Treaties Over Time—Treaty Practice and Interpretation in a Changing World' (Organisation for Economic Cooperation and Development (OECD) 2015) OECD Working Papers on International Investment 2015/2.

16 This was examined in connection to both foreign direct and portfolio investment in Chapter 2.

However, the benefits that arise from foreign investment are not automatic. The Consolidated Method thus presents value to the policymaker in their approach to the international investment law regime in full recognition of the conditional nature of foreign investment's contribution to sustainable development. While the Consolidated Method delivers strategies applicable to both before and after the admission of a foreign investment, the choice to encapsulate them into model provisions is especially relevant to the policymaker. Negotiating comprehensive and progressive terms of international investment agreements is a formidable means to establishing a balance between an attractive investment climate and an ambitious sustainable development programme.

6.1.2 Transnational investor

The implications of the Consolidated Method to the international investor are largely embodied in the broader tectonic changes occurring in the way investment is conceived. Where considering the environmental, social, and governance impacts of an investment were once eccentric considerations, they have quickly become of primary materiality in assessing investment performance.[17] In terms of foreign direct investment (FDI), net-zero declarations by governments[18] make it more difficult to admit investments that are contrary to reaching net-zero without attracting criticism from national and international civil society.[19] Alongside the growth in Sustainable Investment is its substantiation as a concept, not only through research and scholarship, but also in the way that companies and investors have interacted with it. With a growing refinement in the understanding of Sustainable Investment formed clearer demarcations to falsify claims of sustainable development impact. Regulatory authorities have since become more vigilant against SDG-washing or greenwashing in the private sector as a form of consumer protection.[20] Elsewhere, private asset owners have used litigation against companies or institutional investors that misled asset holders on sustainability performance.[21]

17 An overview of this trend was provided in Chapter 4.

18 United Nations, 'Net Zero Coalition' (*Climate Action*) <www.un.org/en/climatechange/net-zero-coalition> accessed 4 August 2022.

19 See, for example, Laura Pitel and Nimet Kıraç, 'Turkey's New Power Plant Exposes "Huge Contradictions" of Net Zero Pledge' *Financial Times* (27 July 2022).

20 One notable example is the Climate and ESG Task Force created by the US Securities and Exchange Commission (Securities and Exchange Commission, United States of America, 'SEC Announces Enforcement Task Force Focused on Climate and ESG Issues' (4 March 2021) <www.sec.gov/news/press-release/2021-42> accessed 4 August 2022). The Task Force brought its first lawsuit against a private sector entity, Vale S.A., for misleading statements in its sustainability reports (Ben Lippard and others, 'First ESG Taskforce Lawsuit Shows SEC Serious on Disclosures' (*Bloomberg Law*, 13 May 2022) <https://news.bloomberglaw.com/esg/first-esg-taskforce-lawsuit-shows-sec-serious-on-disclosures> accessed 4 August 2022).

21 Amy Roy and others, 'Litigation Risks Posed by "Greenwashing" Claims for ESG Funds' (*The Harvard Law School Forum on Corporate Governance*, 25 April 2022) <https://corpgov.law.harvard.edu/2022/04/25/litigation-risks-posed-by-greenwashing-claims-for-esg-funds/> accessed 4 August 2022.

However, as identified in Chapter 4, there remains to be a widely recognized, authoritative standard for Sustainable Investment, especially transnationally. The Consolidated Method is helpful in this regard as its substantive content is derived from multilateral initiatives through the UN system. It remains yet to be seen whether the UN system will continue its present approach, which can be portrayed as facilitating private sector leadership rather than harmonizing standards in effectively what can be described as a free-for-all across very diverse jurisdictions.

While not to the same extent as in the private sector, there also remains a lack of unity and coherence across the UN system in its approach to and conceptualization of Sustainable Investment. As Chapter 4 showed, though remaining loosely linked through UN system-wide mandates, such as the UN Sustainable Development Goals or the Millennium Development Goals before that, there is limited crossover between agencies in the UN system. Thus, one endeavour of the Consolidated Method, particularly through the Notion, was the attempt to form a holistic platform that brought together these disparate initiatives from different agencies based on overlapping attributes and broadly informed by the institutional history of the UN system's engagement in Sustainable Investment.

6.1.3 Investment law practitioner

Without willing investment law practitioners to raise issues such as the incomplete assessment of the right to regulate, the challenges and suggestions identified in this work may never be addressed. Continuing from the fourth pillar in Chapter 2 that examined the incomplete assessment in greater length, the issue can be taken up either by the arbitral tribunal presiding over the investment treaty arbitration or the counsel representing their client. As was also demonstrated in the fourth pillar, however, was that even if one of the parties submits a sustainable development-related challenge, such as in the context of the right to regulate for the public interest, whether and to what extent that submission is considered by the arbitral tribunal remains unpredictable. A common outcome has been for arbitrators to recuse their competency to reflect on such matters as sustainable development, choosing then to focus their deliberations on narrower questions of legality. The fourth pillar, however, managed to curate investment treaty arbitrations that did reflect further on sustainable development-related submissions, identifying three forms of incomplete assessment. Within that context, the arbitrator remains an essential stakeholder to whom the Consolidated Method seeks to appeal.

Institutional change, especially at the multilateral level, takes time; Working Group III of the UN Commission on International Trade Law commenced in November 2017 and in September 2022 released its first draft provisions.[22] Meanwhile, according to data collected by the UN Commission on Trade and Development, there remain 370

22 United Nations Commission on International Trade Law (UNCITRAL), 'Working Group III: Investor-State Dispute Settlement Reform | United Nations Commission On International Trade Law' (*Working Groups*) <https://uncitral.un.org/en/working_groups/3/investor-state> accessed 20 May 2020.

investment treaty arbitrations pending and an average of 77 new arbitrations initiated every year since 2015.[23] Considering that an investment treaty arbitration takes on average four years to conclude and can cost the respondent state an average of USD 2.6 million,[24] the accumulation of arbitral proceedings can be consequential. For this reason, grounded in the evolutionary position to which this work subscribes, the Consolidated Method works from within the existing mechanism of investment treaty arbitration to identify and employ means that can address the issue of incomplete assessments, at least in part, both effectively and expeditiously.

Without systemic change, however, the degree to which an arbitral tribunal explores questions of sustainable development in the context of the right to regulate for the public interest remains limited to the domain of their judicial discretion. The model provisions introduced in Section 5.4 addressed a few of the core attributes of the incomplete assessment, each of which were addressed by the two tenets of applying the Consolidated Method treated in Chapter 5. Namely, when confronted with matters involving sustainable development in the context of the right to regulate for the public interest, the arbitrator may ask a few essential questions about the interpretation of sustainable development being employed as applies to the Action. First, is the interpretation of sustainable development in relation to the impacts of the Action aligned with the national sustainable development strategy of the host state? Equally important is to consider whether that interpretation is aligned with multilaterally accepted standards of sustainable development. Third, are the means to measure, report, and verify sustainable development impact aligned with existing standard practice in the analysis of Sustainable Investment, especially those multilaterally recognized such as those backed by the UN system?[25] By beginning with these questions, the arbitrator gains access to a whole corpus of multilaterally sourced materials and standards that may arm them against falling back into the incomplete assessment.

6.2 Final observations

Sustainable development-related concerns and their relevance to the international investment law regime can also be located at a much more fundamental level such as at the level of the investment itself—as this work attempted to do in connection with Sustainable Investment. For instance, issues not examined in this work include transnational investors eluding climate change-induced risk assessment of investment by selecting host states with lower vulnerability to the effect of climate change—though this practice is quickly becoming a moot strategy. In fact,

23 United Nations Trade and Development (UNCTAD), 'Investment Dispute Settlement Navigator' (*Investment Policy Hub*) <https://investmentpolicy.unctad.org/investment-dispute-settlement> accessed 5 August 2022.

24 Matthew Hodgson, Yarik Kryvoi and Daniel Hrcka, *2021 Empirical Study: Costs, Damages and Duration in Investor-State Arbitration* (British Institute of International and Comparative Law (BIICL) and Allen & Overy International Arbitration Group 2021).

25 As defined in Chapters 4 and 5, the main attributes of such an assessment may include science-based, net positive, or additionality.

transnational investors and their investments were shown to have the same or higher levels of climate change–related risk than local firms in a host state due to such exogenous factors as information asymmetries regarding the host state's climate change response strategy or related administrative procedures.[26] Furthermore, as the FDI-environment nexus is better understood,[27] strategies such as leveraging lax environmental standards to pull in more foreign investment (the pollution haven hypothesis) have shown to incite higher costs than rewards.[28] As such studies demonstrate, the application of interdisciplinary approaches to international investment law research remains a bountiful and much warranted task.

At the core of the research that seeks to strengthen the bond between international investment law and sustainable development, as this book also attempted to do, is both the resigned acceptance of the limitations facing the international investment law regime and an inexorable belief in its potential. The international investment law regime can be seen as ensnared in the restrictions and obligations owed to a conservatism in thinking about foreign investment and its governance. At the same time, the international investment law regime is capable of evolving and adapting to new realities, facilitating the search for intergenerational economic, social, and environmental justice where otherwise there would only be a patchwork of legal systems engineered around national interests. For that reason, it remains a powerful tool in braving the meeting of two opposing forces: the unpredictable vicissitudes that await humanity at the mercy of a rapidly changing planetary host and the need for capital to sow the foundations for a flourishing, sustainable economy that is in harmony with its environment.

26 Xia Li and Kevin P Gallagher, 'Assessing the Climate Change Exposure of Foreign Direct Investment' (2022) 13 Nature Communications 1451.

27 The FDI-environment nexus has been widely subject to study, essentially testing for either a pollution halo hypothesis, which is that the benefits of foreign direct investment such as technology transfers can help reduce environmental impact, or the pollution haven hypothesis, which is that foreign investors will look for lax environmental regulation to house their investments. See, for instance, António Cardoso Marques and Rafaela Vital Caetano, 'Do Greater Amounts of FDI Cause Higher Pollution Levels? Evidence from OECD Countries' (2022) 44 Journal of Policy Modeling 147; Prajukta Tripathy and others, 'Dynamic Link Between Bilateral FDI, the Quality of Environment and Institutions: Evidence from G20 Countries' (2022) 29 Environmental Science and Pollution Research 27150; Xue Gao and others, 'Decomposing the Asymmetric Effects of Terrorism and FDI on Carbon Emission: Evidence from Fragile Economies' (2022) 29 Environmental Science and Pollution Research 41125; Ashis Kumar Pradhan and others, 'Do Foreign Direct Investment Inflows Affect Environmental Degradation in BRICS Nations?' (2022) 29 Environmental Science and Pollution Research 690.

28 See, for instance, Muhammad Farhan Bashir, 'Discovering the Evolution of Pollution Haven Hypothesis: A Literature Review and Future Research Agenda' (2022) 29 Environmental Science and Pollution Research 48210; M Scott Taylor, 'Unbundling the Pollution Haven Hypothesis' (2005) 4 Advances in Economic Analysis & Policy. Another approach has been to measure foreign direct investment inflows at different levels of environmental degradation. See, for instance, Eric Evans Osei Opoku and others, 'Does Environmental Sustainability Attract Foreign Investment? Evidence from Developing Countries' (2022) 31 Business Strategy and the Environment 3542–3573.

References

Alejandro Diego Díaz Gaspar v Republic of Costa Rica (ICSID Case No ARB/19/13), Award (29 June 2022)

Bashir MF, 'Discovering the Evolution of Pollution Haven Hypothesis: A Literature Review and Future Research Agenda' (2022) 29 Environmental Science and Pollution Research 48210

Behn D, Fauchald OK and Langford M, 'The International Investment Regime and Its Discontents' in Daniel Behn, Malcolm Langford and Ole Kristian Fauchald (eds), *The Legitimacy of Investment Arbitration: Empirical Perspectives* (CUP 2022)

Bohmer L, 'Analysis: Unpacking the Reasons Why the Diaz v Costa Rica Tribunal Split on the Merits, but Unanimously Declined to Award Damages to the Claimant' (*Investment Arbitration Reporter*, 8 July 2022) <www.iareporter.com/articles/analysis-unpacking-the-reasons-why-the-diaz-v-costa-rica-tribunal-split-on-the-merits-but-unanimously-declined-to-award-damages-to-the-claimant/> accessed 29 July 2022

Caervantes-Knox K and Thomas E, 'Ecuador Terminates 12 BITs—a Growing Trend of Reconsideration of Traditional Investment Treaties?' (*DLA Piper* 2017) <www.dlapiper.com/en/mexico/insights/publications/2017/05/ecuador-terminates-12-bits-a-growing-trend/> accessed 12 August 2022

Gao X and others, 'Decomposing the Asymmetric Effects of Terrorism and FDI on Carbon Emission: Evidence from Fragile Economies' (2022) 29 Environmental Science and Pollution Research 41125

Gordon K and Pohl J, 'Investment Treaties Over Time—Treaty Practice and Interpretation in a Changing World' (Organisation for Economic Cooperation and Development (OECD) 2015) OECD Working Papers on International Investment 2015/2

Hodgson M, Kryvoi Y and Hrcka D, *2021 Empirical Study: Costs, Damages and Duration in Investor-State Arbitration* (British Institute of International and Comparative Law (BIICL) and Allen & Overy International Arbitration Group 2021)

Li X and Gallagher KP, 'Assessing the Climate Change Exposure of Foreign Direct Investment' (2022) 13 Nature Communications 1451

Lippard B and others, 'First ESG Taskforce Lawsuit Shows SEC Serious on Disclosures' (*Bloomberg Law*, 13 May 2022) <https://news.bloomberglaw.com/esg/first-esg-taskforce-lawsuit-shows-sec-serious-on-disclosures> accessed 4 August 2022

Marques AC and Caetano RV, 'Do Greater Amounts of FDI Cause Higher Pollution Levels? Evidence from OECD Countries' (2022) 44 Journal of Policy Modeling 147

Opoku EEO and others, 'Does Environmental Sustainability Attract Foreign Investment? Evidence from Developing Countries' (2022) 31 Business Strategy and the Environment 3542–3573

Pitel L and Kıraç N, 'Turkey's New Power Plant Exposes "Huge Contradictions" of Net Zero Pledge' *Financial Times* (27 July 2022)

Pradhan AK and others, 'Do Foreign Direct Investment Inflows Affect Environmental Degradation in BRICS Nations?' (2022) 29 Environmental Science and Pollution Research 690

Roy A and others, 'Litigation Risks Posed by "Greenwashing" Claims for ESG Funds' (*The Harvard Law School Forum on Corporate Governance*, 25 April 2022) <https://corpgov.law.harvard.edu/2022/04/25/litigation-risks-posed-by-greenwashing-claims-for-esg-funds/> accessed 4 August 2022

Securities and Exchange Commission, United States of America, 'SEC Announces Enforcement Task Force Focused on Climate and ESG Issues' (4 March 2021) <www.sec.gov/news/press-release/2021-42> accessed 4 August 2022

Simmons BA, Tienhaara K and Thrasher R, 'How Treaties Protecting Fossil Fuel Investors Could Jeopardize Global Efforts to Save the Climate—and Cost Countries Billions' *The Conversation* <http://theconversation.com/how-treaties-protecting-fossil-fuel-investors-could-jeopardize-global-efforts-to-save-the-climate-and-cost-countries-billions-182135> accessed 4 August 2022

Taylor MS, 'Unbundling the Pollution Haven Hypothesis' (2005) 4 Advances in Economic Analysis & Policy

Tripathy P and others, 'Dynamic Link Between Bilateral FDI, the Quality of Environment and Institutions: Evidence from G20 Countries' (2022) 29 Environmental Science and Pollution Research 27150

United Nations, 'Net Zero Coalition' (*Climate Action*) <www.un.org/en/climatechange/net-zero-coalition> accessed 4 August 2022

United Nations Commission on International Trade Law (UNCITRAL), 'Working Group III: Investor-State Dispute Settlement Reform | United Nations Commission On International Trade Law' (*Working Groups*) <https://uncitral.un.org/en/working_groups/3/investor-state> accessed 20 May 2020

United Nations Trade and Development (UNCTAD), 'Investment Dispute Settlement Navigator' (*Investment Policy Hub*) <https://investmentpolicy.unctad.org/investment-dispute-settlement> accessed 5 August 2022

Appendix 1

International investment–sustainable development framework

Objective 1	Does the Action facilitate greater development impact?	
Strategy 1.1.	Optimize development impact	
Measure 1.1.1. Linkage promotion	T1*	Forming linkages between international investment and domestic economic actors through special rules, preferential treatment, and/or public investment
Measure 1.1.2. Integrated industrial policy	T1	Guiding investment policy through modern industrial policy that is grounded in a country's overall development strategy and optimizing development impact absorption through higher Sustainable Development Goal–aligned standards
Measure 1.1.3. South-South and regional preferences	T1	Showing preference for investments that tend to present greater gains in the context of South-South development cooperation by facilitating the creation of larger markets and harmonizing sustainable development standards
Strategy 1.2.	Enhance policy capacities	
Measure 1.2.1. Measurable policy effects	T2†	Monitoring direct and measurable policy implementation and any need for policy adjustments based on reliable data while accounting for exogenous, multifaceted, and implementation difficulties
Measure 1.2.2. Dynamic policymaking	T1	Promoting public interest goals while being responsive to changing conditions and different stages of development by formulating implementation measures based on performance monitoring
Measure 1.2.3. Parallel instruments	T1	Integrating socioeconomic and environmentally responsible development strategy into investment policy by safeguarding government measures

(*Continued*)

(Continued)

Strategy 1.3.	Target high-impact investment	
Measure 1.3.1. Productive investment	T1	Distinguishing between types of investment that may have a more predictable outcome on development and building on domestic economic linkages to catalyse financial resources and investments into strategic areas
Measure 1.3.2. Sustainable development Sectors	T1	Directing investment to priority sectors for sustainable development based on development challenges and opportunities by targeting vulnerable groups and triggering spillover effects
Measure 1.3.3. Pre–foreign direct investment (FDI) screening	T1	Screening foreign enterprises seeking admission of FDI for favourable characteristics defined with active participation by domestic stakeholders
Objective 2	Does the Action encourage development cooperation?	
Strategy 2.1.	Form robust relationships	
Measure 2.1.1. Clear expectations	T1	Establishing concrete commitments between the host state and transnational corporations in applicable agreements concerning sustainable development
Measure 2.1.2. Multistakeholder consensus	T1	Delineating lines of responsibility and authority through multistakeholder communication to ensure inclusive gains from investment
Strategy 2.2.	Reach a common understanding	
Measure 2.2.1. Administrative procedures	T1	Increasing procedural transparency and consistency in administrative processes involving transnational corporations aware that the main responsibility of ensuring development impact remains with the host state
Measure 2.2.2. Corporate citizenship	T1	Forming commonly understood boundaries of international good corporate citizenship based on standards of social and environmental policy
Strategy 2.3.	Establish equitable standards	
Measure 2.3.1. No lesser standard	T1	Encouraging or requiring international investors to be in compliance with home-state, intergovernmental, and/or multilateral standards related to sustainable development
Measure 2.3.2. Home country measures	T1	Agreeing on strong policy commitments and binding obligations on enrolling into and/or implementing international initiatives on corporate governance

(*Continued*)

(Continued)

Objective 3	Does the Action advance mutual benefit in agreements?	
Strategy 3.1.	Harmonize international investment incentives	
Measure 3.1.1. Conditional incentive-limitation	T1	Coordinating conditional incentive-limitation clauses in investment agreements that require a specific number or set of states to adopt the same clause based on a joint weighing of benefits
Measure 3.1.2. Discouraged incentives	T1	Coordinating identification of objectionable investment promotion incentives to avoid overlapping or conflicting national policy tool kits between states meant to achieve development objectives
Measure 3.1.3. Encouraged incentives	T1	Coordinating identification of investment promotion incentives between states for desirable investments, namely those with high development impact
Strategy 3.2.	Secure responsive contracts	
Measure 3.2.1. Durable contracts	T1	Establishing durable relationships through contracts that can augment, or even overshadow, general laws in the host state when necessary for sustainable development
Measure 3.2.2. Capacity building	T1	Ensuring that domestic public and private sector entities are capable of entering into agreements that boost domestic economic benefit while mitigating investment risks
Objective 4	Are investment laws and policies harmonized with multilateral standards related to sustainable development?	
Strategy 4.1.	Reform approaches to investment agreements	
Measure 4.1.1. Joint interpretive statements	T1	Providing multilateral interpretative guidance (or joint committees) for issues where a broad and unpredictable margin of discretion in the interpretation of international investment agreements may exist, such as in the context of investment treaty arbitration
Measure 4.1.2. New generation agreements	T1	Mainstreaming sustainable development in international investment agreements through an active approach, which includes addressing older investment treaties that cause fragmentation
Strategy 4.2.	Harmonize investment reporting standards	
Harmonized reporting	T2	Pursuing an internationally harmonized approach to measuring and reporting on sustainable development-related factors affected by investment

(*Continued*)

(Continued)

Objective 5	Do investment laws and policies sufficiently prevent abusive practices that hamper sustainable development?	
Strategy 5.1.	Craft preventative arrangements before the admission of investment	
Measure 5.1.1. Backstopping	T1	Establishing multilateral backstopping measures that promote exchange of information on restrictive business practices and protects against the misappropriation of knowledge assets
Measure 5.1.2. Protective carve-outs	T1	Carving out protections for domestic minority shareholders and stakeholders against power differentials against transnational corporations and investors
Measure 5.1.3. Clarified instruments	T1	Clarifying on and/or renegotiating treaty provisions or interpretation to prevent conflicting rules both at the national and international level in order to maximize the gains from international investment
Measure 5.1.4. Linking provisions	T1	Confining the application of the rights and protections to "genuine investors" by refining the definition of covered investor and linking coverage to those circumstances
Strategy 5.2.	Install post-admissions measures that safeguard against abusive practices	
Measure 5.2.1. Reservations	T1	Reserving rights to be invoked in the last instance, such as counterclaiming on grounds of the opposing party's misconduct or retaining "golden shares"
Measure 5.2.2. Safety valves	T1	Reserving rights through safeguards to afford policy space and regulatory flexibility to implement strategies that best fit national priorities important to sustainable development

* In reference to the First Tenet (T1), coherence with sustainable development, introduced in Chapter 5. More specifically, the Action is aligned with existing policies meant to advance sustainable development and/or aligned with multilaterally accepted standards of investment in connection to sustainable development.

† In reference to the Second Tenet (T2), contribution to sustainable development, introduced in Chapter 5. More specifically, to what extent the contribution to sustainable development by the Action is falsifiable based on a threshold of empirical and/or science-based evidence as well as whether the Action promotes more investors and/or investments to become aligned with sustainable investment.

Appendix 2

Notion of sustainable investment

Key feature 1	Scope	
Element 1.1. Net positive impact	*Summation of positive and negative impacts of the investment, including extra-financial values*	
	Characteristics	
Key Sustainable Development Goal (SDG) sectors	T2*	Multiplier effect for investments in sectors that represent development priorities, such as core infrastructure
Level of analysis	T2	Differentiated assessment of an investor at the firm level and investment at the operational level
Impact thesis	T2	Contextual impact assessment (outcome and key performance indicators), accounting for impact risk appetite (threshold of permissible risk burden)
Stakeholder analysis	T2	Stakeholder-based impact analysis accounting for disparities in absorptive capacities
Do no significant harm	T1†	Safeguard against backpedalling in different dimension of sustainable development (positive impact in one dimension at the cost of backtracking another dimension)
Element 1.2. Catalyst effect	*Investors and/or investments as means to catalyse sustainable development*	
	Characteristics	
Stewardship	T1	Investors as holders of equity use voting rights to influence corporate behaviour to be more SDG aligned
Theory of change	T1	Investments in sectors with high exposure to climate change and systemic vulnerabilities are better positioned to catalyse SDG alignment
In tandem capital allocation	T1	Investors coordinate allocation of their capital to create clear risks and rewards for investee companies in firm-level decisions that converge or diverge from the SDGs
Active ownership	T1	Conceptualizing "alpha" to consider both financial and extra-financial performance in investment strategies
Policy advocacy	T1	Mobilizing capital in a uniform manner to send policy signals to regulators to catalyse change
Listing requirements	T2	Imposing SDG-aligned requirements for companies before they can list on a stock exchange to catalyse firm-level change

(*Continued*)

(Continued)

Key feature 2	Indicators	
Element 2.1. Real-world impact	*Verification of investment's actual sustainable development impact*	
	Characteristics	
Science based	T2	Aligning performance targets and assessment based on a threshold of current scientific understanding and/or remains updated to the most recent science
Realistic portfolio impact	T2	Drawing on best available and relevant impact data in connection with the SDGs in determining risk
Forward-looking	T2	Upscaling both impact commitments and extent to which data comprehensive captures impact (e.g. including Scope 3 emissions)
Element 2.2. Additionality	*Added engagement in the sustainability contributions of investment*	
Universality	T2	Adjusting requirements for participation in sustainable investment so as not to crowd out new participants
Inward-looking	T1	Upscaling internal mechanisms and units to evoke sustainability-aligned internal change
Key feature 3	Metrics and data	
	Characteristics	
Metric tailoring	T2	Normalizing data to account for sectoral idiosyncrasies to permit inherent disadvantaged firms to participate
Accounting	T2	Accounting for both mitigative and adverse impacts (outcome risks) on metrics for a resultant net balance
Aggregation	T2	Calculating a highly aggregate score or set of scores in order to raise public awareness on progress towards sustainable development
Adjustments	T2	Reflecting differences in time (e.g. short vs long run, size of firm) in metric performance

* In reference to the First Tenet (T1), coherence with sustainable development, introduced in Chapter 5. More specifically, the Action is aligned with existing policies meant to advance sustainable development and/or aligned with multilaterally accepted standards of investment in connection to sustainable development.

† In reference to the Second Tenet (T2), contribution to sustainable development, introduced in Chapter 5. More specifically, to what extent the contribution to sustainable development by the Action is falsifiable based on a threshold of empirical and/or science-based evidence as well as whether the Action promotes more investors and/or investments to become aligned with sustainable investment.

Index

[Note: numbers in **bold** indicate a table and numbers in *italics* indicate a figure on the corresponding page]

FSC
www.fsc.org
MIX
Papier | Fördert gute Waldnutzung
FSC® C083411

Kolibri 360 GmbH
Ferdinand-Jühlke-Straße 7
99095 Erfurt, Deutschland
produktsicherheit@kolibri360.de